D.I.S.C.I.P.L.E.R.S
Daily Devotional

D.I.S.C.I.P.L.E.R.S
Daily Devotional

12 Pathways to Spiritual Progress

Dean De Castro

XULON PRESS

Xulon Press
2301 Lucien Way #415
Maitland, FL 32751
407.339.4217
www.xulonpress.com

Paperback ISBN-13: 978-1-6628-5678-5
Ebook ISBN-13: 978-1-6628-5679-2

Three Keys to Spiritual Growth
Dean De Castro

*But grow in the grace and knowledge of
our Lord and Savior Jesus Christ.*
—2 PETER 3:18

God's goal for every Christian is not sinless perfection but spiritual progress. As we grow spiritually, we can sin less and less and less. So, how do we grow spiritually? In 2 Peter 3:18, I discovered three keys to spiritual growth and maturity.

Principle. Peter urges us to grow in God's grace. Knowing, understanding, believing, and accepting God's grace are essential to spiritual maturity. What is grace? Grace is experiencing **G**od's **R**esources **at** Christ's expense. God blesses us first under the covenant of grace, and His blessings, unmerited favor, forgiveness, and overflowing love lead us to repentance (Rom. 2:4).

Practices. Hebrews 5:14 indicates that we need to practice several spiritual disciplines to grow as mature and responsible Christians. For several years, I tried to practice twelve spiritual disciplines based on the acrostic DISCIPLERS:

- **D**aily devotion (2 Cor. 11:3).
- **I**n love with people (Eph. 5:2).
- **S**uffering for Christ (Phil. 1:29).
- **C**ultivate Christlike character (Gal. 5:22–23).
- **I**nvestment for Eternity (1 Tim. 6:18–19).
- **P**ursue holiness (Heb. 12:14).
- **L**ordship of Christ (Time) (Ps. 31:15).
- **L**ordship of Christ (Talent) (1 Pet. 4:10–11).
- **L**ordship of Christ (Temple) (1 Cor. 6:19).
- **E**vangelism (Acts 1:8).

- **R**eproduction (Matt. 28:19–20).
- **S**mall group (Eccl. 4:9–12).

Now, to be honest, I have not consistently practiced most of these. However, that doesn't stop me, and it shouldn't stop you either; just because you can't do everything doesn't mean you shouldn't do anything.

Priority. Peter also commands us to grow in our Lord and Savior's knowledge. Our focus in life is on knowing God and developing an intimate relationship with Him. Grace is not just a concept; it is God in human form (Titus 2:11). The best way to know Christ personally with ever-deepening intimacy is to fellowship with Him through daily Bible meditation and prayer.

> *Father God, let our practice of all the spiritual disciplines lead us to know and love our Lord. In Jesus's name, amen!*

_____

_____

_____

_____

The Discipline of Daily Devotion
Dean De Castro

...by constant use have trained themselves...
—HEBREWS 5:14

Spiritual maturity is not automatic. It does not happen by accident. In Hebrews 5:14, the word "trained" means learning a custom or habit. Christian growth requires the discipline of godly habits practiced daily. The most important discipline is to cultivate a personal time with God. Most people call it *quiet time*. I prefer to call it *daily devotion*.

The practice of daily devotion. Whatever we call this practice, it should include a specific place and time we choose to meet with God. In this sacred space, we listen to what God says from His words and talk to Him sincerely from our hearts through prayer. Many keep a journal to record their biblical insights and even write down their prayers. You might also include periods of silence or the singing of worship songs.

The purpose of daily devotion. Whatever we do in our daily devotion, the motivation is to keep alive our simple and pure devotion to our Lord Jesus Christ (2 Cor. 11:3b). These two words, simple and pure, aptly describe our love for Christ when we put our faith in Him.

Just like in a marriage, a couple must nourish their relationship by spending quality time together. Similarly, every devoted follower of Christ needs to develop the discipline of investing time connecting with their Bridegroom, the Lord Jesus Christ.

The problem of daily devotion. In 2 Corinthians 11:3a, Paul anticipates that Satan wants to distract Christians from keeping their devotion to Christ. He deceives their minds—just as he lied to Eve in the Garden of Eden by doubting God's goodness. Satan's greatest deception is that we can fulfill our God-given, legitimate needs and desires (physical, psychological, and spiritual) through earthly pleasures and personal achievements.

Christ, however, is the source of true satisfaction. He is the living water and the bread of life (John 4:13; 6:35). Oswald Sanders writes, "There is only one Being Who can satisfy the last aching abyss of the human heart, and that is the Lord Jesus Christ." And daily devotion, according to Stephen Olford, "is absolutely vital to a life of sustained spirituality, effectiveness, and love."

Father God, as the deer pants for streams of water, so our souls pant for You (Ps. 42:1). In Jesus's name, amen!

_____

_____

_____

_____

The Importance of Daily Devotion
Dean De Castro

We have not stopped praying for you.
—COLOSSIANS 1:9–11

In today's passage, we see the spiritual benefits of spending time with God. As we develop the discipline of daily devotion, we will gradually witness all these spiritual traits manifest in our daily conduct.

First, we are filled with the knowledge of God's will (v. 9). As we read God's words during our quiet time, we will learn more about God and discover His will in every area of our life.

Second, we have the wisdom to apply God's word (v. 9). The Spirit of truth will help us rightly interpret God's words and gain the spiritual insights needed to change our behaviors.

Third, we live a life worthy of the Lord (v. 10). Walking worthily doesn't mean we now deserve God's favor due to any "good behavior" on our part. Instead, it is His grace that enables us to live a life that glorifies God.

Fourth, we can please God in every way (v. 10). As we draw near to God regularly, it's easier to feel the heartbeat of God and do whatever pleases Him by faith. And without faith, it is impossible to please God (Heb. 11:6).

Fifth, we bear fruit in every good work (v. 10). Our Lord promised us in John 15 that if we abide in His love through prayer and Scriptures, we will bear much fruit. The purpose of spending time with God is not to be self-focused but God-focused and other-focused. As the love of God fills our hearts, we feel grateful to share God's love with others.

Sixth, we grow in the knowledge of God (v. 11). There's a big difference between seeking knowledge *about* God and the knowledge *of* God. Don't let the factual knowledge about God sidetrack us from knowing God Himself. The purpose of quiet time is to seek God Himself—nothing more, nothing less, and nothing else!

Seventh, we are strengthened with all power (v. 11). Finally, prayer is a significant part of the discipline of daily devotions. As we wait upon God, we receive power from above (Isa. 30:15). The more we pray, the more power we have.

Father God, let us see the value of spending
time with You. In Jesus's name, amen!

New Every Morning
Dean De Castro

Yet this I call to mind...
—LAMENTATIONS 3:21–23

The phrase "I call to mind" indicates the action of remembering and meditating on a particular thing.

In verses 19–20, Jeremiah is depressed, thinking about his afflictions and bitterness. And yet he chose to recall God's mercy and faithfulness. As a result, he found strength and hope.

Meditating on God's love every morning produces the following positive results:

It gives us hope. "And therefore I have hope" (v. 21). It has been said that man can live three months without food, three days without water, and three minutes without air, but hardly three seconds without hope.

Our hope is in God and not in ourselves or our circumstances. We are hopeful because we have a faithful God "Who is the same yesterday and today and forever" (Heb. 13:8). Hope in God gives us the power to obey His will and overcome Satan's temptations. Without it, we are easy prey to discouragement and despair.

It shows us the greatness of God's love. "Because of the Lord's great love we are not consumed, for His compassions never fail" (v. 22). God's love is so great that it never ceases nor fails. It's like digging through a great treasure chest just to revel in all that is there.

It is so easy to go through the day and never once remember God's great love for us. So we can easily get caught up and entangled in the affairs of everyday life that we miss this great source of hope. Psalm 103:11 says, "For as higher as the heavens are above the earth, so great is His love for those who fear Him."

It reveals something new about God's love. The most famous phrase in this passage is "They are new every morning" (v. 23). As we meet God during our daily devotions, God is willing to make Himself known to us every day in a new and refreshing way.

This phrase also lovingly warns us: If God's love is new every morning and we let other priorities squeeze our time with Him, we will miss the opportunity to learn something new about His love for us.

Father God, we praise and worship You, for Your mercies are new every morning. In Jesus's name, amen!

_____

_____

_____

_____

Morning Prayer
Dean De Castro

Let the morning bring...
–PSALM 143:8

In this morning prayer, the psalmist asks God for two things: to remind him of God's unfailing love and show him God's unfailing way.

God's unfailing love. "Let the morning bring the word of Your unfailing love, for I have put my trust in You."

When we read God's Word during our daily devotions, the Holy Spirit will show us the love of God revealed (directly or indirectly) in every passage of the Scriptures. Putting our trust in God's unconditional love will save us from being addicted to man's approval.

We need to remember that God created us for relationships. According to Augustine, "To live is to love." Only God's love can truly satisfy our deep longing for intimate relationships. When our soul is filled only with God's satisfying love, we stop striving for love from people. Instead, we love securely, from the posture of knowing that we are loved. As 1 John 4:19 tells us, "We love because God first loved us."

God's unfailing way. "Show me the way I should go, for to You I lift up my soul."

Every morning during our quiet times, we humbly lift our souls to seek God's guidance and direction for the coming day. God guarantees that the Holy Spirit will guide us because those who the Spirit of God leads are children of God (Rom. 8:14).

In *Daily in Christ*, Neil Anderson writes about a young and inexperienced pilot who was having difficulty landing his plane in a blinding fog. But with the words of the flight manual that he memorized and firmly placed in his mind, along with the gentle voice of the air traffic controller that he couldn't see, guiding him around obstacles and potential collisions, the fearful and anxious pilot landed safely at last.

Anderson writes, "The Holy Spirit guides us through the maze of life much like an air traffic controller. The controller assumed that the young pilot understood the instructions of the flight manual. He guides based on that. Such is the case with the Holy Spirit. He leads us if we know God's Word and His will established in our minds."

Father God, let Your unfailing love and unfailing way help us navigate our life here on earth. In Jesus's name, amen!

The Example of Jesus

Dean De Castro

Very early in the morning...Jesus...went off
to a solitary place, where He prayed.
—MARK 1:35

If we carefully study the context of this passage, we see a flurry of activities the night before.

Jesus had taught, healed, and performed many miracles (v. 34). Our Lord had every reason to get up late the next day. But communion with God was so high on His list of priorities that He got up before dawn to spend time alone with the Father. From our Lord's example, we can see how He generally followed the pattern of morning prayer laid out in Psalm 143:8.

God's unfailing love. After such a day of miracles in Galilee, both the disciples and the crowd expected to witness a similar spectacular display of Jesus's power the next day: "Simon and his companions went to look for Him, and when they found Him, they exclaimed: 'Everyone is looking for you!'" (Mark 1:36–37).

Luke adds that the same group who witnessed the miraculous performance by Jesus the night before "tried to keep Him from leaving them" (Luke 4:42). To the dismay of the disciples and the crowd, however, Jesus refused their requests to return to Capernaum.

It is human to feel needed by people who put expectations on us. But spending time with God keeps us from the temptation of seeking the recognition of others. Satan once tempted Jesus to jump from the top of the temple to impress and gain people's approval, yet our Lord resisted the same temptation and trusted in God's love instead.

God's unfailing way. During His quiet time with the Father, Jesus remembered that God sent Him into the world (John 16:28) and not just to a specific place or city in it. That particular morning, the Holy

Spirit revealed to Jesus that He was done ministering in Galilee and needed to proceed to Judea (Luke 4:44).

Jesus responds to the demands that He stay by proclaiming the broader nature of His mission: "Jesus replied, 'Let us go somewhere else—to the nearby villages—so I can preach there also. That's why I have come'" (Mark 1:38). "But He said, 'I must preach the good news... to the other towns also because that is why I was sent'" (Luke 4:43).

Father God, help us imitate our Lord's example to trust
Your love and follow Your way. In Jesus's name, amen!

Satan Opposes Daily Devotion

Dean De Castro

*But I am afraid that just as Eve was deceived by the
serpent's cunning, your minds may somehow be led
astray from your sincere and pure devotion to Christ.*
–2 CORINTHIANS 11:3

In today's passage, Paul brings us back to what happened in the Garden of Eden.

Unfortunately, Adam and Eve sinned, which led to the downfall of humanity. However, the father of lies continues to attack God's children today.

Satan, our chief opponent, does not want us to spend quiet time with God. He puts erroneous beliefs in the minds of Christians to discourage them from keeping their daily appointment with God. The enemy's goal is to deceive our minds and lead us astray from keeping alive our simple and pure devotion to our Lord Jesus Christ. Satan knows that the more time we spend with God, the more like God we will become, and the more successful we will accomplish God's plan and purposes on this earth.

Many Christians claim they are too busy or too tired to meet with God regularly; they make excuses for why they can't make time for God. But as Corrie Ten Boom warns us, "If the devil cannot make us bad, he will make us busy."

We keep busy fulfilling our responsibilities at home and at the workplace. But making time for God should be our top priority. It is worth our effort, commitment, and discipline. Our Lord Jesus set an excellent example for us concerning daily devotions. Despite His hectic schedule, He regularly connected with the Father.

Of course, personal devotions can be challenging to prioritize. It's tempting to make excuses or simply not bother. So, the next time you find it difficult to get alone with God, remember who is standing in your way: Satan, the Prince of the Air! But God is greater still "because the One who is in you is greater than the one who is in the world" (1 John 4:4).

God longs to spend time with us. Consider what He was willing to give up to reunite us with Him. Is it asking too much that we devote daily time to Him?

> *Father God, let us resist Satan and maintain our simple*
> *and pure love for You. In Jesus's name, amen!*

_____

_____

_____

_____

Intimacy with Christ

Edward Dennett
Adapted from Grace Fellowship International

I have called you friends.
–JOHN 15:15

If you meditate upon these words, you will never reach their profound depths, not even in eternity.

For who is able to say what friendship with Christ involves? No one can or will ever gauge the potential intimacy that it holds out to us.

We should diligently cultivate the enjoyment of the love of Christ so that we may become molded by it. Our intimacy with Christ will manifest itself in our demeanor and create a holy atmosphere that surrounds us.

I do not know of any happier activity than sitting down quietly before the Lord and letting Him make impressions on your heart—to let Him move you with His presence and produce whatever influences He will upon you. By sitting at the feet of Jesus, we shall both delight His heart and find ourselves in a place of untold and unfathomable blessings.

Many people think communion with God is just about having happy feelings. But connection with God is actually about doing the right things, at the right moment, and in the right way. Once you get out of close fellowship with God, you cannot do anything right.

Are we satisfied with just receiving great insights from the Scriptures instead of cultivating a love for God? The more revelation, the better—if affection goes with it. But if the light of God's words is held without the heart, it will not benefit us.

John 20 illustrates this. John had more revelation about the resurrection than Mary, yet when he came to the tomb and found it empty, he went home. Mary had no light about the resurrection, yet as she waited there, weeping, Jesus revealed Himself to her.

It is to the heart and not to the head that Christ reveals Himself. The more passion you have, the more you will be able to receive manifestations of Him. To be near Christ is the greatest enjoyment of spiritual life. Even in heaven itself, you would not be content if you never came into contact with Christ. So, have you come into contact with Him today?

Father God, let us draw near to You, not only with our head but most importantly with our heart. In Jesus's name, amen!

_____

_____

_____

_____

How to Experience Intimacy with God

Dr. Carol Peters-Tanksley, MD
Adapted from drcarolministries.com

These men had been with Jesus.
—ACTS 4:13

God created us for intimacy with Himself.

When we have an intimate relationship with God, people around us can sense that we "had been with Jesus." Here are five ways to experience intimacy with God:

Take time. Intimacy with God takes time to develop. Don't just read something and recite a prayer listing your requests in your daily time with God. Those things are good but are not enough to create and sustain a real relationship. Instead, take time to share your heart with Him. And then stay a little longer to be quiet and listen.

Open door. In the allegory *My Heart – Christ's Home,* our life is compared to a home with many rooms. If you want intimacy with God, He needs access to every room in your heart and life. In twenty-first-century English, that means your schedule, entertainment, bank account, and sexuality.

Follow where He leads. Throughout your life on earth, the Holy Spirit will regularly put His finger on something in your life He wants you to change. So when He tells you to do something, do it. God is a good Father, a good Shepherd. He has a promising future for you. And the way to experience that bright future is to follow Him in each small step along the way.

Listen for His heart. The closer you come to God, the more you sense what He cares about and how He feels. Intimacy with God is not about goosebumps and feelings that stay locked inside you; rather, it's for the benefit of all His children. So, who is He putting in your sphere of influence to impact His kingdom? Whose pain has He allowed you to feel? As you listen for His heart, you will naturally become His hands and feet to people around you.

Stay close. Intimacy with God is not a one-time thing. True intimacy is a lifestyle. As with human relationships, a relationship with God has seasons. There are times when you experience God's sweet presence, and other times you work with Him to press back the kingdom of darkness. Through all this, stay close. Keep coming back into His presence, allowing Him to change you and show you His heart.

Father God, let us take time to spend time
with You. In Jesus's name, amen!

_____

_____

_____

_____

Have You Left Your First Love?

Greg Morse
Adapted from desiringGod.com

*Yet I hold this against you: You have
forsaken the love you had at first.*
−REVELATION 2:4

Even though I love Jesus, my love threatens to grow cold when distractions intrude on my best attempts to have quiet moments with God.

After commending the church at Ephesus concerning their zeal for orthodoxy, Jesus confronts them for abandoning their pure love for Him (Rev. 2:4). But Jesus still loves His church, and He counsels us in three ways:

Remember. Remember, therefore, from where you have fallen. Look back upon former days. Do you remember when God first awakened your soul? Do you remember the excitement you had when He plucked you out of darkness? When He saved you, transforming you from an orphan to a son, a dead sinner to a resurrected saint, an enemy of God to His beloved?

Remember those quiet mornings when you sat at His feet, filled with "joy unspeakable" (1 Pet. 1:8). Remember that you run to prayer, not out of duty, but because your Great Love was waiting for you there (see Ps. 73:25).

Repent. Go to God in the blood of His Son and cry out for mercy, confessing you've grown cold. Tell Him you've entertained other loves. Repent to your God for not loving Him as He deserves. Nevertheless, He stands ready to forgive and restore you. Your High Priest will sympathize with you; therefore, "Let us come boldly unto the throne of grace, that we may obtain mercy, and find grace to help in time of need" (Heb. 4:16, KJV).

Return "and do the works you did at first." God calls us to return to where we have fallen from. He calls us to that new fire of love towards Him. It is a command to keep ourselves in the love of God (Jude 21).

It is worth considering what makes your heart sing for Jesus Christ. Is it long walks in nature, early mornings with your guitar, or reading Christ-exalting fiction? You can have a sweet relationship with God in Christ again. As the prodigal son returned to his father, show yourself on the horizon, and God will run to you in due time (see Luke 15:20).

Father God, refresh our first love for
You. In Jesus's name, amen!

_____

_____

_____

_____

How to Develop the Habit of Daily Devotion

Dean De Castro

Three times a day he got down on his knees and prayed,
giving thanks to his God, just as he had done before
—DANIEL 6:10B

Many Christians believe in the importance of spending regular daily time in God's Word and in prayer.

Yet many of us struggle to do this consistently. Therefore, developing and following a simple plan is imperative for making daily communion with God second nature.

Start with a short opening prayer to prepare yourself. I suggest using Psalm 143:8 as a basis of your brief prayer: *Father God, let the morning bring me word of Your unfailing love, for I have put my trust in You. Show me the way I should go, for I lift my soul to You.* Try to memorize this and recite it in your opening prayer.

Read through a book of the Bible in an orderly fashion. Do not use the "random dip" method—a passage here, a chapter there, what you like here, an exciting portion there. Instead, you could use a Bible reading plan or pick a book and work your way through its entirety over time.

Use the HEAR model created by Replicate Ministries. The acronym stands for **h**ighlight, **e**xplain, **a**pply, and **r**espond. Let me briefly explain this method.

Highlight. Read a section of the Scripture and highlight a verse or two that quickens your spirit and speaks to you directly.

Explain. Ask the Holy Spirit to help you understand what you're reading. Use the six interrogative questions: who, what, where, when, why, how.

Apply. With the help of the Holy Spirit, attempt to uncover the significance of these verses to you personally. Use the acrostic

SAFEPACK: **S**in to avoid. **A**ction to do. **F**aith to exercise. **E**xample to follow. **P**romise to claim. **A**ttitude to change. **C**hallenge to meet. **K**ey to victory in my life today.

Respond. End your quiet time with a prayer of response. Use the PRAY model of prayer: **P**raise. **R**epent. **A**sk. **Y**ield.

Daniel had developed the habit of spending time with God (Dan. 6:10). Like Daniel, we should use the habit-forming power God has given us to make communion with Him follow a godly pattern of behavior.

Father God, help us develop the godly habit of daily
devotions by Your Spirit. In Jesus's name, amen!

_____

_____

_____

_____

HEAR: Highlight

Dean De Castro

*They read from the Book of the Law of God, making
it clear and giving the meaning so that the people
could understood what was being read.*
—NEHEMIAH 8:8

The first step in the HEAR plan of daily devotions is to read a passage of Scripture and highlight the verse or verses that have spoken to you deeply.

In *Conformed to His Image*, Kenneth Boa offers some suggestions for purposeful Scripture reading. Here are some of the recommendations for you to consider:

1. Try to be systematic in selecting your Scripture texts. For example, you can start reading from Genesis 1 to Revelation 22; you can follow a daily reading program that includes readings from the Old Testament, the New Testament, and the book of Psalms; or your passage can come from a devotional guide.
2. To avoid distraction, it is better to use a Bible without study notes. Use an accurate translation rather than a paraphrase.
3. Keep the passage brief—do not confuse quantity with quality.
4. Read the verse you have selected to focus on slowly and prayerfully, and repeat until you have almost memorized it.
5. Try making your first readings audible since that will make them slower and more deliberate.
6. Listen to the words in humility, accompanied by the willingness to obey. Be open to being addressed by the Word in your attitudes, habits, choices, and emotions.

7. Pray as you read the text by asking, "Lord, what are you saying to me in this passage?"

8. Approach reading with no conditions, demands, or expectations. The Word may not meet your perceived needs, but it will touch your actual needs—even when you don't discern them yourself.

For example, the Scripture that stands out for me in reading Matthew 4:1–11 is verse 4: "Man does not live by bread alone, but by every word that comes from the mouth of God." Here are some truths I've learned: Man needs food to live physically; he also needs spiritual food (God's Word) to connect with God. Therefore, we must believe every Word that comes from the mouth of God and not those from the mouth of Satan or other people.

Father God, let Your Word speak to us
today. In Jesus's name, amen!

_____

_____

_____

_____

HEAR: Explain

Dean De Castro

*Just as our dear brother Paul also wrote you with the wisdom
that God gave him...His letters contain some things that are hard
to understand, which ignorant and unstable people distort.*
—2 PETER 3:15–16

In today's passage, Peter warns us to be careful in interpreting
what God said.

The second step in the HEAR plan of daily devotion is to explain
the verse you have chosen to meditate on. We need to learn some
specific and simple rules for interpreting the Bible lest we are found
guilty of distorting its original intention.

Let me cite two examples of how we can misinterpret the Bible.

Flip and dip. There's a story about a Christian who believed in
a Bible reading practice called the "flip and dip" method. He prayed
about a problem, flipped open the Bible, and his finger settled on
Matthew 27:5: Judas "went away and hanged himself." That didn't
sound like the best answer to his problem, so he flipped again. This
time he landed in Luke 10:37: "Go and do likewise." That wouldn't
do either. He was nervous but decided to try it again. He prayed and
flipped the pages, and his fingertip alighted on John 13:27: "What you
are to do, do quickly."

The story is humorous, but it is not without an important message
for us. It points out a problem in biblical interpretation: The wrong
approach and faulty understanding can lead to disaster.

666. Revelation 13:18 states that the number of the beast is 666.
Years ago, as Secretary of State Henry Kissinger made news daily
while on his peace missions in the Middle East and Vietnam, someone
discovered that if you transliterate "Henry Kissinger" into Hebrew
and give a numerical value to each letter, you come up with 666.

Therefore, as this theory goes, he was the Antichrist prophesied by the apostle John.

Of course, this isn't accurate biblical interpretation but a sensationalized coincidence.

How we interpret what the Bible says is critical to its successful use in our everyday life. Faulty interpretation will lead to incorrect application. Therefore, we should seek to accurately understand the meaning of God's words with the Holy Spirit's help.

> *Father God, grant us wisdom to understand Your*
> *Word correctly. In Jesus's name, amen!*

HEAR: Apply

Dean De Castro

But whoever looks intently into the perfect law that gives freedom, and continues in it—not forgetting what they have heard, but doing it—they will be blessed in what they do.
—JAMES 1:25

In the HEAR process of daily devotions, the letter *A* stands for "apply."

This step bridges the gap between the ancient world and your world today. It provides a way for God to speak to you and your life using a specific passage or verse from the Bible.

Merely reading, meditating, and studying God's words are not enough. The ultimate purpose of spending time with God is to love God by obeying all of Christ's words in the power of the Holy Spirit, one choice at a time. I consider this my personal mission statement in life.

The Bible was not given to increase our knowledge but guide our conduct. As German poet Johann von Goethe tells us, "Knowing is not enough; we must apply. Willing is not enough; we must do." And James 1:25 promises us that God will bless us if we lovingly meditate on His words and obey them.

I would suggest using the acrostic SAFEPACK as an aid to help you apply the Scriptures to your life. Mark Littleton recommends these questions in his book, *Delighted by Discipline*: Is there any **S**in to avoid? **A**ction to do? **F**aith to exercise? **E**xample to follow? **P**romise to claim? **A**ttitude to change? **C**hallenge to meet? **K**ey principle to obey in my life today? This doesn't solve all application problems, but it's a good start.

Always remember to make a conscious effort to apply the Scriptures. Always keep in mind this one question: What can I use from this passage in my life today?

In *Personal Bible Study Methods*, Rick Warren suggests four factors that should be involved in coming up with applications: They should be personal, practical, possible, and provable. For example, Ecclesiastes 6:7 says, "All man's efforts are for his mouth, yet his appetite is never satisfied." The four factors in the application could be written out as follows:

Personal: "I need to..."
Practical: "I need to lose some weight."
Possible: "I need to lose 10 pounds."
Provable: "I need to lose 10 pounds before the end of the month."

Father God, let us grow spiritually as we lovingly meditate
on Your words and obey them. In Jesus's name, amen!

HEAR: Respond
Dean De Castro

If you remain in Me and My words remain in you, ask
whatever you wish, and it will be done for you.
—JOHN 15:7

One of the essential components of time with God is time in His Word—the Scriptures.

But another critical factor goes hand in hand with this is prayer. It is a two-way street: talking to the Lord and letting Him speak to us. In John 15:7, our Lord combines keeping His words and praying to Him as the vital parts of abiding in His love.

In our plan of daily devotions, the last letter, *R*, stands for respond. The best way to respond to what God has said through His Word is to pray to Him. To put the essential components of prayer into practice, I would like you to remember the acrostic PRAY suggested by Rick Warren.

Allow me to briefly introduce this prayer model today and explain it in more detail in the days to come.

Praise the Lord. Begin your prayer time by praising God for who He is (adoration) and what He has done (thanksgiving).

Adoration entails giving God the worship He alone deserves. Identify some of His attributes you find particularly meaningful, and take some time to praise God for who He is (1 Chron. 16:25–29). During your daily devotions, thank God for the many blessings in your life, and take a moment to ask God what you need to be thankful for (Ps. 100:4).

Repent of your sins with a prayer of confession. First, ask God to bring to your mind anything that needs to be dealt with, and admit the sin(s) before Him (1 John 1:9). Then, after acknowledging your sins, ask God to help you turn away from them. The Bible calls this repentance (Prov. 28:13).

Ask for yourself and others. Bring personal requests and needs to God (petition) (Phil. 4:6). Also, pray for others (intercession) (1 Sam. 12:23).

Yield yourself to God's will. Your prayer time should end with a time of personal rededication to the Lord.

Reaffirm the lordship of Jesus Christ in your life and pledge your submission and obedience that day to Him (Rom. 6:13; 12:1–2).

Father God, teach us to pray. In Jesus's name, amen!

_____

_____

_____

_____

Three Purposes of Prayer

Dean De Castro

Apart from Me you can do nothing.
—JOHN 15:5

Prayer is crucial because our Lord teaches us that we can do nothing apart from Him.

In 1 Peter 5:5b–10, Peter shows us three reasons prayer is essential in Christian life.

To learn humility (vv. 5b–6). If you only pray when you are in trouble, you have a problem with pride. And as Proverbs 16:18 warns us, "Pride leads to destruction."

When the Israelites trusted and obeyed God's specific instructions to march around the city of Jericho for six days and then seven times on the seventh day, they experienced God's miraculous deliverance (Josh. 6).

But when they fought the small town of Ai, they failed miserably. They were defeated due to the sin of pride. This time, their leader, Joshua, did not inquire about God's direction. Joshua may have thought that this town was so small that they could win the battle without depending on God. Clearly, he was wrong.

To learn dependency (v. 7). Prayer is the tangible expression of our absolute dependency on God. He wants us to cast all our cares on Him and depend entirely on His provision, protection, and power. He wants us to trust Him with all our needs and problems, big or small.

It is dangerous to assume that we don't need God's assistance just because a task appears to be minor or easily done. God is just as concerned with the insignificant troubles in our lives as with the enormous misfortunes. He wants us to acknowledge Him in all the ways we can, and He will direct our path (Prov. 3:5–6).

To resist the enemy (vv. 8–9). Remember, God kicked Satan out of heaven because of the sin of pride. He knows that it is the fundamental sin from which many other sins originate.

A long time ago, in the garden of Eden, Satan tempted Adam and Eve to act independently of God. Since then, he still entices people to the sins of self-sufficiency and misplaced dependency.

Resist the enemy's lie that we are independent creatures who can make it through life on our own. Instead, stand in the truth that we can do everything only through Christ who strengthens us (Phil. 4:13; also see 2 Chron. 7:14).

> *Father God, let us humble ourselves and live a*
> *prayerful life. In Jesus's name, amen!*

PRAY: Praise

Dean De Castro

Let everything that has the breath praise
the Lord. Praise the Lord!
—PSALM 150:6

After God has spoken to you through His Word, respond by talking to Him in prayer.

Start your prayer by praising who He is and what He has done for you. The former is called adoration, and the latter is thanksgiving.

Adoration. Before we repent, ask, and respond to God's words, we should first focus on God's holiness and power. But unfortunately, too much preoccupation with our self-worth makes it easy for us to forget the greatness and beauty of our Creator.

One of the reasons we need to practice the principle of adoration is to remind ourselves daily of God's majesty and glory. When we praise God for who He is, we fulfill the purpose of God in creating us (Rev. 4:11). As humans, we were created for worship. If we fail to worship the true God, we will worship idols by default.

Spending time with God reminds us that God is far greater than our little minds imagine. Therefore, the more our views of God grow, and the more our understanding of Him comes into focus, the more we will become like Christ (2 Cor. 3:18).

We may practice praising God by singing some great hymns of worship from a hymnbook, reading the Psalms, like those in chapters 145–150, and meditating on the different names of God (1 Chron. 16:25–29; 29:10–13).

Thanksgiving. One of the vital ingredients in spending time with God ought to be the practice of giving thanks. As Romans 1:21 implies, ingratitude is a sin.

Adam and Eve had a million reasons to give thanks. Then Satan maliciously planted in the first couple's minds the thought that Eden wasn't enough for them. Christian thinker Os Guinness writes, "Rebellion against God does not begin with clenched fist of atheism but with the self-satisfied heart of the one for whom 'thank you' is redundant."

God doesn't need our gratitude, but He certainly deserves it. In actuality, the need is on our part; it guards our hearts against selfishness. Starting and ending our day in adoration and thanksgiving will keep us focused on God. It reminds us that what matters is God and the glory He receives from our lives.

Father God, to You I give thanks and praise
(Dan. 2:23). In Jesus's name, amen!

_____

_____

_____

_____

PRAY: Repentance

Dean De Castro

*Whoever conceals their sins does not prosper, but the
one who confesses and renounces them finds mercy.*
—PROVERBS 28:13

In the PRAY plan of communicating with God, *R* stands for
"repentance."

After worshipping God with our praise and thanksgiving, we are
now ready to confess and repent of our sins to Him, which always
involves the principles of conviction and forgiveness.

Understanding these four interconnected concepts is important
because they keep our fellowship with God intimate and unbroken.

Conviction. There is a big difference between the Holy Spirit's
conviction and Satan's condemnation. Our great advocate, the Holy
Spirit (John 16:8), will convict us of our sin with repentance and restoration in view, while Satan's condemnation always keeps us down
and miserable.

Whenever Satan or his emissaries bring any charge against us,
remember that "There is now no more condemnation for those who
are in Christ Jesus" (Rom. 8:1). There's no charge pending against any
believer in the court in heaven (Rom. 8:33b–34).

Confession. When the Holy Spirit does convict us, we must
respond with a confession. If we do, the sin will be put behind us and
no longer affect our fellowship with God. But if we don't, our hearts
will become hardened, and we will not enjoy intimacy with the Father.

Don't go looking for something to confess. Instead, ask God to
search your heart (Ps. 139:23–24). Then, if we sincerely desire to
please God, His Holy Spirit, who indwells us, will reveal any sin that
needs to be confessed.

Repentance. The word "confess" in 1 John 1:9 means "to say the same thing" or "to agree" in Greek. In other words, confessing our sins means we agree with what God says about our sins. Genuine repentance acknowledges that we feel sorry for our sin and are also willing to forsake it. Honest confession always leads to repentance (Prov. 28:13).

Forgiveness. God's forgiveness is multidimensional. God promises to remove our transgressions as far as the east is from the west (Ps. 103:12). It is also complete. He will remember all our sins no more (Heb. 10:17); he will "hurl all our iniquities into the depths of the sea" (Mic. 7:19).

Father God, let us confess and forsake
our sins. In Jesus's name, amen!

_____

_____

_____

_____

PRAY: Ask

Dean De Castro

You may ask me for anything in my name, and I will do it.
—JOHN 14:14

In the PRAY plan of communion with God, *A* stands for "ask." This involves asking God for your personal needs and the needs of others. These are the prayers of petition and intercession, respectively.

Petition. Throughout the Bible, God urges us to ask for things for ourselves in prayer. For example, our Lord promises us in John 4:13–14 that we can ask for whatever we want as long as we pray in His name.

In what is commonly called the Lord's Prayer, Jesus wants us to pray to God about our different relationship needs. In the text of the Lord's Prayer in Matthew 6:9–13, we see four types of relationships that we need to ask God for help with.

Relationship with God. "Our Father in heaven, hallowed be Your name, Your kingdom come, Your will be done" (vv. 9–10). We need to pray that our heavenly Father is glorified in everything we ask Him to do for us. Our motive in praying is not to advance our kingdom and seek our will but to work for God's plan and His purposes.

Relationship with ourselves. "Give us today our daily bread" (v. 11). Once we seek God's kingdom and His righteousness, then we can pray for God to provide, protect and heal us.

Relationship with others. "Forgive us our debts, as we also have forgiven our debtors" (v. 12). We can ask God for healthy and harmonious relationships with all the people in our lives.

Relationship with Satan. "And lead us not into temptation, but deliver us from the evil one" (v. 13). We can ask God to protect us from the tempting lies of Satan.

Intercession. The Bible calls on Christians to intercede for others (see 1 Sam. 12:23–24).

So, who are the people in our lives that God would have us pray for? The Bible lists the following groups that we should intercede for:

- Church leaders who have spiritual oversight on us (Heb. 13:7)—pastors, elders, and deacons
- Those under our spiritual charge (1 Sam. 12:23–24)—children, spouses, Sunday school students, and small group members
- God's people, Israel (Ps. 122:6)
- Government leaders (1 Tim. 2:1–2)
- The sick (James 5:15–16)
- Missionaries (Eph. 6:19)
- Our enemies (Matt. 5:8)

Father God, let us pray and trust You can meet
all our needs. In Jesus's name, amen!

_____

_____

_____

_____

PRAY: Yield
Dean De Castro

*But yield yourselves unto God, as those
that are alive from the dead.*
—ROMANS 6:13B, KJV

In the PRAY model of talking to God during our daily devotions, the last letter, *Y*, stands for "yield." Your prayer time should end with a personal commitment to the Lord.

Reaffirm the lordship of Jesus Christ in your life and pledge your submission and obedience to Him for that day. As Romans 6:13 instructs us, we need to yield every member of our body to serve God and please Him.

Handmaidens. "As the eyes of slaves look to the hand of their master, as the eyes of a maid look to the hand of her mistress, so our eyes look to the Lord our God, till He shows us His mercy" (Ps. 123:2).

The setting of this Psalm seems to be a banquet. The hostess, usually unseen by the guests, trains her maids to watch her hand gestures for any instructions she gives. This is the reason they are sometimes called handmaidens.

As the meal progresses, the hostess notes that one of her guests needs a glass of water, a piece of bread, or another pat of butter, and she gives a very subtle hand signal. As the nearest handmaiden sees the movement, she responds, and the guest's need is met.

This psalm underscores the importance of keeping our eyes on the Lord moment by moment so that we can yield every member of our body as "instruments of righteousness" for God.

Medical assistants. It is imperative for a surgeon's medical assistants to observe the hand signals of the doctor and hand him whatever instruments he needs for the operation.

Likewise, during our daily devotions, we need to be alert to get the necessary signals from God, directing us how to spend the day and walk in His ways. Then, we choose by an act of will to obey whatever God lays in our hearts as we meditate His words, praising Him through the actions of adoration and thanksgiving, confessing and repenting our sins, and asking for God's mercy through petition and intercession.

Father God, teach us to focus our minds on You so that we may sense and diligently obey Your will. In Jesus's name, amen!

_____

_____

_____

_____

A Pattern of Prayer

Stephen Olford

Adapted from *Windows of Wisdom*

Lord, teach us to pray.
—LUKE 11:1

After observing Jesus always praying, the disciples requested, "Lord, teach us to pray" (Luke 11:1). The Lord answered their appeal with what we know as the Lord's Prayer (Matt. 6:9–13). This pattern stresses three aspects of a prayerful life.

Prayer should reflect the devotion of a Son. "Our Father in heaven" (v. 9). In John 17, our Lord refers to God as His Father six times. Notice the progression: "Father" (vv. 1, 5, 21, 24), "holy Father" (v. 11), "righteous Father" (v. 25).

Prayer should reflect the submission of a servant. "Your kingdom come, your will be done" (Matt. 6:10). Our learning and adjusting to God's will are critical parts of prayer. And we learn God's will from reading His words during our quiet time. As you pray back to God what He has already said to you from His Word, your will is adjusted to fit His will. Now you can establish on earth what God has already said in heaven.

Prayer should reflect the petition of a supplicant. First, the daily business: "Give us this day our daily bread" (Matt. 6:11). Nothing is insignificant in the sight of God. As suppliants, we must come to God in simple faith, believing that He will hear our requests and answer our prayers.

Second, the daily burden: "Forgive our debts, as we forgive our debtors." The burden of sin is a constant issue in our walk with God. But thank God our Lord carried the burden of human sin and bore that burden on Calvary's cross so that we might know forgiveness and cleansing.

Third, the daily battle: "And do not lead us into temptation, but deliver us from the evil one" (Matt. 6:13). Certainly, the devil will tempt us, particularly concerning our devotional life. But you and I can know victory in Jesus (1 John 2:14).

As we trust the Lord Jesus to do in us and through us what we cannot achieve for ourselves, we can be "more than conquerors through Him who loved us" (Rom. 8:37).

Holy Spirit, teach us to pray as our Lord taught
His disciples. In Jesus's name, amen!

_____

_____

_____

_____

Overcoming Everything with Prayer

David Jeremiah

Adapted from *Overcoming*

Always keep on praying.
—EPHESIANS 6:18

Prayer is the secret lifeline that connects us to God, giving us His strength and direction daily. Paul devoted a unique space to prayer following his discussion of the believer's armor (Eph. 6:10–16).

Pray on all occasions. Whether you're sitting at a stoplight, waiting at school, seeing the doctor, doing the laundry, or mowing the lawn—any time you have a spare moment, keep the communication lines open between you and the throne of God.

We should pray at public occasions, such as church meetings (Acts 12:5) and prayer groups (Acts 12:12). In addition, we should pray at social and festive events, such as weddings, parties, or dinners.

Pray in all places. New Testament people prayed in the following locations: in a solitary place (Mark 1:35), on a mountain (Matt. 14:23), in the temple (Luke 2:37), on a housetop (Acts 10:9), in a house (Acts 19:30), in the church (Acts 12:5), at a riverside (Acts 16:13), on a ship (Acts 27:29), and in prison (Acts 27:29).

Pray at all times. The New Testament records prayers being offered before daylight (Mark 1:35), on the Sabbath day (Acts 16:13), when alone (Luke 9:18), when together (Acts 2:42), all night (Luke 6:12), night and day (1 Tim. 5:5), and continually (Acts 6:4). So, we can and should pray at any hour.

Pray for all things. We should pray for personal things, household concerns, business, and work items. *All* things should be covered by prayer. If it's something you're concerned about, it's something you should pray about often.

As you embrace the practice of prayer, you'll find many ways to fill your life with it. First, pray in the ways that come naturally, then grow and mature your practice of prayer steadily. This is how to prepare yourself with your Commander as you engage in life's daily battles.

Our goal as overcomers is to be able to reach out in prayer at any moment and immediately be in touch with God. Our whole life can be a prayer as we walk daily with Him. Don't sweat the details; leave those to God. Just pray!

Father God, let us learn prayer as the vital foundation
to life as an overcomer. In Jesus's name, amen!

_____

_____

_____

_____

The Discipline of Reading God's Word

Donald S. Whitney
Adapted from *Spiritual Disciplines for the Christian Life*

Have you not read?
—MATTHEW 19:4, ESV

Jesus often asked questions about people's understanding of the Scriptures: "Have you not read?" He assumed that those claiming to be God's people would have read the Word of God.

Spiritual disciplines are scriptural paths where we encounter the transforming grace of God. And the most critical spiritual exercise is the intake of God's Word. In order to be changed and become more like Christ, discipline yourself to read the Bible regularly.

Here are the three practical suggestions for consistent success in Bible reading.

First, find the time. Then try to make it the same time every day. Did you know that if you set aside fifteen minutes a day, you can read through the Bible in less than a year?

Second, find a Bible reading plan and stick to it. It's no wonder that those who open the Bible to read from a random text each day soon drop the discipline.

Third, take at least one thing you've read and think deeply about it for a few moments. Your insight into Scripture will deepen, and you'll better understand how it applies to your life.

In *The Wonder of the Word of God*, Robert L. Sumner tells of a man who lost his eyesight in an explosion. He had just become a Christian when the accident happened, and one of his disappointments was that he could no longer read the Bible.

Then he heard about a lady in England who read braille with her lips. So, hoping to do the same, he sent for some books of the Bible in braille. But he discovered that the nerve endings in his lips had been too severely damaged to distinguish the characters.

One day, as he brought one of the braille pages to his lips, his tongue touched a few of the raised characters, and he could feel them. Then, in a flash, he thought, "I can read the Bible using my tongue." By the time Summer wrote his book, the blind man had read through the entire Bible four times.

If he could do that, do you think you can discipline yourself to read the Bible?

Father God, help us discipline ourselves in reading
Your Word every day. In Jesus's name, amen!

_____

_____

_____

_____

Seven Things the Bible Will Do for You!

Dr. Stanley Toussaint
Adapted from *Veritas*, vol. 12, no. 1 (January 2012)

All Scripture...is useful.
—2 TIMOTHY 3:16

Psalm 19:7–11 shows us different aspects of God's Word. It also tells us at least seven things the Bible will do for you.

The Bible will restore you. "Reviving" or "restoring" (v. 7a, NASB) communicates the idea of refreshing or encouraging us (see Ps. 23:3). The Word of God replaces our weakness and weariness of soul with strength and vitality (see Isa. 40:31).

The Bible will make you wise. "Make wise the simple" (Ps 19:7b). Intelligence and wisdom are vastly different. I have seen brilliant people make foolish decisions. And ordinary people make wise decisions because their priorities are right.

The Bible will give you joy. "Giving joy to the heart" (v. 8a). The presence or absence of joy is a dead giveaway as to whether the Word of God is impacting your life. The apostles, for example, came away "rejoicing" after being flogged because they had preached the gospel (Acts 5:41).

The Bible will be your spiritual "vitamin." "Giving light to the eyes" (Ps. 19:8b) literally means that God's Word will provide you with "bright eyes." Just as food refreshes and strengthens the body, the Word of God will give you "bright eyes" because it will be your spiritual vitamin (see 1 Sam. 14:29).

The Bible will be your enduring hope. There is nothing that can wear away the Word of God; it endures forever. It is more precious than gold (Ps. 19:9–10). So, if you build your life and hope on the foundation of the Bible, it will never collapse or erode beneath you.

The Bible will warn you of danger. "By them is your servant warned" (v. 11a). The Bible both marks out for us the path God wants His people to follow and warns us of the danger and foolishness of disobeying Him and wandering off into sin.

The Bible will tell you of God's rewards. "In keeping them there is great reward" (v. 11b). There is excellent reward both in this life and the life to come for those who believe and keep God's Word.

Father God, when You speak, may Your servants
listen and obey. In Jesus's name, amen!

_____

_____

_____

_____

The Discipline of Bible Meditation
Dean De Castro

May the words of my mouth and the meditation
of my heart be pleasing in Your sight.
—PSALM 19:14

Here are seven steps on how to meditate on the passage of Scripture that speaks to you personally while reading it during your quiet time.

Vocalize. Reading the verse audibly helps you concentrate and also forces you to slowly engraft God's words onto the depths of your heart (Josh. 1:8).

Analyze. Ask the six questions: Who were the people involved? What was taking place in this passage? Where was it taking place? When did it happen? Why did God include it in the Bible? How did it happen?

Don't be concerned if you can't find the answer to each question. There are many types of literature in the Bible, and not all the questions will apply in every case.

Personalize. This is when we take the Bible and treat it autobiographically. So, for example, in meditating on John 3:16, you could personally insert your name and apply the verse to yourself. This makes you feel God speaking to you directly.

Visualize. Our imagination is a gift from God to be used wisely. A sanctified imagination can help make the Bible alive for us. For example, when you read Mark 4:35–40, can you imagine yourself amid the storm and identify with the disciples' terrifying experience?

Summarize. Try to write out an explanation of what you think the verse means. Then paraphrase the verse like you would teaching it to a child. Why? To simplify and make a truth understandable, you must first understand it yourself.

Memorize. Memorizing the Scriptures enables us to mull over God's thoughts during the day quickly, even when asleep at night (Ps. 119:11).

Actualize. The heart of understanding the Bible is applying it in every area of our lives. God wants us to follow His commands and take action (James 1:22–26).

As we meditate on God's truths and understand them, we can follow in the steps of the ancient Ethiopian who, after a better understanding of the Scriptures, "went on his way rejoicing" (Acts 8:39).

Father God, let us delight in Your Word and meditate
on it day and night. In Jesus's name, amen!

_____

_____

_____

_____

Meditate on the Lord Jesus Christ

Daniel Henderson
Adapted from strategicrenewal.com

Remember Jesus Christ.
—2 TIMOTHY 2:8

I wrote an acrostic to meditate on the names of the Lord Jesus Christ. Let these names empower your trust and obedience as you follow Him.

Light of the world. I invite God's light to expose and cleanse my sin and selfishness (John 8:12).

Only wise God. I ask and receive from Him all necessary guidance and direction for my life today (Col. 2:3).

Rock of my salvation. I feel secure knowing that my Lord has already done everything to save and keep me in His love forever (1 Cor. 10:4).

Desire of all nations. I will passionately proclaim His beauty, expressing to others the delight I have found in Him (Phil. 4:4).

Justifier. I do not have to work to be accepted by God because He has already made me righteous in His sight (2 Cor. 5:21).

Emmanuel. I will enjoy and practice His incredible presence, knowing He is always with me (Matt. 1:23).

Strength of my soul. I delight in my weaknesses so that God may demonstrate His power through me (2 Tim. 2:1).

Unchanging friend. I rest in Jesus's faithful companionship and total commitment to me (John 15:15).

Savior. I kneel before His cross in grateful worship and live by faith because He loved me and gave Himself for me (1 Tim. 4:10).

Cornerstone. I allow Christ to build my life by His strength and stability (Eph. 2:20).

Healer of my soul. Christ heals all my hurts, disappointments, and fears through His supernatural touch of wholeness, encouragement, and peace (Ps. 147:3).

Resurrection and the life. Christ lives through me today in the triumph He has already achieved over all sin and death (John 11:25).

Image of the invisible God. I gaze upon Christ in intimacy today that He might reveal the fullness of the Father, Son, and Holy Spirit to my heart (Col. 1:15).

Shield of my salvation. I trust Christ today to protect my faith and preserve my life by His promise and power (Ps. 18:2).

Truth. I entrust to Christ all my questions, receiving counsel from His word to live with confidence in this world (John 14:6).

Father God, let us meditate on our Lord Jesus
Christ day and night. In Jesus's name, amen!

_____

_____

_____

_____

Beholding Christ in the Scriptures

Dean De Castro

*But we all, with open face beholding as in a glass the glory of
the Lord, are changed into the same image from glory to glory.*
—2 CORINTHIANS 3:18, KJV

The glass or mirror is a symbol of God's Word (James 1:23). And Jesus
Christ is the central theme of the entire Bible. As you study the character of Christ in each book of the Scriptures, the Holy Spirit gradually transforms you into the likeness of Christ, from glory to glory.

The Old Testament. The thirty-nine books of the Old Testament set
the scene for Christ, create the need for Him, and predict His coming.

On the road to Emmaus, the resurrected Christ explained to two
depressed followers, "beginning with Moses and all the prophets,"
what the Old Testament says concerning His death and resurrection
(Luke 24:27). Watch the change in these disciples' demeanor, "Were
not our hearts burning within us while He talked with us on the road
and opened the Scriptures to us?" (v. 32).

The four Gospels. The Gospels reveal our Lord's glory and beauty.
First, in Matthew, we see Christ as the King of our life. Second, Mark
teaches us to serve as Christ served—selflessly. Third, we learn compassion from Luke, as Christ came to seek and save the sinners. Finally,
through John, Jesus Christ promises us abundant life.

The Acts of the Apostles. This book primarily highlights the works
of Peter (chapters 1-12) and Paul (chapters 13–28). It is incredible
to see the power of the Holy Spirit change a fearful Peter into a fearless apostle.

Likewise, Paul's miraculous conversion on the way to murder
Christians demonstrates the ability of the gospel to change lives from
the inside out.

The Epistles. From Romans to Revelation, we learn the gospel of God's grace justifies sinners to stand righteous before God and transforms believers to become saints in practice. The gospel is not only given to the unbelievers but also the born-again Christians.

As Jerry Bridges challenges us, "We must preach the gospel to ourselves every day...none is more important than the discipline of beholding the glory of Christ in the mirror of the gospel."

Father God, let us behold the glory and beauty
of Christ in Your Word. Change us to become
more like Him. In Jesus's name, amen!

_____

_____

_____

_____

The Discipline of Memorizing Scriptures
Charles Swindoll
Adapted from *Growing Strong in the Seasons of Life*

My son, keep my words and store up my commands within you.
—PROVERBS 7:1

Memorizing the Scriptures is a significant part of biblical meditation. In fact, it can be the most rewarding spiritual practice in the Christian life.

There are many benefits in storing up God's words in our hearts: It will strengthen your prayer life. Your attitudes and outlook will begin to change. Your mind will become alert and observant. Memorizing Scriptures will enhance your confidence and assurance. It will solidify your faith.

Here are several helpful tips for you to consider:

1. Choose a time when your mind is free from outside distractions, perhaps soon after getting up in the morning.
2. Learn the reference by repeating it every time you say the verse(s).
3. Read each verse several times, both in a whisper and aloud.
4. Break the passage into natural phrases. Learn the reference and then the first phrase. Then repeat the reference and first phrase as you go to the second phrase.
5. Learn a little bit perfectly rather than a great deal poorly. Do not go on to the next verse until you can say the previous one(s) perfectly without looking at your Bible.
6. Review consistently. Review the verse immediately after you have gone through this process. Then, twenty to thirty minutes later, repeat what you've memorized. Before the day has

ended, firmly fix the verse in your mind by going over it fifteen to twenty more times.

7. Use the verse orally as soon as possible. After all, the purpose of Scripture memorization is practical, not academic. Therefore, use the memorized Scriptures in conversation, correspondence, teaching, counseling, and witnessing. Relate what you've learned to your daily situation.

8. Start with an easy verse that won't discourage you. A short verse, like "Jesus wept" (John 11:35), has meaning and value. But move on to longer passages as soon as possible.

9. Choose Scripture that is personal to you. Select verses you can use to defend against Satan as Jesus did (Matt. 4:4, 7, 10).

10. Ask someone to support you in doing this.

Father God, help us hide Your words in our hearts
lest we sin against You. In Jesus's name, amen!

Six Big Reasons You Fail at Quiet Times

Rachel Dawson
Adapted from crosswalk.com

Come near to God and He will come near to you.
—JAMES 4:8

So many of us have struggled to keep consistent quiet time practices, but we might not even seriously and carefully think about why that is.

Here are a few common obstacles to our daily devotions.

Not having enough structure. If your only plan is to let your Bible fall open before you, it can be hard to feel engaged in your quiet times. Instead, try starting with a reading plan that gives you a designated passage of Scripture (or several) to read each day.

Having too much structure. Quiet times may include journaling, deep Bible study, and comparing Bible translations. However, it's unrealistic to accomplish too much in a small chunk of time.

Instead, focus on just one or two elements to include in your quiet time, such as reading the assigned passages from your reading plan and then journaling some thoughts or prayers. Then, as you build the habit of daily devotions, you can add more components to your study.

Fighting your natural rhythms. You should work with your nature instead of against it. For example, if mornings and evenings are challenging times for you, consider another chunk of time that will work well with your schedule, such as a lunch break or during your child's nap.

Not eliminating distractions. Turn your TV and phone off (or on silent mode) and leave them out of arm's reach, go somewhere you can be alone, turn off all electronics and noise-making devices around you, and straighten up the area so messes or other distractions nearby don't steal your attention.

Not knowing your purpose. If you open your Bible without any real goals in mind, you're unlikely to feel productive and purposeful. Even if your objective is just to read one chapter, having a manageable plan helps you stay focused and on track.

Being too ambitious. Trying to read the entire Bible in a few months during your daily devotions can be overwhelming. Instead, start with a certain length of time, perhaps twenty minutes a day, to stay committed and move forward.

Father God, help us overcome the obstacles of maintaining
our daily devotional time. In Jesus's name, amen!

_____

_____

_____

_____

The Cure for Distraction

J. D. Greear
Adapted from jdgreear.com

*Lord, don't you care that my sister has left me to
do the work by myself? Tell her to help me!*
—LUKE 10:40

Martha's rebuke of her sister Mary, who sat at Jesus's feet listening to Him instead of helping Martha serve their guests, reveals that Jesus was not in the right place in Martha's heart.

Martha's problem. Martha's failure to sit at Jesus's feet like Mary showed that her soul craved the significance that came from serving.

Martha should have been fellowshipping with Jesus and doing His will such that she didn't feel the need to prove herself. Hence, she could have sat when Jesus wanted her to sit and gotten up and served if and when He called her to do that.

Like Martha, when our soul is out of fellowship with Jesus, we crave all the more for the next enticement that crosses our path. But as Christ's followers, we are supposed to have such satisfaction in knowing and doing the will of God that we are not susceptible to other cravings.

Mary's example. In Mary, we see the antidote to distraction. Mary sat at the feet of Jesus, listening to His words. In the Bible, getting down at someone's feet means you are under their authority. That means Mary was both focused and submissive.

Personal application. Don't just sit through an occasional sermon and equate it with sitting at Jesus's feet. Sitting at Jesus's feet means setting aside a devoted, sacred time when you pay attention to Him and His Word. Consequently, you'll feel the warmth of Jesus's love and won't feel the burden of always trying to prove yourself or carry the weight alone.

Second, because you'll be more in touch with His Spirit, you'll be more aware when something is not a distraction but a divine interruption.

Martin Luther once said that he had to get up even earlier on his busiest days to spend more time with God. The more active the day, the more we needed to fellowship with God and prevent busyness from distracting us from Him.

Don't let today's distraction destroy the peace and satisfaction that come from learning and resting at the feet of Jesus.

> *Father God, save us from worldly distractions that keep us from spending time with You. In Jesus's name, amen!*

_____

_____

_____

_____

Phases of Daily Devotions

Dean De Castro

God goes with you; He will never leave you nor forsake you.
—DEUTERONOMY 31:6

Early in my Christian life, several older and more mature believers taught me the importance of developing the discipline of daily devotions.

So, whenever we met at the church, they would ask me the same question: "How is your daily devotions habit?" To impress them, I faithfully kept my appointment with God every morning. I did this consistently for almost a year and found it personally delightful; I was quite satisfied in God's presence.

One day, I woke up and did my usual morning devotions, but I felt dead in my spirit this time. I also felt guilty. I thought I may have sinned against God, and I tried to confess every sin I could think of.

Like me, many Christians have learned the importance of meeting with God regularly. So, they try to do it for a while, then often give up when they don't experience the presence of God. Some even feel condemned whenever people inquire about their daily devotional practice.

Unfortunately, most Christians conclude that it is possible to be a mature Christian without having this life-changing ritual established in their busy schedules.

I struggled in my devotional life for many years until I read the pamphlet *Quiet Time Dynamics* by Stephen Eyre. He argues that whatever our quiet time experience look like, there is no place for self-condemnation or pride.

It is undoubtedly a gift of His grace to us whenever we do well. When we do poorly, we shouldn't be surprised. God isn't. We should keep in mind that God's love is not based on whether or not we maintain a quiet time. Nevertheless, it's best to just do it even when you don't feel like it. It will build your character.

If you are experiencing a lapse in your relationship with God, you may not have the healthy habit of seeking God's face daily. I also pray that the reflections here on daily devotions and quiet times will comfort you, reminding you that wherever you are in your walk with God, He will never leave you nor forsake you.

Father God, when we fail to keep our daily devotions, we know that You still love us. In Jesus's name, amen!

_____

_____

_____

_____

Living Loved
Dean De Castro

He...will rejoice over you with singing.
—ZEPHANIAH 3:17

The secret to loving is living loved.

God loves you. Nothing in you gave rise to it, and nothing in you can extinguish it. So, accept and enjoy God's love. And to the degree you do, you will be able to give that love to others.

Personal testimony. I grew up in a Christian school where I learned that Jesus loves me because the Bible tells me so (John 3:16). Then, in 1997, I attended a three-week intensive course at the Counseling Institute in Great Britain, which was founded and run by Rev. Selwyn Hughes.

During the training, God used Zephaniah 3:17 to reveal that He loves me and *likes* me. He delights in me to the point that He serenades me with joy. I remember not sleeping several nights, thinking that God still wants me despite my many imperfections and shortcomings.

King David. In Psalm 18:19, King David also shared a similar experience: "He brought me forth also into a large place; He was delivering me because He was pleased with me and delighted in me" (AMP).

David mentions this again in 2 Samuel 22:20. He was far from perfect, but he believed God was pleased with him. And God indeed took pleasure and delighted in him.

The prodigal son. God may not be pleased with all our behavior. He knows that often we would act like the prodigal son, who might run away from Him and disobey Him. But just as the prodigal son's father waited patiently for his child to come home, our heavenly Father is waiting to welcome and embrace us when we decide to return to His bosom.

Therefore, we need to accept and work on our weaknesses while allowing God to love us as we are.

You are loved by God even when nobody loves you. Your parents may abandon you. Your spouse may divorce you. Your friends may betray you. Your children may ignore you. But God will still love you. Psalm 27:10 assures us of God's passionate and unrelenting love: "Though my father and mother forsake me, the Lord will receive me."

Father God, help us accept and enjoy Your love so that we can love others the way You love us. In Jesus's name, amen!

Love Ourselves Correctly

Dean De Castro

Love your neighbor as yourself.
—MARK 12:31

As we focus on how God loves us, we must first apply His love in the way we relate to ourselves.

Failure to love ourselves appropriately keeps us from loving God and our neighbors. As Charles Stanley writes, "We can't fully love God or anyone else unless we love ourselves."

I grew up listening to sermons that were against teaching the importance of a positive self-image or growing in self-esteem. Many well-meaning Christians believe that psychology belongs to the devil. I got the mistaken impression that God would automatically take care of my mental, emotional, and physical well-being if I just cared for my spiritual health.

There are numerous biblical commands concerning our relationships with God and others. But have you considered the other instructions given in the Bible regarding our responsibility toward ourselves?

- Examine our faith (2 Cor. 13:5)
- Exercise self-control (Gal. 5:23)
- Guard our hearts with all diligence (Prov. 4:23)
- Present our bodies to God as living sacrifices (Rom. 12:1)
- See ourselves as dead to sin and alive to God (Rom. 6:11)
- Make a covenant with our eyes (Job 31:1)
- Save ourselves from this corrupt generation (Acts 2:40)
- Train ourselves unto godliness (1 Tim. 4:8)
- Discipline our bodies like athletes (1 Cor. 9:27)
- Encourage ourselves (Ps. 42:5, 11)
- Build ourselves up (Jude 20)

- Work out our own salvation with fear and trembling (Phil. 2:12)
- Do not think too highly of ourselves (Rom. 12:3)
- Do not deceive ourselves (Gal. 6:7)
- Do not be distressed and hate ourselves (Gen. 45:5)

How we treat ourselves will determine how we treat others. If we reject ourselves, we will unconsciously pass along some form of rejection to those closest to us. As a result, we will attract people into our lives who will give us just the rejection we so ardently seek.

God has accepted us in Christ (Eph. 1:6). Jesus died for us so that we don't have to reject ourselves. If we learn to obey God's commands to love and respect ourselves in a healthy and balanced way, we will love people compassionately and love God completely.

Father God, let us accept and appreciate our worth and importance in Your sight. In Jesus's name, amen!

_____

_____

_____

_____

The Golden Rule (1)

Dean De Castro

Do to others what you would have them do to you,
for this sums up the Law and the Prophets.
—MATTHEW 7:12

This Scripture gives us the best explanation of what it means to love your neighbor as yourself.

People universally demand respect, love, and appreciation, whether they deserve it or not. Jesus understood this innate desire and used it to promote godly behavior. Do you want to be shown respect? Then respect others.

This Golden Rule of relationships is consistent with the other teachings in the Scripture: "Do not be deceived: God cannot be mocked. A man reaps what he sows" (Gal. 6.:7). "Do not judge. For in the same way you judge others, you will be judged, and with the measure you use, it will be measured to you" (Matt. 7:1–2).

Self-worth is important. Seeing our worth from God's perspective is not narcissism or egotism. As believers, we belong to God, "marked in Him with a seal, the promised Holy Spirit" (Eph. 1:13). So, shouldn't we love ourselves appropriately and treat ourselves as people of God, with dignity and respect?

Mother Teresa of Calcutta felt that each person she met was "Jesus in disguise." She recognized that God loves even the unbelievers since they have the image of God in them. Hence, we should not curse people but always treat them with honor and respect (James 3:9).

Balance is crucial. As with many other truths in the Bible, maintaining a balanced perspective is vital. For example, Philippians 2:4 states, "Each of you should look not only to your own interests but also to the interests of others." Notice the words "not only...but also." This verse teaches us to look for the interests of others. But it does not say that we ought to neglect our own needs. On the contrary, both self-interest and other-interest must be balanced properly.

Romans 12:3 says, "Do not think of yourself more highly than you ought, but rather think of yourself with sober judgment." Considering ourselves with sober judgment means not overestimating ourselves, our abilities, or our importance. But it's also wrong to think too lowly of ourselves. We need to follow Paul's advice here and keep the right balance.

Father God, let us learn to love ourselves in a godly balanced way. In Jesus's name, amen!

The Golden Rule (2)
Adapted from gotquestions.org

Do to others what you would have them do to you,
for this sums up the Law and the Prophets.
—MATTHEW 7:12

Liberal critics and secular humanists contend that Jesus's Golden Rule shares a common ethic with all religions. A quick survey of the sayings of Eastern religions will make this plain:

- Confucianism*:* "Do not do to others what you do not want them to do to you" (*Analects* 15:23)
- Hinduism: "This is the sum of duty: do not do to others what would cause pain if done to you" (*Mahabharata* 5:1517).
- Buddhism: "Hurt not others in ways you yourself would find hurtful" (*Udanavarga* 5:18).

These sayings are similar to the Golden Rule but are stated *negatively* and rely on passivity. Jesus's Golden Rule is a positive command to show love proactively. The Eastern religions say it is enough to hold your negative behavior in check; Jesus says to look for ways to act positively.

Because of the "inverted" nature of these non-Christian sayings, they have been described as the "silver rule."

Who borrowed from whom? Some have accused Jesus of "borrowing" the idea of the Golden Rule from the Eastern religions. However, the texts from Confucianism, Hinduism, and Buddhism, cited above, were all written between 500 and 400 BC at the earliest.

Jesus takes the Golden Rule from Leviticus, written about 1450 BC. So, Jesus's source for the Golden Rule predates the "silver rule" by about one thousand years.

Love your enemies. The command to love separates the Christian ethic from every other religion's ethic. The Bible's championing of love includes the radical command to love even one's enemies (Matt. 5:43–44; cf. Exod. 23:4–5). This is unheard of in other religions.

Obeying the Christian imperative to love others is a mark of a genuine Christian (John 13:35). Christians cannot claim to love God if they don't actively love other people. "If anyone says, 'I love God' and hates his brother whom he has seen, cannot love God whom he has not seen" (1 John 4:20). The Golden Rule encapsulates this idea and is unique to the Judeo-Christian Scriptures.

> *Father God, let our relational style of loving others as we love ourselves distinguish our love from the love of the unbelievers to each other. In Jesus's name, amen!*

_____

_____

_____

_____

The New Commandment

Dean De Castro

A new command I give you: Love one another.
As I have loved you, so you must love one another.
—JOHN 13:34

The command to love people appeared numerous times in the Old Testament. So, in that sense, it is not new. But Jesus called it a new command for three reasons:

New pattern: Christ's love. "As I have loved you." In the Old Testament, God gave a general command for people to love their neighbors as themselves. But in the New Testament, our Lord's entrance into humanity and the way He related to people gave a new focus for love that the Old Testament had not been able to do.

By Jesus washing all of the twelve disciples' feet (including Judas's, who later betrayed Him), our Lord put nuance into the word "love": God's unconditional love is demonstrated in loving service and limitless sacrifice.

The most loving Christians have a profound understanding of how much God loves them.

New power: The Holy Spirit. After Jesus commanded His disciples to love one another, He immediately talked about the coming of the Holy Spirit, who would empower them to walk in divine love (John 14:14–15).

Loving people is a risky endeavor and involves messy relationships and maybe even rejection and loneliness. However, loving people without self-protection is the path of self-denial and cross-bearing. Unless a person is born again and has the Holy Spirit dwelling in them, no human being can love the way Jesus loved.

New purpose: Evangelism. "By this all men will know that you are my disciples, if you love one another" (John 13:35). The most effective strategy for evangelism is the love and unity of the church. When relationships break down among Christians, those outside the faith become more convinced that Christianity lacks the very things they need—love, affirmation, and integrity.

Conflicts in the church prove to the world that Christianity does not work. The world will not see God's love for all unless we Christians model it. For example, the early church in Jerusalem experienced tremendous growth because believers loved Jesus and faithfully obeyed His command to love in the way they were loved (Acts 2:42).

Father God, let the world see in us Your love
for them. In Jesus's name, amen!

_____

_____

_____

_____

Love Is Patient and Kind

Dean De Castro

Love is patient, love is kind.
—1 CORINTHIANS 13:4A

Loving others is an overflow of God's love for us.

In 1 Corinthians 13, Paul spells out how we can love people the way God loves us. The first two characteristics Paul mentions to describe this love are patience and kindness.

Some people are naturally patient in temperament, but they are not necessarily kind in deeds. On the contrary, they might be passive and lazy. However, the Bible combines patience and kindness in describing the attitude of mature believers.

Patient. The word "patient" in Chinese consists of two characters: the word "dagger" on top of the word "heart." What a fitting way of describing the pain involved in controlling one's temper. Such difficulty is why so many people are impatient and ill-tempered.

A patient person is tolerant of other people's weaknesses and is willing to adjust and be flexible. Many marriages could be saved if couples learn to accept each other and give up trying to change the other person. "We who are strong ought to bear with the failings of the weak and not to please ourselves" (Rom. 15:1).

If we lack patience, we can always ask God for it (see Jam. 1:5). But be ready to deal with difficult people that God may bring into your life. It's humanly impossible to develop the virtue of patience when there is no opportunity to exercise it.

Kind. True love finds what people need tries to provide it. Therefore, to show our love, we must show kindness to others in our words and deeds.

We are kind, for example, when we say encouraging words to people around us (Eph. 4:29). The leadership expert John Maxwell has a thirty-second rule he practices. Whenever he goes and meets people, it's his habit to use the first thirty seconds of his time to compliment people. This are not meant to patronize people but to build them up.

We also show kindness through our actions and deeds (1 John 3:18). As the poet Henry Burton writes,

> Have you had a kindness shown?
> Pass it on;
> 'Twas not given for thee alone,
> Pass it on;
> Let it travel down the years,
> Let it wipe another's tears,
> Till in Heaven the deed appears—Pass it on.

> *Father God, let us bear the pain of patience and the effort of kindness. In Jesus's name, amen!*

_____

_____

_____

_____

Love Is Humble

Dean De Castro

It does not envy, it does not boast, it is not proud.
—1 CORINTHIANS 13:4B

Pride causes people to boast about what they have and do.

Arrogant people are also jealous of other people's possessions and accomplishments. For good reason, pride and envy are mentioned together in Galatians 5:26. Therefore, it is fair to conclude that proud people desire to keep glory for themselves and, at the same time, want other people's prestige as well.

Pride. A haughty spirit permeated the church at Corinth and generated many of its problems. Arrogance is contrary to love because it focuses on one's self more than others. Pride, therefore, can easily lead to envy and boasting.

True love, however, thinks humbly and modestly about oneself and others (Rom. 12:3). The spirit of love says, "Do not be haughty, but associate with the lowly. Never be conceited" (Rom. 12:16). Our Lord is our best example: "gentle and lowly in heart" (Matt. 11:29).

Envy. Envy and jealousy are not the same. Jealousy desires what someone else has. But envy is jealousy with malice, an intent to hurt or bring another person down. Envy comes with bitterness and anger, and so it naturally leads to strife. And as James 3:16 states, where envy and strife are found, you will also find confusion and Satan's evil works.

On the other hand, God's love rejoices in others' talents and successes. As John MacArthur writes, "When love sees someone who is popular, successful, beautiful, talented, it is glad for them and never jealous or envious."

Boast. The church at Corinth was guilty of boasting. They bragged about their speaking ability, broad knowledge of God's truth, and diverse spiritual gifts (1 Cor. 1:5, 7). In 1 Corinthians 1:10, 12, believers also bragged about their famous leaders, like Peter, Apollos, and Paul, and some even boasted of only following Christ.

But boasting does not honor Christ. Instead, it intimidates and divides people. It provokes others to envy. Humble people, on the other hand, are not self-absorbed braggarts. Instead, they praise others according to love's "more excellent way."

Jealous people tear others down, braggarts build themselves up, but loving and humble people build others up.

Father God, let us humbly praise others and rejoice in their abilities and accomplishments. In Jesus's name, amen!

_____

_____

_____

_____

Love Is Courteous

Dean De Castro

It is not rude, it is not self-seeking.
—1 CORINTHIANS 13:5A

Selfishness is the root; rudeness is the fruit.

People are rude because they only think about their own opinions and comfort. A loving person will not intentionally do or say anything that will embarrass another person, either publicly or privately.

Loving Christians "show proper respect to everyone, love the brotherhood of believers" (1 Pet. 2:17a). Here are three key things that we need to respect about other people.

Respect people's feelings. A lack of love was evident in the rude behavior of the church at Corinth. In 1 Corinthians 14, Paul describes an incident where members were rude and disrespectful.

Some people were eager to exercise their spiritual gifts in sharing God's words, monopolizing the time and hindering others from expressing their own gifts. They were being rude and unloving, with no regard for others. Paul instructs them to take turns in speaking, ensuring that "everything should be done in a fitting and orderly way" (v. 40).

Courteous conduct honors God and His children. In *A Love Worth Giving*, Max Lucado writes, "When you make an effort to greet everyone in the room, especially the ones others may have overlooked, you honor God's children."

Respect people's opinions. In 1 Corinthians 8, some church members at Corinth thoughtlessly used their so-called superior knowledge and liberties to trample on the consciences of their weaker brothers and sisters. For example, they ate foods offered to pagan idols, which created confusion and caused some believers to violate their beliefs.

Loving Christians are willing to respect others' opinions—even if they disagree. The best guideline to follow when believers disagree about debatable doctrines can be summed up in just a few words: In essentials unity; in nonessentials liberty; in all things charity.

Respect people's dignity. James 3:9 tells us not to curse people because they carry the image of God within them.

Our Lord is not rude. He always knocks before entering. "Behold, I stand at the door and knock" (Rev. 3:20, NASB) And when you answer, He awaits your invitation to cross the threshold. If anyone has the right to barge in, Christ does. But He doesn't. He respects people's right to decide who comes into their lives and determine their own futures.

> *Father God, let us be sensitive to the feelings, opinions,*
> *and dignity of our fellow men. In Jesus's name, amen!*

The Most Unselfish Man

Selwyn Hughes

Adapted from *Christ Empowered Living*

It is not self-seeking.
—1 CORINTHIANS 13:5

Jesus was the least selfish and self-seeking man who ever walked the earth.

Take His last hours, study His demeanor from Judas's traitorous kiss until His final moments on the cross, and you will see that His thoughts are always for others.

His silence in the judgment hall is partly explained by the high priest's question about His disciples; He was determined to say nothing about them.

In the garden, He hastened to identify Himself to the officers in charge of the soldiers so that His disciples could get away quickly (John 18:4–8). Always, He was other-centered.

After leaving the high priest's palace, He turned to Peter and, with just a look, unsealed a fount of tears as Peter went out and wept bitterly. What was it about that look that turned Simon Peter to tears? Was it a look of contempt? No. Derision? No. Resentment? No. I believe it was a look that showed hurt but not rejection.

Our Lord thought so little of Himself on the road to the cross that He paused to speak to the weeping women.

And when the hammers swung through the air, driving the iron nails through His hands and into the cross, His prayer was not for Himself but others. He did not say, "Are these the brutes for whom I am dying?" No. He prayed, "Father, forgive them; for they know not what they do" (Luke 23:34, KJV).

When the cross was uplifted and dropped with a thud into its socket, He was still concerned with others. He comforted the penitent thief and made provision for His disconsolate mother.

How sad that we who follow the One whose life was limitless service to others are so often preoccupied with ourselves. Even at the point of death, our Lord's mind was not preoccupied with Himself but with how He could bring His Father's love to the men and women who crossed His path.

No wonder E. Stanley Jones could summarize a core aspect of our faith by saying, "Christianity is the science of relating well to others in the spirit of Jesus Christ."

Father God, let the loving service and limitless sacrifice of our Lord flow freely through us to others. In Jesus's name, amen!

_____

_____

_____

_____

Love Forgives

Dean De Castro

Love...is not easily angered. It keeps no record of wrongs.
—CORINTHIANS 13:5B

Another way of putting it: Love is not overly sensitive.

Love forgives. In other words, touchy people may harbor unforgiveness and resentment in their hearts. It is because they cannot let go of their past hurts.

Love forgives. Some people are easily angered or temperamental because they still harbor bitterness toward people who had hurt them in the past. They have not learned to forgive.

In the busy and crowded hallways of life, it's inevitable that we bump into each other and hurt each other. That is why Jesus commanded us to forgive "not seven times but seventy-seven times" (Matt. 18:22), which means we must forgive people frequently and freely.

Ephesians 4:26 teaches that it's human nature to be angry when people hurt us. However, it's destructive and unhealthy to suppress these feelings and not express them responsibly. Unrestrained anger could lead to sinning if not handled properly and quickly, before the sun goes down. And according to verse 27, anger will allow Satan to do his evil work through us.

Remember: Being upset is Satan's preferred setup for destroying us.

We need to readily and promptly forgive people because that's how our God forgives us: "Forgive each other, just as in Christ God forgave you" (Eph. 4:32b).

Love forgets. A husband once told his pastor that his wife became "historical" whenever she got upset. Puzzled by the statement, the pastor asked, "Do you mean she became hysterical?" The husband replied, "My wife gets historical because she will repeat all the wrong things I've done before." I'm sure we all have had similar experiences. We need to always keep in mind that love keeps no record of wrong.

But choosing the path of love doesn't mean we don't feel the pain of emotional wounds or struggle with bad, hurtful memories. On the contrary, it means we deliberately forget the wrongs suffered, we let them fade into the past.

As Alexander Strauch explains in his book *Leading with Love*, "Life lived according to the 'more excellent way' doesn't keep a journal of injustices and emotional hurts. It makes no plan to get even. Instead, love is generous in her forgetfulness. Love forgives and blesses those who have caused offense."

Father God, let us quickly forgive and deliberately
forget people's offenses. In Jesus's name, amen!

_____

_____

_____

_____

Self-Talk and Anger

Dr. David Stoop

Adapted from *Self-Talk: Key to Personal Growth*

Be ye angry, and sin not.
—EPHESIANS 4:26A, KJV

Be angry. In the original language, God *commands* us to get angry. This is for at least three reasons.

First, anger is a valid and natural human emotion. It is a part of our emotional makeup, created by God. Anger is like the check engine light on your car's dashboard. Pay attention to it and fix the underlying problem.

Second, God's anger punctuates the Old Testament. There are over 450 places in the Old Testament where over 75 percent of the words related to anger are in reference to God's righteous indignation.

Third, Jesus was angry at times. Mark 3:5 states, "And He looked around at them with anger," He was also angry with the merchants who made God's temple "a den of thieves" (Mark 11:15–19).

And sin not. Anger could lead to sin when we hurt the people who offended us through our harsh words (Eph. 4:28–31) or vindictive actions (Rom. 12:19).

Anger is a killer emotion. To deny or be unaware of anger not only wears us out emotionally but also wears us down physically, leaving us vulnerable to all kinds of diseases.

Eliminate demands. Do you feel angry? Look for the "shoulds" or "shouldn'ts" in your self-talk. These words often reflect the irrational demands we impose on a situation, a person, or even ourselves. When we set up demands that are impossible to reach, we create an emotional tension within that results in anger.

God did not allow Moses to enter the Promised Land because he failed to resolve his emotional issues. He disobeyed God by twice striking a rock out of anger (Num. 20:10).

Moses's self-talk might have sounded something like, "I *shouldn't* have to fetch them water!" But his complaints would be futile because in reality he does have to find water for the Israelites—that's part of his job. His demands will do nothing to change reality except make him angry.

Instead, Moses might have said to himself, "Lord, I don't like this job, but with Your help, I can survive." Moses would have resolved his anger if he removed the unrealistic demands he imposed on God, the people, and himself.

Father God, help us get rid of our irrational demands and love people unconditionally. In Jesus's name, amen!

_____

_____

_____

_____

Clear All Your Records

Joyce Meyer

Adapted from *The Love Revolution*

Love...keeps no record of wrongs.
—1 CORINTHIANS 13:5C

Are you a good accountant? Do you keep precise, detailed records of the wrongs that people did to you?

For many years, each time Dave and I argued, I would dig into my mental files and remind him of past mistakes he had made that I felt were wrong. And it amazed him that I even remembered many of them because they were so old.

I know from experience that keeping mental records of offenses poisons our lives and does not change others. We often waste a day being angry at someone who doesn't even realize they did anything that bothered us. They are enjoying their day, and we are wasting ours.

If you are going to keep records, then why not keep records of the good things people say and do rather than their mistakes?

If you write down people's good traits, you will be surprised to see that the positive list is longer than the negative. We should look for and celebrate the good in people because we overcome evil with good (Rom. 12:21).

Why not get out all the past-due accounts you have kept on anyone and mark them "Paid in full"? "Blessed is the man whose sin the Lord will never count against him" (Rom. 4:8). It does not mean that God does not see the sin. It means that He does not charge it against the sinner because of love.

Love can acknowledge that a wrong has been done and erase it before it becomes lodged in the heart. Love does not register or record evil; this way, resentment does not have a chance to grow.

Clearing all your records will produce good results. It will relieve pressure and improve the quality of your life. Forgiving people their wrongs will restore your intimacy with God, and your joy and peace will increase.

Your health may even improve because a calm and undisturbed mind and heart are the life and health of the body (Prov. 14:30). Resentment builds walls. Love builds bridges!

Father God, help us not forget what we should remember and remember what we should forget. In Jesus's name, amen!

Forgive As Forgiven

Max Lucado

Adapted from *How Happiness Happens*

...forgiving one another, just as God in Christ forgave you.
—EPHESIANS 4:32

John 13:3–5 records the events on the eve of the crucifixion and Jesus's final meal with His followers.

Jesus was sure about His identity and destiny. Because He knew who He was, He could do what He did (John 13:3). Jesus even forgave His betrayers before they betrayed Him.

John vividly describes the seven steps our Lord took to prove His perfect and forgiving love towards His disciples:

- He got up from the meal table
- Took off His outer clothing
- Wrapped a towel around His waist
- Poured water into a basin
- Stooped down (implied)
- Washed the disciples' feet
- Dried them with the towel wrapped around His waist
- Wearing the towel and holding the basin, Jesus says to His disciples, "Now that I, your Lord and Teacher, have washed your feet, you also should wash one another's feet. I have set you an example that you should do as I have done for you" (John 13:14–15).

In this context, Paul urges us to follow Jesus's lead in giving grace rather than seeking retribution. We give grace not because our enemies deserve it but because we have already been doused with it. "Forgiving one another, even as God in Christ forgave you" (Eph. 4:32).

When people offend us, we take the towel. We fill the basin. We wash one another's feet. We forgive one another.

If you are secure in your identity as a child of God destined to spend eternity with Him, you can do what Jesus did. Throw aside the robe of rights and expectations and make the most courageous moves. Wash feet.

Forgiveness is the act of applying your undeserved mercy to your undeserved hurts. You didn't deserve to be hurt but neither did you deserve to be forgiven. Being the recipient that you are of God's great grace, does it not make sense to give grace to others?

It's time to follow the example of Jesus in the upper room in John 13. It's time to forgive, just as God, in Christ, forgave you.

Father God, let us offer others the grace of forgiveness
You've given us in Your Son. In Jesus's name, amen!

Love Your Enemy

Paul E. Miller

Adapted from *Love Walked among Us*

Love your enemies.
—MATTHEW 5:44

True to form, Jesus's advice goes against every instinct we have when someone hurts us. He tells us to love our enemies, actively seek their interests, and care for those we can't stand.

Overcome evil with good. Moses was the first to say "an eye for an eye, and a tooth for a tooth" (Matt. 5:38). It was not a prescription for revenge but for curbing our natural reactions.

Instinctively, we take two eyes for one, two teeth for one. We don't want equal justice; we want to punish, to extract more from them than they took from us.

Here, Jesus raises the bar of love to extraordinary heights, commanding that we love our enemies and actively seek their good.

Lest we miss the point, He mentions the legal rights of a Roman soldier to force a person to take his pack one mile. Not only are we to take the pack, but we also offer to take it a second mile (Matt. 5:41). So, instead of exacting twice the revenge, we are to give twice the love.

Bitterness dies, peace ensues. When people hurt us, we obsess about what they did to us. Then bitterness slowly eats away at us like cancer of the soul. Bitterness quietly transforms us, so we become just like our enemies.

Love breaks the vicious cycle, keeping us from becoming like the enemy. Instead, we become like Jesus and are no longer controlled by the other person's sin.

Jesus's command to love your enemies takes the energy out of bitterness. Instead of plotting revenge, we plan how to do them good. We reflect on their needs and how to help them. We offer to take the soldier's pack a second mile because he is tired and weak. Love like this takes our hearts by surprise, and healing begins. Bitterness dies for lack of fuel.

Jesus's teaching to love your enemies reflects the ancient Jewish prophecy that the Messiah would be a "Prince of Peace" (Isa. 9:6–7). Thus, by loving our enemies, we become peacemakers.

Father God, set us free from bitterness by teaching us
how to love our enemies. In Jesus's name, amen!

_____

_____

_____

_____

Love Confronts

Dean De Castro

Love does not delight in evil but rejoices with the truth.
—1 CORINTHIANS 13:6

True love confronts.

Without correction, love becomes sentimental. Parents who never say "no" to their children don't love them more. There is a wise saying that "The negatives in love are hedges along the path so that love will not stray."

Genuine love confronts people when they act contrary to God's will. But on the other hand, love rejoices when believers walk in God's truth.

Love condemns evil. Please note that love doesn't charge the sinners but their evil actions (see Psalm 97:10). A godly person will confront a sinning Christian because they care about the negative consequences of unrighteous actions in people's lives.

For example, in Galatians 2, Paul sternly and publicly rebuked Peter in Antioch because his behavior contradicted the gospel of grace. He gradually disassociated himself from the fellowship of the Gentile believers when prominent church leaders from Jerusalem came to visit the Antioch church (vv. 11–14).

Love that confronts is painful and risky. It calls for sacrifice for truth's sake. Paul had to risk his reputation by correcting Peter, the old chief apostle who had a large following. Nevertheless, God's love is precisely what motivated Paul to condemn Peter's wrong behavior.

"Better is open rebuke than the hidden love" (Prov. 27:5). In other words, true love is not shy in correcting people when they violate the moral truth of God.

Love commends righteousness. "Love rejoices in the truth." In this context, the word truth is being used in the sense of righteous behavior or a principle of conduct that corresponds to the truth of the gospel message.

As New Testament scholar Gordon Fee explains, "The person full of Christian love joins in rejoicing on the side of behavior that reflects the gospel—for every victory gained, every forgiveness offered, every act of kindness."

Paul openly rebuked the church at Corinth for their many failures. However, when they repented of their ways, he rejoiced in all that the Corinthians did that was right and good. One of the greatest delights of Christian leaders and teachers who walk in love is to see those they lead grow in love and live obedient lives for Christ.

Father God, let us live with a love that confronts evil and commends righteousness. In Jesus's name, amen!

_____

_____

_____

_____

Love Is Tenacious

Dean De Castro

*It always protects, always trusts, always
hopes, always perseveres.*
—1 CORINTHIANS 13:7

Paul concludes and summarizes his descriptions of love with four short, positive clauses that tell us what love does.

Love always protects. There's a time to confront people acting outside of God's will as Paul did to Peter in Antioch. But true love also seeks to come up with excuses when people make mistakes. As Proverbs 10:12 says, "Hatred stirs up dissension, but love covers over all wrongs" (see 1 Pet. 4:8).

True love doesn't gossip about people's weaknesses and failings behind their backs. "A gossip betrays a confidence, but a trustworthy man keeps a secret" (Prov. 11:13). A caring person does not delight in exposing people's mistakes with the malicious intent of hurting their reputation. True love always covers and protects people's dignity.

Love always trusts. Trust is the glue that cements any relationship together. And when trust is broken, the relationship goes sour and eventually dies. So, I would rather err on the trusting side than always doubt people's motives and intentions. God's love always trusts and believes in the best of people.

Love always hopes. Godly love does not give up hope in anyone. Never say to a person, "You're hopeless. You'll never change!" Some people are stubborn enough that they'll do foolish things to prove to you that you're right.

Romans 15:13 states that our God is God of hope, and He will fill our hearts with hope by the power of the Holy Spirit. So ask God to give you hope when the person you care about seems hopeless. The situation in the Corinthian church was a mess, but Paul never gave up hope (see 2 Cor. 7:4, 14–16).

Love always perseveres. The word "persevere" is the same translated as "patience" in verse 4. There the emphasis is patience with people. Here, in verse 7, the focus is patience under challenging circumstances.

Everything around us may crumble, but ultimately love wins. It gives a person the power to endure things. Genuine love perseveres in the face of opposition, weakness, and difficulties. It never gives up because it knows that it isn't over until it's over.

Father God, grant us the power to be strong
and tenacious. In Jesus's name, amen!

Love Is Eternal

Dean De Castro

Love never ends.
—1 CORINTHIANS 13:8A, RSV

There will be no need for faith and hope in eternity. But at the same time, "Love never ends." In other words, love is eternal because God is love (1 John 4:16).

Both the apostles James and John reveal that love will be the standard by which God will judge every believer in the future. Indeed, all believers will stand before "the judgment seat of Christ, that each one may receive what is due him for the things done while in the body, whether good or bad" (2 Cor. 5:10).

The basis of the believer's judgment. James 2:12 states, "Speak and act as those who are going to be judged by the law that gives freedom." This law of freedom that will be the basis of the future judgment of the believers is also called the royal law of love in verse 8: "If you really keep the royal law found in Scripture, 'Love your neighbor as yourself.'"

James calls loving people the royal law because it's the law that governs the children of the Most High King (Eph. 5:1–2).

James assures us that if we love our neighbors, then we "are doing right" (James 2:8b), which means we will pass the test on Judgement Day—God will show mercy to us. However, if we disobey the law of love and live only for ourselves, God will instead show judgment without mercy (James 2:13).

Therefore, be merciful to people, and God will be gracious to us when we need it on Judgment Day.

The confidence on Judgment Day. The apostle John referred to this coming judgment of believers in 1 John 4:16–19. We will have confidence and boldness at the judgment seat of Christ because, in this world, we are like the Lord who loved and served people while He was on earth (v. 17).

We will have no fear of punishment on Judgment Day because our maturity (the correct definition of the word "perfect") in love drives out fear (v. 18). On the other hand, selfish and self-centered Christians are immature believers who fear losing their rewards (Rev. 3:11).

Father God, help our imperfect love as we try our best to love as you loved and as we are loved. In Jesus's name, amen!

Mature in Love

Selwyn Hughes

Adapted from *Divine Love*

*When I was a child, I talked like a child, I thought
like a child, I reasoned like a child. When I became
a man, I put the ways of childhood behind me.*
—1 CORINTHIANS 13:11

Maturity in life—particularly the Christian life—means maturity in love.

We are mature to the extent that we can love selflessly. Sometimes, however, we love with the wrong kind of love—a self-seeking and, therefore, immature love. Immaturity in love is made evident in several ways.

Immature love. First, it shows itself in being preponderantly physical. When love focuses on the physical love (eros) and is not held in control by spiritual love (agape), it is a fitful, immature kind of love and soon fizzles out.

As a marriage counselor for many years, I have concluded that emotional immaturity in loving people is high on the list of causes of marriage breakdowns. Many marriages get on the rocks because one or both partners have not grown up emotionally.

Another mark of immaturity is a demanding attitude. This kind of love focuses on wanting to be loved. It is a possessive love: "I want them for myself." Consciously or unconsciously, the emphasis here is on what I can get out of it.

Mature love. Mature love, on the other hand, is directed towards self-forgetfulness and self-sacrifice.

I once read the story of Harold Groves, a missionary to India who traveled to Bombay to visit some friends. The hosts sent their servant to the railway station to meet him, and when he asked how he might recognize the missionary, they said, "Look for a white man helping somebody—that will be him."

So, the servant saw a white man helping an old lady step down from the train, went up to him, and said, "Are you Mr. Grooves?"—and he was.

If you want to recognize a mature person—mature in love—look for someone helping someone else. We are as mature as we are mature in sacrificial love. Our attitudes to life are mature or immature according to the degree of sacrificial love present.

Father God, help us grow emotionally and
spiritually by living a life of loving service and
limitless sacrifice. In Jesus's name, amen!

Love People Compassionately
Dean De Castro

Love one another. As I have loved you, so
you must love one another.
—JOHN 13:34

Jesus has called us to love people as He has loved us. But what is more challenging to learn than love?

How do you love someone when you get no love in return—only withdrawal or ingratitude? How do you love without being trapped or used by the other person? How can you love someone who is selfish, vindictive, and narcissistic?

Loving well is a mark of spiritual maturity. However, it is easier said than done. Let me share two skills for how to love people compassionately.

God's poetry. Ephesians 2:10 states that we are God's "handiwork." This word comes from the Greek word *poiema*, which could be translated as "poetry." *We* are His poetry. You aren't God's poetry. I'm not God's poetry. But together, we are God's poetry.

In *How Happiness Happens*, Max Lucado writes, "Independently we are nothing but small pieces on God's page. You may be a verb, she may be a noun, and I'm probably a question mark. We're just letters, marks from God's hand.

"What letter, then, has a right to criticize another? Dare the *p* to accuse the *q* of being backward? Dare the *m* mock the *w* for being too open-minded? Who are we to tell the writer how to form us or when to use us? We need each other. By ourselves, we are just letters on a page, but collectively we are poetry."

I-thou relationship. In such a relationship, we don't see people as things to be used and abused. Instead, we recognize that every human being is created in the image of God. Therefore, each person is a "thou" and not an "it" to us. Every encounter we have with people unfolds in the presence of God.

As Peter Scazzero writes in *Emotionally Healthy Spirituality*, " Out of our contemplative time with God, we are invited to be prayerfully present to people."

Mother Teresa felt that each person she met was "Jesus in disguise," even the unbelievers. Therefore, we should treat people, even the most difficult ones, with dignity and respect because they have the image of God in them (James 3:9).

Father God, let us esteem others as bearers of Your image.
In Jesus's name, amen!

_____

_____

_____

_____

Practice the Presence of People

Peter Scazzero
Adapted from *Emotionally Healthy Spirituality*

Love your neighbor as yourself.
—MATTHEW 22:39

As a pastor, I have found that telling people to love better and more is not enough.

They need practical skills incorporated into their spiritual formation to grow into emotionally mature Christians. One of the practical skills involved in loving well is practicing the presence of people.

God invites us to practice His presence in our daily lives (see Phil. 4:5a). At the same time, He invites us to practice the presence of people within an awareness of His presence in our daily relationships.

When pushed to the wall to separate this unbreakable union, Jesus refused to separate the practice of God's presence from actively engaging with people.

He summarized the entire Bible for us: "'Love the Lord your God...' This is the first and greatest commandment. And the second is like it: 'Love your neighbor as yourself.'" (Matt. 22:37–40).

Jesus's profound, contemplative prayer life with His Father resulted in a reflective presence with people.

Love means "to reveal the beauty of another person to themselves," writes Jean Vanier. Jesus did that with each person He met. This ability to listen and pay attention to people was at the heart of His mission. It could not help but move Him to compassion.

In the same way, out of our devotional time with God, we are invited to be prayerfully present to people, revealing their own beauty to them.

The religious leaders of Jesus's day never made that connection. They were diligent, zealous, and committed to having God as the Lord of their lives. They memorized Moses' entire five books, prayed five times a day, tithed all their income, and gave money to the poor. But they never delighted in people.

They did not link loving God with the need to grow in their ability to love people. For this reason, they criticized Jesus repeatedly for being a "glutton and a drunkard, a friend of tax collectors and 'sinners'" (Matt. 11:19). They thought that Jesus delighted in people too much.

> *Father God, help us develop the spiritual*
> *discipline of being prayerfully present to the*
> *people around us. In Jesus's name, amen!*

_____

_____

_____

_____

Ten Ways to Love Your Neighbor as Yourself

Courtney Whiting
Adapted from ibelieve.com

Who is my neighbor?
—LUKE 10:29

When the Jewish lawyer asked Jesus, "Who is my neighbor?" Jesus told the story of the Good Samaritan to define what it means to love your neighbor.

Here are ten ways we can love our neighbors as ourselves.

Love is proactive. The Samaritan saw the injured man and stopped. So likewise, in a fast-paced world where it's easy to overlook the needs of others, we need to be aware of those needy people around us.

Love is observant. The Samaritan first saw the hurting man, "and when he saw him, he took pity on him" (v. 33).

Love is compassionate. The Samaritan responded to the injured man's needs rather than simply feeling sorry for him.

Love is responsive. When the Samaritan saw the man, he responded immediately to help meet the man's needs. He bound his wounds using the resources he had on hand.

Love is costly. When the Samaritan tended to the victim's wounds, he gave up his own resources. It costs the Samaritan at least two days' wages and also his time.

Love is inopportune. The Samaritan physically lifted the man onto a donkey. That was not an easy task, and it was likely messy, given the man's injuries. Yet he set the man on his animal to take him to a place of safety.

Love is healing. After the Samaritan bound the man's wounds, he continued his care by taking him to an inn and looking after him.

Love is sacrificial. The Samaritan gave two denarii to the inn-keeper, which was approximately two days' worth of earnings. Yet the only instruction he gave was to care for the wounded man. He expected nothing in return.

Love is communal. When the Samaritan had to leave, he entrusted his care to the innkeeper instead of leaving the man alone. Loving a neighbor sometimes means involving others in the process.

Love is promising. When the Samaritan left the inn, he promised the innkeeper to return and cover the cost of any extra care the man needed even though he owed nothing to the victim.

> *Father God, let us feel compassion and show mercy to*
> *the needy people around us. In Jesus's name, amen!*

_____

_____

_____

_____

Encouragement Changes Everything

John C. Maxwell

Therefore encourage one another and build each other up.
—1 THESSALONIANS 5:11

Encouragement is incredible.

Its impact can be profound—nearly miraculous. To encourage people is to help them gain the courage they might not possess— courage to face the day, do what's right, take risks, and make a difference.

When we encourage people, we often see their lives change forever. And sometimes we see them change the world.

A lot of people have encouraged me along the way in my life. One of those people was Glen Leatherwood, one of my godly Sunday school teachers. We were an unruly group: constantly wiggling, squirming, talking, fighting—doing everything but listening.

One day, with tears streaming from his eyes, he asked the other three boys and me to stay after the class. He told us that God would call all four of us into the ministry. Glen laid his hands on our heads and prayed for us. And he was right. All four of us later become pastors in the church.

How can you help other people feel like they are valuable? By seeing them as a "10." For the most part, I believe that people respond to our expectations of them. If you think the best of them, they generally give you their best. If you treat people like a 10, they respond like a 10. If you treat someone like a 2, he responds like a 2.

People want recognition and affirmation. It is a deep human desire, and we can help people become great simply by believing in them.

If you are a parent, you are responsible for encouraging your family members. If you are an organizational leader, you can increase dramatically your team's effectiveness in proportion to the amount of encouragement you give the people you lead. If you are married, a word of encouragement could save your marriage.

As a friend, you have the privilege of sharing encouraging words that may help someone persevere through a rough time. As a Christian, you have the power to represent Jesus by loving others and lifting them with an encouraging word.

Father God, let us join the love revolution by
encouraging one another. In Jesus's name, amen!

The Importance of Relationships

Selwyn Hughes

Adapted from *Christ Empowered Living*

Be devoted to one another in brotherly love.
—ROMANS 12:10, NASB

It's been said that the whole theme of the Bible is about relationships: perfect relationships in the Trinity, broken relationships in Eden, restored relationships in Christ.

But why are relationships so crucial? One of the most important reasons is this: To be is to be in relationships. To be fully human and fully alive, then, we must learn something about how to relate.

Through our relationships with other image-bearers, our characters are molded. God uses people to help refine people.

Non-Christians go to their graves with their character flaws largely unchanged and unaltered, but it's different with you and me. God wants to make us like Jesus, and one of the ways He goes about doing that is to place people who might rub us the wrong way among us. He will finish His work of transforming us when we see Christ. But our characters' significant shaping occurs here and now—through our relationships.

Do you realize that the Lord handpicks the people you work with and relate to, exposing your temper, your pride, your stubbornness—whatever your failings are? And running away from them is not worth it because God has many more He can maneuver into position to replace them.

Make a list of all the people you don't get along with and ask yourself, "What is God trying to show me about myself through them?"

Where do we find a better place to put Scripture principles into operation than in close relationships? Take marriage, for example: How often do we hear of two Christians seeking a divorce because they believe they are incompatible. "Incompatibility," said someone, "is not a reason for divorce. Incompatibility is the reason for marriage."

Opposites attract, and two people in a marriage who are opposites in temperament have the opportunity to apply the grace of God to their differences and learn to adjust. There would be fewer marriage breakups if couples understood and applied this principle.

Father God, thank You for using difficult people in our lives to make us more like Christ. In Jesus's name, amen!

Relationships Hurt

Selwyn Hughes

Adapted from *Christ Empowered Living*

[Jesus] entrusted Himself to Him who judges justly.
—1 PETER 2:23

Relationships sometimes hurt.

Hurt people hurt people. The more we relate to people, the more we are guaranteed to get hurt.

One of the best definitions of love is this: "Love is moving toward others without self-protection." An excellent example of this type of love is our Lord's encounter with Simon Peter.

In John 21:15–17, our Lord asks Simon Peter three times, "Do you truly love me ?" In his translation, J. B. Phillips says that the word "love" in Jesus's question used twice is the strongest word in the Greek language—*agape*, which means "unconditional love."

However, Peter's consistent reply contained a weaker Greek word, *phileo*, meaning "fondness of friendships." Phillips translates Peter's response thus: "You know that I am your friend."

Our Lord, longing for a positive response from Simon Peter, put the question to him for the third time, but on this occasion, he took the word "friend" (*phileo*) off Peter's lips and put it on His own: "Simon, son of John, are you my friend?"

Stubborn Peter responded the third time in the same way: "You know I am your friend." Peter failed to come through in the way Christ desired, but Peter's coldness did not freeze the stream of the Savior's love.

He continued to love him, and on the day of Pentecost, He fulfilled His promise to Peter by giving him the keys to the kingdom. Through one sermon, Simon Peter opened the doors of the church, and three thousand souls came in.

How could Jesus love so well? According to the Apostle Peter, our Lord was able to respond to all kinds of suffering, insults, scorn, and ridicule because He entrusted Himself to God, who judges justly (1 Pet. 2:20–23).

Our Lord rested securely in His Father's love. The strength of His Father's love flowing through Him enabled Him to keep on loving. Do you trust God to look after your total welfare so that you are free to direct your energies toward others?

Father God, we acknowledge that people might hurt us, but they could not destroy Your love for us. In Jesus' name, amen!

The Keys to Overcoming Rejection
Dean De Castro

He entrusted Himself to Him who judges justly.
—1 PETER 2:23

According to the late Selwyn Hughes, there are three styles of relating with people: One is moving towards others to get something from them. Another is moving away from them to avoid them. The third is moving against others to be hostile to them.

The divine way of relating, however, is to move toward others without fear of rejection.

The night before Jesus died, He showed His disciples that "He loved them to the end" (John 13:1b) by serving as a slave, washing all His disciples' feet, including Judas's, who later would betray Him.

When it was Peter's turn for Jesus to wash his feet, he rejected Jesus's offer (v. 8). Even after Jesus explained why Peter had to accept the Master's service, Peter again rejected Jesus indirectly by being too slow to understand the meaning of God's plan of salvation (vv. 9–10).

How could Jesus love so well? How did He overcome the fear of rejection?

Jesus knew God's sovereignty. "Jesus knew that the Father had put all things under His power" (John 13:3a).

Jesus could love without the fear of rejection because He knew that He had full authority from the Father to win the victory of the cross.

So, when bystanders asked Jesus to jump down from the cross, He refused. He had the power to command more than twelve legions of angels to rescue Him from suffering on the cross (Matt. 26:53), yet He willingly gave up His life because of His great love for us.

Jesus knew His identity. "Jesus knew...that He had come from God and was returning to God; so, He got up" (John 13:3–4a).

The relationship Jesus had with His Father in eternity past made Him the most secure man who ever lived. Even when His disciples withdrew their love and support as He neared the cross, He could go on loving them just the same.

The strength of His Father's love flowing through enabled Him to keep on loving. Only as we focus on how God loves us can we find the love we freely give to others.

Father God, let us trust You to meet our basic need
for love and acceptance. In Jesus's name, amen!

The Five Love Languages

Gary Chapman

Adapted from *The Five Love Languages*

...speaking the truth in love...
—EPHESIANS 4:15

There are five languages of love each person speaks.

Each language corresponds to the types of actions or behaviors that make someone feel the most loved. Once you learn which language of love your partner speaks, you can start to address them through that language and fill up their love tank.

Words of affirmation. For people whose primary love language is words of affirmation, supportive and complimentary words make them feel the most loved. Speaking this language means finding small or large ways of expressing approval and gratitude for who they are and what they do.

Quality time. People with the love language of quality time require moments of undivided attention from their partners. When you spend quality time with your partner, you are telling them they are important.

Receiving gifts. A gift is a representation of thought. For the person with the love language of receiving gifts, that thought means more than anything else in the relationship. It means you consider who they are and what they like. It is not the size of the gift that matters. The gesture of making the effort of obtaining and giving a gift is everything.

Acts of service. The language of acts of service encompasses the act of the partner doing things for the other person. These actions are made without prompting and with the sole intention of pleasing the other. Whether an act of service makes life easier for your partner or fulfills a known desire, your partner's love tank will fill with love.

The main message of an act of service is forethought and consideration. When done without resentment, the thought and action together signify love for your partner.

Physical touch. The act of touching is a surefire way of expressing emotional connection. You hug your friends when they are upset. You embrace and kiss your children to show you love them. You cuddle and are physically intimate with your partner. For the person with this love language, physical touch is the supreme representation of love.

> *Father God, help us fill the love tanks of the people*
> *around us by understanding and speaking their*
> *unique love languages. In Jesus's name, amen!*

Love is a Choice

Gary Chapman
Adapted from *The Five Love Languages*

Love...always perseveres.
—1 CORINTHIANS 13:7

Love doesn't erase the past, but it makes the future different.

When we choose the active expression of love in the primary love language of our spouse, we create an emotional climate where we can deal with our past conflicts and failures.

People often ask me this question: "What if your spouse's love language is something that doesn't come naturally to you?" And my typical answer is, "So?"

For example, my wife's love language is acts of service. One of the things I do for her regularly is vacuum the floors. Do you think that vacuuming floors come naturally to me? When I was a child, my mother used to make me vacuum. I hated doing it because I couldn't play ball on Saturday until I cleaned the entire house.

But I vacuum our house now, and I do it regularly. You couldn't pay me enough to vacuum our house, but I do it for love. When an action doesn't come naturally to you, it is a greater expression of love. Love is something you do for someone else, not something you do for yourself.

Most of us do many things each day that do not come "naturally" to us. That is getting out of bed in the morning for some of us. We go against our feelings and get out of bed. Why? Because we believe there is something worthwhile to do that day. And usually, before the day is over, we feel good having gotten up. Our actions preceded our emotions.

The same is true with love. We discover the primary love language of our spouse, and we choose to speak it whether or not it is natural for us. We are simply choosing to do it for their benefit.

We want to meet our spouse's emotional needs, and we reach out to speak their love language. In so doing, their emotional love tank is filled, and chances are they will reciprocate and speak our language. But when they do, our emotions return, and our love tank begins to fill.

Father God, let us love others even if we don't
feel loving. In Jesus's name, amen!

The Law of Christ

Dean De Castro

Carry each other's burdens, and in this way
you will fulfill the law of Christ.
—GALATIANS 6:2

What is the *law of Christ*? It is what Christ stated as the two greatest commandments in response to the question of a scribe: Love God with all our being and love our neighbors as ourselves (Mark 12:28–31).

The greatest commandments. Both Jesus and the scribe agreed that those two commands are the core of the entire Old Testament law. They comprise the Ten Commandments. The first four commandments refer to our relationship with God, and the last six refer to our relationship with others. The second tablet of the law was based on the first and cannot be accomplished apart from it (Matt. 22:36–40).

In John 13:34–35, Jesus restates this law of love as the *new commandment* whereby the standard for love is Christ's love that He had shown toward His followers by washing their feet (John 13). It is a spiritual fruit (Gal. 5:22) produced not by the compulsion of an external code but by the transformation of the heart by the Holy Spirit (see Rom. 8:4).

Love fulfills the law of Christ. Christians obey the law of Christ by lovingly and humbly restoring a sinning Christian who unwittingly falls into moral lapses (Gal. 6:2). God's love always seeks the welfare and highest good of its object; that is why "love is the fulfillment of the law" (Rom. 13:10b).

As Homer Kent Jr. tells us, "Regeneration by faith produces within the heart a love which desires to accomplish the very things that the law specified but could not produce."

Love prevents the license to sin. Christ's love also prevents the license to sin and leaves the believer a free man who willingly serves the good of others.

For the followers of Christ, the motivation not to sin is out of love for God and love for others. We love and obey God because He first loved us (1 John 4:19). We love others not out of compulsion and false guilt but because Christ's love compels us and we want to follow His example in expressing love to others.

> *Father God, help us love You and people not because we have to but because we want to. In Jesus's name, amen!*

Biblical Views About Suffering and Pain
Dean De Castro

Suffering is beneficial for us. "It was good for me to be afflicted so that I might learn your decree" (Ps. 119:71).

Trials are to be welcomed and not avoided. "When all kinds of trials and temptations crowd into your lives, my brothers, don't resent them as intruders, but welcome them as friends!" (James 1:2, Phillips).

Suffering kills sin in the flesh. "Therefore, since Christ suffered in His body, arm yourselves also with the same attitude, because he who has suffered in the body is done with sin" (1 Pet. 4:1).

Suffering is God's blessing. "For it has been granted to you on behalf of Christ not only to believe on Him, but also to suffer for Him" (Phil. 1:29).

God's discipline produces righteousness and peace. "No discipline seems pleasant at the time, but painful. Later on, however, it produces a harvest of righteousness and peace for those who have been trained by it" (Heb. 12:11).

Suffering leads to glory. "...if indeed we share in His sufferings in order that we may also share in His glory" (Rom. 8:17b).

Suffering is part of our calling and destiny. "We must go through many hardships to enter the kingdom of God" (Acts 14:22). "We sent Timothy...to strengthen and encourage you in your faith, so that no one would be unsettled by these trials. You know quite well that we were destined for them" (1 Thess. 3:2–3).

Hardships allow God's grace to flourish. "That is why, for Christ's sake, I delight in weaknesses, in insults, in hardships, in persecutions, in difficulties. For when I am weak, then I am strong" (2 Cor. 12:10).

Our troubles allow us to empathize with hurting people. "...the God of all comfort, who comforts us in all our troubles, so that we can comfort those in any trouble with the comfort we ourselves received from God" (2 Cor. 1:3–4).

Suffering is only for a season. It, too, shall pass. "Weeping may remain for a night, but rejoicing comes in the morning" (Ps. 30:5b).

> "It is doubtful that God can bless a man greatly until He has hurt him deeply."
>
> —A. W. Tozer

> *Father God, let us suffer for our Lord*
> *gracefully. In Jesus's name, amen!*

Why Does God Allow Suffering?

David Jeremiah
Adapted from davidjeremiah.org

I will rather boast in my infirmities.
—2 CORINTHIANS 12:9, NKJV

In 1994, I was diagnosed with cancer.

Thanks to God's power and the expert care of many dedicated health professionals, I survived my lymphoma. Here are the five principles that help me see my suffering from God's perspective.

Suffering teaches us to trust God. When we believe God lovingly permitted and even intended our ordeal, we will find ourselves saying, "God, You have allowed this in my life. I don't understand it, but I know that it couldn't have happened to me unless it passed through Your loving hands. This thing is from You, and I accept it."

Suffering builds character. Character is shaped in the crucible of adversity. Unless there is a pain in the formula, we will never stop and listen to what God is saying. Sometimes He allows us to stumble because He is determined to teach us and make us wiser and stronger. God is more concerned with our holiness than our comfort or happiness.

Suffering draws us near to God and prepares us to be productive. It has been said, "The Father is never closer to the vine than when He is pruning it." So, just as a loving and dedicated gardener prunes the plants in his garden to thrive and blossom, likewise, our loving heavenly Father disciplines us for our good. Our part is to lean into Him, study His Word, and trust Him to provide for our needs.

Suffering produces dynamic growth. God never allows pain without a purpose. Instead, He uses your suffering to dispense His power. And His power cannot rest upon you unless you realize that you'll never make it without depending utterly upon Him and going in His strength. Some pruning will take place, but you'll grow toward heaven after that pruning is accomplished.

The outcome of our suffering depends upon our response. When I was diagnosed with cancer, I started to ask many *why* questions. God reminded me instead of asking *why* questions, I can ask *what* questions: "*What*, Lord? *What* would You have me do? *What* are You trying to teach me?"

Father God, show us the lessons You want us to learn through our suffering. In Jesus's name, amen!

_____

_____

_____

_____

The Purpose of Trials

Joel Osteen
Adapted from *Your Best Life Now*

These trials are only to test your faith.
—1 PETER 1:7, TLB

God allows the trials and temptations of life to test your faith.

All through life, you will face various tests, and even though you may not enjoy them, God will use those trials to shape you into the person He wants you to be.

We often pray, "God, if you will change my circumstances, then I'll change." In actuality, God is more interested in changing you than He is in changing your circumstances. God will keep bringing up the same issue, again and again, until you pass the test.

Many years ago, the codfish fishing industry faced a significant problem in the distribution aspect of their business. Because the fish were inactive in the tank, they became soft and mushy and gradually lost their taste.

One day, somebody decided to put some catfish in the tank with the codfish. As the tank traveled across the country, the codfish had to stay alert and active and watch out for the catfish. Amazingly, when the tank arrived at its destination, the codfish were as fresh and tasty as they were in the Northeast.

If we are to strengthen our spiritual muscles and grow stronger, we must have adversities to overcome and attacks to resist. It is the struggle that gives us strength. Without opposition or resistance, there is no potential for progress.

Without the resistance of air, an eagle can't soar. Without the resistance of water, a ship can't float. Without the resistance of gravity, you and I can't even walk.

When you go through difficult times, make sure you pass the test. Don't give up. Don't quit. The trial is a test of your faith, character, and endurance. Don't whine and complain, saying, "God, why is all this happening to me?"

Unfortunately, there are no shortcuts; there's no easy way to mature physically, emotionally, and spiritually. You must remain determined and work with God. Constantly work with God, dealing with the issues He brings up and keeping a good attitude, fighting through until you win the victory.

Father God, thank You for using adversity to keep us
fresh, alive, active, and growing. In Jesus's name, amen!

Five Purposes for Suffering

John Piper
Adapted from desiringGod.org

All things work together for good.
—ROMANS 8:28, KJV

We seldom know the *micro* reasons for our sufferings. But the Bible does give us faith-sustaining *macro* reasons.

Here are the five macro purposes of God in our sufferings. Remember the five *R*'s:

Repentance. Suffering calls us and others to turn from treasuring anything on earth above God. "Or those eighteen on whom the tower in Siloam fell and killed them: do you think that they were worse offenders than all the others who lived in Jerusalem? No, I tell you; but unless you repent, you will all likewise perish" (Luke 13:4–5).

Reliance. Suffering is a call to trust God and not the life-sustaining props of this world. "We were so utterly burdened beyond the strength that we despaired of life itself. Indeed, we felt that we had received the sentence of death. But that was to make us rely not on ourselves but on God who raises the dead" (2 Cor. 1:8–9).

Righteousness. Suffering is the discipline of our loving heavenly Father so that we come to share His righteousness and holiness. "The Lord disciplines the one He loves and chastises every son whom He receives…He disciplines us for our good that we may share His holiness. For the moment, all discipline seems painful rather than pleasant but later yields the peaceful fruit of righteousness to those who have been trained by it" (Heb. 12:10–11).

Reward. Suffering is working for us a great reward in heaven that will make up for every loss here a thousandfold. "This light momentary affliction is preparing for us an eternal weight of glory beyond all comparison" (Heb. 12:10–11).

Reminder. Suffering reminds us that God sent His Son into the world to suffer so that our suffering would not be God's condemnation but His purification. The Son was sent "that I may know Him and the power of His resurrection, and may share His sufferings" (Phil. 3:10).

Don't let the micro reasons of suffering—why now, why this way, why this long?—cause you to overlook the massive help God gives in His word by telling us His macro purposes for us.

Father God, let us see your great purposes in
allowing us to suffer. In Jesus's name, amen!

_____

_____

_____

_____

Four Reasons for Rejoicing in Suffering
Dean De Castro

Count it all joy...when you meet trials.
—JAMES 1:2–4, ESV

Today's Scripture tells us at least four reasons why we should rejoice in our trials and suffering:

Suffering brings joy. It is our human nature to resist difficulties instead of embracing them. Phillips' translation states, "Don't resent them as intruders, but welcome them as friends."

Randy Alcorn shares how he rejoiced in his suffering: "This trial is difficult, but God is sovereign, loving, and kind. Through His grace and empowerment, I will become more like Jesus and closer to Him. And I will be eternally grateful for what God did through these hard times."

Suffering is multifaceted. The phrase "trials of a various kind" indicates that troubles come in many shades, shapes, and degrees. Our suffering can be mental, physical, emotional, or spiritual. Whatever their nature or severity, these various trials make us "mature and complete, lacking in nothing" (v. 4).

These multifaceted adversities advance our spiritual maturity and allow our personality to reach its complete and balanced development. Moreover, they enable us to display all those virtues that characterize mature believers in Christ.

Suffering purifies faith. A goldsmith uses heat under a smelting pot to bring the impurities to the top and skim them off, leaving only the pure gold behind. The smelter knows the gold is ready to come off the heat when he sees the reflection of his face in the melted metal. He knows the precious metal is ready to be molded into what he desires.

Likewise, in the heat of tribulations, God purifies our faith and takes away the impurities in our character that obscure the reflection of Christ's image through us.

Suffering is productive. Our sufferings are never wasted. On the contrary, they are productive and purposeful. They produce in us steadfastness or patience (v. 3). We believe our suffering has a meaning and purpose in God's eternal plan.

People who hurt us give us opportunities to forgive. Our physical ailments teach us to depend on God. Everything that is hard and seems wrong in our lives is a divine invitation to turn to God.

Father God, help us think of our trials as seeds that will ultimately bring us a harvest of joy. In Jesus's name, amen!

_____

_____

_____

_____

Rejoicing in Pain

Selwyn Hughes

Adapted from *How to Live the Christian Life*

*When all kinds of trials and temptations crowd
into your lives...welcome them as friends!*
—JAMES 1:2–3, PHILLIPS

God allows sufferings to occur in our lives for a very significant purpose. And a proper response to the problems of life can determine the rate of progress in our Christian experience. We are what we respond to.

So, when problems or trials and difficulties crowd into my life, what should I do? I will meet them head on with *praise*, welcoming them (as the Scripture says) as friends.

God's obligation. If we face an adverse situation or hostile environment that after prayer is not removed, God will provide a unique stream of grace to enable us to rise above the problem with a song of praise in our hearts and joy that knows no despair (2 Cor. 12:9).

The same God who allowed His Son to die in apparent failure on a cross, yet wrought from it the most significant victory the world has ever known, is in charge of my life.

I belong to God, and I am His responsibility. Thus, I firmly believe He would not allow anything to happen to me that could not be turned into my ultimate good (Rom. 8:28).

Man's responsibility. While praising Him for the problems, however, I will not allow myself to become insensitive to any deficiencies in me that may have caused the problem and will seek to examine my life at every single opportunity.

I will ask myself, "Did I cause this problem by something I failed to do?" If I did, then I would correct the fault at once and praise God even further that the problem has enabled me to add something to my character.

Knowing me as He does, He has a plan for my life that cannot be frustrated. He will allow nothing to happen to me that will not contribute to His glory and my good. I will respond to His love and grace with all the enthusiasm I can muster. In this thrilling revelation, I will continuously rejoice and be glad.

Praise the Lord!

> *Father God, let us rejoice in our sufferings as Paul*
> *did (Col. 1:24). In Jesus's name, amen!*

_____

_____

_____

_____

The Gift of Misery

Dan Stone and David Gregory
Adapted from *The Rest of the Gospel*

You meant evil against me, but God meant it for good.
—GENESIS 50:20, ESV

There is a gift from God that we often don't recognize as a gift.

I call it the gift of misery. Often in the Scriptures, God's primary way of preparing people for Him was the gift of misery.

In the Old Testament, Joseph was tossed into a pit by his brothers, sold into slavery, falsely accused, put into prison, unjustly forgotten, and left to languish. Eventually, he became prime minister of Egypt. Humanly speaking, he had a right to be bitter.

When his brothers were at his mercy, however, what was his response? "You meant evil against me, but God meant it for good in order to bring about this present result" (Gen. 50:20).

God used misery in Joseph's life not only to mature him in his faith but also to bring temporal salvation to his father's household—the entire Jewish nation at that time. Joseph could see the evil of his brothers, or he could see the purpose of God. He chose to see the purpose of God.

When we signed on with God, we gave Him rights and privileges over our lives to do with them as He pleases. Of course, we thought life with God would always be pleasant. That's how we feel when we're still babes.

But now, as we look back, we can say, "Lord, that time I was miserable, that's when You became real in my life. And through that experience, You remade my life into that of a disciple who is not above his Master."

Thank God for your misery. It prepares you to be a vessel for His use. It doesn't seem to make sense, but in your weakness is your strength. In your misery is your hope. In your death is your life. In your nothing is His everything.

Thank God for your pain. Don't attribute it to the devil. But if you do, respond like Joseph: "The devil meant it for evil, but God turns his tricks on him and works it for good."

Father God, we realize that when we're miserable
enough, You're ready to bless us. In Jesus's name, amen!

_____

_____

_____

_____

The Discipline of Adversity

Jerry Bridges
Adapted from *The Discipline of Grace*

God disciplines us for our good, in order
that we may share in His holiness.
—HEBREWS 12:10

As devoted disciples of Jesus Christ, we must practice specific disciplines if we are to make progress in the pursuit of holiness. One of the spiritual disciplines necessary in the process of sanctification is the discipline of adversity or hardship.

Adversity is not a discipline we undertake ourselves but is imposed by God on us as a means of spiritual growth. As Hebrews 12:10 says, the purpose of adversity is to make us holy.

In verse 7, the writer of Hebrews instructed us "to endure hardship as discipline." Notice there is no qualifying adjective before the word hardship. He did not say, "Endure all hardship"; neither did he say, "Endure some hardship as discipline."

Without a qualifying adjective, we must understand him to have meant *all* hardship. That is, all hardship of whatever kind has a disciplinary purpose for us. There is no such thing as pain without reason in the life of a believer.

I don't want to trivialize hardship. However, we all know that there are varying degrees of adversity. Some are life-shattering, such as the death of a loved one or a permanently disabling injury. At the opposite end of the spectrum are situations that are no more than temporary nuisances, such as an unexpected visitor dropping by when you are working against a tight deadline.

All of these circumstances and events, whether trivial or severe, are intended by God to be means of developing Christlike character. The only way we develop Christlike character is in the crucible of real-life experience. God, by His providence, continually brings us into situations requiring the exercise of obedience.

Remember, God is the one in charge of sanctification in our lives. He is the one who orchestrates and superintends those particular circumstances that each of us needs. He knows what and how much adversity will develop more Christlikeness in us, and He will not bring nor allow anything to come into our lives any more than is needful for His purpose.

Father God, let us persevere in our suffering to produce more Christlike character (Rom. 5:3). In Jesus's name, amen!

_____

_____

_____

_____

Journey Through the Wall

Peter Scazzero
Adapted from *Emotionally Healthy Spirituality*

All things work for good.
—ROMANS 8:28, NAB

Every follower of Jesus at some point will confront the Wall.

Or, as the ancients called it, "the dark night of the soul." Failure to understand its nature results in long-term pain and confusion. Receiving the gift of God in the Wall, however, transforms our lives forever.

There is an old story about a wise man in China. One day, for no apparent reason, his son's horse ran away. Everyone tried to comfort the family for the young man's bad fortune, but his wise father said, "What makes you so sure this is not a blessing?"

Months later, his horse returned, bringing with her a magnificent stallion. This time everyone was full of congratulations for the son's good fortune. But now, his father said, "What makes you so sure this isn't a disaster?"

Their household became richer by this fine horse that the son loved to ride. But one day, he fell off his horse and broke his hip. Once again, everyone offered their consolation for his bad luck, but his father said, "What makes you so sure this is not a blessing?"

A year later, nomads invaded across the border, and every non-disabled man was required to go into battle. As a result, the Chinese families living in the village lost nine of every ten men. Only because the son was lame did the father and son survive to care for each other.

What appeared like a blessing and success was actually a terrible thing. But conversely, what has seemed a terrible event often becomes a rich blessing.

One of the blessings of going through the Wall of pain and suffering is a childlike, deepening love for mystery. We can rest more easily and live more freely on the other side of the Wall, knowing that God is in control and worthy of our trust.

"Oh, the depth of the riches of the wisdom and knowledge of God! How unsearchable His judgments, and His paths beyond tracing out!... To Him be the glory forever! Amen" (Rom. 11:33–36).

Father God, let us trust You despite our inability to know Your mysterious ways. In Jesus's name, amen!

_____

_____

_____

_____

Pruning the Branches
Neil and Joanne Anderson
Adapted from *Daily in Christ*

*Every branch that bears fruit, He prunes
it, so that it may bear more fruit.*
—JOHN 15:2, NASB

Our goal is to abide in Christ, not to bear fruit.

Jesus promised that if we abide in Him, we will bear much fruit (John 15:5). To bear more fruit, God the Father prunes us. Sometimes, well-meaning Christians have cut too much too soon, hindering growth. A dear but sadly abused child of God pictured her experience in the following poem:

A friend of mine whose grapevines died was about to throw them away.

I said, "I'll take care your vines and make something special of them today."

As I gently bent one vine, entwining round and round,

A rustic wreath began to form, potential did abound.

One vine would not go where it should, and anxious as I was,

I forced it so to change its shape, it broke—and what the cause?

If I had taken precious time to slowly change its form,

It would have made a lovely wreath, not a dead vine, broken, torn.

As I finished bending, adding blooms, applying trim,

I realized how that rustic wreath is like my life within.

You see, so many in my life have tried to make me change.

They've forced my spirit anxiously, I tried to rearrange.

But when the pain was far too great, they forced my fragile form;

I plunged far deeper in despair, my spirit broken, torn.

Then God allowed a gentle one who knew of dying vines,

To kindly, patiently, allow the Lord to take His time.

And though the vine has not yet formed a decorative wreath,

I know that with God's servant's help one day when Christ I meet

He'll see a finished circle, a perfect gift to Him.

It will be a finished product, a wreath with all the trim.

So as you look upon this gift, the vine round and complete,

Remember God is using you to gently shape His wreath.

Father God, just as a gardener is never closer to the vine than when he is pruning it, likewise, we are never closer to You than when You discipline us. In Jesus's name, amen!

Brokenness

Alan Nelson

Adapted from *Discipleship Journal*, issue 94 (1996)

A broken and contrite heart, O God, you will not despise.
—PSALM 51:17, ESV

Psalm 51 is David's soul-wrenching response to the prophet Nathan confronting him over his sin with Bathsheba.

At the core of his confession, David realizes that God allows us to go through a period of brokenness to prepare us for a new level of fruitfulness (See John 15:2).

Times of brokenness may come in many shapes and forms. For some, it takes a shattered marriage, losing a loved one, a failed job, or ruined finances. For others, the discovery of cancer or an emotional collapse may trigger a season of brokenness.

God can use any of these episodes to tame our souls. But the cause of the situation is not nearly as important as how we respond to it. Although the circumstances may be diverse, the divine goal is straightforward—brokenness. God uses brokenness to get our attention. His desired result is the surrender of our will.

Just because we have experienced brokenness does not guarantee that we reflect its benefits. We must check our attitudes regularly to see if our souls are tamed. Here are a dozen questions to ask:

- Am I willing to let go of my dreams and ambitions if it is God's will?
- Am I defensive when accused, criticized, or misunderstood?
- Am I coveting what others have instead of waiting for heaven's rewards?
- Do I forgive when offended, with or without an apology?
- Am I complaining or arguing because of unsurrendered rights?

- Am I thinking of others first out of love?
- Am I proudly appearing to be always right or to know all the answers?
- Am I practicing the spiritual disciplines (prayer, fasting, solitude, simplicity, etc.)?
- Am I being silent regarding self-promotion and letting God do my public relations?
- Am I daily saying, "God, whatever it takes, I'm willing to submit to your leadership?"
- Am I expressing joy in the difficulties that refine me?
- Am I taking risks out of obedience to Christ instead of giving in to fear, pride, or denial?

Father God, when we undergo intense times of brokenness, may You prepare us for greater fruitfulness. In Jesus's name, amen!

_____

_____

_____

_____

The Crucifixion of Jesus

Selwyn Hughes
Adapted from *Every Day with Jesus* (March/April 1996)

When they came to the place called the
Skull, there they crucified Him.
—LUKE 23:33

Crucifixion was the most brutal event on this planet.

But it happened nevertheless, and we must face that fact, no matter how distasteful it may be to our human sensibilities. We should not shrink from looking at the horrible truth of crucifixion because it will bring home to our hearts more powerfully what it means for our Lord to suffer and die for our sins.

Physical torture of crucifixion. Crucifixion was one of the most atrocious and horrifying forms of execution in which a living, breathing man was fastened to some timbers and allowed to hang there for days. This form of torture was devised to produce the maximum pain over the most prolonged time.

A few ancient manuscripts tell us how crucifixion was conducted. First, a victim was flogged, then forced to carry the horizontal piece of the cross to the place of execution. Next, the wood was laid on the ground, and he was fixed to it with ropes or nails.

Then he was lifted and secured to the main post (which sometimes was a permanent structure left in position as a warning), at which point his feet would be tied or nailed to the upright.

It was not unusual for a person to survive on a cross for days. However, exposure, fever, hunger, shock, and exhaustion were usually the immediate causes of death.

Social stigma of crucifixion. Death by crucifixion was the most shameful way of bringing someone's life to an end. Yet this was the manner of death assigned to the Son of God.

The idea of a crucified Messiah was repugnant to the Jews. However, Galatians 3:13 shows that our Lord carried the curse upon all sinners through His death on the cross. Thus, the sinner who would be condemned to death by the law can now be alive to God. Free from the curse, he is open to the blessings of God that come through Christ.

The cross is a sublime paradox: a great crime and love.

Father God, had our Lord not suffered crucifixion, we would never have been saved. Thank You! In Jesus's name, amen!

Reflections on the Cross: A Prayer of Devotion
Anonymous

For My yoke is easy and My burden is light.
—MATTHEW 11:30

O MY SAVIOUR,
I thank You from the depths of my being
for Your wondrous grace and love
in bearing my sin in Your own body on the tree.
May Your cross be to me
as the tree that sweetens my bitter Marahs,
as the rod that blossoms with life and beauty,
as the brazen serpent that calls forth the look of faith.
By Your cross crucify my every sin;
Use it to increase my intimacy with Yourself;
Make it the ground of all my conduct,
the liveliness of all my duties,
the sum of all Your gospel promises,
the comfort of all my afflictions,
the vigour of my love, thankfulness, graces,
the very essence of my religion;
And by it give me that rest without rest,
the rest of ceaseless praise.

O MY LORD AND SAVIOUR,
You also appointed a cross for me to take up and carry,
You have appointed it to be my portion,
but self-love hates it,
carnal reason is unreconciled to it;
without the grace of patience I cannot bear it,
walk with it, profit by it.

O blessed cross, what mercies do you bring with you!
You are only esteemed hateful by my rebel will,
heavy because I shirk your load.
Teach me, gracious Lord and Saviour,
that with my cross You send promised grace
so that I may bear it patiently,
that my cross is Your yoke which is easy,
and Your burden which is light.

*Father God, as we remember Christ's journey to the
cross, let us bear patiently and with gratitude the personal
cross You want us to carry. In Jesus's name, amen!*

_____

_____

_____

_____

Christ's Continuing Afflictions

Selwyn Hughes
Adapted from *Every Day with Jesus* (March/April 1996)

I fill up in my flesh what is still lacking in regard to Christ's
afflictions, for the sake of His Body, which is the church.
—COLOSSIANS 1:24

The crucifixion of Jesus was a once-and-for-all event about two thousand years ago. However, there is a sense in which the suffering of our Lord continues.

Paul's suffering for the church. The verse before us says that Paul rejoiced in his sufferings because they helped make up for what was lacking in Christ's afflictions. But Paul was not talking about the price Christ paid for our redemption on the cross. There is no deficiency in the atoning work of Christ; no one can add to His finished and perfect work.

Instead, Paul refers to the afflictions God called him to bear "for the sake of...the church." When Paul was suffering for the sake of the church, Christ, too, was suffering in Paul's sufferings. In other words, Paul's pain was Christ's pain.

The sins of the church. Christ also suffers in the gross misconduct and failures of His church. The account of the seven churches in the book of Revelation shows our Lord was hurting because they misrepresented our Lord's holy name.

How do you think Christ felt when churches split over some minor issues in the church's practices, such as the modes of baptism, the styles of worship, which Bible versions to use, etc.? Does Christ bleed when divisions occur among His people?

Hebrews 6:6 informs us that it is possible to crucify the Son of God afresh. It happens when those who have "been enlightened, who have tasted the heavenly gift...fall away" (vv. 4–6) and deny the faith.

Of course, few believers would openly deny Christ and pledge to have nothing more to do with Him. But do we realize that when we profess to be one of Christ's followers and yet refuse to obey His commands and deliberately choose our way rather than His, the Savior bleeds again, metaphorically speaking?

Our Lord's pain did not end when He died on the cross. The suffering of our Lord continues every time we put our interests before His.

Father God, help us live so that nothing we do brings
You grief and pain. In Jesus's name, amen!

_____

_____

_____

_____

The Pain of Bearing the Cross

Watchman Nee
Adapted from *The Spiritual Man,* vol. 2

*Then He said to them all: "Whoever wants to be My disciple must
deny themselves and take up their cross daily and follow Me."*
—LUKE 9:23

The purpose of bearing the practical cross God gives us has always
been to crucify our selfish desires. No other part of our whole being
suffers the pain of the cross more than the emotions. Therefore, the
cross must cut deeply into all that belongs to our self-life.

The emotion of hastiness. If a believer has not put his emotion on
the cross, he cannot walk according to the Spirit. And a person who
walks by the Spirit must not be hasty.

An emotional believer will not wait for God because they like to
do everything independently. They cannot trust God because this
requires self-denial. They love to help God—as if God were too slow
and needed their help.

God knows that our flesh is impatient; therefore, He uses our
coworkers, family, environment, and material things to hinder us and
slow us down. He wants our hastiness to die so that He can work on us.

Self-vindication. Every time a believer receives a cross, they go
through its crucifixion once more. However, if they vindicate themselves according to the desire of the self, they will learn that the power
of self is more difficult to subdue the next time.

The Lord often desires that His people commit all things unto His
hand and not vindicate themselves. God wants us to remain silent
to enable the cross, which He has arranged for us to accomplish its
work. Whenever a believer shuts their mouth in their affliction, they
see the cross working.

Once the Holy Spirit has worked intensely through the cross, a believer no longer loves anything according to their own preferences. God fills their desires; hence, they desire nothing.

We must practice taking the cross every day according to God's will. Every cross has its particular mission to fulfill as part of God's work in us. Therefore, may we not allow any cross to come upon us in vain.

Father God, may your appointed cross do its work freely in us. In Jesus's name, amen!

_____

_____

_____

_____

Jesus, I My Cross Have Taken

Henry Francis Lyte (1793–1847)

*For it has been granted to you on behalf of Christ not
only to believe in Him, but also to suffer for Him.*
—PHILIPPIANS 1:29

Jesus, I my cross have taken,
All to leave and follow Thee.
Destitute, despised, forsaken,
Thou from hence my all shall be.
Perish every fond ambition,
All I've sought or hoped or known.
Yet how rich is my condition!
God and heaven are still my own.
Man may trouble and distress me,
'Twill but drive me to Thy breast.
Life with trials hard may press me;
Heaven will bring me sweeter rest.
Oh, 'tis not in grief to harm me
While Thy love is left to me;
Oh, 'twere not in joy to charm me,
Were that joy unmixed with Thee.
Go, then, earthly fame and treasure,
Come disaster, scorn and pain
In Thy service, pain is pleasure,
With Thy favor, loss is gain.
I have called Thee Abba Father,
I have stayed my heart on Thee
Storms may howl, and clouds may gather;
All must work for good to me.
Haste thee on from grace to glory,

Armed by faith, and winged by prayer.
Heaven's eternal days before thee,
God's own hand shall guide thee,
Soon shall close thy earthly mission,
Soon shall pass thy pilgrim's days,
Hope shall change to glad fruition,
Faith to sight, and prayer to praise.

Father God, in You, pain is pleasure and
loss is gain. In Jesus's name, amen!

_____

_____

_____

_____

The Confession of A Preacher

Hershael York
Adapted from preaching.org

Preach the Word...in season and out of season.
—2 TIMOTHY 4:2

When Jesus said that I had to deny myself to follow Him, I thought He meant relinquishing some future CEO position that I certainly would have attained had I not gone into ministry. Or perhaps it meant a willingness to tackle Satan and bind him hand and foot in some public spectacle of spiritual commitment.

The fantasy of immense sacrifice holds much greater appeal than the reality of the routine surrender of my rights. But later, I realized that giving my life to Christ means being faithful to fulfill my calling as a preacher. Moreover, it means doing the small things faithfully throughout my life.

Sermon preparation. Above all other facets of ministry, preaching has demanded a denial of self I never anticipated. As a result, I have regularly incurred the cost of countless hours of Bible study, sermon planning, and the excavation of a hundred mediocre illustrations to unearth the one perfect jewel, all the while assiduously strategizing how to speak resonantly without sounding hollow or contrived.

Jesus never asked me to die while taking the gospel to heathen lands. Still, every Monday morning, He commands me to lay my precious week on the altar and eliminate the extraneous things that impeded my obedience to my initial call.

Sermon delivery. Nothing, however, demands self-denial like a sermon's delivery. On the contrary, it necessitates a disregard for the nagging self-doubts that turn my attention from the text and the seductive confidence of weekly routine and years of experience that lure me to pride.

Every sermon acts against the sovereignty of self and capitulates to the cross of Christ and its claim on my life. My personality, self-consciousness, mood, and comfort become irrelevant when I step into the pulpit.

When a preacher denies self and takes up the cross of Christ in the pulpit, CNN doesn't cover it; the videos don't go viral and get a million hits, and hardly anyone calls it heroic. But it's enough to bring the enemy down and save those who need it.

Father God, let us be faithful in surrendering our rights daily to accomplish Your will in our lives. In Jesus's name, amen!

Pain: A Touchstone

Ron Walters
Adapted from *Preaching* (May/June 2015)

When He has tested me, I will come forth as gold.
—JOB 23:10B

Pain is nature's flashing yellow light, a built-in warning signal.

For example, a child afflicted with the genetic disorder dysautonomia feels no pain because the condition short circuits the autonomous nervous system.

Hence, there is no way to know if the child has a broken bone, an infected ear, or a decayed tooth. The eyes become dry and insensitive to foreign objects. Burns doesn't register. Cuts go unnoticed.

Of the few who survive adolescence, 95 percent develop spinal curvature, pneumonia, depression, and hypothermia from the lack of pain.

The New Testament's most common word for pain is *basanos,* which means "a touchstone" made of velvet-textured black quartz. This very dense stone was used in ancient days to assay gold ore.

A strong-armed goldsmith would rub pure gold against the flat touchstone, leaving a gold-colored streak. Then the suspect alloy would be struck repeatedly beside the golden mark. After rinsing away the broken debris, the goldsmith would compare the two colors and determine the authenticity of the alloy.

The process may seem unfair, but God's methods of testing our faith always have included pain. The pain we feel is real, and it serves an essential purpose. God intended it to serve us and others.

- The cross served as Jesus's touchstone. His pain and death were cruel and excessive but revealed His pure gold.

- Abraham's touchstone was a mountain on which God asked him to sacrifice his precious Isaac. The result was pure gold.
- Job's cataclysmic losses and the unfair accusations of his friends, ultimately revealed pure gold.
- Joseph's betrayal by his brothers began a downward spiral in every conceivable dignity. Yet he became pure gold.
- Paul's hostile receptions, beatings, and prison time revealed the purity of his gold.

Each was struck hard against a personal touchstone. Each felt intense pain, but each revealed pure gold. Is it possible to turn pain into pure gold? What do you think?

Father God, in our trials and the center of our pain, we know that You comfort us, teach us, and sustain us so that our faith will come forth as gold. In Jesus's name, amen!

_____

_____

_____

_____

Paul's Thorn in the Flesh

Dean De Castro

There was given to me a thorn in the flesh.
—2 CORINTHIANS 12:7, NASB

What was the Apostle Paul's thorn in the flesh? I found at least two plausible views, each with Scriptures to back them up.

Poor perception. Some Bible teachers think the thorn in the flesh refers to a chronic eye problem. After all, when Paul saw the risen Lord with all of His glory, he became blind for three days.

In Galatians 6:11, Paul says, "See with what large letters I am writing to you with my own hand." Perhaps Paul wrote in such big letters because his eyesight was poor. Relatedly, Paul also says that the Galatians were willing to pluck out their own eyes for him (Gal. 4:15).

Personal persecution. Another popular theory explaining Paul's thorn in the flesh is the personal harassment he received from the religious leaders who fiercely opposed him. These people included the Judaizers, who followed Paul wherever he went and tried to make some converts adhere to the old Jewish laws and customs (Gal. 5:11–12). He also reports that some false brethren were constantly trying to challenge his position of authority in the local churches (Phil. 1:17).

Paul's petitions. Paul asked the Lord three times to remove this source of pain from him (2 Cor. 12:8). But the answer from God was "No." So, instead of removing the problem, whatever it was, God gave Paul more overwhelming grace: the grace to accept the "No," grace to endure the discomfort, and grace to handle the pain.

God humbled Paul so that he would constantly need God's grace. Moreover, God granted Paul compensating strength. As a result, Paul learned that God's "power is made perfect in weakness" (v. 9).

The exact nature of Paul's thorn in the flesh is uncertain. However, God likely wanted Paul's suffering to be described in general terms so it could be applied to any problem we may face now. Thus, whether the "thorn" we struggle with today is physical, emotional, or spiritual, we can know that God's grace is all-sufficient and that when we are weak, He is strong.

Father God, You never allow a problem to remain in our lives without providing us with the grace and strength that see us through. In Jesus's name, amen!

_____

_____

_____

_____

Nothing I Suffer Surprises God

Vannetha Rendall Risner

Adapted from desiringGod.org

Call to Me and I will answer you.
—JEREMIAH 33:3

Recently, I was concerned about an unexplained new health issue, uncertain of the underlying problem. I was reading God's words in Scripture, but my mind was somewhere far away.

I grabbed my phone and put my questions into Google. Using different terms and queries, I searched to figure out what my symptoms indicated. I found a few hopeful answers but still felt vaguely unsettled. I went back to reading my Bible, wishing I hadn't interrupted my time with God for that.

Then I read, "God is our refuge and strength, a very present help in trouble. Therefore we will not fear though the earth gives way" (Ps. 46:1–2). I realized how foolish I'd been. Why was I looking elsewhere first for answers? Why did I want reassurance from Google rather than from God?

As I sat there praying, I reminded myself that whatever comes to pass has been determined by God (Isa. 37:26). Not a sparrow falls to the ground apart from the Father's will (Matt. 10:29). Nothing is too hard for Him (Jer. 32:17).

I confessed how often I don't even bring God into my worries. I may mouth a quick prayer, but practically I act as though everything depends on my own wisdom.

But when I remember that God makes foolish the understanding of the world (1 Cor. 1:20) and that the foolishness of God is wiser than men (1 Cor. 1:25), I realize that more information won't help me, at least not in the ways I need most.

I am not implying I shouldn't research within reason to understand the perplexing realities happening to me or around me. There may be steps like that that I need to take. But regardless, I need to invite God into the process, seeking the guidance of the Holy Spirit.

So, I pray that when I am afraid, I will not turn to Google over God, and I will rest knowing that God will be there with me even if I walk through the valley of the shadow of death (Ps. 23:4).

Father God, help us trade our irrational fears of
an uncertain future for the loving assurance of an
unchanging God. In Jesus's name, amen!

God Is in Control

Denise A. Dewald

Be still, and know that I am God.
—PSALM 46:10A

*And we know that in all things God works for the good of those
who love Him, who have been called according to His purpose.*
—ROMANS 8:28

Nothing in life happens by chance
It's all part of a plan—
And no matter what we go through,
God holds us in His hand.
Before your panic can begin
Remember to look above—
God waits to hear your heartfelt prayer
And give to you His love.
His love for us is far beyond
What we can understand;
Reach out to Him in greatest need,
He'll gladly take you hand.
Whatever happens in this life
Know that God is in control—
And He is ever waiting to
Comfort you, and console.
Recall how past trials in your life
Have helped your spirit grow—
It was then you called out to God,
And His love you came to know.
And as His love builds in your heart
With every burden you bear,

There'll be too much for you to hold...
With others you will share.

> *Father God, we firmly believe that You can turn*
> *our mess into positive messages that we can*
> *share with others. In Jesus's name, amen!*

_____

_____

_____

_____

This Thing Is From Me

Laura A. Barter Snow

This thing is from Me.
—1 KINGS 12:24, KJV

My child, I have a message for you today. It is short—only five words—but let them sink into your innermost soul: THIS THING IS FROM ME.

Have you ever thought that all that concerns you concerns Me too? For "he that touches you touches the apple of His eye" (Zech. 2:8). You are very "precious in My sight" (Isa. 43:4).

Are you in money difficulties? Is it hard to make ends meet? This thing is from Me, for I am your purse-bearer and would have you draw from and depend upon Me. My supplies are limitless (Phil. 4:19).

Are you passing through a night of sorrow? This thing is from Me. I am the "Man of Sorrows and acquainted with grief" (Isa. 53:3). I have let earthly comforters fail you, that by turning to me, you may obtain everlasting consolation (2 Thess. 2:16, 17).

Have your plans been upset? Are you bowed down and weary? This thing is from Me. You made your plans then came asking Me to bless them. But I would have you let Me plan for you, and then I take the responsibility, for "this thing is too much for you, you are not able to perform it by yourself" (Exod. 18:18).

Have you longed to do some great work for Me and instead been laid aside on a bed of pain and weakness? This thing is from me. I could not get your attention during your busy days, and I want to teach you some of My deepest lessons.

"They also serve who only stand and wait." Some of My greatest workers are those shut out from active service, so they may learn to wield the weapon of prayer.

This day I place in your hands this pot of holy oil; make use of it freely, My child. Let every word that pains you, every interruption that would make you impatient be anointed with it! Remember, interruptions are divine instructions. So, the sting will go as you learn to see Me in all things.

Father God, all our sufferings were filtered through
Your loving hands. In Jesus's name, amen!

Footprints in the Sand

Anonymous

Come to me, all you are weary and burdened, and I will give you rest. Take My yoke upon you and learn from Me, for I am gentle and humble in heart, and you will find rest for your souls. For My yoke is easy and My burden is light.
—MATTHEW 11:28–30

One night a man had a dream. He dreamed
he was walking along the beach with the Lord.
Across the sky flashed scenes from his life.
For each scene he noticed two sets of
footprints in the sand; one belonging
to him, and the other to the Lord.
When the last scene of his life flashed before him,
he looked back at the footprints in the sand.
He noticed that many times along the path of
his life there was only one set of footprints.
He also noticed that it happened at the very
lowest and saddest times in his life.
This really bothered him and he
questioned the Lord about it.
"Lord, You said that You'd walk with me all the way.
But during the most troublesome times
in my life, there is only one set of footprints.
"Why did You leave me when I needed You most?"
The Lord replied: "My precious child,
I love you and would never leave you.
During your times of trial and suffering,
when you see only one set of footprints,
It was then that I carried you."

Father God, how glad we are that You thrust Your shoulder beneath the cross we are called to carry. In Jesus's name, amen!

_____

_____

_____

_____

The Suffering of Job

Dean De Castro

Though He slay me, yet will I hope in Him.
—JOB 13:15A

In one afternoon, Job lost all his material possessions, seven children, and his health.

Then, adding anguish upon anguish, his friends condemned him rather than consoled him. Furthermore, God seemed to ignore Job, refusing to answer and rise to his cause for a long time.

Job's three friends. They believed God was punishing Job for sins in his life. But Job proved them wrong by showing no correlation between righteousness and prosperity or between wickedness and suffering in this world.

It is just a fact that bad things sometimes happen to good people and good things happen to bad people. Job's suffering did not come because he was wrong but because of his unwavering faithfulness to God (Job 1:8).

Elihu. In chapters 32–37, Elihu rebuked Job and his three friends. First, he criticized Job for saying foolish and presumptuous things about God to justify himself. He charged Job's three friends for their superficial theology of suffering.

According to Elihu, God used pain and suffering to purge out of Job's life a residue of pride that had lain quietly and deeply within. Then, when Job was shaken after suffering long enough, the sediment of pride was stirred up and showed itself when Job tried to justify himself at God's expense.

God. In chapters 38–41, God confronts Job for his pride. Instead of addressing Job's particular situation, the Almighty One takes Job on a virtual tour of the universe. God asks Job if he understands how the universe works or how to take care of it and keep it running.

The intention behind God's questions seems to be to demonstrate to Job that he couldn't comprehend the complexity of the reality of how God manages the world even if he wanted to. It's simply too big for him.

Through to the end of the book, Job never learns why he suffers. Instead, he comes to understand that God is God and He knows what He is doing. As Max Lucado writes, "When you can't trace His hand, trust His heart."

Father God, let us trust in You even though we may
not know why we suffer. In Jesus's name, amen!

_____

_____

_____

_____

The Testimony of Carole Carlson

David Jeremiah
Adapted from *When Your World Falls Apart*

Comfort one another.
—1 THESSALONIANS 4:18, NKJV

Kent was in a thankful mood, incredibly grateful for the airplane he and his dad had just purchased. His dream was to become a missionary pilot.

On Thursday night, he called home and said, "Mom, I'm just going to go and practice a few touch and goes. Hold supper for me—I'll be home by nine." Kent never came home.

In a clump of trees at the edge of a small country airport lay the crashed plane and the body of Kent. On that warm June night, God chose to take one of our precious children. How does a parent continue to exist after that moment?

In the weeks and months to follow, I learned more about God's love than I had in all my years of being a Christian.

When I felt helpless to do even the small tasks of the day, I'd repeat, "I can do all things through Christ who strengthens me" (Phil. 4:13). I remembered the verse Kent had underlined in his Bible: "But I do not want you to be ignorant, brethren, concerning those who have fallen asleep, lest you sorrow as others who have no hope" (1 Thess. 4:13).

When I began to indulge in self-pity, I'd embrace my husband, Ward. He was suffering as intensely as I was, and we remembered that God says, "Therefore comfort each other and edify one another, just as you also are doing" (1 Thess. 5:11).

The grace of God gave us comfort, but it also pierced us with the urgency to reach out to others. Ward and I grew closer together as we needed to console other parents who had suffered a loss. As a result, we've developed an uncommon boldness in ministering to those who are hurting.

I hope no one experiences losing a child. But a far greater tragedy is to lose the opportunity to know Jesus Christ intimately. How grateful we are that our children learn and love Him. Life has meaning for us simply because we have the assurance that we will be reunited when this life is over.

Father God, let us worship You with a grateful heart
in times of pain and crisis. In Jesus's name, amen!

_____

_____

_____

_____

The Testimony of Steve Garrison

David Jeremiah

Adapted from *When Your World Falls Apart*

I will turn the desert into pools of water.
—ISAIAH 41:18

The slowdown in commercial real estate began late in 1990. My company had built thirty-six buildings to sell or lease in five industrial parks during the two previous years. But now it was early in 1991, and all the commercial and industrial buildings stood tenantless, with no buyers in sight.

So my wife and I reluctantly cashed in our IRAs to meet our financial obligations, and in April of 1991, the doors to Garrison Development were shut and locked for the last time.

I'd come to my bend in the road. And just around the turn, I found myself in an arid spiritual desert. I began to see that my walk with God gradually eroded during years of fruitfulness. Finally, with the blinders removed from my eyes, I saw myself in an unflattering new light.

God showed me hard truths about myself that I didn't want to see. For example, I'd had no idea that I'd allowed my reputation, the esteem of my colleagues, and my net worth and assets to become pagan idols in my life.

These things shocked me because I thought I had it all together. But instead, God was "lovingly beating me up." These were difficult lessons to learn, but I sat at His feet and listened to His Word. And amid the discipline, I came to love Him more than I had in the past.

In time, God led me to launch my real estate consulting business. That was the right move because the Lord is the One who established it. Of course, my business today is not as lucrative as it was in the "good old days," but I think my work life is just where God wants it to be.

These years have built my faith like nothing else could have done. I've learned the incredible power of praising God in adversity. I've discovered how to step back and look at my life concerns from an eternal perspective, and it's been wonderful to find how many anxieties fade away when I do that.

Father God, thank You for those spiritual deserts where
we get to know You better. In Jesus's name, amen!

Battling Fear Over the Coronavirus (COVID-19)

Dr. Carol Peters-Tanksley
Adapted from drcarolministries.com

In the world you have tribulation.
—JOHN 16:33, NASB

How do you battle fear over the coronavirus (COVID-19)? For those of us who believe in Jesus, fear is not an option.

Hundreds of times, the Scriptures tell us to fear not. One of my favorite passages is Jesus's words in John 16:33: "I have said these things to you, that in me you may have peace. In the world you will have tribulation. But take heart, I have overcome the world." So how do you get to "no fear here?"

Remember, God is in control. Do you think this is a surprise to God? He knows the absolute truth about how this pandemic started. And He knows how it will end. He knows how many people will get sick (or die) and the impact on the economy.

He knows how governments and other authorities will respond and what our healthcare resources can and cannot do. And He knows how these events will impact you and your family personally. And beyond knowing, He cares about the whole situation and you personally.

We still face troubles. Sometimes we think trusting God's care means He will make everything OK. But remember, Jesus did promise tribulation (John 16:33).

It's a gnarly time for humans to be alive in this world. We are in the mopping-up time in the battle between God's kingdom of light and Satan's kingdom of darkness. God can miraculously bring meaning and good things even out of tragedy. But we will still face troubles.

Wisdom and trust. So, what do you do right now, today? Use wisdom. Wash your hands. Use social distancing. Calmly talk with your family about what actions you will take during this time.

And at the same time, stay on your knees. Prayer changes things. Prayer is not a heavenly vending machine where you put in a prayer and get out the blessing you desire.

But prayer still makes a difference. Prayer keeps your mind in a healthy place. But especially in difficult times, we must take our cues first from our Heavenly Father. His shoulders are big enough to handle all your cares, both today and tomorrow.

> *Father God, let us trust your wisdom and have peace during this pandemic. In Jesus's name, amen!*

Pandemic Diseases

Adapted from gotquestions.org

I will forgive their sin and will heal their land.
—2 CHRONICLES 7:14

Question: "What does the Bible say about pandemic diseases and sicknesses?"

Answer. Various outbreaks of pandemic diseases, such as Ebola or the coronavirus, have prompted many to ask why God allows—or even causes—pandemic diseases and whether such illnesses are a sign of the end times.

Old Testament. The Old Testament describes numerous occasions when God brought plagues and diseases to His people. For example, after giving the Mosaic law, God commanded the people to obey it or suffer many evils, including something that sounds like Ebola: "The Lord will strike you with wasting disease, with fever and inflammation...which will plague you until you perish" (Deut. 28:22).

It's sometimes hard to imagine our loving and merciful God displaying such wrath and anger toward His people. But God's punishments always have the goal of repentance and restoration (2 Chron. 7:13–14).

New Testament. In the New Testament, Jesus healed "every disease and every sickness" as well as plagues in the areas He visited (Matt. 9:35; 10:1; Mark 3:10). Just as God chose to use plagues and disease to show His power to the Israelites, Jesus healed as an exhibition of the same power to verify that He was indeed the Son of God.

End times. The spread of Ebola and the coronavirus is a foretaste of pandemics that will be part of the end times. Jesus referred to future plagues associated with the last days (Luke 21:11). The two witnesses of Revelation 11 will have the power "to strike the earth with every kind of plague as often as they want" (Rev. 11:6).

Since no one knows the time of Jesus's return, we must be careful about saying global pandemics prove that we are living in the end times.

The appearance of pandemic diseases may or may not be tied to God's specific judgment of sin. They could also simply be the result of living in a fallen world.

There is no way to determine whether or not a pandemic has a specific spiritual cause, but we know that God has sovereign control over all things (Rom. 11:36) and will work all things together for the good of those who know and love Him (Rom. 8:28).

Father God, forgive our sins and heal our
land. In Jesus's name, amen!

How to Suffer Well

Marshall Segal

Adapted from desiringGod.org

...those who suffer according to God's will...
—1 PETER 4:19

The Apostle Peter wrote his first letter to help Christians suffer well. Here are the three ways to prepare now:

Imagine what waits for you. "Born again to a living hope...kept in heaven for you" (1 Pet. 1:3–4). If we were more familiar with heaven, we would experience suffering differently. But instead, heaven will establish you, forever free from sin and suffering, in God's painless and thrilling presence.

As Randy Alcorn explains, "Anticipating heaven doesn't eliminate pain, but it lessens and puts it in perspective. Meditating in heaven is a great pain reliever. It reminds us that suffering and death are temporary conditions. Our existence will not end in suffering and death—they are but a gateway to our eternal life of unending joy."

Receive the preciousness of refining. "That the tested genuineness of your faith—more precious than gold that perishes" (1 Pet. 1:6–7). Suffering shows us what is holding us back from God. What has subtly displaced Him as our refuge? How have we slowly begun to compromise with the desires of the flesh? In what ways have we wandered from the narrow path that leads to life (Matt. 7:13–14)?

The shadows of suffering light the long road of sanctification like nothing else. God wants it to be the fire that builds our faith in Him.

Know that you are not alone. "Knowing that the same kinds of suffering are being experienced by your brotherhood throughout the world" (1 Pet. 5:9). If you are suffering more than those around you, you are not as alone as you might feel. Think about how many more have suffered since Peter wrote those words—churches suddenly shut down in China, believers beaten and disowned by their own families in Iraq, Christians targeted and killed by terrorists in Kenya.

Peter says we will find the strength to persevere in our suffering by watching the armies of saints, across oceans and over centuries, endure the same and worse because God was and is with them.

Father God, show us how to suffer well, just as our Lord suffered well when He was on earth. In Jesus's name, amen!

Soldiering for the Lord
Anonymous

Endure hardship as a good soldier of Christ Jesus.
—2 TIMOTHY 2:3, NKJV

I am a soldier in the army of my God.

The Lord Jesus is my commanding officer. The Holy Bible is my code of conduct. Faith, prayer, and the Word are my weapons of warfare.

I have been taught by the Holy Spirit, trained by experience, tried by adversity, and tested by fire. I am a volunteer in this army, and I am enlisted for eternity.

I am faithful, reliable, capable, and dependable. If God needs me, I am there. I am in place, saluting my King, obeying His orders, praising His name, and building His kingdom.

I am a soldier. I am not a baby. I do not need to be pampered, petted, primed up, picked up, or pepped up.

I am a soldier. No one has to call me, remind me, write me, visit me, entice me, or lure me.

I am a soldier. I am not a wimp. No one has to send me flowers, gifts, food, cards, or candy or give me handouts.

I do not need to be cuddled, cradled, cared for, or catered to.

I am committed. I cannot have my feelings hurt badly enough to turn myself around. I cannot be discouraged enough to turn me aside. I cannot lose enough to cause me to quit.

I am more than a conqueror. Devils cannot defeat me. People cannot disillusion me. Weather cannot weary me. Sickness cannot stop me. Battles cannot beat me. Money cannot buy me. Governments cannot silence me, and hell cannot handle me.

I am a soldier. Even death cannot destroy me. I will retire in this army at the rapture or die in this army, but I will not get out, sell out, be talked out, or pushed out.

I am a soldier in the army, and I'm marching, claiming victory. I will not give up. I will not turn around. I am a soldier, marching heaven-bound. Here I stand!

And when my commander calls me from this battlefield, He will promote me to captain and then allow me to rule with Him.

Father God, help us to fight the good fight
of faith. In Jesus's name, amen!

The Pain of Responsibility

Dean De Castro

Work out your own salvation.
—PHILIPPIANS 2:12, KJV

Knowing the Philippian believers' faithful adherence to his teachings, Paul encouraged them to keep his instructions even during his absence (Phil. 2:12).

Obedience is a form of work that requires intense effort and willingness to sacrifice. It involves constantly considering the balance between the reward of obedience and the pain of regrets. When the pleasure of obeying God outweighs the perceived pain of remorse, it will provide strong motivation to do God's will.

The promise of obedience. Psalm 128 presents a perfect picture of a blessed man. It names three rewards for those who fear God and obey His will.

First, they will enjoy the fruit of their labor (v. 2a). Nothing is more painful than a successful person who is not happy and fulfilled in his career.

Second, due to one's diligence and excellence in performing their job, God will bless and prosper them financially (v. 2b).

Third, an obedient believer will enjoy a wonderful family with a supportive and successful wife (v. 3a: "Your wife will be like a fruitful vine within your house."). And his children will treasure the company of their parents (v. 3b: "your sons will be like olive shoots around your table.")

The pain of regrets. In *Disciples Are Made Not Born*, the author imagines that when he dies, God will take him aside and say to him, "Henrichsen, let Me show you what your life could have been like *if only* you had done what I asked, *if only* you had been faithful to me, and *if only* you had disciplined your life and made it count as I wanted you to."

After King Saul disobeyed God, he experienced great remorse over losing his kingship. Likewise, the Apostle Paul was concerned that after leading many people to Christ, he might be disqualified from receiving God's promised reward due to undisciplined living (1 Cor. 9:27; see 1 Cor. 3:14–15).

Remember: The pain of obedience weighs ounces; the pain of regret weighs tons. Even when self-denial hurts, obeying God ultimately brings joy.

Father God, teach us to pursue the pleasure of obedience
and avoid the pain of regret. In Jesus's name, amen!

_____

_____

_____

_____

Becoming Like Christ

Dean De Castro

For those God foreknew He also predestined to
be conformed to the image of His Son.
—ROMANS 8:29

Today's verse gives the most concise revelation of God's ultimate goal in saving sinners—that we become "conformed to the image of His Son."

This doesn't mean you're going to become like a little god. Instead, God wants you to take on the godly character traits of Jesus and display all the fruits of the Holy Spirit (Gal. 5:22–23).

The process. This process of becoming like Christ was conceived before the foundation of the world. "For those God foreknew He also predestined to be conformed to the image of His Son" (Rom. 8:29).

But it is also being realized as a divine-human process in the present. "Work out your salvation yourself...for it is God who works in you " (Phil. 2:12). It will be completed when we stand in the presence of His glory, "blameless with great joy" (Jude 24).

Romans 12:2 and 2 Corinthians 3:18 describe this process of spiritual transformation in the believer's life. The word Paul used is translated in English as "metamorphosis," which is the process of how a caterpillar changes into a butterfly.

Theologians call this process in our lives *sanctification.* "Sanctification is the work of the Holy Spirit in us," Jerry Bridges writes, "whereby our inner being is progressively changed, freeing us more and more from sinful traits and developing within us over time the virtues of Christlike character."

Human responsibility. As disciples of Jesus Christ, we are responsible to Cultivate Christlike Character daily. This involves our loving response in obedience and the diligent use of the spiritual disciplines that are instruments of sanctification.

Obedience is the crux of the Christian life; it is faith in action. And without action, nothing changes. The Holy Spirit is willing to help us, but He will not do the obeying for us.

Any spiritual discipline you practice is a seed you sow to reap a godly habit and noble character. As the saying goes, "Sow an action, you reap a habit; sow a habit, you reap a character." And character is who we are when no one is looking.

Father God, let the world see the beauty of Jesus
in us for Your glory. In Jesus's name, amen!

_____

_____

_____

_____

Signs of Becoming Like Christ

Jerry Bridges
Adapted from *The Discipline of Grace*

...transformed into the same image from glory to glory...
—2 CORINTHIANS 3:18, NASB

Christlikeness is God's goal for all believers.

And that should be our goal also. So, how can we know we are becoming like Christ? Here are the four signs:

Hate sin. Christ "loved righteousness and hated wickedness" (Heb. 1:9). In His humanity, Jesus loved equity, fairness, justice, and upright dealings with others. Yet, at the same time, He hated wickedness. He hated sin for what it is—a rebellion against God's authority, despising His person and defying His commands.

Do we hate sin because of its despicable nature or due to the feelings of guilt that follow it? To the extent that we hate sin as our Lord did, we are transformed into His likeness.

Obey God. Jesus's entire goal on earth was to do the will of His Father even though that would culminate in giving up His life for His sheep. "For I have come down from heaven not to do My will but to do the will of Him who sent Me" (John 6:38).

To be like Jesus is always to seek to do the will of the Father. But unfortunately, we frequently desire to do our own will, resulting in actions that may not appear to be sinful. But they are in fact evil if they are not the Father's will.

Delight in God. Psalm 40:8 tells us that Jesus delighted in doing the will of the Father. "I desire to do Your will, O my God." To become like Jesus is to come to the place where we delight in doing the will of God, however sacrificial or unpleasant that will seem to us at the time, simply because it is *His* will.

Please God. Everything Jesus did was to please the Father. "For I always do what pleases Him" (John 8:29). How often do we think, speak, or act to please the Father? We may do or say the right thing outwardly, but what is our motive? Is it to feel good about ourselves, look good to others, or please the Father?

Father God, help us grow in the likeness
of Your Son. In Jesus's name, amen!

_____

_____

_____

_____

The Character Crisis

John MacArthur

Adapted from *The Quest for Character*

Love does not delight in evil but rejoices with the truth.
—1 CORINTHIANS 13:6

Personal character hardly seems to matter very much nowadays—at least in mass media, entertainment, politics, and pop culture. People today entertain themselves with iniquity, heedlessly applauding those who sin most flagrantly (see Rom. 1:28–32).

We live in a culture where personal character and individual virtue rapidly evaporate on almost every level. We live in a materialistic culture where prestige, prosperity, and popularity are valued more than genuine integrity.

Yet God designed us to be men and women of exemplary character. From cover to cover, the Scripture condemns iniquity and exalts virtue. In 1 Thessalonians 5:21–22, God commands us to "hold fast what is good and abstain from every form of evil."

But where do we go to learn how to do that? Popular culture will not point the way for us. Scripture alone is a reliable lamp for our feet and light for our path (Ps. 119:105). God's Word shows the way in the quest for moral character.

The Bible contains numerous lists of positive character qualities. In 2 Peter 1:5–8, for example, we find a catalog of virtues, and we are urged to add them to our faith. The fruit of the Spirit in Galatians 5, the qualities of authentic love in 1 Corinthians 13, and the Beatitudes in Matthew 5 all mention similar traits that characterize true excellence of character.

Real character is not merely the sum of several disconnected virtues. Instead, it is a reflection of the moral nature of God Himself. For that reason, all virtues are interdependent and closely related. And all of them are the fruit of God's grace.

I challenge you to study seriously the biblical inventory of character traits outlined in those four passages—with an eye to personal and practical application.

May you perceive the true beauty of Christ's character in these Scriptures and desire to see it reproduced in your own life.

Father God, may the beauty of Christ's character
be seen in us. In Jesus's name, amen!

Everything You Need

David Jeremiah
Adapted from *Everything You Need*

[God] has given us everything we need for life and godliness.
—2 PETER 1:3, BSB

According to Peter, God has given us everything we need to grow spiritually.

God has given us His power, His promises, and His purposes to be spiritually mature and responsible followers of Jesus Christ.

God's power. Peter began his letter by telling us about God's power to live a godly, Christlike life on earth: "His divine power..." (v. 3).

Have you ever had the frustrating experience of charging your phone only to realize hours later that you didn't plug it into the wall? Similarly, if you're not experiencing the power of God in your life, check your connections—you might not be plugged into the right energy source.

God's endless energy and omnipotent power radiate from His Word. If you feel overwhelmed with life, immerse yourself in the Scriptures. Spend time with God in prayer. And let His power lift you, sustain you, and strengthen you as He has promised.

God's promises. In verse 4, Peter says that God communicates His power to us through His promises, which sustain our faith. Whatever you need is already stored away in the vault of Scripture, and you can open it with the key of faith.

God has given us His Word. His promises provide an endless supply of grace for us every day. All God's promises are available to enrich you and meet all your needs (see 2 Cor. 1:20).

God's purpose. Why did God provide you with His divine power through His promises? God's purpose for you is to be "partakers of His divine nature" (v. 4). That doesn't mean you're going to be God

Himself. Only God is God, and living a godly life doesn't turn us into little gods.

Rather, it means God's divine power transmitted through His promises can make you more like Him. At the same time, you'll have a more remarkable ability to say no to "the corruption in the world caused by evil desires" (v. 4b). Put simply, God's goal is for you to be more like Jesus and less like the world.

Father God, thank You for giving us the power
to live a godly life. In Jesus's name, amen!

The Eight Character Qualities of a Godly Life

David Jeremiah

Adapted from *Everything You Need*

Add to your faith.

—2 PETER 1:5–7

In today's Scripture, Peter lists eight character qualities we need to develop a godly life.

Diligence. To experience actual character transformation takes intense effort in diligently applying God's Word to every area of our lives. We cannot expect to grow and abound in "the precious faith" (v. 1) without such a zealous endeavor (Heb. 6:11).

Virtue. The biblical quality of virtue always includes moral and sexual purity. Therefore, it pleases God when we stay away from all sexual sins and pursue holiness (1 Thess. 4:3–4).

Knowledge. Peter isn't talking about educational degrees or IQ levels. Instead, he's telling you to enroll in God's classroom and do as Jesus says in Matthew 11:29: "Take My yoke upon you and learn from Me" (see 1 Pet. 2:2; 2 Pet. 3:18).

Self-control. Author and pastor Randy Frazee says, "Self-control is not only about the discipline to stop doing things that destroy us but also about the discipline to do the things that build us up." Self-control is a make-or-break discipline. It's the difference between success and failure in living a godly life (Prov. 16:32).

Perseverance. This is the quality of remaining steadfast in the face of severe trials, obstacles, and suffering. It is striving to finish what we begin, accomplishing difficult things, and demonstrating God's grace in all seasons of life (see Luke 8:15).

Godliness. This means increasingly becoming more like Christ all the time. Study our Lord's walk and His talk from the gospels and repeatedly ask yourself that famous question: "What would Jesus do?" (see 1 Tim. 4:7).

Brotherly kindness. One secret to brotherly kindness is to take care of someone in need. As Paul puts it in Ephesians 4:28, we should work hard and share God's blessings with those who have need. Does anyone in your circle of contacts need a little extra help?

Love. This is the crowning quality that completes Peter's list because it's the most important—it gives meaning to the rest. This self-sacrificing love motivates people to share and do their all for God and others (1 John 4:19).

Father God, grant us the diligence and perseverance to train
ourselves in cultivating godly character. In Jesus's name, amen!

_____

_____

_____

_____

The Blessing

David Jeremiah
Adapted from *Everything You Need*

For if you possess these qualities...they will keep you...
—2 PETER 1:8–11

In these precious verses, Peter reveals seven incredible blessings when you diligently develop the eight qualities he lists in 2 Peter 1:5–7. God has given you everything you need so He can bless you in every imaginable way!

Godly maturity. "For if these things are yours and abound." (v. 8). "These things" refers to all the eight traits that can abound in you. Let these qualities abound in you, and in that process, maturity happens.

Growing productivity. "They will keep you from being...unproductive" (v. 8b). The key to productivity in Christian ministry is the diligent development of godly character in your life. As God works *in you*, developing you into a mature believer, He'll then also work *through you* so you can be a blessing to others.

Greater clarity. "For he who lacks these things is shortsighted" (v. 9). When you diligently seek to grow in Christlike character, you'll never forget how Christ has forgiven you of past sins. Instead, you'll learn to be thankful to Him every day.

Genuine stability. "Make your calling and election sure" (v. 10). Peter was not saying you can work your way to heaven. Rather, he was concerned about genuine believers not exhibiting their salvation in their growth in godliness and stability. They will experience the serenity of heart, mind, and soul.

Guaranteed security. "You will never stumble" (v. 10b). Peter doesn't mean you will never make a mistake or commit a sin. He meant instead that you never have to worry about your eternal salvation. As you grow in the eight qualities Peter described, you won't stumble into doubting your salvation.

Glorious eternity. "And you will receive a rich welcome into the eternal kingdom of our Lord and Savior Jesus Christ" (v. 11). Peter isn't suggesting we get into the Lord's kingdom by building character in our lives.

We can't work our way into heaven on our own merits or efforts. Instead, he's saying that if we diligently add these qualities to our Christian lives, we will get to heaven triumphantly.

God has indeed given you everything you need.

Father God, thank You for giving us everything we need
to grow and glorify You. In Jesus's name, amen!

The Character of Love

Dean De Castro

And over all these virtues put on love, which
binds them all together in perfect unity.
—COLOSSIANS 3:14

Starting today, we will look at the fruit of the Spirit listed in Galatians 5:22–23a.

These nine godly traits result from the Holy Spirit working in the lives of committed believers who actively pursue Christlikeness.

The fruit of the Holy Spirit. Notice that Paul didn't say the "fruits" of the Holy Spirit but the "fruit" of the Spirit. Love is not simply the first fruit mentioned—it is the fruit itself. All the others are merely expressions of love. Ultimately, love is the basis for all other positive character traits.

Paul says in Colossians 3:14 that love binds together all the virtues of Christian character. As Jerry Bridges explains, "Love is not so much a character trait as the inner disposition of the soul that produces them all."

A life of love. God has granted us His eternal life, and that life, as shown by Jesus, is a life of loving service and limitless sacrifice. The resurrected Christ comes into our hearts through the indwelling Holy Spirit so that He might pass through us and bless others.

Loving well is the goal of the Christian. The core of our maturity as Christians is visible in how we relate. We become more like Christ "because in this world we are like Him" (1 John 4:17). We can love just as Jesus loved.

The most unselfish man. Jesus was the most unselfish man who ever walked the earth. In John 13, just hours before His death, our Lord demonstrated His love to all His disciples (including Judas) in a selfless act of service: He washed all the twenty-four dirty feet of His disciples.

Jesus knows that these men will betray and forsake Him. He knows that they will bury their heads in shame and look at their feet in disgust. And when they do, He wants them to remember how He loved them to the end by washing their feet.

The same love they received from Him for three years endured to the end. It never faltered. It never failed.

Father God, let us not allow a lack of love for someone to reside in our hearts unchecked and unchallenged. In Jesus's name, amen!

_____

_____

_____

_____

The Character of Joy

Dean De Castro

Always be joyful...for this is God's will for
you who belong to Christ Jesus.
—1 THESSALONIANS 5:16A–18B, NLT

The Bible teaches that only those who believe in Jesus, although they have not seen Him, are filled with an inexpressible and glorious joy (1 Pet. 1:8).

It's one thing to have the joy of the Lord; it's another thing to keep the command "Be joyful always." It's easy to be happy when everything is going our way. But what about when everything around us is falling apart? In these instances, we can only cultivate the character of joy and stay optimistic through the power of the Holy Spirit (Rom. 14:17 ;15:13).

Why be joyful at all times? Our joy glorifies God. We are like Christ when we are joyful Christians. Jesus was joyful and brought joy to the people of first-century Palestine.

People liked Him and invited Him to their weddings. He performed His first miracle, turning water into wine, at a wedding party. He went to so many parties that His enemies criticized Him for hanging out with people of ill repute. But Jesus was happy and wanted us to be the same.

To be joyless is to dishonor God. As John W. Sanderson says, "It is practical atheism, for it ignores God and His attributes." To be *joyless* is to deny God's love and control over our lives. On the other hand, to be *joyful* is glorifying God by demonstrating to the unbelieving world that our loving and faithful Heavenly Father cares for us and provides us with all we need.

How to be joyful at all times? One way to develop inner joy is serving others. Joy comes as we focus less on ourselves and concentrate more on helping others. Rick Warren writes, "The happiest people are usually too busy serving and helping others to ask themselves, 'Am I happy?'"

The level of our joy matters to God. He wants us to glorify Him by our joy and serve people to gain happiness. Are you willing to give some thought to the importance God places on the fruit of joy in your life?

> *Father God, many of us are not more joyful by nature*
> *than others. Please help us to cultivate the character*
> *of joy nevertheless. In Jesus's name, amen!*

_____

_____

_____

_____

The Character of Peace
Dean De Castro

The fruit of the Spirit is...peace.
—GALATIANS 5:22

Paul listed peace as the third character quality of the fruit of the Spirit because he was concerned with the lack of peace and unity among the believers in Galatia.

He warned them against "biting and devouring each other" (Gal. 5:15). Their lack of love for one another contradicted their high standing as the children of God. Instead of being peacemakers (Matt. 5:9), they become troublemakers.

Peace should be a hallmark of the godly person because it is a Godlike trait: God is called the "God of peace" several times in the New Testament: "May God Himself, the God of peace, sanctify you through and through" (1 Thess. 5:23a); "And the God of peace will be with you" (Phil. 4:9b).

Peace is also a Christlike trait that Christians need to develop. Christ came to this world to bring peace to men (Luke 2:14). Herod and Pilate, who used to be enemies, became friends because of Jesus (Luke 23:12). Also, a follower once asked Jesus to be an mediator between him and his brother to divide their parents' inheritance (Luke 12:13). And our Lord constantly intervened to resolve the ongoing disputes among His disciples (Luke 22:24). Let us be like Him in sowing peace throughout our lives. Our Lord was a peacemaker. And He wants us to be the same.

Lord, make me an instrument of Your peace
Where there is hatred, Let me sow love;
Where there is injury, Let me sow pardon;
Where there is doubt, Let me sow faith;

Where there is despair, Let me sow hope;
Where there is darkness, Let me sow light;
Where there is sadness, Let me sow joy.
Lord, grant me that I may seek
Rather to comfort than to be comforted;
To understand than to be understood;
To love than to be loved.
For it is by giving that one receives;
By forgiving that one is forgiven;
And by dying that one awakens to eternal life.

—Francis of Assisi (1181–1226)

*Father God, help us be peacemakers like our Lord
so that the unbelieving world recognizes that we
genuinely are Your children. In Jesus's name, amen!*

The Character of Patience

Dean De Castro

Be patient with each other, making allowance
for each other's faults because of your love.
—EPHESIANS 4:2, NLT

Are you a patient person?

Perhaps you're like the person who prayed, "Lord, give me patience, and I want it right now!" Be careful about asking God for patience—you might get it. And then God will allow people or circumstances to test your patience to answer your prayer.

God wants us to cultivate the character of patience. Patience reveals the nature of Christ in us.

It is evidence of our love for people. Love makes you patient when people do things that irritate you and provoke anger.

John Sanderson observes, "Hardly a day passes but one hears sneering remarks about the stupidity, the awkwardness, the ineptitude of others."

Parents lose their patience when their children do things that embarrass them. Wives lose their patience when their husbands are inept at fixing the broken washer. Every day, we are tempted to become impatient with our friends, neighbors, and loved ones.

The key to patience under provocation is to remember that our faults and failures before God are so much more serious and dire than the petty actions of others that tend to irritate us. Therefore, God calls us to bear the weaknesses of others graciously (Eph. 4:2).

It is evidence of our faith in God. One aspect of patience involves enduring abuse. The biblical response to suffering at the hands of others is characterized as "long-suffering" in the King James Version. The virtue of patience gives us the ability to suffer a long time under the mistreatment of others without growing resentful or bitter.

How can we exercise patience under the ill treatment of others? Peter tells us to follow the example of Christ: "When they hurled their insults at Him, He did not retaliate; when He suffered, He made no threats. Instead, He entrusted Himself to Him [God] who judges justly" (1 Pet. 2:23).

The patient Christian who suffers is confident that God will render justice. So, instead of waiting for an opportunity for revenge, he prays for God's forgiveness of his tormentors, just as Jesus and Stephen prayed for their executioners.

Father God, let us learn from our Lord's perseverance
(2 Thess. 3:5). In Jesus's name, amen!

The Character of Kindness

Dean De Castro

*Be kind and compassionate to one another, forgiving
each other, just as in Christ God forgave you.*
—EPHESIANS 4:32

In this passage, Paul explains that kindness means being compassionate toward people's backgrounds and quickly forgiving their offenses.

Remember: Hurt people hurt people. We need to understand that not everyone has the skill to initiate, build, and sustain good relationships. Many people grew up in dysfunctional families and never had positive relationships.

Being sympathetic about people's families of origin can help us be compassionate to them and then forgive them just as God in Christ forgave us.

In *How Happiness Happens*, Max Lucado suggests a few practical steps we can take to forgive:

Decide what you need to forgive. Get specific. Narrow it down and identify the particular offense. "He was a jerk" does not work. "He promised to leave his work at work and be more attentive at home" is better.

Ask yourself why it hurts. Do you feel betrayed? Ignored? Isolated? Do your best to find the answer before taking it out on the offender.

Take it to Jesus. Let this wound be an opportunity to draw near to your Savior. Talk to Jesus about the offense until the anger subsides. And if it returns, talk to Jesus again.

Tell your offender. Do this when it feels safe. Then with a clear head and pure motives, file a complaint. Be specific. Not overly dramatic. Explain the offense and the way it made you feel. If done respectfully and honestly, this is a step toward forgiveness. By bringing it up, you give forgiveness a chance to have its way and win the day. However, there is no guarantee.

Pray for your offender. You cannot force reconciliation, but you can offer intercession. As Jesus commands us, "Pray for those who persecute you" (Matt. 5:44). Here is one final idea:

Conduct a funeral. Bury the offense. Place it in a casket (a shoebox will suffice), and bury it in the cemetery known as "Moving on with Life." When the anger surfaces again, tell yourself, "It's time to walk boldly into a bright future."

Father God, forgive our debts just as we forgive
our debtors. In Jesus's name, amen!

_____

_____

_____

_____

The Character of Goodness

Dean De Castro

The fruit of the Spirit is...goodness.
—GALATIANS 5:22

We must develop the character of goodness if we want to be more like Christ.

Goodness characterized the life and personality of our Lord: "Jesus of Nazareth, who went about doing good" (Acts 10:38). Goodness is love in action—words and deeds.

Good words. As Proverbs 18:21a reminds us, "The tongue has the power of life and death." We have to be watchful of what we say to people. We can use our words to either build people up or put them down; our words can encourage or discourage others.

When people verbally abuse us, our natural response is to strike back. Pride prompts us to return hurt for hurt and insult for insult. However, our Lord instructs us: "Love your enemies, bless them that curse you" (Luke 6:28a).

The Greek word for "bless" is where we got the word "eulogize." It means "to speak well of." When we bless our enemy, we speak well of the person to them and others.

Jesus set an example for us to follow. He was reviled, mocked, and ridiculed by His persecutors. And yet, He returned blessing for cursing and committed Himself into His heavenly Father's care (1 Pet. 2:21). So likewise, if we bless those who hurt us, God will take full responsibility for whatever punishment should be administered to our offenders. Our commitment is to overcome evil with good, and speaking words of blessing is one way to do that.

Good deeds. 1 Timothy 5:8 teaches that good deeds should begin at home: "If anyone does not provide for his relatives, and especially for his immediate family, he has denied the faith and is worse than an unbeliever."

Somehow, it seems more spiritual to babysit some other person's children for free than to help mom with the dishes after Sunday dinner. On the other hand, for a Christian husband who hates to take out the garbage, the distasteful duties of the home should provide him with the opportunity of doing good deeds and developing the character of goodness.

If we are out doing good deeds for others while neglecting our family's needs, we are not practicing the grace of goodness.

Father God, help us be sensitive to meet the needs
of those around us. In Jesus's name, amen!

_____

_____

_____

_____

The Character of Faithfulness

Dean De Castro

The fruit of the Spirit is…faithfulness.
—GALATIANS 5:22

In our effort to become Christlike, we need to cultivate the character of faithfulness. God is faithful, and He wants us to be the same.

The faithfulness of God. There are more than sixty references in the Bible to the faithfulness of God. Consider the absolute necessity of God's faithfulness in our life:

- God is faithful to keep all His promises (Ps. 145:13b).
- God is faithful to limit the intensity of our temptation and make a way of escape (1 Cor. 10:13).
- God is faithful to forgive our sins when we confess them to Him (1 John 1:9).
- God is faithful to establish us and keep us from evil (2 Thess. 3:3).
- God is faithful to remain with us in suffering (1 Pet. 4:19).
- God is faithful every day to demonstrate His mercy to us (Lam. 3:22–23).
- God is faithful to reward our work and love for Him (Heb. 6:10).
- God is faithful to keep us until He takes us home to heaven (1 Thess. 5:23–24).

The faithfulness of man. The faithful person is sincere, trustworthy, and loyal. However, faithfulness is not a natural virtue. Many people will profess faithfulness, but few will actually demonstrate it in their lives (Prov. 20:6).

The main reason faithfulness is such a rare virtue in this modern world is that it hurts. But Psalm 15:4b says that a godly person "keeps his oath even when it hurts." Consider the following questions and what your answers say about your own faithfulness:

- Do you pretend to be something you are not?
- As a taxpayer, do you fail to report all of your income?
- As a car dealer, how much do you tell a prospective buyer about a used car?
- Do you tell a lie because it is expedient?
- Do you exaggerate?
- Do you manipulate the facts of a story just a bit to impress people?

Summarizing much of what God wants us to know about faithfulness, Rick Warren writes, "Whether it's keeping your promises, honoring your marriage, being committed to your church, doing your best at work, or being loyal to your friends, God will honor your faithfulness. Why? Because He wants us to become more and more like Christ, who was faithful unto death."

Father God, may we be faithful when it costs us our comfort or even our life (Rev. 2:10). In Jesus's name, amen!

_____

_____

_____

_____

The Character of Gentleness

Dean De Castro

The fruit of the Spirit is...gentleness.
—GALATIANS 5:22–23

A Christian is to be gentle because God is gentle (Isa. 40:11) and our Lord calls Himself "gentle and humble in heart" (Matt. 11:28–29).

Billy Graham defines gentleness as "mildness in dealing with others...it displays a sensitive regard for others and is careful never to be unfeeling for the rights of others." In other words, gentleness is respectful and considerate of other people's dignity and opinions.

Gentle people are respectful. Gentle people treat others with respect even when they don't share their values.

Our Lord's encounter with the Samaritan woman beautifully illustrates His gentleness. Firmly yet gently, Jesus continued to probe her need until she recognized it herself and turned to Him to meet it. He didn't confront the woman for having multiple husbands until she was ready to disclose it.

As 1 Peter 3:15 says, "Always be prepared to give an answer to everyone who asks you to give the reason for the hope that you have. But to do this with gentleness and respect."

When we witness to people, we must respect and accept them. That doesn't mean we must approve of their sinful lifestyle. There's a difference between acceptance and approval. I can take you as a person of worth without agreeing with everything you do. And I must respect your right to be treated respectfully.

Gentle people are considerate. Gentle people are always considerate of other people's rights to their opinions. When people disagree with them, they disagree agreeably. Paul told Timothy, "The Lord's servant must not quarrel...Those who oppose him he must gently instruct" (2 Tim. 2:24–25).

This verse applies to every Christian. The gentle Christian will not feel threatened by opposition or resent those who oppose him. Instead, they are careful with their words and considerate of other people's opinions.

How do others see us? Are we dogmatic and opinionated? Do we appear rigid, unyielding, and inflexible, or do we come across as genial, reasonable, and considerate in our relationships with other people? Do we seek to intimidate or dominate others by the sheer force of our personality?

Father God, help us be respectful and considerate to
the people around us. In Jesus's name, amen!

The Character of Self-Control

Dean De Castro

Like a city whose walls are broken through
is a person who lacks self-control.
—PROVERBS 25:28

In ancient times, the walls of a city were its central defense; without them, the city would be easy prey to its enemies. Likewise, self-control is the believer's wall of protection against the sinful desires that wage war against their soul (1 Pet. 2:11).

Lack of self-control turns anger to murder, social drinking to alcoholism, and unhappiness to chronic depression and suicide.

As we conclude our reflections on the fruit of the Spirit listed in Galatians 5:22–23, notice again Paul's use of the singular—*fruit* rather than *fruits*. The fruit are interconnected. It's enlightening to see the vital connection between this last one and the other eight. The first eight virtues are each connected to the fruit of self-control:

Love. Without self-control, love may become too sentimental and lack boundaries.

Joy. Without self-control, joy may become flippant and revelry.

Peace. Without self-control, the pursuit of peace may lead to a peace-at-any-price attitude.

Patience. Without self-control, patience may become lenient.

Kindness. Without self-control, kindness may become bland.

Goodness. Without self-control, goodness may become self-righteousness.

Faithfulness. Without self-control, faithfulness may become slavishness.

Gentleness. Without self-control, gentleness may become a weakness.

The first appearance of "self-control" in the New Testament is in Acts 24, where Paul reasons with Felix "on righteousness, self-control, and the judgment to come" (v. 25).

According to the Roman historian Tacitus, Felix "reveled in cruelty and lust, and wielded the power of a king with the mind of a slave." Felix began his eight-year tenure as Roman procurator of Judea by seducing and marrying Drusilla, the wife of the king of a small Syrian state.

Paul's discourse on the need for self-mastery met with a response all too common today: Felix was convinced of his condition, even to the point of trembling, but he put it off until "I find it convenient" (Acts 24:25). There is no record that Felix's "convenient time" ever came. Ours won't either. It's never convenient to be self-disciplined—only crucial.

Father God, help us discipline ourselves not for the sake of discipline but godliness (1 Tim. 4:7a). In Jesus's Name, amen!

Jesus Embodies the Fruit of the Spirit
Dean De Castro

Whoever claims to live in Him must live as Jesus did.
—1 JOHN 2:6

If we claim to be disciples of Jesus Christ, we must discipline ourselves to develop His character and personality in order to live as He lived.

Paul lists some of the character qualities of Christ in Galatians 5:22–23; they are known as the fruit of the Spirit. It begins with love and ends with self-control.

Have you ever noticed how Christ perfectly exemplifies all the godly qualities in Galatians 5?

Love. "No one has greater love than the One who lays down His life for His friends" (John 15:13).

Joy. "Looking unto Jesus the author and finisher of our faith; who for the joy that was set before Him endured the cross" (Heb. 12:2, KJV).

Peace. Jesus is called "Prince of Peace" in Isaiah 9:6.

Patience. "I was shown mercy so that in me, the worst of sinners, Christ Jesus might display His unlimited patience as an example for those who would believe in Him" (1 Tim. 1:16).

Kindness. Through the "love and kindness of God our Savior," He saved us (Titus 3:4).

Goodness. Jesus "went around doing good and healing all" (Acts 10:38).

Faithfulness. "The Lord is faithful, who shall establish you and keep you from evil" (2 Thess. 3:3, KJV).

Gentleness. Paul appealed to the Corinthians in the "gentleness of Christ" (2 Cor. 10:1).

Self-control. Jesus set Himself apart so that His disciples may grow in practical holiness by keeping His words (John 17:17, 19).

Jesus Christ was the perfect man who perfectly displayed the image of God on earth (Heb. 1:3). His life on earth embodied all the ninefold fruit of the Spirit. And God's ultimate goal is for us to discipline ourselves to become more like His Son.

It has been said that Christian living is not difficult—it's just humanly impossible. That's why Paul called the character traits in Galatians 5 the fruit of the Holy Spirit. As we learn to walk in the Spirit, He will empower us to obey God's will and manifest the godly qualities of our Lord Jesus Christ.

Father God, may the moral attributes of Jesus be seen in us
more and more to glorify Your Name. In Jesus's name, amen!

_____

_____

_____

_____

Nine Tests for Spiritual Fruit

Scott Hubbard
Adapted from desiringGod.org

The fruit of the Spirit is…
—GALATIANS 5:22–23

In this passage, Paul lists nine character traits that manifest the Holy Spirit's presence in our lives.

Love. Do you labor for the good of your brothers and sisters? Every day, we gladly consider ourselves servants (Gal. 5:13) and ask not, "Who will meet my needs today?" but instead, "Whose needs can I meet today?"

Joy. Do you delight in the Christlikeness of God's people? When we walk by the Spirit, we rejoice when we see the timid speak the gospel boldly and fathers lead their families in fear of the Lord.

Peace. Do you strive to maintain the unity of the Spirit even at a high personal cost? We ask for forgiveness first, even when most of the fault lies with others. And when we engage in conflict, we "aim for restoration" so that we might "live in peace" (2 Cor. 13:11).

Patience. Are you growing in your ability to overlook offenses? Patient people are like God: "slow to anger" (Exod. 34:6) even when confronted with severe and repeated provocation (Rom. 2:4; 1 Tim. 1:16).

Kindness. Do you overlook offenses and repay them with love? Kind people can give a blessing, receive a curse in return, and still bless people (see Rom. 12:19–21).

Goodness. Do you dream up opportunities to be helpful? Those who walk by the Spirit carry a general disposition to be useful, generous, and helpful.

Faithfulness. Do you do what you say you'll do, even in minor matters? Spirit-filled Christians make every effort to do what they say they'll do, even when it hurts (Ps. 15:4b).

Gentleness. Do you use your strength to serve the weak? In the face of personal offense, the gentle person is more concerned with the offender's soul than their self-importance, so they channel their strength in the service of gentle restoration.

Self-control. Do you refuse your flesh's cravings? Self-control hurts. It requires us to say a merciless "No!" to any desire that draws us away from the spirit into the flesh (Titus 2:11–12).

Father God, help us cultivate the nine graces of the
Spirit's fruit daily. In Jesus's name, amen!

_____

_____

_____

_____

A Christian's Character: The Beatitudes

Dean De Castro

Blessed are...
—MATTHEW 5:3–12

In Matthew 5:3–12, Jesus set forth eight qualities of His genuine disciples.

The poor in spirit (v. 3). This phrase means we should acknowledge our spiritual bankruptcy before God and trust in God's unmerited favor to enter His kingdom. It is also essential for enjoying God's blessings in His kingdom (Matt. 6:33).

Those who mourn (v. 4). This refers to godly sorrow, which leads to repentance (2 Cor. 7:10). David cried out to God and humbly confessed his sins. God comforted him by forgiving his sins and restoring the joy of salvation (Ps. 51:12).

The meek (v. 5). The meek are even-tempered, showing displeasure without reacting impulsively (Num. 12:3). As a result, they will inherit the land (Ps. 37:9) and see the goodness of the Lord in the land of the living (Ps. 27:13).

Those who hunger and thirst after righteousness (v. 6). Only God can satisfy the deep longings of man for knowing God. Those who maintain an intimate relationship with God will be satisfied with His goodness (Jer. 31:14).

The merciful (v. 7). God forgives only those who forgive others. Therefore, a person receives mercy only if they are merciful (Matt. 6:12; James 2:13).

The pure in heart (v. 8). Presently, on this earth, the pure in heart shall see God in their lives by seeking to keep their hearts pure. But eternally, the pure in heart shall see God face to face. They shall "see Him as He is" and behold "His face in righteousness" (1 John 3:2).

The peacemakers (v. 9). The peacemakers strive at every opportunity to make peace between others. They work to resolve disputes, reconcile differences, eliminate strife, and build relationships. Believers are peacemakers because they have made peace with God (Rom. 5:1) and know the God of peace (Phil. 4:9).

The persecuted (vv. 10–12). Believers are persecuted because we live and demonstrate a life of righteousness, which Jesus defined in the preceding verses (vv. 7–9). Living in this way exposes the sins of unbelievers, which causes them to hate us (John 15:18).

Suffering produces in us the hope of glory in the future heavenly kingdom, where God will reward us accordingly (Rom. 8:18).

*Father God, help us live on earth as citizens
of heaven. In Jesus's name, amen!*

The Supreme Virtue of Love

Dean De Castro

Love is...
—1 CORINTHIANS 13:4–7

The thirteenth chapter of 1 Corinthians is regarded by many as the most excellent exposition on love ever written. Paul spells out sixteen things about love—eight things that it does and eight things it does not.

Love is patient and kind. Some people are naturally patient in temperament, but they are not kind in their words and deeds. Instead, they might be passive and lazy. The Bible combines both patience and kindness in describing a mature believer.

Love is not envious, boastful, and proud. Pride causes people to boast about what they have and do. Arrogant people are also jealous of other people's possessions and accomplishments. Pride and envy are also mentioned together in Galatians 5:26.

Love is not rude. It is not self-seeking. Selfishness is the root; rudeness is the fruit. People are rude because they only think about their own opinions and comfort. A loving person will not do or say anything that will embarrass another person, either publicly or privately.

Love is not easily angered. It keeps no record of wrong. Another way of putting it is that love is not overly sensitive. Love forgives. In other words, touchy people may harbor unforgiveness and resentment in their hearts. They cannot let go of their past hurts (Eph. 4:32b).

Love does not delight in evil but rejoices with the truth. True love corrects. Without correction, love becomes sentimental. Genuine love confronts when people are acting contrary to God's will. The Apostle Paul sternly rebuked Peter in Antioch because his behavior contradicted the gospel of grace. Mature people, like the apostle John, rejoice when believers walk in God's truths (2 John 4).

Love always protects, always trusts, always hopes, always perseveres. Love protects and covers people's reputations. Trust is important in any relationship. When somebody breaks trust, the connection goes sour and eventually dies. However, godly love does not give up hope on anyone. On the contrary, it perseveres under challenging circumstances because it ain't over yet until it's over.

Love never fails because it is the character of God. God is love. And we are most like God when we walk in love.

Father God, let love be the greatest virtue
in our lives. In Jesus's name, amen!

_____

_____

_____

_____

God's Part in Changing Me

Rick Warren

Adapted from *The Power to Change Your Life*

Work out your salvation...for it is God who
works in you to will and to act.
—PHILIPPIANS 2:12B–13

The Apostle Paul describes the two-part process God uses in the above passage, where he first says, "Work out your salvation," and then turns around and says, "It is God who works in you."

God has a part in our spiritual growth, and we also have a role. So let's look first at God's position in this process and the tools He uses.

God uses His Spirit. When we commit ourselves to Christ, the Holy Spirit comes into our lives to empower and direct us (Rom. 8:9–11). The Spirit of God gives us new strength and vitality and the desire and the power to do what is right.

When the Holy Spirit controls your life, He will produce in you nine positive characteristics called the fruit of the Spirit (Gal. 5:22–23).

God uses His Word. Through the Scriptures, God teaches us how to live (2 Tim. 3:16–17). A converted cannibal in the South Sea islands sat by a large pot reading his Bible when an anthropologist approached him and asked, "What are you doing?" The native replied, "I am reading the Bible."

The anthropologist scoffed and said, "Don't you know that modern, civilized man has rejected that book? It's nothing but a pack of lies. You shouldn't waste your time reading it."

The cannibal looked him over from head to toe and slowly replied, "Sir, if it weren't for this book, you'd be in that pot!" The word of God had changed his life and his appetites.

God uses circumstances. Sometimes it takes a painful experience to make us change our ways. Proverbs 20:30 says, "Blows and wounds cleanse away evil, and beatings purge the inmost being."

C. S. Lewis says that God whispers to us in our pleasure but shouts to us in our pain. God can use our sins, the devil, and problems caused by other people to make us like Jesus Christ. He can use every situation in our lives for our growth.

Father God, help us know Your part in the process of growing into the image of Your Son. In Jesus's name, amen!

_____

_____

_____

_____

My Part in Changing Me

Rick Warren

Adapted from *The Power to Change Your Life*

Be transformed by the renewing of your mind.
—ROMANS 12:2A

Yesterday, we saw God's part in changing us. Now, what about our part? We must make three choices if we want to change.

We must depend on the Holy Spirit. In John 15, Jesus compares our spiritual life to a vine and its branches. "For without Me you can do nothing" (John 15:5, NKJV).

In this illustration, the branch is dependent on the main vine; it cannot produce fruit by itself. Therefore, Christians cannot make changes in their lives on their own. It's the work of the Holy Spirit.

How do we know if we are abiding in Christ? First, look at your prayer life. Your prayers demonstrate your dependence on God. The secret of depending on God's Spirit is being incessantly in prayer. Pray about everything. As we pray, we will start to see the fruit developing in our lives.

We must choose our thoughts. Proverbs 4:23 says, "Be careful how you think; your thoughts shape your life" (GNT). Change always begins with new thinking. We are transformed by the renewing of our minds (Rom. 12:2).

The Bible teaches that how you think determines how you feel and how you feel affects how you act. According to Jesus, "You will know the truth, and the truth will set you free" (John 8:32). That is, you will be set free when you live with the right thoughts based on God's Word. You will find your old habits and feelings and actions falling away.

We must respond wisely to circumstances. We cannot control all the circumstances in our lives, but we can control how we respond. For example, Joseph was betrayed by his brothers and sold into slavery. But years later, he said, "You intended to harm me, but God intended it for good" (Gen. 50:20).

Victor Frankl writes, "The last of human freedoms is the ability to choose one's attitude in a given set of circumstances." So, choose to respond to unpleasant situations as Jesus would. What matters in life is not what happens *to* us but what happens *in* us.

Father God, help us cooperate with You in the life-changing process of becoming like Christ. In Jesus's name, amen!

_____

_____

_____

_____

The Spirit of Transformation

Dean De Castro

...being transformed into His image...
from the Lord, who is the Spirit.
—2 CORINTHIANS 3:18

One of the significant works of the Holy Spirit is transforming us into the likeness of Christ from glory to glory (2 Cor. 3:18).

In his commentary on the book of Romans, John Stott writes, "The Christian life is essentially life in the Spirit which is animated, sustained, directed, and enriched by the Holy Spirit. Without the Holy Spirit, genuine Christian discipleship would be inconceivable, indeed impossible."

Listen to the resident boss. In his classic book *The Normal Christian Life*, Watchman Nee tells the story of a young couple, two converts who were ignorant about Bible. During the cold winter months in Northern China, the man drank wine (sometimes excessively) with his meals.

So, one day, when the husband went to say grace before the meal, he found he could not pray. He asked his wife to open the Bible and see what it says about drinking wine. Being ignorant of the Word, she turned the pages in vain. Finally, the man pushed away from the wine, and together they asked for a blessing on their meal.

Eventually, the man was able to visit brother Nee in Shanghai and told him the story. Then, using a familiar expression in Chinese that best applied in this scenario, he said, "Brother Nee, Resident Boss wouldn't let me have that drink!"

"Very well, brother," Nee said, "You always try to listen to Resident Boss."

Depend on the Holy Spirit. Not regularly asking the Holy Spirit for assistance is the underlying cause of most of our failures in the

Christian life. Freedom to become like Christ is not accomplished by willpower but by the power of the Holy Spirit.

As we discipline ourselves to listen to the still, small voice of the Holy Spirit in our hearts, follow His promptings, and surrender to His control, God will work in us to will and act according to His good purposes (Phil. 2:13).

When we do our part, God will do His part: He will release the power to change and overcome all the sinful patterns in our lives.

Father God, help us obey the still, small voice
of the Holy Spirit. In Jesus's name, amen!

_____

_____

_____

_____

The Discipline of Adversity

Jerry Bridges
Adapted from *The Discipline of Grace*

God disciplines us for our good.
—HEBREWS 12:10

Our heavenly Father uses the pain of adversity to discipline us for our good.

Every form of hardship is painful and intended to make us more Christlike. Therefore, we must accept and submit to God's disciplines even though they might make no sense to us.

The pain of adversity. "No discipline seems pleasant at the time, but painful" (v. 11). All forms of afflictions are painful. We should admit the pain.

I knew a person who suffered some adversities and would put on a forced smile and say, "But we are victorious." She thought believers should not admit pain. But the writer of Hebrews was honest. He says that the discipline of hardship is painful.

The purpose of adversity. God disciplines us so that we may share in His holiness (v. 10). There is no such thing as pain without purpose in the believer's life. All pain we experience moves us closer to the goal of being holy as He is holy.

Our primary response to God's discipline should be humble submission and trust. We should *submit* to God's providential dealings with us, knowing that there is still much in our character that needs improving.

We should *trust* Him, believing that He is infinite in His wisdom and knows precisely the kind and extent of adversity we need to accomplish His purpose.

The perplexity of adversity. Although all pain has a purpose in God's mind, that purpose is often hidden from us. As a result, God's ways will usually remain a mystery (Rom. 11:33).

It is unwise to ask, "Why did this happen to me?" as if we do not deserve such bad treatment from God. We need to realize that it is far better than we deserve, whatever our situation is. None of us wants to receive from God what we deserve, for that will only be eternal punishment.

Submit to whatever God may be doing in our lives even though it doesn't make sense to us. And as we do this, we will see the fruit of the Spirit produced in our lives in due time (v. 11b).

> *Father God, let us submit and trust all Your*
> *workings in our life. In Jesus's name, amen!*

_____

_____

_____

_____

Sow Habit, Reap Character

Dean De Castro

...to impurity and to ever-increasing wickedness...
to righteousness leading to holiness.
—ROMANS 6:19

Today's Scripture reveals some key truths about the development of moral habits in one direction or the other. The more we sin, the more we are inclined to sin—"impurity to ever-increasing wickedness."

On the other hand, as we sow righteous actions, we develop holy habits that eventually lead to Christlike character—"righteousness leading to holiness."

The power of habit. The following piece vividly illustrates the powerful hold of habits in our lives.

I am your constant companion, greatest helper, or heaviest burden. I will push you onward or drag you down to failure. I am entirely at your command. Half the things you do, you might as well turn over to me. And I will be able to do them quickly and correctly.

You must be firm with me. Show me exactly how you want something done. And after a few lessons, I will do it automatically. I am the servant of all great men and all of the failures as well. Those who are great, I have made great. Those who are failures, I have made failures.

I am not a machine, though I work with all the precision of a machine. Plus, the intelligence of a man. You may run me for profit or run me for ruin; it makes no difference to me. Take me, train me, and I will put the world at your feet. Be easy with me, and I will destroy you.

Who am I? I am HABIT!

The power of choices. Choices have consequences. As Romans 6:19 teaches us, we train ourselves in the wrong direction when choosing to sin instead of obeying God's Word. We reinforce the sinful habits we have already developed and allow them to gain greater strength in our souls.

We break the sinful patterns and develop holy habits by choosing to obey God's will. Therefore, each time we are tempted to indulge in the evil compulsive cravings of our bodies, we cry out to God, as Paul did in Romans 7:24–25b, to enable us make godly choices.

> *Father God, help us obey You in the power of the Holy Spirit, one choice at a time. In Jesus's name, amen!*

_____

_____

_____

_____

Put off Sinful Habits, Put on Christlike Character

Jerry Bridges

Adapted from *Disciplined by Grace*

Put off your old self...put on the new self...
—EPHESIANS 4:22, 24

Paul's ethical teaching is characterized by this twofold approach of putting off the sinful habits of the old self and putting on the Christlike character traits of the new self.

The scissors example. This twofold approach of putting off and putting on is best illustrated by the two blades of a pair of scissors. A single scissor blade is useless for doing its job. The two edges must be joined together at the pivot point and work in conjunction to be effective.

The scissors illustrate a spiritual principle: We must work simultaneously to put off the sinful patterns of our old selves and put on the godly traits of our new selves. One without the other is ineffective.

Some believers seem to focus on putting off sinful practices but overlook what they are to put on. Such people probably become self-righteous since they to equate godliness with a defined list of don'ts.

Other believers focus on certain positive traits, such as love, compassion, and kindness. But if they ignore the negative prohibitions of Scripture, they can become careless in morality and ethics. So, we need the dual focus of putting off and putting on, and each should receive equal attention from us.

The biblical example. In Ephesians 4:25–32, Paul gave a series of practical instructions that clearly illustrate the two paths we are confronted with in trying to cultivate godly character:

- Tell the truth or tell a lie (v. 25).

- Deal with anger or let it smolder (vv. 26–27).
- Be honest in our finances or steal from others (v. 28a).
- Share with others in need or spend our resources on ourselves (v. 28b).
- Say what is helpful to others or speak unwholesome words (criticism, gossip, complaining, etc.) (vv. 29–30).
- Be kind, compassionate, and forgiving or harbor bitterness, anger, and resentment (vv. 31–32).

In other words, the practice of putting off sinful actions and putting on Christlike character involves a constant series of choices. And when we obey God one choice at a time, our righteous actions lead to holy character.

Father God, help us obey both the negative prohibitions and positive instructions of Your Word. In Jesus's name, amen!

_____

_____

_____

_____

Five Elements for Lasting Change

Rick Warren
Adapted from *The Daniel Plan*

For I can do everything through Christ, who gives me strength.
—PHILIPPIANS 4:13, NLT

Change occurs not by chance but by choices. True and lasting change requires five elements.

Lasting change requires building your life on the truth. Jesus promises that the truth will make you free (John 8:31–32). But at first, the truth is likely to make you miserable!

We don't like to face the truth about ourselves, our weaknesses, bad habits, and especially our motivations. But until you face the truth about *why* you do what you do and get to the root of your habits, change is likely to be shallow and short-lived.

Lasting change requires making wise choices. Everyone wants to be healthy, but very few people choose to be healthy. You won't change until you *decide* to change your harmful, unhealthy habits.

God offers you His power to make healthy choices (Phil. 2:13). So, you do what you can do, and God does what only He can do.

Lasting change requires new ways of thinking. If you want to change how you act, you must begin by changing how you think. Your thoughts are the autopilot of your life (Rom. 12:2). The biblical word for changing your mind is "repentance."

To repent is to make a mental U-turn, to focus my thoughts in a completely different direction. This new mindset creates new emotions, which give the motivation to change. You do this by filling your mind with the Bible, God's truth.

Lasting change requires God's Spirit in your life. God's Holy Spirit helps us break free from bad habits, compulsions, and addictions. The more I allow God's Spirit to guide and empower me, the more He grows positive character qualities in my life to replace my bad habits (Gal. 5:22–23).

Lasting change requires an open community. God created us to need each other (Gen. 2:18; Eccl. 4:9–12). He designed us for relationships. If you are serious about making lasting changes in your life, you need the support of others. Other people can assist you by praying for you and giving you feedback.

Father God, we believe change is possible. Help us do our part and believe that You will do Your part. In Jesus's name, amen!

_____

_____

_____

_____

Dependent Discipline

Dean De Castro

I have learned the secret of being content...I can do
all this through Him who gives me strength.
—PHILIPPIANS 4:12B–13

The Bible teaches that we must accept our responsibility to develop Christlike character. But the Word of God also teaches us that we must not carry out our duties with our own strength and willpower. Rather, we must depend upon the Holy Spirit to enable us. "'Not by might nor by power, but by My Spirit,' says the Lord" (Zech. 4:6).

Discipline. The Apostle Paul encouraged Timothy to train himself to be godly (1 Tim. 4:7). Just as athletes had to go through strict discipline to win in their respective sports, Christians need to discipline themselves to be godly.

In the same book, Paul associates godliness with contentment (1 Tim. 6:6), which Paul had to learn the hard way (Phil. 4:12).

Of all the Ten Commandments, the most challenging one for Paul to obey was the command not to covet; he struggled with "every kind of covetous desire" (Rom. 7:7–8). As a result, Paul worked very hard to cultivate the virtue of contentment.

He applied rigorous discipline and worked at it diligently. Finally, however, Paul discovered that learning contentment was not to be done with his strength but through "Him who gives me strength" (Phil. 4:12–13).

Dependence. To Cultivate Christlike Character, we must discipline ourselves to be dependent upon the Holy Spirit. Nehemiah, the wall builder, understood the principle of dependent discipline well, the idea that we are both dependent and responsible.

In rebuilding the wall of Jerusalem, Nehemiah faced significant opposition. Nehemiah 4:8–9 states, "All plotted together to come and fight against Jerusalem and stir up trouble against it. But we prayed to our God and posted a guard day and night to meet this threat." Nehemiah depended on God through prayer and accepted his responsibility to stand guard.

Jerry Bridges encapsulates this message: "We must depend upon the Holy Spirit to enable us. But at the same time, we must not assume that we have no responsibility simply because we are dependent. God enables us to work, but He does not do the work for us."

Father God, help us discipline ourselves unto godliness
through Christ, who strengthens us. In Jesus's name, amen!

_____

_____

_____

_____

The Principle of Grace

Dean De Castro

...the God of all grace...
—1 PETER 5:10A

Grace is the operating principle of Christian living. Knowing, understanding, believing, and accepting God's grace are all essential components to growing as children of God.

Spiritual progress and not sinless perfection is God's will for us. As long as we live in this mortal body, we will always struggle with sin and fail. It is impossible to be sinless, but it is possible to sin less and less.

What is grace? Under the covenant of grace, God blesses us first, and then His blessings, unmerited favor, forgiveness, and overflowing love lead us to repentance and change (Rom. 2:4).

After Jesus blessed Peter with two boatloads of fish, Peter then knelt before Jesus and admitted his sinfulness. This miracle of God's goodness led Peter to follow Jesus and become a fisher of men (see Luke 5:1–11).

Paul credited God's grace for changing his life. "But by the grace of God, I am what I am" (1 Cor. 15:10). Paul worked harder than the other apostles because of the power of God's grace working mightily and effectively in his life.

Peter commands us to grow in the knowledge of God's grace (2 Pet. 3:18). But how much do you know of this significant truth? In 1 Peter 5:10, God is identified as the God of all grace. Here are some of the multifaceted aspects of grace mentioned in the New Testament:

Grace justifies. "And are justified freely by His grace" (Rom. 3:24).

Grace qualifies. "Through whom we have gained access by faith into the grace in which we now stand." (Rom. 5:2a).

Grace sanctifies. "For the grace of God teaches us...to say 'No' to ungodliness" (Titus 2:11–12).

Grace glorifies. "He has made us competent as ministers of a new covenant [grace]...we...are being transformed into His likeness with ever-increasing glory" (2 Cor. 3:6, 18).

Grace fortifies. "It is good for our hearts to be strengthened by grace" (Heb. 13:9).

Grace nullifies. "For sin shall not be your master, because you are not under law but under grace" (Rom. 6:14).

Grace multiplies. "And from His fulness have we all received grace upon grace" (John 1:16, RSV).

Father God, may Your amazing grace change us
to become like Christ. In Jesus's name, amen!

_____

_____

_____

_____

The Double Meaning of Grace

Dean De Castro

*My only aim is to finish the race and complete
the task the Lord Jesus has given me—the task of
testifying to the good news of God's grace.*
—ACTS 20:24

The central message that the Apostle Paul faithfully preached world-wide is the gospel of God's grace. He was martyred because he believed the gospel of God's grace was the only message that could change people's lives.

The Bible teaches about both saving grace and sanctifying grace. They are not opposed to one another. A clear understanding of this two-fold aspect of grace, and how both aspects work together, is essential for the life-long pursuit of Christlikeness.

Saving grace is God's unmerited and undeserved favor. He took what we deserved (punishment) and gave us what we didn't earn (eternal life) by sending His Son into the world to save us from the *guilt* of sin.

Sanctifying grace is God sending His Holy Spirit into our born-again human spirits to save us from the *grip* of sin and to produce the character of Christ in our lives. This same grace that saves us also transforms us to live lives pleasing to God.

Below are some of the Scripture passages that will help you differentiate between God's saving grace and sanctifying grace. Although there are more passages in the Bible that deal with sanctifying grace, both sanctifying and saving grace are necessary for us, and we should try to understand them both.

Saving grace

- We are saved by grace through faith (Eph. 2:8).
- Our righteous standing before God is due to grace (Rom. 5:2).
- Forgiveness of sins is by the riches of God's grace (Eph. 1:7).
- Regarding salvation, we are no longer under the law but under grace (Rom. 6:14).
- We are justified by God's grace (Titus 3:7).

Sanctifying grace

- Grace disciplines us to say no to sin (Titus 2:11–12).
- God called us to holy living because of His purpose and grace (2 Tim. 1:9).
- Our heart is strengthened by grace (Heb. 13:9).
- We get grace in times of difficulty and suffering (Heb. 4:16).
- By the grace of God, we are what we are (1 Cor. 15:10a).
- God's grace is sufficient to compensate for our weaknesses (2 Cor. 12:9).
- Paul's success was due to God's grace (1 Cor. 15:10b).

Father God, let the gospel of Your grace inspire us to change to become like Christ. In Jesus's name, amen!

_____

_____

_____

_____

An Exchanged Life
Dean De Castro

Christ, who is your life...
—COLOSSIANS 3:4

It has been said that Christian living is not difficult—it is simply impossible.

The new life we receive at conversion is not a changed life but an exchanged life. It is the very life of Christ living in us and through us in the person of the Holy Spirit. Jesus is the only person who has lived a perfect life, and He is the only one who can enable us to manifest His faultless moral character today.

Reincarnation or regeneration? A man believed that he was the reincarnation of Napoleon Bonaparte and later the mighty Egyptian pharaoh Ramses.

He used to be a fearful person with low self-esteem. But he later became fearless, self-reliant, and highly successful. Whenever he felt insecure, he would think of how the great Napoleon and Ramses would feel.

Christians reject reincarnation, but we do believe in regeneration. At our conversion, the living Christ becomes our life (Col. 3:4). Christ lives in us through the person of the Holy Spirit. Our human spirit and the Spirit of God become one (1 Cor. 6:17). We may not fully understand our union with Christ, though. That is why in Colossians 1:27, Paul calls it a "mystery."

Program or person? After struggling with overcoming his sins, Paul cried out to God to deliver him from constant failures to obey His will.

In Romans 7:24, notice that Paul didn't say *what* would save him from his mortal body. Instead, he asked, "*Who* will rescue me from this body of death? Thanks be to God, through Jesus Christ our Lord!" (v. 25).

No program or set of principles can bring lasting and sustained change in a person's life. Only a personal and intimate relationship with Jesus Christ can make it happen.

Jesus did not come to show us how to do the right things—He is the Way. Jesus did not come to teach us correct theology—He is the Truth. Jesus did not come to shape us up and give us a better life—He is the Life. The only way we will become more like Christ is to believe by faith that Christ is our life.

Father God, grant us wisdom to understand the gift
of our union with Christ. In Jesus's name, amen!

_____

_____

_____

_____

The Discipline of Giving

Dean De Castro

Sell your possessions and give to the poor.
—MATTHEW 19:21

Both the Old Testament and the New Testament teach the importance of giving.

For every ten verses in the Old Testament, one verse directly or indirectly discusses money. In the New Testament, for every twelve verses, there is one verse about money. In all the parables of Jesus, half of them talk about money or financial stewardship.

When the rich young ruler asked Jesus how he could get eternal life, Jesus responded, "Sell your possessions and give to the poor, and you will have treasure in heaven. Then come, follow me" (Matt. 19:21). Notice two important aspects to this teaching:

First, how we handle material possessions has spiritual significance. "Give...and you will have treasure in heaven."

The principle is timeless—there is a strong connection between a person's actual spiritual condition and his attitude and actions concerning money and possessions. Richard Halverson succinctly captures this idea: "Money is an exact index to a man's true character."

When people asked John the Baptist what they should do to bear the fruit of repentance, first, he told them to share their clothes and food with the poor. Then he instructed the tax collectors not to collect and pocket extra money. And finally, he commanded the soldiers not to extort money and be content with their wages (Luke 3:7–14).

The conclusive proof of genuine repentance and conversion was a new perspective and attitude on handling money and possessions.

Second, giving is a discipleship issue. "Come, follow me." Why did Jesus demand the young ruler give up *everything* and follow Him?

Jesus does not call on all His disciples to liquidate their possessions and follow Him. But He knew that money was the rich young man's idol. He knew that no man could enthrone the true God unless he chose to dethrone his other gods. "No one can serve both God and money" (Luke 16:13).

Jesus gauged the rich young ruler's commitment to eternal life by his unwillingness to part with his money. If Jesus is not the Lord *of all,* He cannot be the Lord *at all.*

> *Father God, take our silver and our gold; not a mite would we withhold. In Jesus's name, amen!*

_____

_____

_____

_____

God Owns It All

Ron Blue

Adapted from *Master Your Money*

"The silver is mine and the gold is mine,"
declares the Lord Almighty.
—HAGGAI 2:8

Very few Christians would argue with the principle that God owns it all, and yet if we follow that principle to its natural conclusion, there are three revolutionary implications.

First, God has the right to do whatever He wants, whenever He wants. It is all His because an owner has *rights*, and I, as a steward, have only *responsibilities.*

Believing this also frees me to give generously of God's resources to God's purposes and His people. All that I have belongs to Him. I possess much but own nothing.

Second, my giving decision is a spiritual decision, but every spending decision is a spiritual decision also. There is nothing more spiritual about giving than buying a car, taking a vacation, buying food, paying off debt, paying taxes, etc. These are all uses of His resources, for He owns all that I have.

Think about the freedom of knowing that if God owns it all—and He does—He must have some thoughts about how He wants me to use His property. The Bible reveals specific guidelines for how the Owner wants His property used. As a steward, I have a great deal of latitude, but I am still responsible to the Owner. Someday I will give an accounting of how I used His property.

Third, the truth that God owns it all means that you can't fake stewardship. Your checkbook reveals all that you believe about stewardship. Likewise, a life story could be written from a checkbook. It reflects your goals, priorities, convictions, relationships, and even the use of your time.

A person who has been a Christian for even a short while can fake prayer, Bible study, evangelism, going to church, and so on, but he can't pretend against what his checkbook reveals. Maybe that is why so many of us are secretive about our finances.

I don't understand it, but I know that somehow my eternal position and reward are determined irrevocably by my faithfulness in handling the property entrusted to me by God.

Father God, help us be faithful with whatever resources are entrusted to us. In Jesus's name, amen!

_____

_____

_____

_____

Money—What Does It Matter?

Joby Soriano

But store up for yourselves treasures in heaven.
—MATTHEW 6:20

What is money? Printed ink on a piece of paper;
People lie, cheat, steal, labor, for what will end up one day as a vapor.
It drives many for what they call, seeking for success;
When in the process, they lose the essence of life because they are so filled with stress.
This currency blinds us to reality, causes deafness insensitivity;
Hearts filled with greed, a loss of integrity, minds without serenity.
We think it's our right to use it as we please;
Forgetting it is God's; We should give thanks on our knees.
I obsessed with money, thinking happiness and joy will follow;
Only to be overcome with emptiness, my life was truly hollow.
It cannot buy time, peace, health, friendship or love;
It betrays us and consumes us, leaving us nothing to be proud of.
Wake up to the riches we truly possess in Christ;
It is the freedom from sin that He paid with His sacrifice.
Being blessed with wealth is not a curse or a sin;
For as long as it's not our master or idol or love within.
The incredible investment that outshines all the things that money can buy,
Is sending it on ahead by depositing it in the lives passing by.
You and I today are not defined by what we have to show and display to others;
Our true identity is engraved in the heart of our God who sees us like no other.
Grab hold of what God has given you today and use it, so no one forgets;
As you end your life, you will look back with a smile and have no regrets.

—Taken from Pastor Joby Soriano's message on *No Regrets with Money* at Christ's Commission Fellowship, April 18, 2021, Philippines

Father God, let us leave this world with no regrets about the money You have entrusted to us. In Jesus's name, amen!

Misconceptions about Money

Larry Kreider

Adapted from *The Tithe: A Test in Trust*

It's money that makes the world go around.
—ECCLESIASTES 10:19, MSG

Christians often fall into one of two camps regarding what they believe is God's perspective regarding a Christian's financial style.

Some may think that all Christians should be poor, and others may take the viewpoint that all Christians should be wealthy.

Those who believe all Christians should be wealthy often believe financial wealth is a clear sign of God's blessing. However, although God wants to prosper us in every way, including financially, financial wealth does not necessarily mean God blesses us.

The Laodicean Christians are a case in point. Scripture tells us they were wealthy, yet they were considered spiritually "wretched" (Rev. 3:17). On the other hand, many wealthy people *are* blessed by God because they use their finances unselfishly. For example, Job was a rich and godly man who did not allow his money to become his God (Job 1).

Likewise, before encountering Jesus, Zacchaeus, a wealthy tax collector, trusted his riches instead of believing in the living God. But after he met Jesus, he gave back four times what he had taken from others (Luke 19:8).

In the other camp, they usually fear what money can do to them. They fear its corrupting influence and believe money will cause them to backslide. Therefore, they reject any wealth as having an evil impact.

The truth is that our Lord is not for or against money. Money is amoral in and of itself. It is what we do with it and our attitude toward it that makes it moral or immoral.

Money is not the root of evil (as some people misquote 1 Tim. 6:10.) However, the Lord warns us to beware of the pitfall of *loving* money. The *love* of money is the root of all kinds of evil. We are all subject to becoming lovers of money, whether we have little or much.

Rich or poor, if we begin to love money, it will lead us down the path of greed and cause much pain in our lives and the lives of those around us.

Father God, teach us to love people and use money and
not the other way around. In Jesus's name, amen!

_____

_____

_____

_____

Love of Money

John MacArthur
Adapted from *Giving: God's Way*

The love of money is a root of all kinds of evil.
—1 TIMOTHY 6:10

How do you regard money?

The wrong way to view it is to love it. It's not the money but its love that is the problem. You can have a lot of it and not love it, and you can have none of it and love it. When you derive your sense of security from your money instead of your God, you're trapped in idolatry.

What does loving money lead to?

First, it persuades people to forget God. In Proverbs 30:8, Agur prays, "Don't give me too much, or I may worship my wealth instead of You. I'll become self-sufficient." But also, "Don't give me too little, or I'll steal to meet my needs."

Second, when you love money, Satan can deceive you. In the parable of the sower in Mark 4, Jesus warns us that "the deceitfulness of riches" can choke the word of God sown in our hearts (v. 19, KJV). When you have money, you can quickly think you have everything. It lulls you into a sense of complacency.

Third, the love of money can lead a person to a place where he compromises biblical instruction. What would you sell out for?

Some people (even Christians) would lie to get a job promotion. Some mute the testimony of Jesus so they won't be unpopular. Some people would sell out for intellectual respect, some for the body beautiful, some for golf, hunting, a new car. What's your price? When you start seeking something other than the kingdom of God and His righteousness, you've already sold out.

Achan brought defeat on Israel's army and death to himself and his family for the money. For the money, Balam sinned and tried to curse

God's people. For the money, Delilah betrayed Samson and caused the slaughter of thousands. For the money, Ananias and Sapphira became the first hypocrites in the church, and God executed them. For the money, Judas sold Jesus.

Not very good company for money lovers, is it?

Father God, let us be content with the amount of money
You have entrusted to us. In Jesus's name, amen!

The Parable of the Rich Fool

Gary Inrig

Adapted from *The Parables*

You fool!
—LUKE 12:20

In today's passage, the rich man boasted about his wealth and future expansion plans.

But in a moment, his bubble burst. "You fool! This very night your life will be demanded from you. Then who will get what you have prepared for yourself?" (Luke 12:20).

The Lord's diagnosis was unrelenting in its honesty and revealing in its insight. Three things stand out:

He was a fool, not a success. In the Old Testament language of Psalms and Proverbs, a fool is an individual who makes choices as if God doesn't exist and who lives as if God hasn't spoken. Eleven times over, we hear "I" and "my" in this man's words. For him, God does not exist.

As Jim Elliot says, "He is no fool who gives what he cannot keep to gain what he cannot lose."

He was a servant, not a master. The rich man convinced himself that he was in control of his life and that wealth gave him authority. But God's words told him that he has no power over the present: "This very night your life will be demanded from you."

The fool also had no power over the future: "Who will get what you have prepared for yourself?" As the writer of Ecclesiastes laments, "I must leave [my wealth] to the one who comes after me. And who knows whether he will be a wise man or a fool?" (Eccles. 2:18–19).

He was a pauper, not a rich man. The wealthy farmer realized that he had worked so hard for so little. He had invested in the passing, not the permanent.

What makes death hard is the evaluation of what we lose by it. This man was leaving everything behind—the barns he had built, the people he had controlled, the prestige he had acquired.

Death revealed to him who he was, a man who "stores up things for himself but is not rich toward God" (v. 21).

Father God, let us seek to be rich toward You by investing in the things that will last for eternity. In Jesus's name, amen!

_____

_____

_____

_____

The Parable of the Shrewd Manager

Gary Inrig

Adapted from *The Parables*

The master commended the dishonest manager
because he had acted shrewdly.
—LUKE 16:8A

Why did the master commend the dishonest manager after he was fired and went around calling his master's customers and altering their bills?

It's crucial to see that the manager did not say he was pleased by his steward's actions, but he did say he was impressed.

The word "shrewd" in Greek means "to act with foresight." It is the same word used to describe the five "wise" virgins who brought extra oil, anticipating future needs (Matt. 25:1–13). Therefore, the cunning manager acted decisively with his resources in the present to maximize his opportunities in the future.

In Luke 16:8b–13, Jesus discusses the three principles of shrewd discipleship that every disciple of Jesus has to demonstrate.

Shrewd disciples use money to achieve eternal goals. Jesus says, "Gain friends for yourselves, so that...you will be welcomed [by them] into eternal dwellings" (v. 9). When you use your money to spread the gospel, there will be people lining up in heaven to tell you of your influence in their lives, much of it perhaps unknown or unrecognized by you.

Shrewd disciples use money in light of eternal consequences. The second principle is the reward explained in verse 10: "Whoever can be trusted with very little can also be trusted with much, and whoever is dishonest with very little will also be dishonest with much." It is in the little things that we prove ourselves. Faithfulness with money is primarily an issue of character.

The primary value of earthly wealth is that it is a tool to train us to handle "true riches," which refers to the kingdom's affairs.

Shrewd disciples recognize that stewardship of money prevents bondage to money. Jesus tells us, "You cannot serve both God and money" (v. 13). Either God owns our wealth, or it holds us. Therefore, we must choose our ultimate loyalty. When we determine the Lord as our sole Master, He does not remove our money. Instead, He takes the money and transforms it into an ally.

Father God, may there be eternal friends to meet us
when we get to heaven. In Jesus's name, amen!

Treasure in Heaven

Bruce Wilkinson
Adapted from *A Life God Rewards*

Lay up for yourselves treasures in heaven.
—MATTHEW 6:20, KJV

In today's verse, Jesus shatters three common misconceptions about how we should think about treasure.

What you should do about your treasures—"lay up." The Greek verb translated "lay up" is in the imperative—it's Jesus's command. Laying up treasure in heaven is a directive you should obey; it is God's plan for you.

When the sinful pull of greed, envy, and manipulation is absent in God's kingdom, we will enjoy our treasure, and it will serve a pure and meaningful purpose. God's rewards will allow us to serve, give, accomplish, and enjoy more for Him in heaven.

Who should you lay it up for—"yourselves." If you don't lay up for yourself in heaven, no one can do it for you. That's why Jesus called the man who never laid up treasure for himself a "fool" (Luke 12:13–21).

To lay up treasure for ourselves in heaven, we must first give it to others on earth. "Sell what you have and give alms; provide yourselves-...a treasure in the heavens" (Luke 12:33).

Jesus wasn't telling His disciples that treasure doesn't matter or that He didn't want them to have any. Just the opposite! He wanted them to provide for themselves because He knew that treasure would matter in eternity, and He wanted them to have a lot of it there (see 1 Tim. 6:18–19).

Where you should lay it up—"in heaven." Location matters. If you lay up treasure on earth, it's vulnerable to corruption or loss—"where moth and rust destroy, and where thieves break in and steal" (Matt. 6:19–20). Heaven is the only place where your treasure will be safe.

Jesus also says, "Where your treasure is, there your heart will also be" (Matt. 6:21). So, if you aren't purposely and generously investing your treasure in God's kingdom, your heart isn't there.

You will serve money if you don't serve God with your money. And when you serve money over God, you will inevitably follow your human instincts to keep your treasures here.

Father God, let us invest our treasures today in what matters in heaven. In Jesus's name, amen!

_____

_____

_____

_____

The Treasure Principle

Randy Alcorn
Adapted from *The Treasure Principle*

But store up yourselves treasures in heaven.
—MATTHEW 6:20

The Treasure Principle is simple: You can't take it with you—but you can send it on ahead.

Anything we try to hang on to in this world will be lost. But anything we put into God's hands will be ours for eternity. Here are six keys to the Treasure Principle:

First, God owns everything. I'm His money manager. "Everything under heaven belongs to me" (Job 41:11). If God is the owner, I am the manager. I need to adopt a steward's mentality toward the assets He has entrusted—not given—to me (Rom. 14:12).

Second, my heart always goes where I put God's money. "Where your treasure, there your heart will be also" (Matt. 6:21). As the compass needle follows north, your heart will follow your treasure.

Third, heaven, not earth, is my home. "We are citizens of a better country— a heavenly one" (Heb. 11:16). Where we choose to store our treasures depends on where we think our home is. If heaven is our true home, we'll send our money there. Everything we send on ahead will be waiting there for us.

Fourth, I should live not for the dot but for the line. Our lives have two phases: a dot and also a line extending out from that dot. Our present life on earth is the dot. The line is eternity, which Christians will spend in heaven. So, live for the line, not for the dot.

Fifth, giving is the only antidote to materialism. The faithful "lay up treasure for themselves as a firm foundation for the coming age" (1 Tim. 6:19). Giving breaks me free from the claims of mammon that would enslave me. Giving shifts me to a new center of gravity—heaven.

Sixth, God prospers me not to raise my standard of living but my bar of giving. "You will be made rich in every way so that you can be generous on every occasion" (2 Cor. 9:11). Abundance isn't God's provision for me to live in luxury; it's His provision for me to help others live.

Father God, let us experience the joy of
giving. In Jesus's Name, amen!

_____

_____

_____

_____

Money

Greg Ogden
Adapted from *Discipleship Essentials*

Whoever sows generously will also reap generously.
—2 CORINTHIANS 9:6

A stewardship principle is built into God's economy: You get back what you give. Here's another way of stating it: The extent you provide will be the extent to which you get back.

Here are the seven steps to financial freedom:

Step 1. Give cheerfully. All giving begins with attitude, not the amount. So, the first step to financial freedom is to ask the Lord to show you how outrageously lavish His grace is toward you.

Step 2. Give regularly, not haphazardly. Giving is not just reactive or sporadic but done with forethought. Plan your giving in the same way you would a renovation on your house.

Step 3. Give your first fruit. It was the practice in the Old Testament that people gave the first fruits of the harvest or the best of their flock to the Lord. So, make the first check you write each month for furthering the Lord's work.

Step 4. Give when it's tight. Giving is an act of faith in the ability of God to provide. It allows the Lord to demonstrate His faithfulness in tangible ways. When we trust God even in the lean times and watch Him provide, we have clear evidence that He is real.

Step 5. Give sacrificially. C. S. Lewis put it best: "I do not believe one can settle how much we ought to give. The only safe rule is to give more than we can spare. If our charities do not pinch or hamper us, they are too small. We sacrifice comforts, luxuries, and amusements because our charitable expenditures exclude them."

Step 6. Give a tithe. Giving a tenth of our income is a clear standard for our obedience to God. Write down your annual or monthly income and find what 10 percent of it is. This practice is your starting point. Build from there.

Step 7. Give in faith. Giving should always contain the element of the risk of faith. By faith, set the goal of your giving a little beyond where you know God will provide the resources.

Father God, help us be faithful stewards of all the resources
You have entrusted us here on earth. In Jesus's name, amen!

_____

_____

_____

_____

The Grace of Giving

Richard Foster
Adapted from *Money, Sex and Power*

Share your food with the hungry.
—ISAIAH 58:7

The grace of giving is often a tremendous stimulant to the life of faith.

Giving brings authenticity and vitality to our devotional experience. If our spiritual vitality seems low, if Bible study produces only dusty words, if prayer seems hollow and empty, then perhaps a prescription of lavish and joyful giving is just what we need.

In Isaiah 58, we read of religious people whose pious devotion counted for nothing because it did not match active caring for the poor and the oppressed. "Is not this fast that I choose...to let the oppressed go free...to share your bread with the hungry" (Isa. 58:6–7).

Giving frees us from the tyranny of money. It releases a little more of our egocentric selves and a little more of our false sense of security.

Dr. Karl Menninger once asked a wealthy patient, "What on earth are you going to do with all that money?"

The patient replied, "Just worry about it, I suppose!"

Dr. Menninger said, "Well, do you get that much pleasure out of worrying about it?"

"No," responded the patient, "but I get such terror when I think of giving some of it to somebody."

Now, this "terror" is real. When we let go of money, we let go of ourselves and our security. In a sense, money is coined personality, so tied to who we are that we are giving part of ourselves when we share it. As one economist puts it, "We cannot consistently give money without giving ourselves."

And that is precisely why it is vital to give. It is one way to obey Jesus's command to deny ourselves (Luke 9:23). Money is an effective way of showing our love to God because it is so much a part of us. We consecrate ourselves by consecrating our money.

Money frees us to care. It produces an air of expectancy as we anticipate what God will lead us to give. It makes life with God an adventure of discovery. It allows God to use us to make a difference in the world.

> *Father God, let money be a means of enhancing our love and devotion to You. In Jesus's name, amen!*

Giving—Love, Not Legalism

Donald Whitney
From *Spiritual Disciplines for the Christian Life*

See that you also excel in this grace of giving.
—2 CORINTHIANS 8:7

In 2 Corinthians 8, the Apostle Paul tells the people of Corinth about how some of their fellow Greeks in Macedonia were such good and faithful givers. Then, in verse 7, he tells the Corinthians to "excel in this grace of giving" just as the Macedonians have.

But notice what he says in verse 8: "I am not commanding you, but I want to test the sincerity of your love by comparing it with the earnestness of others." Paul did not use his authority as an apostle of Jesus to command the Corinthians to give. Instead of dictating a law of giving, he says that giving should be a way of proving your love for God.

Notice the absence of a religious demand as a motive to give in the first part of 2 Corinthians 9:7, when Paul writes, "Each man should give what he has decided in his heart to give."

Paul never gives them an external, measurable standard of giving. Instead, he says that giving to God should be measured in the heart and the standard is their love for God.

Suppose I come to my wife, Caffey, on Valentine's Day, give her a dozen of her favorite yellow roses, and say, "Happy Valentine's Day!" And she says, "Oh, they're beautiful! Thank you! You shouldn't have spent so much money." I then respond neutrally to her joy with, "Don't mention it. Today is Valentine's Day, and as your husband, I have to get a gift for you." How do you think she'd feel?

Now suppose I do the same thing but say instead, "There's nothing I'd rather do with my money than use it for you because I love you so much." Same money. Same gift. But one gift is motivated by law, the other by love. And that makes all the difference in the world.

God is just like we are in this regard. He wants your giving to express your love for Him, not legalism.

Father God, we give because You have first given
Your Son to us. In Jesus's name, amen!

The Principle of Tithing

Dean De Castro

Then Abram [Abraham] gave him
[Melchizedek] a tenth of everything.
—GENESIS 14:20

The principle of tithing is timeless. It is for every man in every age and dispensation. The dispensation of the law didn't initiate it, nor did the dispensation of grace terminate it. It was neither given by Moses nor abrogated by Jesus Christ.

Some Bible teachers today are preaching against tithing. They argue that tithing belongs to the Mosaic law. Since we are no longer under the law but under grace (Rom, 6:14), they say, Christians should not give 10 percent of their income to the church.

There are at least three reasons why I believe Christians should practice tithing. If the Hebrews, compelled by the law, gave one-tenth, how can we, constrained by grace, give even one mite less?

The example of Abraham. Genesis 14 shows us that the practice of tithing existed even before the time of Moses. Four hundred years before Moses, Abraham already knew and practiced tithing.

When he came back from winning over the enemies who captured his nephew Lot, Abraham met a priest of Salem named Melchizedek. Genesis 14:20 states that Melchizedek blessed Abraham, and in response, Abraham gave him a tenth of everything that he got from defeating his enemies.

Abraham's action reveals that tithing is our way of returning God's favor and blessings in this life. Tithing also shows one's respect for the servant of God by supplying their practical needs (Gal. 6:6).

The teaching of Jesus. Did Jesus teach anything about tithing? Not much. But in Matthew 23:23, our Lord only rebukes the Pharisees' wrong approach toward tithing. They showed their hypocrisy by tithing faithfully, but they used this as an excuse to mistreat their neighbors.

We can safely conclude that Jesus wanted His disciples to continue giving the 10 percent of their income to God. As a devout Jew, our Lord must have practiced tithing Himself.

The New Testament pattern of giving. In 1 Corinthians 16:2, Paul alludes to the principle of tithing when he instructs the believers to set aside a sum of money in keeping with their income, pooling it at weekly worship it to send on to Jerusalem.

Father God, let us practice tithing as an act of
our love for You. In Jesus's name, amen!

_____

_____

_____

_____

The Blessings of Tithing
Dean De Castro

...and pour out so much blessing...
—MALACHI 3:10

In Malachi 3:10–13, the prophet mentions at least three blessings that God promises to those who obey Him in the area of giving.

God's provision. Malachi 3:10 says, "Bring the whole tithe into the storehouse...and see if I will...pour out so much blessing that you will not have the room enough for it." Instead of arguing whether tithing is biblical, why not try doing it and testing God to see for yourself whether it works.

We love the promise of God in Philippians 4:19: "And my God will meet all your needs." We all wish that God would abundantly supply all our needs. However, we often overlook the condition stated in the preceding verse.

In verse 18, Paul thanks the Philippian church for their generous gift while he was in jail. The challenge is that God will only meet all our needs as we give generously to meet the needs of others. As 2 Corinthians 9:6 states, "Whoever sows generously will also reap generously."

God's protection. In Malachi 3:11, God says, "I will rebuke the devourer for your sake." The ultimate devourer is Satan. When we obey God, especially in the area of giving, God promises to protect us from the attacks of Satan on our finances, our health, our family, and our career.

But if we disobey God, 1 Samuel 15:23 warns us that the sin of disobedience is equivalent to the sin of divination, witchcraft, and idolatry. Disobedience allows Satan to come into our lives and steal our joy, peace, and even our children.

God's prosperity. "Then all the nations will call you blessed, for yours will be a delightful land,' says the Lord Almighty" (Mal. 3:12). The word "delightful" can also be translated as "happy." Unless Christians learn to give on God's terms, they miss the enjoyment and enrichment God has prepared for them.

After all, the Lord Jesus says in Acts 20:35, "Happiness lies more in giving than in receiving" (NEB). We learn from experience that miserly people are miserable and generous people are joyous.

Father God, let us be generous and joyous people
in Your sight. In Jesus's name, amen!

_____

_____

_____

_____

The New Testament Pattern of Giving

Dean De Castro

But everything should be done in a fitting and orderly way.
—1 CORINTHIANS 14:40

This principle also applies to giving.

In 1 Corinthians 16:1–2, Paul lays out his instructions for the pattern and practices of giving in all local churches for all time.

Where? In verse 1, Paul instructs all the local churches concerning financial assistance to the poverty-stricken saints in Jerusalem.

In the New Testament, giving should be done first to the local church because the giver's primary spiritual community and leadership are in the church. These church leaders need financial support to fully devote their time to ministry (Gal. 6:6).

When? "On the first day of the week." The early church met on the first day of the week in commemoration of the resurrection of Jesus Christ. It quickly became the day of worship, giving, and service for the people of God. Giving should be an act of worship to the resurrected and ascended Savior.

In Old Testament times, the tithe, generally speaking, was an annual tax. But in the New Testament, we find that giving to God was a weekly contribution. This reveals that God wants our giving to be systematic and disciplined.

Who? "Let each of you." Paul expects the rich and the poor alike to share in the offering. Our Lord praised the widow's mite and received Barnabas' generous gifts to demonstrate that no one is too poor or rich to sacrifice for God.

How? Giving should be *deliberate.* "Set aside a sum of money." Each believer should set aside their offering at home and then bring it to the church on the first day. This practice excludes any hastiness or pressure from the whole area of giving.

Giving should also be *proportionate,* "in keeping with his income." Paul did not mention any specific amount. However, the tithe is an excellent place to start. But as the Lord gives us more, we should plan to give more.

As Stephen Olford writes, "If there is a genuine consideration of what we receive of God, there will be a genuine calculation of what we return to Him."

Father God, may our giving be in proportion to the
blessings You have given us. In Jesus's name, amen!

_____

_____

_____

_____

The Example of the Macedonians' Giving

Dean De Castro

They first gave themselves to the Lord, and then to us.
—2 CORINTHIANS 8:5, NKJV

In encouraging the Corinthian church to financially support the poor believers in Jerusalem, Paul uses the example of the churches in Macedonia to motivate them. In 2 Corinthians 8:5, he relates the vertical and horizontal dimensions of the Macedonians' commitment.

They gave themselves first to the Lord. It is impossible to grow spiritually without committing one's offering to the Lord. God can have our money without our hearts, but He cannot have our hearts without having all our money. Giving oneself to God is indeed worship (Rom. 12:1).

The exceptional giving of the Macedonians—out of poverty—was the result of their first giving themselves to God. The principle behind this attitude is clear: When all one has is given to God, giving to others becomes the natural reflex of the soul. It is easy to surrender part when we have already offered the whole.

You may be attending church faithfully, enjoying the fellowship of Christians, reading your Bible, and praying regularly and still not growing spiritually. The problem may be that you have not developed the discipline of giving. Remember that giving to the Lord's work is evidence that God has been working in your heart.

They gave themselves to the church leaders in keeping with God's will. The Macedonian churches did not only put themselves at God's disposal; they also submitted to His chosen leaders—the Apostle Paul and his coworkers. They had complied with God's messengers. They did so because it was part of their deeper dedication to God Himself.

As Homer Kent Jr. explains, "As the Macedonians became sensitive to the will of God in their lives, they wholeheartedly dedicated themselves to Him, and this involved accepting the guidance of God's missionaries—the apostolic party."

Giving to the church's needs also involves trusting the church leadership in their financial decisions. Therefore, we support the church's ministries without any strings attached. We may disagree with a particular leadership's decision but still support it because of a consensus. As Paul writes in Romans 12:17, "Be careful to do what is right in the eyes of everybody."

Father God, let us give in keeping with
Your will. In Jesus's name, amen!

Giving Starts in the Local Church

Randy Alcorn

Adapted from *Money, Possessions, and Eternity*

...brought the money from the sales and put it at the apostles'
feet, and it was distributed to anyone who had need.
—ACTS 4:34–35

In today's passage, the early Christians did not discern on their own where the funds they gave to God should go. Instead, they gave these funds to spiritually qualified church leaders, who distributed them according to their cumulative knowledge, collective wisdom, and leading from the Lord.

But you might ask, "How can I give to my church when I don't agree with how the money is spent?"

First, I would ask myself if it may be that the church leaders are in a better position to judge this than I am. Then I would ask if my high opinion of the organization I support instead is based on firsthand knowledge or some media hype.

Furthermore, I would ask myself if I am trying to exercise too much control over the funds. If the Bible tells me to pay taxes (Rom. 13:1–7), knowing full well that the government will waste some of it and even use it for sinister purposes, surely I can give to God even when I don't feel comfortable with every detail of how the funds are used.

Of course, I must draw the line somewhere. Suppose my money goes to liberal seminaries, groups that promote immorality, or other unbiblical causes. In that case, it is time to speak to my church leaders rather than quietly giving my money elsewhere without confronting the problem.

After prayerfully discussing this matter with the church leaders, if you still cannot support your church with a good conscience, then perhaps it is time to ask God to help you find a church where you can give obediently and wholeheartedly.

I do not encourage church shopping or church hopping. But if you are in a church where you honestly feel you cannot give generously in good conscience, then either your convictions must change or your church must change. To go on as you are, not delivering your first fruits to church, in my opinion, is biblically unacceptable.

Father God, let the church leaders of every congregation have the discernment to manage Your children's giving faithfully. In Jesus's name, amen!

_____

_____

_____

_____

Giving and the Great Commission

Randy Alcorn

Adapted from *Money, Possessions, and Eternity*

With Your blood you purchased for God persons from
every tribe and language and people and nation.
—REVELATION 5:9

Paul told us in 1 Corinthians 15:3 that our top priority must be the gospel. Therefore, the spread of the gospel is likewise of first importance.

But what are our priorities in spreading the gospel? Church budgets often designate less than 10 percent of their income to missions. But what is called "missions" often includes ministries to reach our own country or community. This obviously isn't foreign missions.

I have heard people say things like, "We have plenty of needs in our own country and community. People here are just as important as people off in some jungle, aren't they? A soul is a soul—God doesn't care whether it comes from our country or another."

This philosophy requires several responses. First, the needs of those who have no access to the gospel are obviously greater than those of someone living in a country with churches in every community. Why should some hear the gospel many times when others have never heard it?

Furthermore, we must realize God is interested in more than the total number of souls in heaven and *does* in fact care about where they come from. The apostle John was overwhelmed when he saw "a great multitude that no one could count, from every nation, tribe, people and language, standing before the throne and in front of the Lamb" (Rev. 7:9).

We are motivated first by the glory of God, but are also legitimately moved by the eternal needs of people. We decry the fact that religious liberals don't believe in hell. But there is one shame even greater—that we who do believe in hell would make so little effort to keep people from going there.

I am convinced that God has provided Christians of the Western world with such incredible wealth because we may use it to help fulfill the Great Commission. There is no greater way to invest our money in eternity than in the cause of world missions.

Father God, let us see multitudes of people from
all over the world worshipping and praising
You in eternity. In Jesus's name, amen!

_____

_____

_____

_____

The Abundant Life

Charles Swindoll

Adapted from *Swindoll's New Testament Insights*

I have come that they may have life, and that
they may have it more abundantly.
—JOHN 10:10B, NKJV

Most prosperity preachers of the Word of Faith movement interpret "abundantly" to mean creature comforts, a prestigious job, and lots of money and possessions. Yet I see no indication that Jesus offered His followers anything in the realm of material wealth.

So, if "abundance" is not cash, possessions, or comfort, what is it?

In the context of Jesus's proclamation "I am the Good Shepherd" (John 10:11), He describes in verses 28 and 29 the abundant life He promises to those willing to follow Him.

Christ's sheep are confident (v. 28). Domestic sheep and sheep in the wild, while grazing, act quite differently.

Wild sheep remain vigilant against predators; they chew with their heads up, constantly scanning their surroundings for danger. Domestic sheep graze with their heads down, popping up only when a noise draws their attention. When sheep have a good shepherd, they feel secure; they don't live in constant fear.

Believers believe that Christ has done everything to secure their eternal safety. Because He is entirely faithful, we may rest in the assurance that our Lord will preserve us from evil until it no longer exists.

Christ's sheep are secure (v 29). This is a fact, not a feeling. Regardless of how insensitive, disobedient, or fearful the sheep choose to be, their place in the flock is secure.

This is not to suggest the believer's behavior is irrelevant or unimportant. People who willfully resist spiritual growth and who evidence no change in their values or behavior need to question their spiritual condition seriously.

Eternal security, however, like salvation itself, is not based on the goodness of the believer. Therefore, we are just as incapable of holding on to salvation as we were earning it in the first place.

The abundance Jesus offers is a spiritual abundance that transcends circumstances like income, health, living conditions, and even death. So, follow God's leading diligently, and rest in the confidence of His power to protect you from all evil. After all, He's the Good Shepherd, so following Him is for your good.

Father God, lead us to walk in Your righteous
path daily. In Jesus's name, amen!

Basic Attitudes Towards Finances

Bethany World Payer Center
Adapted from *Finding the Rock*

Be content with [food and clothing].
—1 TIMOTHY 6:8

There are basic attitudes towards finances if we want to enjoy the fruit of financial freedom. Here are four basic attitudes that contribute to responsible stewardship:

Be content, not covetous. Paul commands Christians to be content (1 Tim. 6:8). You must realize that you are spirit first, not material. Therefore, you will be using material things for only a short time on this earth before someone else will have them.

The drive to always obtain more is the root of many ills in this country. Moreover, it is the cause of much family pain and suffering (see 1 Tim. 6:10).

Trust in God, not in riches (Phil. 4:19). God is your source for everything in life! God is the one who blesses you financially, and He will take care of you through every circumstance. Your employer, friends, relatives, or the government is not your source!

When you acknowledge God as your source, He will take care of you regardless of the economy or the circumstances of your life.

Be generous, not greedy (Prov. 11:24–25). This passage tells us that generosity and sowing based on the needs of others will be blessed by God. When you give freely, as the Spirit directs, God will bless you for your generosity and willingness to share.

But on the other hand, when you hold on to the little you have and refuse to share, you will only end up losing the little you thought you had!

Dean De Castro   279

Generosity is an attitude of the heart, not a set of amounts. God does not regard the amount you give, but the degree of sacrifice and the willingness on your part to provide it (Luke 21:2–4; 2 Cor. 8:12).

Walk in faith, not fear (2 Cor. 9:8–11). God never rewards the selfishness and fear that keeps you thinking only about yourself. You are called to be a giver, trusting God to provide you with "seed" and meet your needs as you concern yourself with others. If you hoard out of fear that you will not have enough, you limit God's blessings to you.

Father God, let us develop godly attitudes toward
our finances. In Jesus's name, amen!

_____

_____

_____

_____

Basic Principles of Finances

Bethany World Prayer Center
Adapted from *Finding the Rock*

It is more blessed to give than to receive.
—ACTS 20:35

Here are seven practical considerations for handling our finances in a godly fashion.

Tithe ten percent of all your income (Mal. 3:1–12). The tithe is the beginning point in managing your finances. Tithing means you are first giving to God in *gratitude* for the past, then as your *priority* for the present, and finally as your *faith* in the future. He, in turn, will bless you more than you can imagine (Mal. 3:10, KJV).

Save 10 percent of your income (Prov. 21:20). After you give to the Lord, then pay yourself. When you begin saving, set aside three months' income in the bank to hedge against rough times; next, start long-term savings by putting money into safe investments that you do not touch.

Budget the remaining 80 percent of your income. Develop a specific budget for your money. Know your monthly income and expenditures and plan what you will do with your money each month. Most of us have enough money, but we waste it on the wrong priorities.

Curb your spending. Live within your means. Be on guard against the temptation to overspend during holidays and on vacation. Instead, plan for such times. Keep careful track of your spending. There are many good software programs to help.

Use wisdom in investing. Never gamble; there is no "get rich quick" method to solve all your financial worries. Instead, diversify your investments; obtain and follow sound investment advice. If married, both partners must agree on all significant investments and feel comfortable before moving forward.

Avoid borrowing (Prov. 22:7). Instead, only borrow on appreciating items, such as a house. Pay your bills before indulging in luxuries. Never file for bankruptcy, but even if you do, repay your debts.

Be hardworking and diligent (2 Thess. 3:10–12). Be diligent and work hard at your place of employment. Do your job as unto the Lord. Be a good steward of your household. Take care of things that need to be repaired, and teach your children a strong work ethic.

Father God, help us manage wisely all the resources
You have entrusted to us. In Jesus's name, amen!

_____

_____

_____

_____

The Habit of Generosity

Joyce Meyer
Adapted from *Making Good Habits, Breaking Bad Habits*

A generous person will prosper.
—PROVERBS 11:25

God is generous, and those who wish to be like Him must learn to be generous.

It is not wrong to want things. God has given us the ability to create helpful and needful things to enjoy. But He wants us to enjoy them with an attitude of gratitude and a willingness to be generous to others.

What steps can you take to start forming the excellent habit of generosity?

Be generous on purpose. Decide to be more of a blessing to others. Be creative. Ask God to show you ways to bless people. There are endless ways to bless people if we put our minds to it.

Think of people you will be with today, and then think about their needs. For example, perhaps they need to talk, and you can encourage them by listening. Maybe they need help financially, and you could give them a gift certificate to the grocery store or a gas card.

If you don't know what the person needs, begin listening to them, and it won't be long before you hear them mentioning something they are lacking.

At times, I have kept a list of things I have heard various people say what they want or need, and even if I can't do it for them right away, I keep it on my list and do it when I can.

We cannot out-give God. He said if we give, He will give back to us, "pressed down, shaken together, and running over" (Luke 6:38). The more generous you are, the more God will bless your life.

Are you a generous person? If you are not, don't feel guilty. Instead, pray and ask God for help, and do things for people until you develop the habit of generosity.

Giving will become a part of your character. People won't need to convince you to give; instead, you will learn to love giving and always look for ways to do it.

Father God, help us enjoy the gift of giving
and generosity. In Jesus's name, amen!

God's Provision for the Giver

Randy Alcorn

Adapted from *Money, Possessions, and Eternity*

*You will be enriched in every way so that you
can be generous on every occasion.*
—2 CORINTHIANS 9:11

Scripture clarifies that in many cases, God blesses us financially when we give generously (Prov. 11:24–25; Luke 6:38). God's extra provision is usually not intended to raise our standard of living but to raise our bar of giving.

R. G. LeTourneau was an example of a man who understood God's purpose in blessing him financially. The founder of an earthmoving company, LeTourneau reached the point of giving 90 percent of his income to the Lord. As he put it, "I shovel out the money, and God shovels it back to me—but God has a bigger shovel."

Once, my wife and I sensed God's leading to take our daughters and spend two months visiting missionary families in Africa and Europe. We decided to finance the trip ourselves without reducing our giving level.

So, while we would never touch our tithe, we were tempted to rationalize using some of our extra monthly missionary giving for our trip. After all, it was for a missionary purpose! But this didn't seem right.

Two weeks before the trip, we received a fantastic amount of money but were $1,000 short. Meanwhile, there was a special missionary offering at church. Though it didn't make sense in light of the circumstances, we determined to give substantially to this offering, above and beyond our regular giving. It "didn't make sense," but we knew it was right.

Amazingly, within a week of the trip, God gave back the money we had given and more than $1,000 beyond it, enough to give some back to Him before getting on the plane.

We look back at the trip and realize that, humanly speaking, we shouldn't have been able to accumulate the needed funds. But God provided abundantly.

But no matter how much we give, Jesus Christ remains the unmatchable Giver. He left behind the wealth of heaven to grant us infinite riches. So, no matter how much we give, we can never out-give God.

Father God, we acknowledge your extra provision
is not to raise our standard of living but to raise
the bar of our giving. In Jesus's name, amen!

_____

_____

_____

_____

How Much Money Should a Christian Make?

William H. Cook

Adapted from *Success, Motivation, and the Scriptures*

For the love of money is a root of all kinds of evil.
—1 TIMOTHY 6:10A

Is money the root of all evil? Is it just a necessary evil? Is it evil at all?

Money is not the root of all evil. In itself, money is neutral. But the Bible tells us that the love of money (human greed) is a root of all kinds of evil (1 Tim. 6:10a).

Money can ruin you. There are at least five ways money can destroy one's life:

- Too much money can ruin one's worthy goals of service and sacrifice.
- Too much money can ruin one's family.
- Climbing the money ladder can destroy moral character.
- Too much money may push you further and further from the people who need you.
- Too much money may result in ego inflation.

Christians should make money. The Bible teaches that making money is vital for a Christian's life. Therefore, God commands us, "Six days shalt thou labour" (Exod. 20:9, KJV).

Paul wrote to the Christians at Thessalonica, who believed that Jesus would come soon. As a result, they would not work! They wanted to sit on the highest mountain and watch for the return of Christ. But they wouldn't work to feed themselves.

Paul rebuked these disobedient Christians: "Doing your own work, just as we told you before. As a result, people who are not Christians will trust and respect you, and you will not need to depend on others for enough money to pay your bills" (1 Thess. 4:11–12, TLB).

And when some of the church members didn't heed Paul's command, he wrote them again, saying, "If a man does not work, he shall not eat" (2 Thess. 3:10b).

How much money should a Christian make? One day it dawned on me that God knew better than I just precisely how much money it would take to ruin me. Therefore, I should thank God daily that He has never been interested in helping me attain so much that my life would be destroyed by what I had acquired.

Father God, help us work hard, save hard, and give
hard to your cause. In Jesus's name, amen!

_____

_____

_____

_____

Was Jesus Rich or Poor?

Dean De Castro

Give me neither poverty nor riches.
—PROVERBS 30:8

Was Jesus poor or wealthy—and why does it matter?

As followers of Jesus, we need to properly understand what the Bible teaches about our Lord's attitude towards poverty and prosperity.

Jesus's poverty. *Was Jesus homeless?* When Jesus said, "The Son of Man has nowhere to lay His head" (Luke 9:58), He spoke these words to a man who volunteered to follow Him (v. 57), hoping to escape his responsibility.

Unlike foxes and birds that withdraw to their dens and nests for rest, Jesus has no place to rest from His responsibility. Therefore, in following Jesus, one cannot use their faith to avoid fulfilling their human duties and obligations.

Was Jesus poor? This question seems to misunderstand Paul's statement in 2 Corinthians 8:9: "[Jesus] became poor, that you through His poverty might become rich."

In this verse, Paul was referring to Jesus's incarnation. Indeed, to take on human flesh and dwell among sinful people, Jesus had to set aside the wealth of heaven (Phil. 2:7). Thus, Paul was saying that Jesus voluntarily gave up heaven so we could become spiritually rich by trusting Him.

Jesus's wealth. When Joseph passed away, Jesus took over His earthly father's lucrative carpentry business (Mark 6:3). Historians tell us Nazareth was a prosperous town, especially for tradespeople, since it was located near the city of Sepphoris, a luxurious Roman vacation destination that was under constant construction.

During His three years of ministry, Jesus lived by faith, depending mainly on the financial support of His wealthy followers, including Joseph of Arimathea, Nicodemus, Zacchaeus, Levi, and certain unnamed Pharisees.

Jesus had enough money to have a treasurer, Judas (John 12:4–6). When Jesus fed the five thousand, He had two hundred days' wages in the treasury (6:5–7). Jesus gave to the poor from this treasury regularly (13:29).

Based on the Gospels, it is safe to conclude that Jesus was neither rich nor poor. He taught people to avoid the love of money and instead invest it for eternity (Matt. 6:20, 24).

Father God, give us neither poverty nor riches but contentment in both circumstances to honor You. In Jesus's name, amen!

_____

_____

_____

_____

Paul and Prosperity

Dean De Castro

*Command those who are rich...to be
generous and willing to share.*
—1 TIMOTHY 6:17–18

Was Paul from a wealthy family? If so, to what extent did his wealth affect the way he did ministry?

Paul's pre-conversion status. There is ample biblical evidence to suggest that Paul grew up in a moderately wealthy family.

He was a Roman citizen by birth (Acts 16:38). However, to obtain citizenship, one might need to spend eighteen months' wages or more on the gifts necessary to receive that honor.

Paul's educational achievement may also be a hint to his social status. As the son of a Pharisee and a Pharisee himself (Acts 23:6), Paul's family must have been wealthy enough to send him to an expensive rabbinical school in Jerusalem under the tutelage of Gamaliel (Acts 5:34), who was the most excellent scholar of his day.

In Tarsus, Paul was a tentmaker by trade. Tarsus was known for the costly cloth *cilicium*, which was used for tents and saddles. Paul's family may have worked with this expensive material, doing jobs for the wealthy residents of Tarsus.

Paul's after conversion's ministry. Paul's ministry suggests that he had financial resources to support himself and his companions.

His extensive travels with his coworkers were expensive. And in Ephesus, he likely rented space to teach for two years (Acts 19:9–10).

While under house arrest for two years, he lived in a rented home (Acts 28:30). Paul must have had enough money in his savings to rent it since he could not work after the arrest.

In Acts 21, Paul sponsored a Nazarite vow for four Jewish believers (vv. 23–24). The church leadership in Jerusalem urged Paul to pay for the costly expenses of these four men. Acts 24:26 states that Felix "hoped that Paul would give him some money." He probably had a good basis for believing that Paul had some financial resources.

In a number of instances, we see that Paul used his wealth, education, and social status to invest in advancing God's kingdom and ardently encouraged affluent people to do likewise (1 Tim. 6:17–18). In addition, he taught all Christ's followers to work hard to support their livelihood and help others in financial distress (Eph. 4:28).

Father God, let us be faithful stewards of the resources You gave us to lead more people to Your kingdom. In Jesus's name, amen!

Teaching Children Stewardship

Randy Alcorn

Adapted from *Money, Possessions, and Eternity*

Train a child in the way he should go, And
when he is old he will not depart from it.
—PROVERBS 22:6, NKJV

As parents, we should direct and encourage our children to give.

But this needs to be more than simply taking our dollar and giving it to our child to put in the offering. For giving to be giving, it must come from the child's own assets.

In our case, we taught our children to tithe from the very earliest age. No matter where their income came from, even as a gift, 10 percent belonged to the Lord, which was untouchable. If Grandpa gave them ten dollars for Christmas, the question was not "What can I do with ten dollars?" but "What can I do with nine dollars?"

We first started giving our children a salary of fifty cents per week when they were ages three and five. We called it a "salary" because they had to do specific tasks to receive it.

I gave each of the three jars that I had carefully labeled with their names and the designations: "Giving," "Saving," and "Spending." I told them that every time they earned their salary (one dollar per week), they were first to put at least ten percent into the giving jar and then distribute the rest between the other two jars as they wished.

But once they put money in the giving jar, even beyond the tithe, it was dedicated to the Lord, and they could not take it out again. So, every Sunday morning, they would empty their giving jar and bring it to the offering box at church. After that, however, they were free to transfer money from saving and spending to giving or from spending to saving.

It is essential to realize that a child cannot learn money management unless they have money to manage and unless their efforts somehow earn that money. Parents who shovel out money according to the dictates of the moment are not teaching their children stewardship. There must be a regular, earned income for accurate stewardship decisions.

Father God, help every young parent raise their children
with the holy habit of giving. In Jesus's name, amen!

The Sin of Worry

Gary Inrig

Adapted from *The Parables*

You of little faith!...Do not worry about it.
—LUKE 12:28B, 29B

In Luke 12:22–34, Jesus deals with the issue of worry.

The terms of discipleship are demanding. To obey the call is to trust Christ completely. But what are the implications of that obedience? Financial questions loom large. Will the Lord meet my needs if I say goodbye to all my possessions?

People who tell us not to worry seem to be missing something. They usually come across as unrealistic, uninformed, or condescending. However, in today's passage, the Lord encourages us to think about why we have good reason not to worry.

First, worry is foolish (Luke 12:22–24). Worrying may make you fall into the folly of the rich fool who believed that his life consists of his possessions. But life is more than food and clothes, and God has promised us that He will care for us, much more so than He does for His creatures, the birds. To worry is to foolishly forget that we are God's valued children and He is our loving Father.

Second, worry is futile (12:25–28). Anxiety can shorten life, but it can't lengthen it—and God, who gives beauty to the fields, will not strip us bare. Fear denies the care of God—and all to no effect. The alternative is not to be "care-less" but "trust-full."

We must recognize that most worry is about things that can't change (the past), things that can't be controlled (the present), and things that might not happen (the future). How much better it is to entrust ourselves to our God.

Third, worry is faithless (12:29–31). To be absorbed with physical and personal needs is ultimately a sign of unbelief.

The Lord addresses fear in verses 32–34. He tells us not to grasp our possessions or trust them. We are instead to invest them eternally. The crucial issue in life is not the *amount* of our treasure but its *location*.

Our hearts follow our treasure, and if our treasure is in heaven, our hearts will be there also. Our call as a disciple is to be rich toward God and have a treasure in heaven that will not be exhausted.

Father God, forgive us of the sins of worry
and unbelief. In Jesus's name, amen!

_____

_____

_____

_____

Five Reasons to Be Fearless

John Piper

Adapted from desiringGod.org

Fear not, little flock, for it is your Father's
good pleasure to give you the kingdom.
—LUKE 12:32, ESV

God wants us not to be afraid concerning money because fearlessness—that freedom from anxiety—will magnify five great things about Him.

First, fearlessness shows that we treasure God as our *Shepherd*. "Fear not, little flock." We are His flock, and He is our Shepherd. And if He is our Shepherd, then Psalm 23:1 applies: "The Lord is my Shepherd, and I shall not want"—that is, I shall not lack anything I need.

Second, fearlessness shows that we treasure God as our *Father*. "It is your Father's good pleasure." We are not only His flock, but we are also His children, and He is our Father. Therefore, He cares and knows what you need and will ensure you have what you need.

Third, fearlessness shows that we treasure God as our *King*. "For it is your Father's good pleasure to give you the kingdom." He can give us the "kingdom" because He is the King. It adds a tremendous element of power to the one who provides for us.

"Shepherd" connotes protection and provision. "Father" connotes love and tenderness, authority, and guidance. "King" connotes power, sovereignty, and wealth.

Fourth, fearlessness shows how generous and gracious God is. Notice, He *gives* the kingdom: "Fear not, little flock, for it is your Father's good pleasure to give you the kingdom."

He doesn't sell you the kingdom, rent it, or lease it. So, therefore, He is infinitely wealthy and does not need our payments. God is generous and free with His bounty. We magnify God when we are not afraid but trust Him with our needs.

Finally, not being anxious shows that we believe God wants to do this. "For it is your Father's good pleasure to give you the kingdom." It delights Him. He is not begrudging. It makes Him glad to give us the kingdom.

We should treasure God as our Shepherd, Father, and King who is generous and happy to give us His kingdom—to give us heaven, eternal life, and joy and everything we need to get there.

Father God, deliver us from the fear of
poverty. In Jesus's name, amen!

The Discipline of Detachment

Peter Scazzero
Adapted from *Emotionally Healthy Spirituality*

For this world in its present form is passing away.
—1 CORINTHIANS 7:31

The critical issue for our journey with God is not "Am I happy?" but "Am I free? Am I growing in the freedom God gave me?"

Paul addressed this central issue of detachment in 1 Corinthians 7:29–31, calling us to a radical, new understanding of our relationship with the world.

We are to live our lives as the rest of the world—marrying, experiencing joy and sorrow, buying things, and using them. But we live with the awareness that these things, in themselves, are not our lives. Instead, we live in light of eternity, free from the dominating power of things.

The danger of attachment. Along the way, in this journey with Christ, we get attached to (literally "nailed to") habits, things, and people in an unhealthy way. For example, I love my home, car, books, Geri, our four daughters, church, comforts, and good health.

But like you, I rarely realize how attached I am to something until God removes it. Then the power struggle begins. I say, "God, I must have that second car for convenience," God answers, "No, you don't need that. You need Me!"

When we put our claws into something, and we don't want to take them out, we are beyond enjoying them. So, we now *must* have them.

The purpose of detachment. God's purpose for us is to have a loving union with Him at the end of the journey. Therefore, we joyfully detach from certain behaviors and activities for a more intimate, devoted attachment to God.

We are to enjoy the world, for God's creation is good. We are to appreciate nature, people, all God's gifts, and His presence in creation—without being trapped by them. Somebody has rightly said that those who are the most detached are best able to taste the purest joy in the beauty of God's creation.

Detachment is the great secret to inner peace. The journey with Jesus calls us to a life of undivided devotion to Him. It requires that we simplify our lives, removing distractions.

Father God, save us from worldly distractions
and entanglements. In Jesus's name, amen!

_____

_____

_____

_____

The Discipline of Contentment

Dean De Castro

I have learned to be content whatever the circumstances.
—PHILIPPIANS 4:11

While Paul was in prison, he didn't know his future, whether he'd be free, punished, or killed. But he had learned contentment in all circumstances, good or bad.

The struggle with contentment. Even the great Apostle Paul struggled with greed and contentment. Of all the Ten Commandments, the most challenging for Paul to obey was the command not to covet. He battled with "every kind of covetous desire" (Rom. 7:7–8). Paul found it hard to cultivate the virtue of contentment due to the sin of greed in his heart.

For some people, it's hard to learn contentment in times of want and deprivation. However, it was probably much more challenging for Paul to be content when God blessed him abundantly through other people.

So, he wrote a thank you letter to the church in Philippi for their generous supply of monetary gifts and human resources (like Epaphroditus) to meet his practical needs in prison. Moreover, he asked them to stop supporting him because he was content with their offering (Phil. 4:17–18).

Finally, Paul thanked God for teaching him to be content in every situation, whether in want or plenty. He discovered the key to learning contentment was not in his own strength but through Him who gives the power (Phil. 4:12–13).

The source of contentment. Paul realized the source of contentment is believing in God's promise: "My God will supply all your needs according to His glorious riches in Christ Jesus" (Phil. 4:19). These needs include our physical needs for survival and safety.

Moreover, God can also satisfy our spiritual needs (unconditional love and acceptance) and our psychological needs (a sense of respect and importance). God promises that "He will satisfy your needs in a sun-scorched land" (Isa. 58:11a).

Unfortunately, the lack of contentment in Christ drives people to crave other things to satisfy the longings of their hearts, which only the presence of God Himself can satisfy. As Oswald Sanders rightly tells us, "There is only one Being who can satisfy the last aching abyss of the human heart, and that is the Lord Jesus Christ."

Father God, thank You for giving us everything we need
to live godly and contented lives. In Jesus's name, amen!

The Pursuit of Holiness

Dean De Castro

Pursue...holiness, without which no one will see the Lord.
—HEBREWS 12:14, NKJV

One of the most important lessons I've learned about this spiritual discipline is that holiness is not so much a matter of what you achieve as it is the grace that God provides.

John Catoir beautifully expresses this insight in his poem "Holiness Is":

> Holiness is not something that comes from doing good; we do good because we are holy.

> Holiness is not something we acquire by avoiding evil; we avoid evil because we are holy.

> Holiness is not the result of kindness; we are kind because we are holy.

> Holiness is not something that blossoms when we are courageous; we are courageous because we are holy.

> Holiness is not the result of character building; we build character because we are holy.

> Holiness is not a gift we obtain after a lifetime of service; we give service because we are holy.

Our Holiness is God with us, Immanuel. And while it's true that Holiness carries with it both the Cross and Resurrection, it is more a gift than a reward.

I was born and grew up in the Philippines. I learned that for the Catholic Church to confer the title of "saint" to a certain individual, they must fulfill at least two major requirements:

First, only dead people are considered to be candidates for sainthood. The Catholic Church has never conferred the title of saint to somebody still alive. Second, only dead people who had done great service to humanity would be inducted into sainthood.

In 1 Corinthians 1:2, Paul called the Corinthian believers "sanctified in Christ Jesus and holy." This Scripture disproves the doctrine of sainthood taught by the Catholic Church.

The Corinthian Christians were certainly alive when Paul called them "saints." In addition, they were probably the most immature believers in the early church. God knows our flaws and faults, but He chooses to look at us as if we had never sinned.

In *Holiness By Grace*, Bryan Chapell writes, "God looks at us as though we were as holy as His own Son, and treats us lovingly despite our many imperfections."

Father God, let us pursue holiness based on how You see us in Your Son: blameless and holy. In Jesus's name, amen!

Personal Responsibility and Holiness
Dean De Castro

Be holy.
—HEBREWS 12:14

We have settled the fact that holiness is both a gift and a Person: "Christ Jesus...who has become for us...holiness" (1 Cor. 1:30). God has already given us all the divine resources we need to live a godly life (2 Pet. 1:3).

But that doesn't mean we have no part to play in maintaining our holiness. On the contrary, there are some human responsibilities and efforts that help us keep and enjoy our freedom from sin. Let me briefly share two of them.

Refuse Satan's deception. Every person who struggles with any addictive behavior over and again argues, "I'm hopeless. I can't help myself. Change is impossible!" You can justify any addiction if you fall into Satan's deception that you cannot change: "It was born in you. It's your nature. Quit fighting it!"

Our Adversary constantly tempts us to fall back into that deception. The battle is lost once the mind believes the lie that we can do nothing about the problem of our own sins.

With God, there is no such thing as too far down or too late. Therefore, refuse to accept Satan's lie. "With man, this is impossible, but not with God; all things are possible with God" (Mark 10:27). Victory is possible only when the truth dawns that, in Christ, change is always possible!

Recapture your thoughts. The mind is the battlefield. Satan can put evil thoughts into our minds. He did it successfully with Judas (John 13:27), King David (1 Chron. 21:1), and Ananias and Sapphira (Acts 5:3). Therefore, don't accept and believe every thought that pops up in your head. Instead, "Take captive of every thought and make it submit to the obedience of Christ" (2 Cor. 10:5).

Satan is the father of lies (John 8:44). Since the beginning of humankind, his strategy has been to deceive us with his crafty wiles and falsehood (2 Cor. 11:3). His power *lies* in his *lies*.

Therefore, develop the discipline of reading, memorizing, and meditating on God's words (Josh. 1:8–9; Ps. 1:2). Allow the words of Christ to dwell in your hearts by mastering the four Gospels, and only dwell on thoughts that are true and God-glorifying (Phil. 4:8).

Father God, we affirm that change is possible for those
who believe in Christ. In Jesus's name, amen!

_____

_____

_____

_____

The Triumphant Cross of Christ
Dean De Castro

We are more than conquerors.
—ROMANS 8:37

The cross of Christ symbolizes His triumph over His enemies. Through our Lord's death on the cross, we are more than conquerors over our seven spiritual enemies: Satan, sin, old man, flesh, law, world, and death.

Satan. We fight Satan as a victor and not a victim. The cross has disarmed the power of Satan and his fallen angels over God's children (Col. 2:15). God has given us the spirit of power (2 Tim. 1:7a) over Satan's attempt to destroy our destiny (see John 13:2–3a).

Sin. We can say no and resist sin's temptations because Jesus's death on the cross has set us free from the legal ownership of sin over our mortal bodies (Rom. 6:12). We are no longer slaves to sin (Rom. 6:6b) but are now slaves of God and righteousness (Rom. 6:22, 18).

Old man. It refers to our former identity in Adam as Satan's children before conversion (John 8:44). The old self is our old nature that loves to sin but was crucified with Christ and is now gone forever (Rom. 6:6). God put us in Christ with a new heart that is perfect and holy and desires to obey God (Ezek. 36:26–27; Eph. 4:24).

Flesh. When God obliterated our old self with Christ on the cross, He gave us the power to overcome the sinful desires that remain in our brain and body (Gal. 5:24). We can now learn how to renew our minds and create new empowering beliefs, positive emotions, and godly habits.

Law. Jesus died to save us from the guilt and condemnation caused by the law's absolute demands (Col. 2:14; Rom. 8:1). God's love on the cross motivates us to obey all His commands (John 14:23).

World. When we discipline ourselves to keep our daily devotions, no earthly pleasures can match the wondrous treasure that God's love on the cross affords us (see Gal. 1:3–4; 6:14b).

Death. We do not shrink from death because of the Lamb's blood shed on the cross (Rev. 12:11).

> *Father God, may we never boast except in the cross of our Lord Jesus Christ (Gal. 6:14a). In Jesus's name, amen!*

Resist Your Enemy

Dean De Castro

Resist the devil, and he will flee from you.
—JAMES 4:7

Could our struggle with sin have anything to do with Satan and his demonic forces?

The stories of Ananias and Sapphira lying about their giving to the church and Judas betraying Jesus demonstrate that Satan has access to the human mind. The Adversary will deceive us into doubting everything Jesus has accomplished for us on the cross.

Romans 6:6 shows that when Jesus died, you were in Him and died to sin, your evil master. According to 2 Corinthians 5:17, when you are in Christ, the old spirit is gone, the new spirit has come, and you are a new creation.

But Satan never leaves us without a fight. The fact of our co-crucifixion with Christ does not stop the old illicit lover from coming around to harass, seduce, or try to press a new claim on us.

James commands us to "resist the devil and he will flee from you" (James 4:7). Whenever the father of lies attacks us, it is wise to take an inventory and check our armor.

Here are the seven pieces of armor listed in Ephesians 6:12–17. Included is a brief description of what each part ought to mean to us personally.

The belt of truthfulness: an attitude of total honesty and transparency, free from all falsehood, deceit, and hypocrisy (1 Pet. 2:1).

The breastplate of righteousness: appropriating the righteousness of Christ (2 Cor. 5:21) so that we can overcome the evil within us and around us and live righteously (1 Tim. 6:11).

The shoes of peace: being a peacemaker wherever we go as ambassadors of Christ (2 Cor. 5:20).

The shield of faith: a life lived with implicit trust in God and His Word (1 Tim. 6:12).

The helmet of salvation: confidence in the assurance of our salvation (John 20:31) and protection from Satan's deceptions with the wisdom of God (1 Cor. 1:30).

The sword of the Spirit: knowing the specific Scriptures to apply at the point of temptation (Ps. 119:11).

Prayer: an attitude of total dependency by communicating with our Commander to win life's daily battles.

> *Father God, help us be good soldiers of Christ as we*
> *defeat the devil's deceptions. In Jesus's name, amen!*

Some Reasons for Temptation

Erwin Lutzer
Adapted from *How to Say No to a Stubborn Habit*

And lead us not into temptation...
—MATTHEW 6:13A

Why is temptation so powerful? As might be expected, God has a purpose in allowing Satan to tempt us.

A test of loyalty. With all of its frightful possibilities for failure, temptation is God's method of testing our loyalties. We cannot say that we love someone until we have had to make some hard choices on their behalf. Similarly, we cannot say we love God unless we've said no to persistent temptations.

What happens when you are confronted with a tough decision— such as whether you should satisfy your passions or control them? Our response to temptation is an accurate barometer of our love for God.

Transformed passions. Temptation is God's character development curriculum. God uses our temptations and even our sins to help us climb the ladder of spiritual maturity.

Temptation is God's magnifying glass; it shows us how much work He has left to do in our lives. Temptation brings out the best or the worst in us. First, it brings impurities to the surface. Then God begins the siphoning process.

Temptations mean risk. The potential for devasting failure is ever with us. But precisely because the stakes are so high, the rewards of resisting are great. We cannot say no to temptation without saying yes to something far better.

Strength for our weakness. God uses our sins to show us His grace and power. The depressing effect of sin is offset by the good news of God's grace. Thus, Paul writes, "But where sin increased, grace abounded all the more" (Rom. 5:20).

Think about that particular sin of yours—the one that won't move off center stage. Maybe it's an obvious one: drunkenness, gluttony, or sexual misconduct. Or perhaps it's a very private sin in your mind: pride, anxiety, fear, or bitterness.

Whatever it is, God can deliver you from that sin. You and He can track it down, rout, and exterminate it. Sin need not have dominion over you. God will remove evil and replace it with something better.

Father God, may You show us Your strength and grace
as we face temptations daily. In Jesus's name, amen!

_____

_____

_____

_____

Divine Forces to Fight Temptation

Bryan Chapell

Adapted from *Holiness by Grace*

He will not let you be tempted beyond what you
can bear. But when you are tempted, He will also
provide a way out so that you can endure it.
—1 CORINTHIANS 10:13B

How can we stand against temptation?

Paul answers by urging us to put our faith in the divine forces at work to fight the battles of temptation.

A sovereign promise. God promises He will never allow Satan to tempt us beyond our ability to resist. Paul says, "There is a way out; God will always provide a way of escape."

Though our spiritual enemies surround us, God will show us a secret passage, provide us with an overpowering weapon, or cause a weakness in the enemy lines to help us escape temptation. The means are available for rescue from temptation.

A saving plan. When the escape is opened for us, we should not just stand idle. God commands us to flee temptation (1 Cor. 10:14). As Joseph fled temptation when Potiphar's wife tried to seduce him, we must be willing to run from what we know tempts us (Gen. 39:12).

We should understand ourselves well enough to keep distant from situations where it's tough to resist. We should not despise the grace of Christian friends and counselors that God provides in His church to help us become accountable.

The Savior's love. In earlier verses, Paul tells the Corinthians to flee the clutches of sin, but now he reminds them that they must escape to the arms of their Savior. In I Corinthians 10:16–17, Paul discusses the Lord's Supper. Why would Paul introduce this topic?

One reason is that the Corinthians defiled the Lord's Supper with idolatrous practices. But Paul's compassionate intention was to use the love of the Savior's sacrifice to woo wandering souls from spiritual danger. The love of the Savior draws us away from the lure of temptation.

What tempts us is pervasive and powerful, but Christ's love is no match for it all as we survey the wondrous cross and embrace the great escape it provides.

Father God, may we be drawn from the dangers
of temptation into the security of Your strong
and loving arms. In Jesus's name, amen!

_____

_____

_____

_____

Winning the War in Your Mind

Craig Groeschel

Adapted from *Winning the War in Your Mind*

Take captive every thought to make it obedient to Christ.
—2 CORINTHIANS 10:5

Our mind is a battlefield.

And the pursuit of holiness is won or lost in our minds. Satan's winning strategy is to persuade us to believe a lie. Here are four tools to control our thoughts and win the war in our minds.

The replacement principle (2 Tim. 1:7). A lie accepted as truth will affect your life as if it were true. Belief in a lie will also hold you back from doing what God calls you to do.

God has given us a new way to think, but must get on board, agree, and cooperate with Him. We must learn to identify these mistruths, argue with them by asking probing questions, and replace them with God's truth.

The rewire principle (Rom. 12:2). Our brains have neural pathways—mental ruts we create through repeatedly thinking the same thoughts—that trigger our automatic response to external stimuli.

To rewire unhealthy thought patterns in the brain, we seek appropriate Bible verses that directly address our battle against temptations.

We renew our minds by personalizing these Scriptures to form personal declarations, writing, thinking, and confessing until we believe them. These declarations of God's truth will become your new mental pathways to life and peace.

The reframe principle (Prov. 3:5–6). You can't control what happens to you, but you can control how you frame it. And the way you view it will dictate how you respond and behave.

When we reframe what happened from God's perspective, we can experience life without the old, irrational beliefs that have limited us and start seeing our experiences through the lens of God's goodness.

The rejoice principle (Ps. 106:1). It's easy to feel overwhelmed by everything happening around us. Instead of worrying, we put all our fears in our God box, trusting His love and provision for us.

Praying changes our brains, as does praising God. We praise Him for who He is, even if that is not what we want in the moment. As we pray and praise God, He shows up and gives us peace of mind.

Father God, renew our minds and transform
our lives. In Jesus's name, amen!

Old Lies, New Truth

Craig Groeschel

Adapted from *Winning the War in Your Mind*

Take...the sword of the Spirit, which is the Word of God.
—EPHESIANS 6:17

In Matthew 4, Jesus wielded the sword of the Holy Spirit—the Word of God—to overcome Satan's temptations.

So, likewise, we must use this weapon against the enemy's lies. Here are five steps to replace Satan's lies with God's truth.

Identify the problem. The best way to discover the lie holding you captive is by looking at the problems that plague you. They are personal and therefore easy to identify.

Ask probing questions. Pray for help in being honest with yourself, and ask soul-searching questions.

For many years, I struggled with overachievement and became a people-pleaser. So, whenever I am tempted to impress people, I ask myself the following questions: Why am I doing this? Is fear driving this? If so, what am I afraid of? When did this start in my childhood? What is the real need I'm trying to meet with this wrong behavior?

Pinpoint the lie. God showed me that I wrongly believed my worth was based on what other people thought about me.

Find at least one Bible verse to replace the lie. For example, Psalm 139:14 states, "I am fearfully and wonderfully made." "You were redeemed...with the precious blood of Christ" (1 Pet. 1:18–19).

Convert biblical principles into lifelong declarations. The goal of these statements is to have them become our new neural pathway against the lies that tempt. Write your confessions in a way that will speak to and inspire you.

Inspired by the truth of God's Word, here's my faith declaration: *My value is based not on what I do but on Him who made me. I am fearfully and wonderfully made. If God paid the price of His only Son for me, I have infinite value regardless of what other people think of me.*

Here's the plan: You should start your day in God's Word, digging trenches of truth and finding your declarations. Then write it, think it, and confess it until you believe it.

Father God, teach us how to use the Spirit's sword to cut Satan's lies into pieces. In Jesus's name, amen!

_____

_____

_____

_____

Set Your Mind

Bill Gillham
Adapted from *Lifetime Guarantee*

Set your minds on things above, not on earthly things.
—COLOSSIANS 3:2

What "things above" should you be thinking?

Well, don't dwell on golden streets and mansions. That won't transform you. Instead, see yourself seated with Christ in heaven (Eph. 2:6). Picture yourself resting there in Christ. You are a son or daughter in the Father's forever family. You are holy and blameless before Him. You are deeply loved, totally accepted, and incredibly blessed.

While relaxing there, envision the Father reaching around you with His strong right arm and snuggling you up to His chest. Can you smell how clean His robe is and feel its texture on your cheek?

I am not teaching a counterfeit power of positive thinking or Eastern religious meditation. Nor am I espousing human-made psychotherapy with Scriptures merely tacked on.

Setting our minds on something is what we do every day. Let me illustrate:

I want you to set your mind on eating a hamburger at your favorite burger restaurant. It needs just a tad more seasoning. Put some on it. Now take another bite. Ah, that's better. Take a swig of your favorite beverage. Let's make it a sweltering summer day, and you're dying for a drink. Feel it going down? Mmm, so refreshing.

You always set your mind, don't you? It's a daily practice. So why can't we use our sanctified imagination to set our minds on the things above?

God didn't give you an option of setting your mind or not as you choose. He has commanded you to do it. And when you do it, you're walking in *reality*. When you decide not to do it, you are walking in *deception*, controlled through the workings of the Evil One in your mind.

It is only through setting your mind on heavenly and biblical beliefs that you will begin to experience the victory of Christ and the characteristics of your true identity in Christ manifested in your daily life.

Father God, let us rest in our true identity
in Christ. In Jesus's name, amen!

_____

_____

_____

_____

You Can Lessen the Conflict

Erwin Lutzer
Adapted from *How to Say No to a Stubborn Habit*

*I desire to do Your will, O my God. Your
Law is within my heart.*
—PSALM 40:8

Does temptation lose its power?

Not completely. Even when we are motivated by a desire to please God, we experience conflict because God often requires obedience that runs counter to human motivation.

Two magnets. Visualize a piece of steel suspended between two magnets. It fluctuates, unsure whether to swing right or left. Then, for a moment, it wavers. It could go either way because it is simultaneously drawn in two directions.

Then, as it begins to swing to the right, it wavers for a second and continues to move in that direction. Finally, it carries more rapidly to the right; it cannot swing back anymore. It is out of the range of the left magnet's power.

Two choices. You may be hovering between God and the world, between your desires and God's. No one knows what your eventual decision will be. But the farther you go in God's direction, the less attraction the world will have. Saying yes to God can be habit-forming.

I can't resist enticing thoughts simply by saying, "I resist that thought!" The thought returns repeatedly. However, I can push my thoughts toward Scripture—quote a verse, offer praise, or renew my fellowship with God. Only in the presence of the Almighty does the world lose its lure.

God has given you the resources to say no to sin. For "it is God who is at work in you, both to will and to work for His good pleasure"

(Phil. 2:13). God works in us by energizing our will. He helps us make the decisions we ought to make and ultimately really want to make.

Don't think you are powerless against a barrage of temptations. Whatever your sins, there is hope. You can say no to any stubborn habit. And the more you learn to love Christ, the less you will be attracted by the world.

> *Father God, help us constantly turn our eyes upon*
> *our Lord so that the magnetic pull of the law of sin*
> *will lose its power over us. In Jesus's name, amen!*

_____

_____

_____

_____

The Cross Condemned Sin

Dean De Castro

And so He [God] condemned sin in the flesh
[the broken body of Jesus on the cross].
—ROMANS 8:3

Sin is the evil spirit of Satan.

It has produced all kinds of individual sins in this world. It caused all the evils that destroyed the peace and prosperity of humankind. However, the death of Christ on the cross has condemned sin as the tyrant that enslaves humanity.

The cross of Christ has paid the penalty of sin. All have sinned and deserve to die because the penalty for sinning is death (Rom. 6:23). Therefore, someone has to die, either you or a heaven-sent substitute. Thankfully, Jesus was the sacrificial Lamb God killed in our place.

The Chinese word for "righteousness" consists of two characters. On top is "sheep" and under it is "I." The knife of God's punishment fell upon Jesus, the Lamb of God, and His blood cleanses us from all our sins.

The cross of Christ has canceled the propriety of sin. Every human being is a sinner by birth. When Adam and Eve sinned, they sold humanity to sin. Therefore, sin has the legal right to own us. We don't have any choice but to sin; it's our nature.

However, through His death on the cross, Jesus has brought us from the slave market of sin and adopted us into His royal family. Therefore, whenever evil tries to oppress us into following its bidding, we can always present the adoption certificate and claim that "God has adopted us in the Beloved" (Eph. 1:5).

The cross of Christ has suspended the principle of sin. Although the death of Christ has already condemned sin on the cross, unfortunately, it still exists. It continues to exert tremendous power on those who do not know its power has been usurped. However, God has given us the law of the Spirit of life, which suspends the law of sin and death (Rom. 8:2).

It's like the law of aerodynamics, which has the power to overcome the law of gravity. So long as we focus on God and His words, we can overcome the gravitational pull of sin (Ps. 119:11).

Father God, let us resist sin from ruling over
our bodies. In Jesus's name, amen!

The Sequence of Sinning

Watchman Nee
Adapted from *The Spiritual Man*, vol. 1

For we know that our old self was crucified with Him
so that the body ruled by sin might be done away
with, that we should no longer be slaves to sin.
—ROMANS 6:6

This verse presents to us three figures: sin (singular in Greek), the old man, and the body. There are significant distinctions among these three. They each have a different share in the matter of committing sins.

Definitions. Sin here is commonly known as the "root of sin." It exerts its power so that we might obey our old man and commit sins. The old man is our old personality that loves sins and is subject to the power of sin.

The body of sin refers to the physical part of man that is full of sinful desires. Sin is expressed through it; otherwise, sin is merely an unseen power.

The sequence of sinning. Every time a person sins, it results from the collaboration of these three. First, sin exerts its power, then the old man concedes to the suggestion of evil, and finally, the body carries out the act of sinning.

God's way. Some preachers teach that if a man can uproot and eradicate the source of evil, he will no longer sin. On the other hand, ascetics teach people that subduing and suppressing the evil desires of the body will make one holy.

Romans 6:6, however, clearly shows us the way of God. God does not intend to uproot the sin within nor suppress the body without. God deals with the old man in the middle.

When Christ went to the cross, He also brought us there to be crucified with Him *once and forever*. Our co-crucifixion with Christ is an accomplished fact. No one doubts that Christ has been crucified. So, why do we question whether or not our old man has been crucified?

Therefore, brothers, let us pray until God gives us the revelation that will allow us to truthfully and genuinely say "that our old man has been crucified with Christ" (KJV).

Father God, may the Spirit of wisdom and revelation
enlighten the eyes of our hearts (Eph. 1:17) to understand
our co-crucifixion with Christ. In Jesus's name, amen!

Three Key Steps to Experience Freedom from Sin

Chuck Swindoll

Adapted from *Swindoll's New Testament Insights on Romans*

We should no longer be slaves to sin.
—ROMANS 6:6C

Although the death of Christ on the cross has officially emancipated us from the slavery of sin, yet, the majority of Christians today have not learned to turn their legal status as freed slaves into a practical experience as free men and women in Christ.

In Romans 6:2–11, Paul presents three specific steps to experiencing genuine freedom in Christ.

Know the truth. "For we know..." (v. 6). This is the truth of our *identification* with Christ in His death, burial, and resurrection (vv. 2–11). Genuinely, our identity becomes united with Christ such that His experience becomes ours. And this is true whether we know it or not.

Christ died to sin, and we died with Him. Therefore, we have been liberated from bondage to sin (v. 7). Before emancipation, we could not refuse sin's authority, but now we do not have to obey its commands.

We were also identified with Christ in His resurrection to live a new life (v. 4b) and live for God (v. 10b). The power to overcome any evil lives within you: none other than God in the person of the Holy Spirit. Call on Him to help!

Consider the truth. Once we know that God's gift is available, we must reckon this truth as reality (v. 11). Habits are tough to break. Therefore, we must repeatedly and continuously *consider* divine truth and *decide* it is true. Count on it and live it out.

Present our bodies to truth. Having decided something is accurate, we must change our behavior accordingly. We must present ourselves to our new Master to enjoy the benefits of new life. Your mind controls your body, so take command and make your body operate in agreement with what you have accepted as true (vv. 12–13).

Knowing, considering, and presenting is not the entire solution to our problems. And I don't mean to oversimplify the process of spiritual growth. Deeply entrenched patterns of sin require much more attention than a simple accounting procedure. However, it is a necessary beginning.

Father God, let our legal emancipation from sin become
a daily reality in our lives. In Jesus's name, amen!

_____

_____

_____

_____

The Birth of Sin

Dean De Castro

After desire has conceived, it gives birth to sin.
—JAMES 1:15

We usually think of sin as a single act. But today's verse describes it as the result of a process. In James 1:14–15, this process of sin has four stages.

Desire (v. 14). God created us with an innate desire, a legitimate need and want to survive in this world. This is good but can drive us to excess. So, eating is normal; gluttony, however, is a sin. Sleep is normal; laziness is a sin. Sex within the marriage covenant is honorable, but God "will judge the adulterers and all the sexually immoral" (Heb. 13:4). The key to holiness is controlling our God-given desires through the power of the Holy Spirit.

Deception (v. 14). James used the illustrations of a hunter and a fisherman who use bait to entice and catch their prey, "being carried away and enticed." So, likewise, Satan is the father of lies who tempts us with the temporary pleasures of sin (Heb. 12:25). He even deceives us into thinking that temptation comes from God (James 1:13, 16).

As followers of Christ, it's a priority to know the Bible so you can detect the bait and refuse to fall into Satan's trap. God's Word keeps us from sinning (Ps. 119:11).

Disobedience (v. 15). James changed the image from hunting and fishing to the birth of a baby. As John MacArthur writes, "When lust is seduced (so to speak) by the baited hook, it becomes pregnant in the womb of a person's will. Finally, the act of sin occurs."

It is dangerous for Christians to live by their emotions. Feeling-oriented believers easily fall into temptation. Mature believers, on the other hand, obey God's will no matter how they feel. As such, they are willing to endure the pain of denying their sinful cravings and passions.

Death (v. 15). Disobedience gives birth to death, not life. Unfortunately, for some believers, it may mean premature death (1 Cor. 11:30). Therefore, whenever you face temptations, take your eyes off the bait and look ahead to see the consequences of sin. As you heed God's warning and see this final tragedy, it will encourage you not to yield to temptation.

Father God, help us abort the birth of sin through
repentance and confession. In Jesus's name, amen!

_____

_____

_____

_____

Slave of Jesus Christ

Dean De Castro

...slave of God and of the Lord Jesus Christ.
—JAMES 1:1, NLT

"Slave of God and the Lord Jesus Christ" is not a title reserved exclusively for the apostles and full-time Christian workers.

It's the identity and status of every born-again believer. Being Christian doesn't imply that we no longer function as slaves. Either you are a slave of sin (Rom. 6:17a) or you are a slave of God (Rom. 6:22) and righteousness (Rom. 6:18).

Free from sin. Every human being is a sinner by birth (Rom. 3:23). All are born slaves of sin. Some may object that they are free to do whatever they *want*. But the sad reality is that they are not free to do what they *ought*.

Jesus came to set people free from sin. The cross of Christ has condemned sin in His body (Rom. 8:3b). Thus, Romans 6:14 states that sin is no longer our master. The death and resurrection of Jesus Christ have set believers free from the penalty and dominion of sin over their bodies (Rom. 6:23; 6:6–7).

Free to serve. Many Christians have misunderstood the idea of freedom in Christ. Although the Bible teaches that Christians are no longer slaves of sin, this does not imply that we are then free to do whatever we want.

Paul warns us not to use our freedom in Christ as an excuse to indulge in our sinful desires. Instead, we should exercise our freedom to serve God and others (Gal. 5:13–14).

The truth is we were saved to serve God (Phil. 2:11–12), our family (1 Tim. 5:8), our neighbors (Luke 10:25–37), our church (1 Cor. 14:26), and others at the workplace (1 Tim. 6:1–2).

Paul argues that genuine born-again Christians will not continue to practice sin because they have committed to obeying God willingly as slaves (Rom. 6:15–18).

In his commentary on the book of Romans, John Stott explains, "Since through conversion, we offered ourselves to God to be His slaves, and in consequence are committed to obedience, how can we possibly claim the freedom to sin?...Once we offer ourselves to God as His slaves, we are permanently and unconditionally at His disposal. Having chosen our Master, we have no choice but to obey Him."

Father God, we reaffirm our vow to obey You as
our loving Master. In Jesus's name, amen!

The Discipline of Commitment

Jerry Bridges
Adapted from *The Discipline of Grace*

*I urge you...In view of God's mercy, to offer your bodies
as a living sacrifice, holy and pleasing to God.*
—ROMANS 12:1

If we hope to progress in the pursuit of holiness, commitment is essential.

In today's Scripture, Paul calls for commitment from Christ's devoted disciples. We can learn at least three lessons about the level of commitment God expects from us to grow in practical holiness.

The object of commitment. "Pleasing to God." As believers, we can be committed to a set of Christian values or a discipleship lifestyle without being committed to God Himself. It is also possible that our commitment to holiness is a commitment to our self-esteem and not to God.

We should not seek holiness to feel good about ourselves or avoid the sense of shame and guilt that follows the committing of persistent sins in our lives. But instead, we offer ourselves—spirit, soul, and body—to God, and in doing so, commit ourselves to pursue a way of life that is most pleasing to Him.

The act of commitment. "Offer yourselves." The word "offer" conveys the idea of a decisive, once-for-all dedication or commitment. We are to put our bodies at God's disposal with the same finality that an Israelite would bring an animal sacrifice to the temple to be offered to God.

At the same time, it is to be a *living* sacrifice, signifying a constant dedication or a perpetual sacrifice never to be neglected or recalled. So, the commitment to holiness must be a firm commitment that is continually reaffirmed.

Dean De Castro   333

The motivation of commitment. "In view of God's mercy." Because of God's mercy, Paul urges us today to commit our bodies as living sacrifices, holy and pleasing to God. God's mercy is revealed to us in the gospel, and that we have experienced that is the ground for our commitment.

Such a commitment as Paul called for would indeed be legalistic and oppressive if it were not grounded in love. Thus, God has asked us for a response of love and gratitude, which is expressed in loving devotion.

Father God, let us commit to please You by
living a holy life. In Jesus's name, amen!

The Spirit of Revelation

Dean De Castro

May [God] give you the Spirit of wisdom and revelation.
—EPHESIANS 1:17

The Holy Spirit is called the Spirit of revelation in Ephesians 1:17.

Without revelation from the Holy Spirit, all biblical information stored in our brains is useless in changing our character. And this is especially the case in understanding the cross of Christ and its meaning for us.

Many Christians know that Christ died on the cross to forgive their sins. But very few understand that they died with Christ on the cross to be set free from sin. In both instances, we need the Holy Spirit to reveal these mysteries and how they impact our behavior and character.

Christ died for us. We see in 1 Corinthians 2:14 that an unsaved person doesn't know and cannot know that Christ died for them because Satan blinds their mind. Only the Holy Spirit can reveal to them that Jesus Christ is the Son of God and the Savior of the world. Also, only the Holy Spirit can make people believe and accept that their sins are forgiven and they are now God's children (Rom. 8:16).

We died with Christ. Paul states in Romans 6:6–7 that we died with Christ to sin and are free from it. Paul tells us, "When Jesus died, you were in Him, and you died too. The old man is gone, and the new man has come, and you are a new creation in Christ Jesus" (2 Cor. 5:17).

Are you in Christ? If so, then you are a brand new creation. We don't look it all the time. We don't feel it all the time. And we don't think it all the time. But we are. Because God says so. He has made us into His righteousness (2 Cor. 5:21). To God, you are as though you've never sinned. When He looks at you, He sees the divine nature of His Son.

Jesus died on the cross two thousand years ago in this visible and temporal realm. However, the truth that we died with Him to be free from sin belongs to the unseen and eternal realm that only the Holy Spirit can reveal to us.

Father God, help us understand and experience the
reality of our freedom from sin. In Jesus's name, amen!

_____

_____

_____

_____

Functions of Faith

Dean De Castro

Count yourselves dead to sin but alive to God in Christ Jesus.
—ROMANS 6:11

After knowing that your old self is dead and gone, the next step is to believe it by faith.

The word "count" in Romans 6:11 is synonymous with faith. By faith, we believe that in Christ we died to sin and are alive to God. Biblical faith does three things:

Faith sees. By faith, see yourself as a victor and not a victim. Faith makes us "certain of what we do not see" (Heb. 11:1).

We fight sin from a position of strength, not of weakness, because Christ has already condemned and defeated it with His body on the cross (Rom. 8:3).

The Israelites' victim mindset let them see their enemies as giants and themselves as grasshoppers. Unfortunately, their unbelief cost them a generation. On the other hand, David saw Goliath's head in his hand and saved a whole nation. In God's economy, to believe is to see (see John 11:40).

Faith speaks. By faith, declare your new identity in Christ. "With that same spirit of faith, we also believe and therefore speak" (2 Cor. 4:13).

Confess, aloud if opportunity permits, your new identity in Christ. Here are examples of faith declarations:

- I am the righteousness of God in Christ Jesus (2 Cor. 5:21).
- I am perfectly holy and complete in Christ (Heb. 10:14; Col. 2:10).
- I am precious in God's eyes because He loves and honors me (Isa. 43:3–5).

- I am a saint who occasionally sins (1 Cor. 1:2; 1 John 2:1).

Faith acts. By faith, act as Jesus would act. "Faith without deeds is dead" (James 2:26).

Since the resurrected Jesus now lives in you (Gal. 2:20), choose to act like Christ, speaking loving, kind, and inspiring words to the difficult people in your life, even when you feel like tearing them down.

Don't accept Satan's lie that you are a hypocrite when you act contrary to how you feel. Instead, choose to live by faith over your fickle feelings, and your emotions will gradually conform to your deep-seated biblical values and beliefs.

Father God, let us please You with our
faith. In Jesus's name, amen!

_____

_____

_____

_____

The Old Man is Gone

Dean De Castro

*Knowing this, that our old man [self] was
crucified with Him [Christ]...*
—ROMANS 6:6A, NKJV

When Christ died on the cross, God included the old man to die with Him.

God put us in Christ (1 Cor. 1:30). His death and resurrection became ours. Understanding that our old man was put to death and destroyed is essential to living a holy and victorious life.

The meaning of the old man. The term "old man" refers to our old identity with Adam in our unregenerate state. It is who we once were in Adam. Paul describes the unregenerate, in-Adam man in Romans 5.

The old man was the old identity that connected believers to Adam—the head of the ancient race condemned by God. That part of our life history in Adam ended at the cross.

Bishop Handley Moule translates Romans 6:6 as "Our old man, our old state, as out of Christ and under Adam's headship, under guilt and in moral bondage, was crucified with Christ."

The death of the old man. When the Roman soldiers crucified Jesus on the cross, God included the old self to die with Christ. The death of Christ on the cross terminated our old identity as slaves of sin (v. 6c).

Christ's resurrection from the dead gave us a new divine life, the life of Christ Himself. We have become new creatures in Christ who are holy, perfect, and set apart for God. This last description is what the term "saint" means in the original language.

How can we be comfortable calling ourselves saints while fully aware of our shortcomings and failures? At this point, it is essential to understand our new identity in Christ. *One's identity is based not on one's behavior but on one's birth.*

The Bible teaches that we become sinners, not because we sin, but because we are born sinners. Therefore, God calls Christians saints not because they are religious but because they are born of God.

Our identity will change our behavior. Knowing who we are in Christ will remind us to act accordingly. Therefore, we must constantly remind ourselves who we are: beloved children of a holy God.

Father God, help us Pursue Holiness because
You are holy. In Jesus's name, amen!

New Creation in Christ

Dan Stone

Adapted from *The Rest of the Gospel*

Therefore, if anyone is in Christ, he is a new creation. The
old has passed away; behold, the new has come.
—2 CORINTHIANS 5:17, ESV

Are you in Christ?

If so, you are a new creation. At your new birth, God birthed in you a new spirit, created in His likeness, holiness, and righteousness (Eph. 4:24).

David Needham says in *Birthright* that at the moment of conversion, a new person who had never existed before comes into being. You are not a repaint job but a brand new creature.

God has crucified the old you on the cross with Christ. The new you was born of the Holy Spirit, raised with Christ, and seated in the heavens (Eph. 2:6).

The old has passed away. Passed to whom? The old you is gone to the One who is in charge of the universe. To Him, you aren't the same person you were before you entered into Christ. Instead, you're a brand new creation in Christ.

It may not disappear as quickly as you'd like in the visible and temporal realm, but it's gone to God. God sees the unseen and eternal. So, the question is this: Who's keeping the score, you or God?

The new has come. God has a different point of reference for us than we do. He doesn't fasten His attention on our flesh or false self. Instead, God looks at us as new creatures in Christ.

When God looks at you, He sees the nature of His Son. He sees you as love, joy, and peace. He sees you as righteous, redeemed, and justified. He sees you as perfect and complete (Col. 2:10a). You are not only accepted by God; you are acceptable to Him.

In your *spirit*, you are a new creation. Do you look like a new creation? No. You look like the same old Tom or Jane. Externally, you still are. But you have been renewed from within. You are already a new creature. You don't have to try continually to make yourself a new creature. It's a losing proposition.

> *Father God, help us understand the new people that*
> *we have become in Christ. In Jesus's name, amen!*

_____

_____

_____

_____

The New Human Spirit

Dean De Castro

But he who is joined to the Lord is one spirit with Him.
—1 CORINTHIANS 6:17, NKJV

How many Christians have the revelation that they are spiritual beings, have a soul, and live in a body? Remember 1 Thessalonians 5:23b: "May your whole spirit, soul, and body be kept blameless at the coming of our Lord Jesus Christ."

The new human spirit and the Holy Spirit are one. God and we are one. That sounds heretical, but that is what the Bible says in 1 Corinthians 6:17. God has permanently joined Himself to our new regenerated human spirit.

The old human spirit (the old man) we inherited from Adam died with Christ on the cross (Rom. 6:6). God crucified the old man (indwelt by and enslaved to sin) and gave us a new spirit, created "in true righteousness and holiness" (Eph. 4:24). It was the fulfillment of Ezekiel 36:26–27a: "Moreover, I will give you a new heart and put a new spirit within you...and I will put My Spirit within you."

God removed our old sinful human spirit and created a new human spirit, born of Him, and put His Spirit in us. The Holy Spirit is now living in our regenerated human spirit. This truth impacts how we live our Christian life.

The Holy Spirit works directly through our new human spirit. Below are just some of the Scriptures that show the direct relationship between the Holy Spirit and our new human spirit:

- Regeneration occurs in our spirit (John 3:6).
- We worship God in our spirit (John 4:24).
- We pray in the spirit (Eph. 6:18; Rom. 8:26–27).

- The Holy Spirit confirms with our spirit the assurance of our salvation (Rom. 8:15–16).
- The Holy Spirit infuses power into our spirit (inner being) (Eph. 3:16).
- We understand the deep things of God through our spirit (1 Cor. 2:10–11).

Watchman Nee reminds us, "The knowledge most lacking among believers today concerns the existence of the human spirit and its function...Because of this, believers do not know how to cooperate with God, control themselves, and fight against Satan, since all these three things require the work of the spirit."

Father God, thank You for Your Spirit dwelling in the deepest part of our being. In Jesus's name, amen!

_____

_____

_____

_____

Remember Your Identity

Dean De Castro

From now on we regard no one from a worldly point of view.
—2 CORINTHIANS 5:16

This verse says that we are no longer known by our old identity but by who we *now are* in Christ.

Understanding our identity in Christ is one of the most significant principles of Christian living in Scripture. It is the key to unlocking and releasing you from the shackles of whatever may be holding you hostage.

In his book *Grace Revolution,* Joseph Prince wisely observes that many struggling with sin, addiction, and destructive behaviors don't have the revelation of their new covenant identity in Christ. When you see a believer struggling with sin, it is often a case of mistaken identity.

Let's look at what God has to say about our new identity in Christ.

I am holy. "Put on the new self, created to be like God in true righteousness and holiness" (Eph. 4:24). God says that the old you has died, and the newly resurrected you is holy. But you may say, "I don't act holy." The Word doesn't state that you always act holy. Never call unholy what God has called holy (see Acts 10:14).

I am a conqueror over evil. If you are in Christ, you are no longer a victim but a victor. Romans 8:37 says that you are more than a conqueror through Christ. Your experiences may not support this view, but God's Word does. So, rest in His victory.

I am complete. "In Him, you have been made complete" (Col. 2:10). You are complete in Christ. How can you improve on perfect? Hebrews 10:14 says, "Because by one sacrifice He has made perfect forever those who are being made holy."

In short, the process of pursuing practical holiness begins with the fact that we're already holy and perfect. Therefore, changing our actions starts with clarifying our identity.

Satan plans to defeat you by confusing your identity because he knows that our self-perception will affect our decisions and reactions to life's circumstances. Knowing our true identity will increase our confidence to consistently act as who we are in Christ.

Father God, show us our true identity as believers
and empower us to live out that identity by
your power. In Jesus's name, amen!

_____

_____

_____

_____

Overcoming the Flesh

Dean De Castro

And those who belong to Christ Jesus have crucified the flesh.
—GALATIANS 5:24

The flesh is not synonymous with the old man. God obliterated it when Jesus died on the cross (Rom. 6:6). But on the other hand, the flesh remains with us until we die.

The meaning of the flesh. Most of the time, it refers to our physical body, with its appetites and impulses. But metaphorically speaking, it refers to the old man's sinful ways and deceitful desires programmed in the brain and encoded in the body.

John MacArthur notes, "We have been removed from the unregenerate self's presence and control, so we should not follow the remaining memories of the old sinful ways as if we were still under its evil influence."

The things of the FLESH. Romans 8:5 describes believers as those who don't mind the things of the flesh (KJV). So what are the things of the flesh in daily, practical living? Let me share the five elements of our enemy based on the acronym FLESH.

Family upbringing. Whatever sinful behaviors we struggle with could be attributed to our family of origin and culture. For example, Paul persecuted Christians because of his Jewish upbringing (Phil. 3:4–6).

Lies of Satan. The enemy uses lies in deceiving believers to walk in the flesh and not in the Spirit (see Matt. 16:23).

Emotions. If we are not controlled by the power of the Holy Spirit, our toxic feelings and compulsive cravings can lead us to sinful living (1 Pet. 2:11).

Self-will. Romans 7 describes how Paul tried to obey God through his stubborn self-will and failed miserably (see Gal. 3:3).

Harmful habits. Romans 8:13 commands us to kill the evil practices of the body.

The crucifixion of the flesh. In a sense, we crucified our flesh, along with its lusts and passions, when we repented of our sins and made a commitment: "No to ungodliness and worldly passions, and to live self-controlled, upright, and godly lives in the present age" (Titus 2:12; see also Acts 2:40–41).

So, true believers have crucified the flesh and will continue to do so by the power of the Holy Spirit (Gal. 5:16).

> *Father God, let us renew our vow to kill the*
> *flesh daily. In Jesus's name, amen!*

The Discipline of Mortification

Jerry Bridges

Adapted from *The Discipline of Grace*

Ye through the Spirit do mortify the deeds of the body.
—ROMANS 8:13, KJV

The command to "mortify" means to put to death the sinful patterns we commit in thought, word, or deed. How do we then put to death the evil practices of the body?

First, Paul did not say to mortify indwelling sin, but rather *sins,* which are the various expressions of indwelling sin. We cannot eliminate indwelling sin in this life. It will be with us until the day we die.

Second, it means to break the habit pattern we have developed of continually giving in to that particular sin. The goal of mortification is to weaken the habits of sin by making the right choices.

Third, mortification involves dealing with all known sins in one's life. Without a purpose to obey all of God's Word, isolated attempts to mortify a particular sin are of no avail. We must hate all sin for what it is: an expression of rebellion against God.

Fourth, we must put to death the flesh continually as it seeks to assert itself in various ways in our lives. As long as we live, we must make it our business to mortify the indwelling power of sin.

Fifth, we are often troubled with a persistent sin only because it disturbs our peace and makes us feel guilty. Instead, we need to know that whenever we sin, "The Lord was grieved...and His heart was filled with pain" (Gen. 6:6).

Sixth, there is an underlying hostility when the word "mortify" is used in the New Testament (Matt. 26:59). Now apply that sense of hostility toward the sin you wish to kill. See it for what it is—a rebellion against God, breaking His law, despising His authority, and grieving His heart.

Last, we must realize that the sin we are dealing with is none other than a continual exalting of our sinful desires over God's known will. It is always emotionally painful to say no to those desires. That is why Paul used such strong language as "put to death."

> *Father God, let us endure the pain of mortification by Your Spirit's resurrection power. In Jesus's name, amen!*

_____

_____

_____

_____

No More Condemnation

Dean De Castro

Therefore, there is now no condemnation
for those who are in Christ Jesus.
—ROMANS 8:1

Satan loves to torment God's people. He constantly reminds them of their past and holds their sins before them even after God forgave them.

However, today's Scripture comforts us, telling us that we can now live a guilt-free life because of Christ's death and resurrection.

The death of Christ condemns the law. Satan uses God's law—holy, righteous, and good (Rom. 7:12)—to charge people for their failure to keep it perfectly (Gal. 3:10). However, Jesus died to save us from guilt by "nailing it [the law] to the cross" (Col. 2:14).

Jesus's death also liberated us from legalism, the false thinking that people can use their effort and willpower to gain God's approval.

Legalistic people feel condemned most of the time. It is because they love to compare themselves to others, criticize themselves when they fall short of someone else's achievements, and judge others when they violate their standards.

When God forgives our sins, He also chooses to forget them. "For I will forgive their wickedness and will remember their sins no more" (Heb. 8:12; also see Isa. 43:25). God doesn't let our sins keep Him from loving us.

The resurrection of Jesus fulfills the law. When Jesus rose from the dead, He came to dwell in our new hearts through the Holy Spirit (1 Cor. 6:19). Jesus says God's law would never pass away because it reveals God's will (Matt. 5:17–18). But it is only fulfilled when we walk in the Spirit and not in the flesh (Rom. 8:4).

God sent His Son into the world to justify us and His Holy Spirit into our regenerated hearts to sanctify us. Therefore, you "have been chosen...through the sanctifying work of the Spirit, for the obedience to Jesus Christ" (1 Pet. 1:2).

God makes demands through His laws, but He also enables us to meet them through His Spirit. As Charles Swindoll writes, "A rigid master was the law, demanding brick, denying straw; But when with gospel-tongue it sings, it bids me fly, and gives me wings."

Father God, thank You for setting us free from the law's condemnation and enabling us to obey You by Your Spirit. In Jesus's name, amen!

_____

_____

_____

_____

Overcoming the World

Dean De Castro

*...the Lord Jesus Christ, who gave Himself for our
sins to rescue us from the present evil age.*
—GALATIANS 1:3–4

Three times, Jesus referred to Satan as the "ruler of this world" (John 12:31; 14:30; 16:11).

Satan uses the things of the world to entice people to sin against God. Specifically, Satan makes use of the lust of the flesh, the lust of the eyes, and the pride of life (1 John 2:16). I prefer to call them the three *P*'s: pleasure, possessions, and power.

Pleasure. The world only offers the temporary fun of sin (Heb. 11:25). But Jesus is the object of real happiness and satisfaction (1 Pet. 1:8):

> He is the Security you seek in money.
> He is the High you seek in alcohol.
> He is the Ecstasy you seek in sex.
> He is the Song you seek in music.
> He is the Beauty you seek in travel.
> He is the Wisdom you seek in books.
> He is the Peace you seek in worry.
> It is Jesus Whom You seek.

Possessions. In Matthew 6:21–22, Jesus refers to the inner eye and its longing for worldly possessions. But materialism never satisfies and produces happiness. As Jesus warns us, "What good will it be for a man if he gains the whole world, yet forfeits his soul" (Matt. 16:26).

Benjamin Franklin wisely observes, "The more a man has, the more he wants. Instead of its filling a vacuum, it makes one. If it satisfies one want, it doubles and triples that want another way."

Jesus also promises that if we first seek God's kingdom and His righteousness, He will give us all the things we need to sustain life (Matt. 6:33).

Power. Worldly people are willing to sacrifice their moral values and even their families on the altar of power, position, and fame. Yet the Bible teaches that God will award real honor and prestige in His future kingdom (Matt. 25:21).

Unlike the false teachers in Galatia, the Apostle Paul did not seek power and control over his followers. Paul had crucified the world, with its pleasure, possessions, and power, on the cross. These worldly things no longer appealed to him because he had died to them (Gal. 6:14).

Father God, help us to not love the world and the
things of the world. In Jesus's name, amen!

_____

_____

_____

_____

Media Diet

David Murray

Adapted from *The Happy Christian*

Whatever is true...think about such things.
—PHILIPPIANS 4:8

We live in an increasingly pessimistic culture where the internet and TV feed us daily with a gloomy diet of negative news.

As Christians, we can starve ourselves of mental junk and replace it with wholesome thoughts. In Philippians 4:8, Paul lists six characteristics of healthy thoughts.

"Whatever is true." Avoid listening to lies, misrepresentation, imbalance, and distortions on both the left and the right of the political spectrum. Instead, gather facts rather than opinions, and use the truth to influence your outlook and mood. Surround yourself with truth tellers, and avoid muck spreaders.

"Whatever is noble." The media celebrates sinful acts more than righteous acts. People who are striving to live a dignified life do not make news headlines. They are usually caricatured as pitiable, contemptible, or irrelevant if they are ever pictured on TV or on film at all. Paul urges us to seek out and celebrate right behavior.

"Whatever is pure." Most people find it hard to escape the tendency to turn from the light and be attracted to the dark side of life. Partly it's because there is often more darkness around than light. Therefore, it's more important to talk about faithful marriages, outstanding young people, generous philanthropists, and honest politicians.

"Whatever is lovely." Unfortunately, most of us live in places where it's often challenging to locate beauty in our immediate surroundings. We need to get out of the city, see the stunning mountains, savor the fragrance of the forest, taste fresh and healthy produce, and listen

to beautiful bird songs. Find ways to increase your intake of beauty through your various senses.

"Whatever is of good report." Focus on what is constructive rather than destructive. Don't look for what you can critique; look for what you can admire, whether it's a good product, a helpful service, a wise insight, or a superb article, and praise and celebrate it.

"If there is any virtue and if there is anything praiseworthy, meditate on these things." Focusing on these subjects takes enormous mental effort, but the rewards are worth it.

Father God, grant us the grace to remain positive
in a pessimistic world. In Jesus's name, amen!

_____

_____

_____

_____

The Temptation of Technology

J. D. Greear
Adapted from jdgreear.com

...lovers of pleasure rather than lovers of God. . .
—2 TIMOTHY 3:4

Christians who are out of fellowship with God are always craving for more. Their radar is always on, searching for the next excitement. As a result, they become lovers of pleasure rather than lovers of God.

Nowhere is this more evident than in the way we use our phones. Scientists say many of us are so attached to our phones because when we look at social media, a chemical called dopamine is released, the same substance that causes people to get addicted to drugs and porn and other vices. This explains why you instinctively reach for your phone when you are bored.

An article by John Piper gives six reasons why we are so drawn to technology first thing in the morning and at the first sign of a lull:

Novelty candy. We have FOMO (fear of missing out). We're afraid that our friends will know something we don't know. Sociologists have classified a condition where you experience legitimate anxiety of being separated from your phones called nomophobia—i.e., no mobile phobia. Without Jesus, your FOMO will lead to nomophobia. But with Jesus, you'll have NoMoFoMo.

Ego candy. We want to know what people are saying about us, so we get on social media and look for likes and positive comments.

Entertainment candy. We want to feed on what is fascinating, weird, strange, fantastic, or shocking.

Boredom avoidance. We want to put off the day ahead, especially when it looks routine to us.

Responsibility avoidance. We want to put off the responsibilities God has given us as bosses, employees, fathers, mothers, and students.

Hardship avoidance. We avoid dealing with relationship conflicts or the pain, disease, and disabilities in our bodies.

These are signs of an unhealthy soul that needs a hit of an entertainment or distraction drug to find satisfaction and enjoyment.

But as Christ's followers, we are supposed to have such satisfaction in knowing and doing the will of God that we are not susceptible to other cravings.

> *Father God, who have we in heaven but You?*
> *And earth has nothing we desire besides You*
> *(Ps. 73:25). In Jesus's name, amen!*

Overcoming the Fear of Death

Dean De Castro

By His death, He might break the power of him who
holds the power of death —that is, the devil.
—HEBREWS 2:14

The triumphant cross of Christ takes the power of death to push people out of the hands of Satan.

Revelation 12:11 describes the saints on the day of tribulation who are not afraid to die because of the blood shed by the Lamb on the cross.

To die is gain. Paul argues in Philippians 1:21 that it is actually to their own gain for a Christian to die. The believer will gain unlimited access to the glorious presence of God the Father, our Lord Jesus Christ, and the Holy Spirit.

By taking away a child of God to be with Him, God has finally set the person free from the tyranny and torture of sin and suffering. Moreover, according to Psalm 16:11, the deceased Christian is now enjoying the fulness of God's joy in His presence and the eternal pleasures in His right hand.

To rule with Christ. Remember the story of how the resurrected Jesus served His disciples by preparing them breakfast by the sea of Galilee (John 21).

God is an eternal worker (John 5:17) and promises those who are overcomers to rule with the Lord in His glorious kingdom (Rev. 2:26).

To enjoy eternity. Christ's second coming gives hope during death. When Jesus returns, He "will transform our lowly bodies so that they will be like His glorious body" (Phil. 3:20–21). The future resurrection of our bodies is the culmination of the complete salvation God has provided for us through Christ's death on the cross (Rom. 8:17).

Inside your body is the blueprint for your resurrection body. With it, you'll be better able to enjoy an eternity of wonders God has prepared for you.

Joni Ericson Tada puts it well: "Somewhere in my paralyzed body is the seed of what I shall become. The paralysis makes what I will become all the grander when you contrast atrophied legs against splendorous resurrected legs. If there are mirrors in heaven (and why not?), the image I'll see will unmistakably 'Joni,' although a much better, brighter Joni."

Father God, thank You for the happy ending that removes the slavery and fear of death. In Jesus's name, amen!

_____

_____

_____

_____

Trapped Again

Dean De Castro

For although the righteous fall seven times, they rise again.
—PROVERBS 24:16

What should you do when you slip back into the same habitual sins?

Are you tempted to conclude that victory isn't possible after all? Let me share four things we can do to bounce back from our occasional failures to live holy lives.

Accept personal responsibility. James warns us, "When tempted, no one should say, 'God is tempting me,' for God cannot be tempted by evil, nor does He tempt anyone, but each one is tempted…by his own evil desires" (James 1:13–15).

Blaming God, Satan, other people, or adverse circumstances for our moral failures weakens our resolve to subdue the power of the evil desires that entice us into sin.

Beware of perfectionism. Except for Jesus Christ, no one is morally perfect. God's goal for us is not sinless perfection but spiritual progress. You will never be sinless on this planet, but it is possible to sin less and less.

People with perfectionistic tendencies easily give up their fight against sin. They argue, "What's the use of trying when there's no guarantee of complete victory?"

Perfectionists are afraid of failure because their pride can't handle defeat. As such, they are powerless to overcome temptations "because God opposes the proud but gives grace to the humble" (1 Pet. 5:5).

Claim your victory. Romans 8:37 assures us that "we are more than conquerors through Him who loved us." Our victory in Christ is sealed by the faithful intercession of the Holy Spirit (Rom. 8:26–27), by the eternal purpose of Father God in conforming us into the image of His Son (Rom. 8:28–30), and by the unending love of Jesus Christ (Rom. 8:31–39).

Don't give up the fight. Satan and his evil forces do not give up easily. Satan confronted Jesus three times in rapid succession. If Satan assaults you ten times, resist him ten times, but don't give in.

However miserably we have failed, God's grace is greater than our sins. Only God's mercy will give us the courage to get up again and keep on going even after we have failed for the umpteenth time.

> *Father God, thank You for winning the spiritual*
> *war even though we may occasionally lose our*
> *personal battles. In Jesus's name, amen!*

_____

_____

_____

_____

Redeeming the Time

Dean De Castro

...redeeming the time...
—EPHESIANS 5:16, NKJV

If we acknowledge the lordship of Christ in every area of our life, then we should allow Him to have complete control of our time. The acrostic TIME beautifully elucidates this truth.

T—Treasure time. Every morning, God credits you with 86,4000 seconds that carry over no balance, no overdrafts, and will be lost if you fail to invest them for a good purpose. The loss is yours if you fail to spend the day's deposit. There is no drawing against tomorrow. Live in the present and wisely use your God-given time.

I—Invest your time. We cannot delay or hasten, save or lose time. But we can wisely invest it and find time we never knew we had. In *The Time of Your Life*, Mark Porter suggests three techniques to invest our time: fill the space, double up, and delegate.

As examples, Ken Taylor put together the entirety of *The Living Bible* while riding the commuter train between Wheaton and Chicago. Also, Jesus spent the time walking to the next town and eating meals teaching His disciples. And Moses delegated some of his responsibilities to qualified men and was thus able to lead the people of Israel.

M—Manage life's categories. The Bible does not give us a list of priorities but a set of categories we must balance under Christ's lordship. God is not simply the top priority in a list of responsibilities. He's the Lord of life who intervenes in everything we do.

In 1 Peter, we see this comprehensive view of life clearly outlined: personal (2:11–12), family (3:1–7), work (2:18–25), church (4:7–11, 5:1–5), and community (2:13).

E—Entrust everything to God. After the command to redeem our time, Paul also commands us to be filled or controlled by the Holy Spirit (Eph. 5:18b).

We may read all the books and attend all the workshops available on time management, but if we don't apply our knowledge under the leadership of the Holy Spirit, we will be controlled by the power of sin to waste our time. The Holy Spirit helps us plan and carry out our projects according to God's will.

Father God, teach us a balanced view of life that helps us keep things in perspective. In Jesus's name, amen!

_____

_____

_____

_____

The Days Are Evil

Dean De Castro

...because the days are evil.
—EPHESIANS 5:16B

Paul commands us to use our time wisely "because the days are evil." Our days are evil because every temptation and evil force are engaged during them.

We live in a world where evil overtakes everything, and unless we redeem it—buy it from the devil through godly planning and organization—these evil days will keep us from living a victorious life.

We face three vicious time robbers that tempt us to fritter away our lives with trivial things. These three enemies are the world, the flesh, and the devil.

The world. We live in a world that is not conducive to living a godly life. Instead, it provides a steady barrage of diversions and socially acceptable preoccupations that distract us from spending quality time with God.

We must carefully discipline ourselves in how we live in this world, lest we conform more to its evil ways rather than to the practices of Christ.

The flesh. Our bodies are addicted to ease, pleasure, gluttony, and sloth. Unless we exercise self-control, our bodies will tend to serve evil more than God.

We must also discipline our thoughts. Otherwise, like water, they tend to flow downhill or stand stagnant. Therefore, we need to take the time to learn and study God's word—line by line, verse by verse, moment by moment, and day by day.

Without this conscious, disciplined setting of the directions of our thoughts, they will be unproductive at best and evil at worst.

The devil. We are at the center of the most costly and decisive battle in history—the struggle between God and Satan. The devil has a million ways of deceiving us to waste our time: TV, movies, social media, hobbies, work, personal problems—you name it.

So, be prepared for Satan to throw in your way a barrage of diversions, detours, and roadblocks to get you sidetracked. But don't panic. "The One who is in you is greater than the one who is in the world" (1 John 4:4).

God will give us the grace to resist Satan and use our time wisely as we advance His cause in this world.

Father God, let us live a godly life in these
evil days. In Jesus's name, amen!

_____

_____

_____

_____

Personal Purpose Statement

Dean De Castro

Understand what the Lord's will is.
—EPHESIANS 5:17

Discovering your purpose in life is the foundation of effective time management.

It is the basis for setting long-range goals, planning action steps, and prioritizing daily tasks to achieve God's will for our lives.

Tommy Newberry writes, "A purpose statement is a written, present-tense articulation of exactly what type of person you believe God wants you to become."

About eleven years ago, God revealed the purpose statement that guides me daily in managing my time wisely: *Love God by obeying all of Christ's words in the power of the Holy Spirit, one choice at a time.*

To love God. I practice daily devotions to remind myself that God loves me and also *likes* me. He is not mad at me but is madly in love with me. Whenever God thinks of me, He sings with joy and serenades me with delight (Zeph. 3:17). And I love Him because He first loved me (1 John 4:19).

By obeying all of Christ's words. According to John 14:15, obedience is the mark of loving God. "If you love me, you will obey what I command." Our love for God causes us to want to do everything He wants us to do (see Gen. 29:20).

Obedience or the lack of it does not increase or minimize God's unconditional love for us, but it does enlarge our capacity to receive God's love and love Him in return.

In the power of the Holy Spirit. Although the Holy Spirit indwells and seals us immediately upon salvation, His work within each believer takes a lifetime.

He is our constant Helper who transforms us into Christ's image and empowers us to face our daily challenges. In all our difficulties, conflicts, and heartaches, He guides our way, guards our hearts, and grants us wisdom.

One choice at a time. It is in our moments of choice that our destiny is shaped. We can choose to trust God and grow spiritually, or we can choose to live in our strength and fail miserably. The choice is ours!

> *Father God, let us love and obey You, not in our*
> *strength, but in the power of the Holy Spirit, one*
> *decision at a time. In Jesus's name, amen!*

_____

_____

_____

_____

Understanding God's Will

Dean De Castro

Understand what the Lord's will is.
—EPHESIANS 5:17

After Paul commands us to redeem the time (Eph. 5:16), he warns us not to manage our time without first knowing God's will wisely (v. 17). How, then, can we discover God's will and direction for our lives?

In his book, *The Time of Your Life*, Mark Porter suggests four channels for God's guidance. He calls them the compass of God's guidance. Imagine a compass with its four directions:

West. This refers to the Word of God. "Your Word is a lamp to my feet and a light for my path" (Ps. 119:105). Over 90 percent of God's will for our lives is found in the Bible. If we act on the clear teachings of the Scriptures, God will supply the missing instructions.

South. This refers to the Spirit of God. As to areas the Bible is silent on, such as God's will for your career, let the Holy Spirit guide you through the principles of the Scriptures.

The Holy Spirit will whisper to your ears, saying, "This is the way; walk in it" (Isa. 30:21). Listen and obey the inward promptings of the Holy Spirit by faith.

East. This refers to events or circumstances. When Paul was heading for Asia to preach the gospel, the Holy Spirit forbade him and finally directed him to Macedonia (Acts 16:6–10). Be sensitive to God's guidance when it comes through the ordering of circumstances.

North. This refers to the counsel of godly neighbors and friends in the Lord. The Holy Spirit used Ananias to open the eyes of Paul and delivered to him God's will and purpose for his life (Acts 9:10–17).

Prayer. Imagine prayer as the fulcrum of the compass. Prayer is the key that unlocks each channel for guidance. Pray God will bring Scripture to light, revealing His will. Pray the Holy Spirit will give peace about the right way; open and shut doors to indicate His path and confirm it through two or three witnesses (godly counsel).

Before we feel the urgency to do God's will, we must make sure it is the King's business (1 Sam. 21:8).

Father God, let us use our time wisely according to Your will for our lives. In Jesus's name, amen!

Pray for Wisdom

Dean De Castro

So teach us to number our days, that we
may apply our hearts unto wisdom.
—PSALM 90:12, KJV

In Psalm 90, Moses writes about the transitoriness of man and the eternity of God. God is timeless (v. 4), while man's earthly life is like the grass that soon withers and dies (vv. 5b–6). Here are three reasons to number our days:

Life is short. God gives man only seventy or eighty years of life because of sin. But even if you have a longer life, "You are a mist that appears for a little while and then vanishes" (James 4:14). Even the most extended life is brief in comparison to eternity.

Pray God will grant you wisdom to maximize your time on earth as you strive for a productive and God-honoring life.

Live in light of eternity. Our commitment to redeeming the time must be with eternity's values in view. We live in time to prepare for eternity. Therefore, time is best used in ways that prepare us properly for eternity. The following poem best expresses this purpose:

> We live in time so little time
> And we learn all so painfully,
> That we may spare this hour's term
> To practice for eternity.

There is a direct connection between what you do today and what you will experience in eternity. Your belief in Christ determines your eternal destination. However, how you spend eternity is based on your behavior. Jesus promises "to reward each according to his works" (Matt. 16:27).

Time is elastic. We all have the same number of hours in our day. But the time we have at our disposal each day is flexible. So, for example, a mother who has ten children to support with an eight-to-five job does not have as much time at her disposal as another woman with one child who lives on investments from an inheritance.

Don't try to live the life of another person. You are a unique individual with a definite mission from God (Eph. 2:10). Be true to your calling and bloom where you're planted. You may not look successful in the sight of man, but God will reward your faithfulness and obedience in eternity.

> *Father God, grant us wisdom to take careful*
> *inventory of our time. In Jesus's name, amen!*

Seven Keys to Good Time Management

Charles Stanley
Adapted from *Success God's Way*

Live the rest of their earthly lives...for the will of God.
—1 PETER 4:2

God wants us to use our time according to His will.

Below are seven keys to good time management that help us adjust our schedules according to the Lord's priorities for each day of our lives.

Assume responsibility. Ephesians 5:16 challenges you to make the most of your time to the best of your ability. If you don't manage your own time, somebody else will.

Seek God's guidance. Ask God each morning for guidance in your time at work. Ask Him to manage your time with your wife and family. Also, ask the Lord to help you manage your recreational time for maximum relaxation benefits to renew your creative energy.

Plan your schedule. Schedule your goals in the context of deadlines. Ask the Lord to show you how to set your schedule on any given day, week, and year to allow for a good balance of work and rest, alone time and family time, and input and output.

Stay organized. Ask the Lord to help you remove the things that pull you away from your God-given purpose and goals and the things that clutter your schedule with unimportant activities and obligations.

Rely on God's wisdom. As you plan projects or break down large goals into specific tasks, ask the Lord, "Am I sequencing activities or tasks in the proper order? Am I allowing the appropriate amount of time for each facet of this project? Have I set the correct deadlines?"

Eliminate the unimportant. Eliminate anything that doesn't fit into your life purpose. For example, my life purpose is to get the gospel to as many people as possible, as quickly as possible, as simply stated as possible, as irresistibly as possible, in the power of the Holy Spirit, to the glory of God

Every day, I evaluate my to-do list by asking, "Am I progressing toward fulfilling my life mission through these tasks?" If the answer is no, I don't do them.

Review your day. Compare what you did with what you intended to do. Thank God for your accomplishments. However, if you fail, ask for God's forgiveness and help to do better the next day.

> *Father God, help us discipline ourselves in the*
> *wise use of our time. In Jesus's name, amen!*

_____

_____

_____

_____

The Tyranny of the Urgent

Charles Hummel

Adapted from *The Tyranny of the Urgent*

I have finished the work which Thou gavest Me to do.
—JOHN 17:4, KJV

How could Jesus use the word "finished"?

His three-year ministry seemed all too short. He did not finish all the urgent tasks in Palestine or the other things He would have liked to do, but He did finish the work God gave Him to do.

The Gospel records show that Jesus worked and worked hard. After describing a busy day, Mark writes that the whole city gathered together as Jesus healed many diseases and cast out many devils (Mark 1:32–34).

On another occasion, the demand of the ill and maimed caused Him to miss supper and work so late that His family thought He was beside Himself (see Mark 3:21).

One day, after a strenuous teaching session, Jesus and His disciples went out in a boat. Even a storm didn't awaken Him (see Mark 4:37–38). What a picture of exhaustion.

Yet His life was never feverish; He had time for people. He could spend hours talking to one person, such as the Samaritan woman at the well. When His brothers wanted Him to go to Judea, He replied, "My time is not yet come" (John 7:6). Jesus's life showed an outstanding balance and a sense of timing.

What was the secret of Jesus's work?

We find a clue by following Mark's account of Jesus's busy day. Mark observes that "in the morning, rising a great while before day, He went out, and departed into a solitary place, and there prayed" (Mark 1:35).

Here is the secret of Jesus's life and work for God: He prayerfully waited for His Father's instructions. Jesus had no divinely drawn blueprint. Instead, He discerned the Father's will daily in a life of prayer. Through this means, He warded off the urgent and accomplished the important.

When our days end in this life, are we confident that we have finished the work God gave us to do? As we learn from Jesus's example to wait for God's instructions through prayer, our Lord will also free us from the tyranny of the urgent.

Father God, help us discern what is urgent and
what is Your will. In Jesus's name, amen!

_____

_____

_____

_____

The Example of Jesus

J. Oswald Sanders
Adapted from *Spiritual Leadership*

Are there not twelve hours of daylight?
—JOHN 11:9

Philosopher William James affirmed that the best use of one's life is to spend it on something that will outlast it. Life's value is not in its duration but its donation—not how long we live but how fully and well.

Our Lord set the perfect example of the strategic use of time. He admitted to His disciples that there are twelve hours in the day. There are twelve hours in the day, but He fully used them to accomplish God's plan for His life.

Divine serenity. The secret of Jesus's serenity lay in His assurance that He was working according to the Father's plan for His life. This plan embraced every hour and made provisions for every contingency.

Through communion in prayer with His Father, Jesus received each day both the words He would say and the works He would do. "The words I say to you are not just my own. Rather, it is the Father, living in me, who is doing His work" (John 14:10).

Divine timing. Jesus was conscious of divine timing in His life. Even to His beloved mother, He said, "My time has not yet come" (John 2:4). And in responding to Mary and Martha's distress, Jesus declined to change His schedule by two days (11:1–6).

Jesus completed His life's work without any part spoiled by undue haste or half-done through lack of time. He wasted no time on things not vital. On the contrary, His twenty-four hours a day were sufficient to meet the whole will of God.

Divine interruptions. The Gospel accounts contain no hint of any interruption ever disturbing Jesus. On the contrary, when a person approached Him for help, Jesus gave the impression that He had no more important concern than the needs of His visitor.

To Jesus, there were no such things as unexpected interruptions. On the contrary, He always foresaw "unexpected" events as part of the Father's planning and was therefore undisturbed by them. True, there was hardly time to eat at some points, but time was always sufficient to accomplish all the Father's will.

Father God, teach us to respond to divine
interruptions gracefully. In Jesus's name, amen!

Controlled by God

Paul E. Miller

Adapted from *Love Walked among Us*

For you any time is right.
—JOHN 7:6

Notice Jesus's dependence on His Father when His brothers suggest changing His schedule (John 7:2–6, 8–9). Jesus tells His brothers, "For your time is right," implying that they are free to do what they want when they want to do it.

But of Himself, He says, "The right time for me has not yet come." Jesus is aware that the Father controls His schedule, even when He should go to the Feast of the Tabernacle.

People's agendas. When the Jews celebrated the Feast of the Tabernacle, the population of Jerusalem swelled to over a million. His family assumes that, like them, Jesus loves the cheer of the crowd.

The brothers want Jesus to do miracles at the Feast so that millions will see and make Him famous and influential. And, of course, He would remember His family when He becomes a power broker.

But Jesus doesn't care about fame or power, only the will of God, so He tells them no. Jesus's brothers would have interpreted His freedom as self-will because, in the first century, one didn't think and act against or outside the interests of their extended family.

Jesus's submission. Jesus refuses to allow His brothers' agendas to control His time. He knows that performing miracles at the Feast would not be an act of love but manipulation for power.

Jesus has a different center of gravity. He has the love of God in His heart (see John 5:41–42, 44). He doesn't need love from other sources. His bondage to His Father frees Him to say no to His brothers and yes to people in pain.

Dean De Castro   379

Without His underlying submission to God, other people's agendas would have distracted Jesus from doing God's will. He would be hurrying off to Jerusalem with His brothers, partly trying to keep His family happy, partly trying to become famous.

Dependence on God means surrendering my will to His. It means saying to God, "You're the boss." Indeed, God is in control of our time, and we depend on Him for accomplishing *what* He wants us to do *when* He wants us to do it.

> *Father God, we commit our time into Your hands*
> *(Ps. 31:15a). In Jesus's name, amen!*

_____

_____

_____

_____

Living on Purpose

Joyce Meyer
Adapted from *Seize the Day*

I must proclaim the good news of the kingdom of God to
the other towns also, because that is why I was sent.
—LUKE 4:43

When we get past the age of fifty or sixty, we begin to think quite differently about what we want to do with our time. We become more determined to make the most of our time.

I am usually a very goal-oriented individual, and I am motivated by accomplishment. But in the past year, I found myself looking at things I needed and wanted to do and becoming so double-minded about which one to do first that I often ended up doing nothing.

I felt overwhelmed, and that was unusual for me. I felt like life was ordering me around rather than me ordering my life, and I knew something was wrong. So I prayed about it and wanted to hear what God would say to me about the situation.

As I prayed about it, God began showing me the importance of living life "on purpose"—something I had done most of my life but had somehow gotten off track. As I started listening to people, I found that many live their lives without accomplishing much of what they truly intended to do.

I wonder how many people feel they lived the life they were meant to live at the end of their time. How many have only regrets about what they did or did not do during their lives? You only have one life, and if it is not going in the direction you want, now is the time to make changes.

When we live unproductive lives, we should not blame it on circumstances, other people, the way the world is today, or anything else.

God created man and gave him free will. That means we can make choices in literally every area of life.

God has a will and purpose for each of us, and He desires that we use our free will to choose His will so we can enjoy the best life possible. So learn to seize the day and start making the moments you have count toward fulfilling your potential!

Father God, save us from the sin of
passivity. In Jesus's name, amen!

A Model of Life

Dough Sherman and William Hendricks
Adapted from *How to Balance Competing Time Demands*

*Whatever you do, whether in word or deed, do
it all in the name of the Lord Jesus.*
—COLOSSIANS 3:17

In Europe, one of the most prestigious and demanding athletic contests is the pentathlon.

It requires the athlete to compete in five events: a 4,000-meter cross country race; a 300-meter freestyle swim; a 5,000-meter, thirty-jump equestrian steeplechase; pistol shooting at 25 meters; and epee fencing.

The pentathlon is comprehensive; you must do well in five areas to win. Likewise, to "win" in the biblical pentathlon, you must pursue growth in all five areas.

In 1 Peter, we see this comprehensive view of life clearly outlined: personal (2:11–12), family (3:1–7), work (2:18–25), church (4:7–11, 5:1–5), and community (2:13).

Each believer has a unique walk with God. Consequently, we must answer to God for how we respond to Him in each of the five areas, knowing that our approach may be different from someone else's. For example, if you're single, you'll approach the biblical pentathlon very differently than a married person with children.

No athlete ever arrives at perfection in any event. The way he improves is by setting limited goals in each of the five areas and then striving to meet those goals. In the Christian life, we'll never "arrive." But we can set limited goals in each of the five areas of life and grow in Christlikeness.

In the pentathlon, each event affects all the others. Remember, life is interrelated and dynamic. I've represented the five categories of the pentathlon as though they were five mutually exclusive parts of life, but in actuality they overlap considerably.

If we're going to have a list, Jesus shouldn't be at the top of the list; He shouldn't even be on the list! That's because He's not just another item, another responsibility, another entry on the checklist. Instead, Jesus is the Lord of life whom we should seek to please in everything we do (Col. 3:17). He's the Lord of life who must be at the center of everything we do.

Father God, help us live a well-rounded and
balanced Christian life that honors You as Lord and
Master over our lives. In Jesus's name, amen!

_____

_____

_____

_____

Goal Setting and Contentment

William Cook

Adapted from *Success, Motivation, and the Scriptures*

I press on toward the goal to win the prize.
—PHILIPPIANS 3:14

Most Christians wrestle with goal setting. Either they hate the idea of goal-setting or they set insignificant goals.

Some years ago, a newspaper headline told of three hundred whales that suddenly died. The whales were pursing sardines and found themselves stranded in a bay. According to a report, "The small fish lured the sea giants to their death....They came to their violent demise by chasing small ends, by prostituting vast powers for insignificant goals."

Only a few Christians have the habit of setting goals. One reason is an incorrect interpretation of biblical contentment.

Some misinterpret the following Scriptures: "Be content with what you have" (Heb. 13:5). "For I have learned to be content with whatever the circumstances" (Phil. 4:11). "But godliness with contentment is great gain" (1 Tim. 6:6).

Lordship (having Christ in the control tower) should be the primary prerogative in the study of every Christian concept. What will my Christian contentment mean if Christ is in the control tower?

Let me submit how I understand Paul's concept of Christian contentment:

- I am thrilled today with what God has given me. I am wonderfully satisfied.
- My thrill today is no guarantee that God intends me to be thrilled tomorrow with the same things.

- I want my desires limited (if need be) to what God wants me to have and what God wants me to achieve.
- I also want my passions stretched (if need be) to that which I am convinced God wants me to have and succeed in.

There's a picture of contentment under the lordship of Christ. Whether the desires need to be limited or stretched will be a matter of daily wisdom to be achieved in time alone with God.

God may more often require stretching rather than shrinking! He rebukes us for our failure to push, for not thinking big. "Ye have not because ye ask not" (James 4:2, KJV).

Goal setting for the Christian means planning, organizing, and stretching under the lordship of Christ.

> *Father God, let us wisely redeem our time to know and carry out Your will for our life. In Jesus's name, amen!*

_____

_____

_____

_____

Setting SMAC Goals

Doug Sherman and William Hendrick
Adapted from *How to Balance Competing Time Demands*

Without vision, people cast off restraint.
—PROVERBS 29:18, CUV

Without direction, most of us will wander around without purpose and growth. Therefore, you must go beyond good intentions and *plan steps* for accomplishing them.

When it comes to setting goals, I've found a little acronym to be helpful: SMAC. As you set goals, you'll want to make them specific, measurable, achievable, and compatible.

S—Specific. The more specific you can make your goals, the better. For example, "I'm going to pray with my wife for five minutes before bed once before the end of this week."

M—Measurable. Set a goal to determine whether you can achieve it with a simple yes or no. "I'm going to help my daughter learn to ride her new bike this Saturday morning after breakfast." You'll be able to tell people at noon on Saturday whether you've done this.

A—Achievable. We need to build realism into our goals. When it comes to goals, less is usually more! We'll accomplish more over time if we bite off less at a time. For example, "Saturday morning, I'm going to get all my bank statements out and balance my checkbook." This goal should be relatively easily achievable for someone who wants to start working on their family finances.

C—Compatible. Your goals must be compatible with your circumstances. For example, "I plan to go to my health club three mornings a week, between 6:15 and 7:30, for a workout." This goal is specific, measurable, and achievable. But it is not compatible with the life of a single parent who has to work and take care of children in the early morning.

Some sample goals:

- Personal life: Read the Bible fifteen minutes a day, five days a week.
- Family life: Pray together as a family for five minutes each day.
- Work life: Leave the house no later than _____ each morning to get to work on time.
- Church life: Meet with my child's Sunday school teacher to learn what my child is learning.
- Community life: Pray for government officials by individual names each week.

Schedule these activities into your calendar and *do them*!

Father God, guide us to set goals, plan action steps, and diligently execute them on our path toward godliness. In Jesus's name, amen!

_____

_____

_____

_____

Overcoming Procrastination

Mark Porter

Adapted from *The Time of Your Life*

I will hasten and not delay to obey Your commands.
—PSALM 119:60

One meaning of the phrase "redeeming the time" is to seize the opportunity before it is lost. Some prospects will be lost unless they are taken "before winter." For Timothy, it was before winter or never!

Procrastination is bad. Paul, sensing the time of his departure is at hand, writes to Timothy, "Make every effort to come before winter" (2 Tim. 4:21). Suppose Timothy had said to himself, "Yes, I must go to Rome; but first of all, I must clear up some matters here at Ephesus."

Eventually, Timothy sets out for Troas to get a ship for Rome. Upon arrival, he seeks out Paul's prison—only to be told he was beheaded last month.

Procrastination is good. Is procrastination always bad? In John 11, we read that the Lord Jesus deliberately delayed when He heard that Lazarus was sick. For Mary and Martha, His procrastination seemed tragic. "Lord, if you had been here, my brother would not have died" (vv. 21, 32).

In the wisdom of Jesus, the delay was designed to bring glory to God. "I am glad for your sakes that I was not there, so that you may believe...if you believe, you will see the glory of God...Many, therefore of the Jews, who had come to Mary and beheld what He had done, believed in Him" (vv. 15, 40, 45).

Stubborn as mules. The Lord says, "I will instruct you and teach you in the way which you should go; I will counsel you with My eye upon you. Do not be as the horse or as the mule which has no understanding, whose trappings include bit and bridle to hold them in check; otherwise, they will not come near to you" (Ps. 32:8–9).

Dean De Castro   389

Sometimes, we are as stubborn as mules that seldom go when we want them to. On the other hand, there are times when we are as wild as horses—running ahead of the Lord and not waiting for Him. Both can be equally bad. We need to keep in step with God.

Father God, we will hasten and not delay to obey
Your commands. In Jesus's name, amen!

_____

_____

_____

_____

The Discipline of Concentration

Mark Porter

Adapted from *The Time of Your Life*

...one thing I do...
—PHILIPPIANS 3:13

The clothes dryer had been on the blink for three weeks. So, first thing Saturday morning, I tore into the dryer. After removing the back, I was uncertain how to proceed, so I decided to get the instruction manual filed away upstairs. When I got to the file cabinet, I noticed a stack of materials waiting to be put in.

While filing them, I noticed a letter I should have answered three months ago. My friend had asked if he could borrow a pamphlet I had, so I went off to find the brochure. After several minutes of fumbling in a dark closet, I decided to get a flashlight. Unfortunately, the batteries were dead, so I went to the kitchen and put batteries on my wife's grocery list.

While in the kitchen, I noticed the faucet was dripping, so I got my tools to replace the washer and accidentally cut my finger. I bandaged my finger and returned to the kitchen to add Band-Aids to my wife's grocery list.

My wife asked if I was hungry. It was lunchtime! "By the way," she asked, "did you get the dryer fixed?"

When Paul writes, "One thing I do...I press on toward my goal" (Phil. 3:13–14), he is implying that there are diversionary activities that keep us from our number one priority. These additional activities can be harmless and legitimate, but they can also distract us from our primary goal.

Jesus knew when to say no to diversionary activities. When He sent out the seventy, His instructions were to "greet no one on the way" and "do not keep moving from house to house" Luke 10:4, 7). It was not because He was antisocial but because these activities would divert from His goal.

When Elisha sent Gehazi, his servant, to raise the Shunammite's son, his instructions were "Gird up your loins...and go your way; if you meet any man, do not salute him, and if anyone salutes you, do not answer him" (2 Kings 4:29). There was no time for socializing when a boy lay dead.

Father God, save us from the many distractions
that keep us from focusing on our Spirit-
directed tasks. In Jesus's name, amen!

Embracing Interruptions in a Distraction-Filled World

J. D. Greear

Adapted from jdgreear.com

They tried to enter Bithynia, but the Spirit
of Jesus would not allow them.
—ACTS 16:7

Jesus seemed to be entirely *indestructible* on the one hand but imminently *interruptible* on the other. So, He'd be doing something and then stop when some opportunity would arise.

If we are going to follow the Holy Spirit, we are to live in the same way. We need the focus and indestructibility of John 4 combined with the flexibility and interruptibility of John 5.

Jesus's indestructibility. In John 4, not even His own hunger can keep Jesus from pursuing God's will. When His disciples went to get something to eat, Jesus stuck around to minister to the Samaritan woman at the well. Then, a few hours later, they return to find Jesus still sitting there.

"Aren't you hungry?" they ask, to which Jesus says, "My food is to do the will of the One that sent me" (John 4:34). If there is one thing that can distract me from focusing in ministry, it is hunger—I'm not great at counseling when I'm *hungry*. But Jesus was so locked into God's will that even hunger could not affect His disposition.

Jesus's interruptibility. In John 5, Jesus freely allows His Sabbath to be interrupted by a man who needs healing. In verse 17, Jesus explains His openness to being interrupted by saying, "My Father is still working, and I am also working."

In other words, Jesus recognizes that His Father is always at work around Him, and sometimes the Father will invite Him into something He is doing, and Jesus is ready to respond.

The best moments. Have you noticed that the best moments in our lives often come through unexpected interruptions?

The best parenting moments rarely happen on our schedules. Likewise, the best witnessing encounters never happen on schedule—God puts us next to somebody who needs a word from Him, and it's up to us to respond.

A healthy Christian life is one in which you learn to live free of devilish distractions so that you can be open to divine interruptions and obedient to the Holy Spirit.

Father God, let us be open to divine interruptions
and respond accordingly. In Jesus's name, amen!

_____

_____

_____

_____

How to Waste Your Time

Joel Osteen
Adapted from *The Power of I Am*

...redeeming the time...
—EPHESIANS 5:17, KJV

Time is more valuable than money.

You can make more money, but you can't make more time. Just like you spend your money, you are spending your time. Are you investing in it or wasting it?

Here are three ways to waste your precious time:

Fighting the wrong battle. Realize every battle is not worth fighting. You don't have time to engage in conflicts that are not between you and your God-given destiny.

You don't have to resolve disputes with every person. Some people don't want to be at peace with you. That's a distraction. Don't waste your valuable time fighting battles that don't matter.

Unforgiveness. Ephesians 4:26 says, "Don't let the sun go down on your anger." Here's the problem: If the sun goes down with resentment, it comes back up with bitterness, which blocks God's blessings and keeps you from seeing the bright future.

If you want the sun to shine brightly in your life again, you need to pray before you go to bed each night, "God, I forgive the people who did me wrong today. I'm going to bed in peace." Don't go to bed with any hatred still in your heart.

When you do that, the sun will go down with nothing blocking it. When it comes back the next morning, you'll have a new spring in your step. You'll be excited about the day and ready for your future.

Wrong friendships. To whom are you giving your time and attention? Please don't waste it with people who drag you down. This may mean you have to change who you eat lunch with at the office daily. That person who's always finding fault, being critical, and bad-mouthing the boss, you don't need that poison in your life.

Ask God to give you new friends, people who inspire you, sharpen you, and push you toward your destiny. Surround yourself with people who model excellence, integrity, character, and godliness.

Don't waste another day. God has given you a present. It's called "today." This day is a gift. Make sure you're investing your time and not wasting it.

Father God, help us live well-spent lives. In Jesus's name, amen!

What Is a Waste of Time?

Charles Stanley
Adapted from *Success God's Way*

Live—not as unwise but as wise.
— EPHESIANS 5:15

Wasting time is a sin.

But only God can define what waste is. It is anything that does not contribute to fulfilling His plan and purpose for us.

Are recreation and play wastes of time? Not necessarily. God intends for you to rest and to relax and have moments of pure enjoyment. That's part of His plan to rejuvenate your body, mind, and spirit.

Is spending time alone, listening to the Lord, and quietly waiting in His presence a waste of time? No. God delights in having fellowship with you. Spending quiet time with the Lord is vital to building a relationship with Him. It lets you discern what God wants you to do with your time and energy.

Do prayer and conversations about God wastes time? Never! If you are sitting in traffic, doing a menial task, or waiting for an appointment, use that time to talk to God or to strike up a conversation about the love of God.

Are reading and studying wasting time? No. Not if you are reading something valuable to fulfilling your God-given goals. You develop talents and gifts by studying. It is not a waste of time if you are learning the right things for the right reasons.

Is it a waste of time to be a workaholic and spend eighteen hours a day, seven days a week, on a job or a ministry? Yes. Working continually is not a balanced approach to time; a person's physical strength and energy suffer over the long haul. Instead, the person's relationships with God, family, and friends—connections that are priorities in God's plan for everyone—weaken.

But playing when you should be working, sleeping when you should be awake, or spending time doing frivolous things at the expense of spending time with the Lord or family and friends is a waste.

Nothing is a waste of time if it is a part of a balanced plan to fulfill God's purposes for maximum usefulness, productivity, and efficiency in using your talents and gifts.

Father God, help us use our time with wisdom
and balance. In Jesus's name, amen!

_____

_____

_____

_____

No Time Like the Present

Charles E. Hummel

Adapted from *The Tyranny of the Urgent*

I am with you always.
—MATTHEW 28:20

We have only today within our grasp. The past is past, and the future is yet to be; we can do nothing about either of them. But we can deal with what is happening moment by moment.

The sacrament of the present moment. In *Abandonment to Divine Providence,* Jean-Pierre de Caussade (1675–1751) writes, "If we have abandoned ourselves to God, there is only one rule for us: the duty of the present moment."

He also calls this the "sacrament of the present moment." He recognizes that most of us are ordinary creatures with humdrum lives of trivial tasks and decisions—some pleasant, many boring, others tedious or tragic.

Yet we need to recognize that God speaks through what happens to us. Therefore, we are to welcome all the present circumstances of our life as an expression of God's will. No matter how difficult it is to understand them, the events of each moment are stamped with God's will (see Rom. 8:28).

The practice of the presence of God. At the age of fifty-five, Nicholas Herman (1611–1691) served as a lay brother among the Carmelites Dechausses (bare-footed) in Paris, where he served in the community kitchen. He then became known as Brother Lawrence.

In the book *The Practice of the Presence of God*, Brother Lawrence points out that we establish a sense of God's presence by continually conversing with Him, speaking to Him frankly and plainly, and imploring His assistance in our affairs just as they happen.

Dean De Castro   399

For Brother Lawrence, the set times of prayer are not different from other times since he continues his fellowship with God in those activities. For him, prayer is not an escape from the world, a "sacred" period removed from daily life. He considered those tasks, performed with a motive of love, a form of prayer.

When we grasp the importance of the present, we learn to prize the "now" of our existence. We then can say with the psalmist, "This is the day the Lord has made; let us rejoice and be glad in it" (Ps. 118:24).

Father God, let us see the present as Your precious present to accomplish Your plans for our lives. In Jesus's name, amen!

Practical Tips to Redeem Your Time

Edmund Chan

Adapted from the message preached by Rev. Edmund Chan at
the 105th Anniversary Worship Service, Cebu Gospel Church,
Philippines, March 21, 2021

...making the most of every opportunity...
—EPHESIANS 5:16

To redeem the time means living in the present and making the most of every day's opportunities.

Most people live in the past with hurts and regrets, while others live in the future and worry about life's uncertainties. We can't live in the past because we can't go back and change it. The future is beyond us and out of our control. Only God knows and controls the future.

The only thing we have in our hands is today. Don't take your today for granted. Redeem your today and make the most of today's opportunities.

Remember, today is yesterday's tomorrow. Learn to live today well. Your tomorrow changes in how you live today. *You are changing your past for tomorrow by living today well.*

Below are some practical tips for living today well:

- Allow yourself to relax.
- Get enough sleep. Rest well.
- Take time to unplug.
- Enjoy a quiet time with God.
- Have deep conversations with kindred spirits.
- Encourage somebody today.
- Keep a gratitude journal. Look for the joy in each day.
- Set a portion of your income to give away. A spirit of generosity expresses a heart of gratitude.

- Declutter your life. Clean your stuff to use, throw, give away, or donate.
- Schedule your priorities. Left unscheduled, good intentions are good priorities vaporized.
- Develop healthy routines. Good routines build strong habits.
- Do something that will grow you.
- Ask yourself, "What did I learn today?"
- Have a stop-doing list. Some things are not helpful. Stop doing them.
- Don't just focus on what you *can* do but on what you *must* do.

Create your list and make the most of every opportunity to please God. Allow me to share my philosophy of life: *My life is a gift from God. And what I make of my life is my gift back to God.*

Father God, let us live in the present well and offer our
best life as a present to You. In Jesus's name, amen!

_____

_____

_____

_____

Getting Unstuck...Past, Present, and Future

Dr. Carol Peters-Tanksley
Adapted from drcarolminsitries.com

My times are in Your hands.
—PSALMS 31:15

Your past, present, and future are all vital if you want to become who God needs you to be. You need to understand where all three aspects come into play

Where have you come from? You cannot escape the impact of your history until and unless you own it. Your family of origin has indelibly imprinted itself in your DNA. For example, how you were exposed to sex may color how you handle your sexuality today.

But don't stay there! Examining where you came from doesn't excuse any of your behavior. However, this examination can provide a level of understanding you can't get any other way.

Where are you now? If you want to stay stuck, ignore the truth. Jesus never ignored the truth. He said to the woman at the well, "You've had five husbands" (John 4:18). To Peter, He said, "You will deny me" (Matt. 26:75). Shining the light of honesty on where you are now may feel uncomfortable, but it makes the next step possible.

There are a million variations of wherever you might be right now. And like a physician making a diagnosis before suggesting treatment, you need some sense of your present reality before you can continue the journey.

The fantastic news is that Jesus doesn't leave you where He finds you. Instead, He makes it possible for you to get from where you are now to where He created you to be.

Where do you want to go? If your life continues on its current trajectory, where will you be in a year? Five years? Ten years? Do you like what you see? Looking to the future is necessary if you want that future to be any different than your life right now. So, even Jesus had to keep His eyes on the future (Heb. 12:2).

What has He planted in your heart? Whose pain would you give anything to alleviate? What change in the world would you gladly invest your life to make happen? Those questions can help you imagine the future God has created you for.

Father God, our times, past, present, and future,
are in Your hands. In Jesus's name, amen!

Motivational Quotes on Time

Teach us to number our days, that we
may gain a heart of wisdom.
—PSALM 90:12

Don't count the days; make the days count. —Anonymous

Today is the first day of your life. —Peter Tan-Chi

Yesterday is history, tomorrow is a mystery, but today is a gift; that's why we call it the "present." —Anonymous

Time is free, but it's priceless. You can't own it, but you can use it. You can't keep it, but you can spend it. Once you've lost it, you can never get it back. —Harvey Mackay

Just like you spend money, you are spending your life. You're either investing in it or wasting it. —Joel Osteen

Either you run the day, or the day runs you. —Jim Rohn

The way we spend our time defines who we are. —Jonathan Estrin

Time must be the servant of eternity. —Erwin Lutzer

Every day is yours to use or lose. —Anonymous

You can't have more time, only better choices. —Tommy Newberry

I refuse to entertain negativity. Life is too big and time is too short to get caught up in the empty drama. —Anonymous

Time slips away like grains of sand, never to return again. — Robin Sharma

Your time is limited, so don't waste it living someone else's life. — Steve Jobs

Living with the thought of eternity in mind helps us make better choices about what we do with our time. —Joyce Meyer

If you love life, don't waste your time, because time is life. – Dean De Castro

Father God, grant us the wisdom and motivation
to number our days. In Jesus's name, amen!

_____

_____

_____

_____

My Pacesetter

Anonymous
From *The Time of Your Life* by Mark Porter

The Lord is my Shepherd.
—PSALM 23:1

The Lord is my pacesetter,
I shall not rush.
He makes me to stop
for quiet intervals.
He provides me with images of stillness
which restore my serenity.
He leads me in ways of efficiency through calmness of mind,
and His guidance is peace.
Even though I have a great many things
to accomplish each day,
I will not fret
for His presence is here.
His timelessness,
His all-importance
will keep me in balance.
He prepares refreshment
In the midst of my activity
By anointing my mind
with His oil of tranquility.
My cup of joyous energy overflows.
Surely harmony and effectiveness
shall be the fruit of my hours.
And I shall walk
In the pace of the Lord
and dwell in His house

forever.

*Father God, we surrender the control of our time
into Your hands. In Jesus's name, amen!*

_____

_____

_____

_____

My First Lesson on Time Management

D. F. Kehl

Adapted from *Control Yourself*

Just as people are destined to die once, and
after that to face judgment.
—HEBREWS 9:27

Andrew Marvell once wrote, "At my back always I hear; Time's winged chariot hurrying near."

I suppose I first heard time's chariot hurrying at my back most vividly when I was a graduate student at the University of Wisconsin. After having some tests done at the university hospital, I was informed that I was a diabetic.

The doctor told me that people with diabetes face the likelihood of early death due to complications. And he gave no assurance that such eventualities wouldn't ultimately occur even with the utmost self-discipline. That's a complex message for a previously healthy and unrestricted twenty-one year old to accept. But the alternatives were considerably less desirable.

This news left me wondering what part would go first—maybe my heart? Or a kidney? Or my eyes? Or perhaps a toe or two? I'm becoming too morbid, you think. Well, maybe you can understand why I need to number my days. You see, I *have* to be self-disciplined, like it or not.

But is it much different with you or anyone else? Aren't we *all* under the sentence of death? The appointment with death is already made (Heb. 9:27). So, unless Jesus returns and takes us home without dying, it's only a matter of time for all of us.

Since that March day in Wisconsin, I have frequently asked God for more time, but then it occurred that I have no right to request more time unless I'm using the present time in the most effective, efficient way possible.

And I don't think you have that right either. That's like singing about and praying for a *thousand* tongues when I don't' make effective use of the *one* tongue I have. Why would God let me have more time just to see me waste it?

Of one thing we may be sure: God has tasks for each of us, and He will give us sufficient time to complete those tasks if we are faithful to Him and use our time wisely.

*Father God, help us live and use our time in light of
our impending death. In Jesus's name, amen!*

_____

_____

_____

_____

Live in Light of Christ's Return

Dean De Castro

*Our salvation is nearer now...The night is
nearly over; the day is almost here.*
—ROMANS 13:11C–12A

"Salvation" here does not refer to our deliverance from the judgment of sin. That has already been accomplished. Paul refers to the future salvation of our physical bodies (Rom. 8:23) and the whole of creation (Rom. 8:21) at the second coming of our Lord Jesus Christ.

Because the coming of Christ draws ever closer and could occur at any moment, Paul gives several important admonitions in Romans 13:11–14.

Wake up! "The hour has come for you to wake up from your slumber" (v. 11b). In light of Jesus's imminent return, we need to be alert, living in eager anticipation of that day.

As the long night continues before the second coming of Christ, some believers are sleeping spiritually. "Wake up, O sleeper, rise from the dead, and Christ will shine on you" (Eph. 5:14b). As children of light (1 Thess. 5:5), it's the moment for us to wake up and use our time wisely (Eph. 5:16–17).

Dress up! First, we must take off our night clothes and turn away from the deeds of darkness that unbelievers commit. Paul lists the sins in three pairs. The lack of control in drink, sex, and social relationships (vv. 12b–13b).

Next, we must "put on the armor of light" (v. 12b) as suitable daytime protection for the soldiers of Christ. For the Christian, life is not a sleepwalk but a battle.

Finally, we must "put on the Lord Jesus Christ" (v. 14a). To put on something is to believe in it in a certain way and then behave accordingly. Chuck Swindoll comments, "Police officers put on a uniform, which reminds them of their identity and the example they set." We put on Christ to display our identity in Christ and remind us of our responsibility to be His ambassadors in this world.

In contrast to the beautiful clothing in Christ, Paul refers to our ugly, selfish, fallen nature—the flesh—that is still present with us. Therefore, instead of thinking about how to gratify its sinful desires, we need to ruthlessly repudiate and put them to death (Rom. 13:14b; 8:13).

Father God, let us use our time wisely in this dark
and corrupt generation. In Jesus's name, amen!

Three Ways to Live in Light of Eternity

J. D. Greear
Adapted from jdgreear.com

*The Son of Man will come at an hour
when you do not expect Him.*
—LUKE 12:40

In Luke 12, Jesus tells His disciples to think about their present lives from the vantage point of the end. He wants them to learn that it is only by thinking clearly about the future that they will live wisely in the present. In addition, they will gain the strength to obey God's commands by reflecting on how close eternity is.

If you want to live your life in a state of readiness to be faithful, then there are three characteristics you should take on.

Be awake to your task. "Blessed are those servants whom the master finds awake when he comes" (Luke 12:37). Blessed are the people who are active in fulfilling the Great Commission: Make disciples of every nation.

The Greek word for "nations" refers to the different ethnic and language groups in the world, of which there are still 7,413 unreached today.

In Luke 12:42, Jesus describes the "faithful and wise manager" as the one who gives others their portion of food at the proper time. So, to live justly is to use what we have to help meet the physical needs of others and make sure they have had the opportunity to hear the gospel.

Be confident of Jesus's return (Luke 12:40). The servants who got in trouble in this parable were either unsure of their master's return or just forgot about it. We, however, need to be watchful and confident about our Master's return.

We look at everything differently when we are sure Jesus is coming back. We can endure sacrifices on earth because life is temporary and eternity is forever.

Live in a way that only makes sense if Jesus comes soon. That's what it means to live ready.

Be faithful to your charge (Luke 12:45–47). Notice how Jesus describes the fate of those who neglect their master's return. Though they aren't overtly evil people—only people who get distracted and fail to pursue their task—they are actively given severe punishment and assigned a place with the unfaithful.

Faithful disciples are not distracted by the treasures of this world but are focused instead on an eternal inheritance.

Father God, let us live in light of
eternity. In Jesus's name, amen!

Only One Life

C. T. Studd

What is your life? You are a mist that appears
for a little while and then vanishes.
—JAMES 4:14

Two little lines I heard one day, Traveling along life's busy way;
Bringing conviction to my heart, And from my mind would not depart;
Only one life, 'twill soon be past, Only what's done for Christ will last.
Only one life, yes only one, Soon will its fleeting hours be done;
Then, in "that day" my Lord to meet, And stand before His judgment seat;
Only one life, 'twill soon be past, Only what's done for Christ will last.
Only one life, the still small voice, Gently pleads for a better choice,
Bidding me selfish aims to leave, And to God's holy will to cleave;
Only one life, 'twill soon be past, Only what's done for Christ will last.
Only one life, a few brief years, Each with its burdens, hopes, and fears;
Each with its days I must fulfill, living for self or in His will;
Only one life, 'twill soon be past, Only what's done for Christ will last.
When this bright world would tempt me sore, When Satan would a victory score;
When self would seek to have its way, Then help me Lord with joy to say;
Only one life, 'twill soon be past, Only What's done with Christ will last.
Give me Father, a purpose deep, In joy or sorrow Thy word to keep;
Faithful and true what e'er the strife, Pleasing Thee in my daily life;
Only one life, 'twill soon be past, Only what's done for Christ will last.
Oh let my love with fervor burn, And from the world now let me turn;
Living for Thee, and Thee alone, Bringing Thee pleasure on Thy throne;
Only one life, 'twill soon be past, Only what's done for Christ will last.

Only one life, yes only one, Now let me say, "Thy will be done";
And when at last I'll hear the call, I know I'll say "'twas worth it all";
Only one life, 'twill soon be past, Only what's done for Christ will last.

Father God, let us see the brevity of life and use
it wisely for You. In Jesus's name, amen!

_____

_____

_____

_____

God Will Sustain You a Day at a Time

Vaneetha Rendall Risner
Adapted from desiringGod.org

Each day has enough trouble of its own.
—MATTHEW 6:34

My arms ultimately gave out earlier this year as I was getting ready. I couldn't even get dressed by myself. I suffer from post-polio syndrome, and I'm never sure whether some new pain is a daily setback or the new normal.

I cried out to the Lord, "I can't live like this for the rest of my life. I just can't do it." After my lament, I was quiet. Then, in silence, the following words came to my mind: "I'm not asking you to live like this for the rest of your life. I'm asking you to live like this today."

Daily bread. Jesus taught us to pray, "Give us this day our daily bread" (Matt. 6:11). God will meet our needs today. His grace is available for today. Therefore, we should not be anxious about the future, or even tomorrow, for every day has its own trouble (Matt. 6:34).

The future is in God's hands. Tomorrow morning may bring joy and even a miracle (Ps. 30:5), for His mercies are new every morning, and nothing is impossible with God (Lam. 3:22–23; Luke 1:37).

God reassured me that I didn't need to despair over the future. But He wasn't assuring me that my circumstances would change if I trusted Him. Instead, He called me to trust Him day by day, moment by moment, breath by breath. Although the day was hard, God ensured it would not crush me (2 Cor. 4:8–9).

Just today. My pain and strength ebb and flow daily, so I often don't know what to expect until I get out of bed. But even when the day holds suffering, God comforts me to know that He is not calling me to live with this pain and weakness for the rest of my life. Instead, He is just calling me to live with it today.

Some days He will do far more than I could ask for or even imagine (Eph. 3:20). And other days, He will sustain me in the storm. But every day, He will provide all that I need.

Father God, thank You for sustaining us one
day at a time. In Jesus's name, amen!

_____

_____

_____

_____

In His Time

Jon Bloom

Adapted from desiringGod.org

[God] has made everything beautiful in its time.
—ECCLESIASTES 3:11

The Hebrew word translated "beautiful" means appropriate, fitting, right. So, this verse teaches us that God's perfect timing can be trusted even when we don't understand it.

God's perfect timing. God operates on a very different timeline than we do—if "timeline" is even the right word. For God is not constrained by time. On the contrary, He is the Father of time (Gen. 1:1; Col. 1:16). He exists from "everlasting to everlasting" (Ps. 90:2). God is not in time; time is in God (Acts 17:28; Col. 1:17).

In the fulness of time, God sent His Son into the world (Gal. 4:4), where He proclaimed, "The time is fulfilled, and the kingdom of God is at hand" (Mark 1:14–15). While here, He displayed the great wisdom of God's timing, often in ways that surprised and confused His followers (John 4:1–42; 11:1–44).

And when His time had come (John 12:23), Jesus died on the cross, was raised from the dead, and sat down at the right hand of God, waiting for His enemies to be defeated (Heb. 10:12–14). Someday, our Lord will come when it is the time for restoring all the things God promised (Acts 3:20–21).

Trust God's timing. In the life of faith, we must learn to rely on God's timing more than our own. But unfortunately, learning to trust God's timing is not easy. This is partly due to our sin and unbelief. It's also because we can't calculate God's time. As a result, His timing often doesn't make sense to us.

We cry out, "How long, O Lord?" (Ps. 13:1), wondering when He will finally fulfill some promise that we're clinging to. So, in 2 Peter

3:8, Peter urges us not to overlook that God-time is not man-time. "With the Lord, one day is as a thousand years, and a thousand years as one day."

As children of God, we must not be perplexed by our heavenly Father's apparent slowness. In actuality, God "is not slow" as man counts slowness (v. 9). On the contrary, He makes everything beautiful in its time—the time He purposefully chooses for it.

Father God, let us trust Your timing even when we
don't understand it. In Jesus's name, amen!

_____

_____

_____

_____

Watch Out for the Enemy!

Doug Sherman and William Hendricks
Adapted from *How to Balance Competing Time Demands*

...my grace...my power...
—2 CORINTHIANS 12:9

As you attempt to balance competing time demands, two potential dangers can bring you down: trying to become like Christ through merely human effort and legalism.

Beware of merely human effort. Sometimes, when people hear about setting goals to grow spiritually, they think that becoming Christlike happens through mere human effort. But unfortunately, that's a misperception—even our best efforts to live the way God wants us to fall short of Christ's perfection.

Our growth toward Christlikeness is a joint venture with God. Picture Alexander Graham Bell working with his grandson to construct a toy steamboat made from an egg, powered by a candle. One is a world-class inventor, and the other is a boy enjoying an intriguing new venture. So, which of their efforts accounts for that toy boat?

It is analogous to our walk with Christ. He is the mastermind behind our life and the power working in and through our feeble efforts to make us like Himself. Because He loves us deeply and delights in seeing us grow, He invests our efforts with meaning and power.

Christian growth doesn't mean we accomplish amazing things on God's behalf. Instead, it's Christ changing us through His Holy Spirit, both for His sake and ours.

Beware of legalism. This is a way of thinking that holds something like, "God accepts me because of what I've done or failed to do." It's a relationship with God based on law, not grace. The "law" here is an image you have of a moral law against which God is measuring you.

Dean De Castro   421

That moral law may be expressed for you through the Ten Commandments, the Golden Rule, the Sermon on the Mount, or even the harsh, unrealistic standards of a neurotic parent.

Whatever the source, if you're a legalist, you'll constantly be comparing yourself to others, condemning yourself when you fall short of someone else's achievements, and condemning others when they violate your standards. You'll also live with guilt, constantly weighed down by a sense of God's displeasure and disapproval.

Father God, help us manage our time with
Your grace. In Jesus's name, amen!

_____

_____

_____

_____

Change Takes Time

Dean De Castro

The Lord your God will drive out those
nations before you, little by little.
—DEUTERONOMY 7:22A

People look forward every four years to the glorious Summer Olympics, with the world's great athletes converging in one place to compete for the elusive gold medal.

One of the most exciting events is the race to determine the world's fastest man—the 100-meter dash. According to the race clock one year, the difference between the gold medalist and his second-place competitor was only 11/1000ths of a second! So, the difference between winning and second was nothing more than a *slight edge.*

As we seek to apply the truths of God's words in every aspect of our life, we need to remember the slight edge principle. Change is possible, but it takes time.

We can learn this powerful principle of success through Deuteronomy 7:22. God promised His chosen people that he would drive out their enemies in the land of Canaan *little by little.* Consider how this might shift our perspective:

- We can love and obey God one choice at a time.
- We can read and master the Bible one chapter at a time.
- We can lose excess weight one bite at a time.
- We can learn a new language one word at a time.
- We can fulfill the Great Commission one soul at a time.
- We can clean up and organize our garage one box at a time.
- We can change our character one habit at a time.
- We can retire comfortably by saving one penny at a time.
- We can finish reading or writing a book one chapter at a time.

Dean De Castro   423

- We can live by faith and please God one day at a time.

According to recent research, it takes at least sixty-six days to develop a new habit. Because it takes a lot of neural energy to interrupt an old behavior, hence, to build a new practice, we must repeat a new behavior hundreds of times before it sticks. Eventually, though, it will become second nature.

Keep looking at our Lord in the gospel of His grace, and God will gradually change us to become like Christ from glory to glory (2 Cor. 3:18).

Father God, grant us the patience of Job as You mold us into the image of Your Son, Jesus Christ. In Jesus's name, amen!

_____

_____

_____

_____

God's Ordained Purpose and Mission

Dean De Castro

Before you were born...I appointed you as a prophet.
—JEREMIAH 1:5

The Bible teaches that God has an ordained purpose and mission for each of His children, even before they are born (Jer. 1:5).

Therefore, whatever spiritual gifts God has given you, and whatever stage of life you are in, He wants you to use them so that your success glorifies God and blesses other people (1 Pet. 4:11).

Anne Sullivan's testimony. When Hellen Keller went to study at the Perkins School for the Blind in Boston, she was constantly bitter and angry. Finally, a tutor, Anne Sullivan, was assigned to work with her.

With Sullivan's help, Helen graduated with honors, having mastered several languages. Helen Keller achieved her goals, despite her physical deficiencies, because Anne Sullivan believed in her.

Sullivan's patience, wisdom, and teaching ability combined made her a uniquely gifted teacher for Helen.

My personal testimony. As of March 2019, I officially retired from serving in the local church. However, as I was praying for my next assignment from God, He reminded me of the vision He gave me when I was fifteen and I was praying for God's guidance on what to major in in college after graduating high school.

I was reading the book of Exodus during my devotional time when God spoke to me. God told Moses to write down everything God had said to him on the mountain. The word "write" showed up several times, and I felt God wanted me to be a writer. So, I went on to study journalism and mass communication.

A year later, God led me to study at a Bible school to become a Bible teacher. Fifty-two years have passed since then, and now in my retirement, I am fulfilling my dream of becoming a Christian writer, sharing what God taught me through all these years.

What spiritual gifts and natural talents do you have? Are you committed to finding out God's unique plan and purpose for your life? God has a great future for you. All you have to do is to believe and embrace it.

I did.

Father God, let us embrace Your perfect plan for
our life here on earth. In Jesus's name, amen!

_____

_____

_____

_____

Saved to Serve

Dean De Castro

For we are God's handiwork...to do good works.
—EPHESIANS 2:10

Have you ever wondered why God doesn't immediately take us to heaven after He saves us?

The Bible says God saved us to serve Him (Eph. 2:10), and we serve God by serving others. God wants us to use our God-given talents and spiritual gifts to fulfill His purposes here on earth.

Talents and spiritual gifts are not the same things. Talents are natural skills and gifts that God, out of His abundance, gives to Christians and non-Christians alike. For example, Carl Lewis was a gifted track star because he could run faster and jump farther than many other human beings.

On the other hand, spiritual gifts are only for those indwelt by the Holy Spirit. God gives every born-again Christian at least one spiritual ability to build the Body of Christ and extend its influence in an unbelieving world.

Talents and skills. As a follower of Christ, you must use your God-given aptitudes and skills to glorify God in your workplace. Remember that you work for Christ; He is your ultimate boss. "It is the Lord you are serving" (Col. 3:24b).

As Martin Luther King Jr. puts it, "If it falls your lot to sweep streets in life, sweep streets like Beethoven composed music. Sweep streets like Shakespeare wrote poetry. Sweep streets so well that all the hosts of heaven and earth will have to pause and say, 'Here lived a great street sweeper, who swept his job well'" (see Titus 2:10).

Spiritual gifts. According to 1 Peter 4:10, "Each one should use whatever gift he has received to serve others." "Each one" means that God has gifted every Christian to serve Him well in the church.

There is a story about Michelangelo pushing a massive piece of rock down the street. A curious neighbor sitting lazily on his porch called out, "Hey, Mike, why are you laboring so hard over an old piece of stone?" Michelangelo answered, "Because there is an angel in that rock that wants to come out."

What spiritual gifts in you want to come out to build fellow Christians and fulfill the Great Commission?

> *Father God, let us use our God-given talents and spiritual gifts to glorify You and serve others. In Jesus's name, amen!*

_____

_____

_____

_____

Spiritual Gifts and Talents in the Ministry
Dean De Castro

Each one should use whatever gift you have received to
serve others...If anyone speaks...if anyone serves...so that
in all things God may be praised through Jesus Christ.
—1 PETER 4:10–11

According to the Apostle Peter, God has given us different talents and spiritual gifts to serve others. Let me share seven insights about ministry based on today's passage.

First, "each one" means God gives every Christian the ability to do at least one thing well for Him. In other words, there is something you can do for God that no one else could.

Second, our responsibility is to "use whatever gift you have received to serve others." If you don't use it, you'll lose it. As Neil Anderson warns us, "Tragically, many people go to the grave with their music still in them, never contributing to the symphony of God's work."

Third, talents and spiritual abilities are God's "gifts and grace" to be faithfully administered. Rick Warren writes, "Faithful servants don't leave a job half undone, and they don't quit when they get discouraged. They are trustworthy and dependable."

Fourth, spiritual gifts come in "various forms." Peter lists two of them: speaking and serving. Paul lists seven gifts in Romans 12, eleven in 1 Corinthians 12, and four in Ephesians 4.

Fifth, those with the gifts of words (prophecy, teaching, exhortation, etc.) must speak according to God's words and not their own human opinions and ideas.

Sixth, those who have the gift of serving (leading, helps, administration, etc.) must do so with God's strength.

Seventh, the ultimate goal of the ministry is "that in all things God may be praised through Jesus Christ. To Him be the glory and the power forever and ever. Amen!"

We must understand that no one else can develop our potential for us. Instead, we must discover our own God-given gifts and talents and then put ourselves to the task of developing these skills and abilities to their fullest extent.

> Serving mankind is the rent we pay for occupying a space here on the planet earth.
>
> —Anonymous.

Father God, let us not go to the grave without
knowing and using our gifts and talents to glorify
You and edify others. In Jesus's name, amen!

_____

_____

_____

_____

Your Place in the Body

Selwyn Hughes

Adapted from *How to Live the Christian Life*

All of you together are the one Body of Christ.
—1 CORINTHIANS 12:27, TLB

What is the church?

Is it Gothic architecture, elegant masonry, and stained-glass windows? Is it a building on which stands a steeple? No! The church is the Body of Christ.

The church—His Body. When Jesus was here on earth, He was God in human flesh. But after His return to heaven, He sent back the Holy Spirit to form a new Body so that His life could continue here on earth.

That Body consists of millions of believers, redeemed by His blood, and now part of that mystical union that stretches around the globe.

As members of that Body, we are also members of one another, and the purpose of our spiritual gift is not simply to express ourselves but to *build up that Body.*

Our place in the Body. As in the human Body, each part functions in complete harmony and interdependence. So, in the Body of Christ, He has positioned each one of us to perform a task that we are capable of.

Once we understand our specific place in the Body of Christ, we need to commit to using every ability God has given us—first, to bring ourselves into Christ's likeness and seek to bring others to spiritual maturity.

Maximum effectiveness with minimum weariness. When a person begins to work the way God has planned for them, this service is not a grinding struggle but sheer delight.

Someone might think you ought to be a preacher and go to Bible school or that you ought to sing in the choir or sit on a particular committee. You must learn to say, "Let me pray about it first and find out whether this is in line with what the Lord has planned, and I will let you know."

Recognize that God has made you the way you are for a purpose. Don't model yourself on anyone else or copy the ministry of others, but find out what God has for you, then work with Him.

Father God, let us discover our primary spiritual gift and exercise it as You have planned. In Jesus's name, amen!

_____

_____

_____

_____

A Basic List of Gifts

Mark Porter
Adapted from *The Time of Your Life*

We have different gifts, according to the grace given to us.
—ROMANS 12:6–8

Paul provides a more extensive list of spiritual gifts in 1 Corinthians 12, but they are all derived from the essential list of seven in Romans 12. And the Word of God commands every believer to practice all seven of these gifts to varying degrees.

Prophesying. Speaking to others for God (1 Cor. 14:1)

Serving. Meeting the needs of others (Gal. 5:13)

Teaching. Helping others understand and apply God's truth (Col. 3:16)

Exhorting. Stimulating the faith and works of others (Heb. 13:3, KJV)

Giving. Sharing yourself and your goods to meet the needs of others (Rom. 12:13)

Leading. Coordinating the activities of others to achieve common goals (1 Tim. 3:4)

Showing mercy. Comforting and empathizing with others (Col. 3:12–13)

Bill Gothard, founder of the Institute in Basic Youth Conflicts, compares the seven gifts of the Spirit by showing how each gift might be used to respond to an accident at dinner. For example, the hostess drops the dessert on the floor.

The server says, "Here, let me clean it up."

The leader says, "Jim, would you go get the mop? Then, Sue, if you help me clean up, Mary and I will fix another dessert."

The giver says, "I'll go out and buy another dessert."

The merciful says, "Don't feel bad; it could have happened to anyone."

The prophet says, "That's what happens when you're not careful."

The teacher says, "Clearly, it fell because it was unbalanced; the tray was too heavy on one side."

The exhorter says, "To avoid this in the future, you should use both hands."

There is a beautiful balance in the diversity of these seven gifts. But unfortunately, when there is strife and misunderstanding in the church, almost always, we can trace it to a failure to appreciate the function of other gifts in the Body.

Father God, guide us to discover our spiritual gifts
and use them actively and humbly in building
up Your church. In Jesus's name, amen!

_____

_____

_____

_____

Categories of Spiritual Gifts

Greg Ogden

Adapted from *Discipleship Essentials*

There are different kinds of gifts.
—1 CORINTHIANS 12:4A

We can categorize the spiritual gifts listed in different Scriptures into four groups:

Support gifts. Those who have support gifts are responsible for equipping the rest of the church members to exercise their ministry gifts (Eph. 4:11).

Apostle: Missionaries and church planters.

Prophet: Preachers of God's words.

Evangelist: Passionate in sharing the gospel of God's grace.

Pastor-teacher: Shepherd of a flock.

Speaking gifts

Teaching (Rom. 12:7; 1 Cor. 12:28): Teach God's words effectively.

Encouragement (Rom. 12:8): Motivate individuals or groups through exhortation or rebuke.

Wisdom (1 Cor. 12:8): Apply insights from the Holy Spirit to specific needs.

Knowledge (1 Cor. 12:8): Accumulate facts to help upbuild the body.

Sign gifts

Healing (1 Cor. 12:9): Supernatural intervention of physical, emotional or spiritual illness.

Miracles (1 Cor. 12:10): Interrupt the universe's natural laws to glorify God.

Tongues and interpretation (1 Cor. 12:10): Supernatural human or angelic language to praise God.

Service gifts

Help (1 Cor. 12:28): Aide someone to pursue their main call.

Administration (1 Cor. 12:28): Organize people to accomplish goals.

Service (Rom. 12:7): Meet practical or material needs of others.

Giving (Rom. 12:8): Give material goods or resources joyfully.

Leadership/Faith (Rom. 12:8–9): Empower people to fulfill their dreams.

Mercy (Rom. 12:8): Work joyfully with those the majority ignores.

Hospitality (1 Pet. 4:9): Entertain guests at home with joy and affection.

Discernment (1 Cor. 12:10): Judge whether the spirit acting on a person is from God or Satan.

Father God, let us gratefully and faithfully use the spiritual gifts You have apportioned to each of us. In Jesus's name, amen!

_____

_____

_____

_____

Shaped for Serving God

Rick Warren
Adapted from *The Purpose Driven Life*

Your hands shaped me and made me.
—JOB 10:8

God has uniquely designed, or "shaped," us to do certain things.

Whenever God gives us an assignment, He always equips us with what we need to accomplish it. You are a combination of many different factors. I have created a simple acrostic to help you remember five of these factors: SHAPE.

S—Spiritual Gifts. God gives every believer at least one spiritual gift. It's called a gift because you don't deserve it.

Your spiritual gifts were not provided for your benefit but for the good of others. The Bible says, "A spiritual gift is given to each of us as a means of helping the entire church" (1 Cor. 12:7, NLT). Have you taken the time to find your spiritual gifts? An unopened gift is worthless.

H—Heart. The Bible uses this term to describe the bundle of desires, hopes, interests, ambitions, dreams, and affection you have. Your heart represents what you care about the most. Figure out what you are passionate about, and then do it for God's glory.

A—Abilities. Your abilities are the natural talents you were born with. Your abilities were not given to make your living; God gave them to you for ministry. "God has given each of you some special abilities, be sure to use them to help each other, passing on to others God's many kinds of blessings" (1 Pet. 4:10, TLB).

P—Personality. God made you to be you with your unique personality. Your temperament will affect how, when, and where you use your spiritual gifts and abilities. Like stained glass, our different personalities reflect God's light in many colors and patterns. They bless the family of God with depth and variety.

E—Experiences. At least six categories of experience from your past mold your ministry: family, educational, vocational, spiritual, ministerial, and painful experiences. Aldous Huxley rightly reminds us, "Experience is not what happens to you. It is what you do with what happens to you." So, please don't waste your pain; use it to help others.

Father God, help us know how You shape us to be effective
in our ministry for You. In Jesus's name, amen!

_____

_____

_____

_____

Steps in Spiritual Gifts Discovery

Greg Ogden
Adapted from *Discipleship Essentials*

We have different gifts, according to the grace given to us.
—ROMANS 12:6A

There is no exact process for discovering your spiritual gifts. To get a clear picture of yourself, you must come to the discovery process from several different angles.

Explore the possibilities. Be aware of the biblical definition of the different gifts so you can compare your behavior and inclinations with their characteristics.

Discern your motivation. When you operate according to your gifts, you should feel that you are doing what you have been specifically designed by God to do, which will lead to inner satisfaction and fulfillment.

Seek feedback from the Body. Those who know you best and have observed you are the best candidates for giving you their evaluation of your giftedness. Spiritual gifts affect others and build them up. Each gift leaves its imprint.

Test the options. Often, the discovery of a spiritual gift means taking risks and trying new things. Evaluate your past areas of service and attempt to determine which were fulfilling and which were unsatisfactory.

Explore critical feelings. What you criticize in others may be a clue to your giftedness. It could tell giftedness because you have identified something in another that you feel capable of doing yourself. However, it could also mean that you have a critical spirit and need repentance.

Subjective inventory of gifts. On a piece of paper, complete the following statements as quickly as possible, writing down your initial thoughts:

- In my work or church ministry, I find myself most fulfilled when _____.
- Others have told me I am most helpful when _____.
- People have often asked me to _____ (e.g., teach or clarify a confusing concept).
- As a Christian, I most often picture myself as _____ (e.g., a coach)
- I believe God has given me the responsibility of _____ in my congregation.
- My biggest concern for this church is _____.
- If I were confident in not failing in ministry, I would _____.
- After reviewing my answers, I think I have the gifts of _____. (List as many as you like.)

*Father God, help us discover and affirm each other's gifts
in building up Your Body. In Jesus's name, amen!*

_____

_____

_____

_____

Obstacles to Discovering Our Gifts

Mark Porter
Adapted from *The Time of Your Life*

Do not neglect the spiritual gift within you.
—1 TIMOTHY 4:14–15, NASB

In Romans 12, Paul tells us about four obstacles that prevent the discovery and development of spiritual gifts. Just as God seldom reveals His will to someone unwilling to obey, we will remain in a fog concerning our spiritual gifts until we root these attitudes out of our lives.

Selfishness. The word "sacrifice" in verse 1—"present your bodies as a living sacrifice"— signals the very antithesis of selfishness. Our bodies are to become living sacrifices, including all our members, faculties, and natural talents.

Therefore, a prerequisite for developing spiritual gifts is making ourselves available. Talents and faculties used for only ourselves will never develop into spiritual gifts.

Pride. Nothing squelches a spiritual gift faster than pride. Therefore, "I say to every man among you not to think highly of himself than he ought to think" (v. 3a).

Churches have split because some in the congregation thought they had a monopoly on spiritual gifts. As a result, they looked down with disdain on others who didn't have the skills they had. For the sake of our communities and the churches, we need to recognize and accept our limitations.

Envy. We are so envious of other people's gifts that we become blind to our own. The Apostle Paul urges us to evaluate our gifts with sound judgment "as God has allotted to each a measure of faith" (v. 3b). An underestimate of one's gift can be as bad as an overestimate.

Don't look at other believers and say, "Oh, if I were as gifted as she is..." because there is a real sense in which no one else can do what God gifted you to do.

Laziness. Developing a spiritual gift can be hard work. But "if it is leadership, let him govern diligently" (v. 8). The same applies to all spiritual gifts.

For example, you may have the gift of teaching, but you will never be able to teach the Word of God effectively until you become familiar with the whole counsel of God. To be an effective Bible teacher is a lifelong process.

Father God, whatever spiritual gifts You have given us, let us polish them like a diamond in the rough. In Jesus's name, amen!

_____

_____

_____

_____

Motivations in Ministry

Donald Whitney
Adapted from *Spiritual Disciplines for the Christian*

Serve the Lord with gladness.
—PSALM 100:2, KJV

Motives matter in the ministry. The Bible mentions at least six reasons for serving.

Motivated by obedience. In Deuteronomy 13:4, Moses relates serving God to obeying Him. Any faithful Christian would say that they want to obey God. But we disobey God when we are not serving Him.

Motivated by gratitude. It is no burden to serve God when we consider what great things He has done for us (1 Sam. 12:24). The greatest gift He has given us is His salvation through Christ's sacrifice on the cross.

Motivated by gladness. We are not to serve God grudgingly but gladly (Ps. 100:2). For the believer, serving God is not a burden; it's a privilege. Do your kids get the impression from you that serving God is something that you really enjoy or merely endure?

Motivated by forgiveness, not guilt. In Isaiah 6:6–8, notice how the prophet responds once God forgives him: "Here am I. Send me!" (v. 8). Isaiah wants to serve God, not because he felt guilty, but because God had taken his guilt away (v. 7). God's people do not serve Him to be forgiven but because Christ's death freed us from guilt.

Motivated by humility. By washing His disciples' feet, our Lord set an example of how to serve with humility (John 13:12–16). In the discipline of service, the issue is not always how well you do, for even the world serves well when it leads to profit. But the Christian serves with humility because it leads to Christlikeness.

Motivated by love. There is no better fuel for service that burns longer and provides more energy than love (Gal. 5:13).

A reporter once asked a missionary couple in Africa whether they liked their work. The husband responded. "Liking or disliking has nothing to do with it. We have orders to go, and we go. Love constrains us."

*Father God, purify our motives for serving
You. In Jesus's name, amen!*

The Ministry is War

Dean De Castro

Join with me in suffering, like a good soldier of Christ Jesus.
—2 TIMOTHY 2:3

Paul spoke of the ministry as "fighting the good fight" (2 Tim. 4:7), and he encouraged Timothy to endure hardship as a good soldier of Jesus Christ (2 Tim. 2:3).

In defending his apostolic authority against his worst critics in the church at Corinth, Paul explains his serious attitude towards his ministry in 2 Corinthians 10:1–5.

Paul realizes that the ministry is spiritual warfare. Therefore, he battles not with flesh and blood but with a spiritual enemy who is determined to destroy the church of Christ (Eph. 6:12).

Paul's fighting. Paul admits that he still lives in the flesh (2 Cor. 10:3a, KJV)—possessing a body still subject to human imperfections. However, Paul refuses to rely on the strength of his personality—being bold, aggressive, and confident of winning the war in the ministry. Instead, he learned to rely on the power of the Holy Spirit to rescue souls for Christ (2 Cor. 10:3b).

In contrast, Paul hints indirectly that some of the church leaders in Corinth were fighting the war of rescuing sinners from the kingdom of darkness by using weapons of the flesh (2 Cor. 10:4).

In his commentary on this epistle, Homer Kent Jr. writes, "Human eloquence, manmade schemes, personal magnetism, psychological manipulation, crowd dynamics, and showmanship may achieve temporary results, but ultimately they are no match for the opposing spiritual forces."

Paul's preaching. In 2 Corinthians 10:5, Paul describes how his preaching is so powerful and effective in destroying the human reasonings and excuses that keep unbelievers from accepting God's saving message.

Paul did not use his intellectual acumen and rhetorical skills to persuade sinners to submit to Christ's lordship. Instead, he relied on the power of the Holy Spirit to make every thought of his audience captive to the obedience to Christ's gospel.

As a result, Paul's anointed messages led many unbelievers to come out of darkness and into light. Moreover, they repented of their wrong beliefs about God and His works, becoming submissive to the lordship of Christ in thought and deed.

Father God, help us destroy the devil's deception
in Your strength. In Jesus's name, amen!

_____

_____

_____

_____

Duty and Delight

Dean De Castro

So you also, when you have done everything you were
told to do, should say,..."We have only done our duty."
—LUKE 17:10

Why do you serve the Lord?

Is it because of duty? I believe it is. As slaves of God purchased by the precious blood of Christ, it is our duty and obligation to serve our new Master. Such service is simply a logical and reasonable reaction to what God has done (Rom. 12:1).

Duty. The parable Jesus tells in Luke 17:7–10 teaches us that God is not obligated to reward us after doing everything we have been asked to do. God owes us nothing for having done our duty!

We should not even think we can relax after a hard day's work and do whatever we want. As slaves owned by God, we are always on duty 24/7. We can only rest after completing our assignments from God.

Delight. Remember that we are not hirelings, serving for wages. The Bible teaches that we are not only slaves of God but are also adopted into His household to be His beloved children (Rom. 8:15). We serve God because we are His children, delighting in our Father's work and trusting in His generosity.

In his thought-provoking book *Slave,* John MacArthur writes, "The only begotten Son of God took on the form of a slave (Phil. 2:7) so that the slaves of sin might become both slaves of righteousness and sons of God...Thus, we are simultaneously *sons* and *slaves.* The two realities are not mutually exclusive—even if the metaphors are different. Forever we will be part of His family. Forever we will be in His glorious servitude (Rev. 22:3)."

On December 4, 1857, on the threshold of his return to Africa, David Livingston tried to put into words the motives that shaped his life: "I have never ceased to rejoice that God has entrusted me with His service. People talk a lot about the sacrifice involved in devoting my life to Africa. Can this be called a sacrifice at all if we give back to God a 'little of what we owe Him?' Away with this word. It is anything but sacrifice. Rather, call it a 'privilege'!"

Father God, it's both our responsibility and honor
to serve you forever. In Jesus's name, amen!

_____

_____

_____

_____

Insecurity in the Ministry

Dean De Castro

"No," said Peter, "you shall never wash my feet."
—JOHN 13:8A

When Jesus turned to Peter to wash his feet, Peter reacted strongly, "Lord, you are not about to wash my feet." In Peter's mind, Jesus washing the feet of all the disciples was a demeaning act that made Peter feel extremely uncomfortable.

Christ's identity. Washing feet was the job of the slaves at that time. It's beneath the dignity of Jesus as the teacher of the twelve disciples. So why did Jesus engage in such lowly service?

It didn't bother Jesus to do what no disciple was willing to because He knew who He was. His identity and worth were based on His relationship with the Father (John 13:3).

Your identity. Insecure people are unwilling to accept jobs that they consider "beneath" them. They are constantly worrying about how they appear to others. They are addicted to people's opinions and approval. This is why only secure people are truly free to serve.

To serve people effectively, you must set your identity and worth in Christ. Our identity must be in God, not our achievements (Luke 10:20). Because they know they are loved and accepted unconditionally by God's grace, those who serve God don't need to prove their worth.

Rick Warren emphasizes the importance of security in service, writing, "Servants don't need to cover their walls with plaques and awards to validate their work. They don't insist on being addressed by titles, and they don't wrap themselves in robes of superiority. Servants find status symbols unnecessary, and they don't measure their worth by their achievements."

Similarly, Henri Nouwen says, "In order to be of service to others, we have to die to them; that is, we have to give up measuring our meaning and value with the yardstick of others....Thus we become free to be compassionate."

In *The Crucifixion of Ministry*, Andrew Purves provides a vision for students and clergy "to reclaim the vital connection between Christ and our participation in His ministry today, even if it means we have to let Christ Himself put to death our own ministries to which we cling so closely."

Father God, let us be more concerned about serving others than being validated by men. In Jesus's name, amen!

_____

_____

_____

_____

How Real Servants Act

Rick Warren
Adapted from *The Purpose Driven Life*

Whoever wants to be great must become a servant.
—MARK 10:43, MSG

How can you know if you have a servant's heart? Jesus says, "You can tell what they are by what they do" (Matt. 7:16, CEV).

Real servants make themselves available to serve. Servants don't fill up their time with other pursuits that could limit their availability. Much like a soldier, a servant must always stand by for duty (2 Tim. 2:4, NASB). Servants see interruptions as divine appointments for ministry and are happy for the opportunity to practice serving.

Real servants pay attention to needs. "Whenever we have the opportunity, we have to do what is good for everyone" (Gal. 6:10, GWT). John Wesley's words remind us of our duty: "Do all the good you can, by all the means you can, in all the places you can, at all the times you can, to all the people you can, as long as you ever can."

Real servants do their best with what they have. "If you wait for perfect conditions, you will never get anything done" (Eccl. 11:4, NLT). God expects you to do what you can, with what you have, wherever you are. Less than perfect service is always better than the best intention.

Real servants do every task with equal dedication. Whatever they do, servants "do it with all their heart" (Col. 3:23). The size of the task is irrelevant. Don't look for great tasks to do for God. Before attempting to do the extraordinary, try serving in ordinary ways, and God will assign you whatever He wants you to do.

Real servants are faithful to their ministry. Servants finish their tasks, fulfill their responsibilities, keep their promises, and complete their commitments. They don't leave a job half done, and they don't quit when they get discouraged. They are trustworthy and dependable (Matt. 25:23).

Real servants maintain a low profile. Self-promotion and servanthood don't mix. Real servants don't serve for the approval or applause of others. As Paul says, "If I were still trying to please men, I would not be a servant of Christ" (Gal. 1:10).

Father God, help us serve You and others like our Lord,
with great humility and love. In Jesus's name, amen!

_____

_____

_____

_____

The Example of Jesus

Max Lucado
Adapted from *How Happiness Happens*

The Son of Man did not come to be served, but to serve.
—MATTHEW 20:28

Jesus came to serve.

Jesus served here on earth. In one of His appearances to His followers, they were on the Sea of Galilee when they heard Him call out from the shore. When He told them where to find fish, they realized it was Jesus.

Peter plunged into the water and swam to shore. The other disciples grabbed their oars and paddled. When they reached the beach, they saw the most extraordinary sight. Jesus was cooking! He told them, "Come and eat breakfast" (John 21:12).

Shouldn't the roles be reversed? Jesus had just ripped the gates of hell off their hinges. He'd disemboweled the devil. He'd made a deposit of grace that forever offsets our debt of sin. He'd sentenced the demons to death row and set free every sinner since Adam.

Jesus will serve in the future. Jesus, the unrivaled Commander of the Universe, wore the apron? Even more, He has yet to remove it. He promises a feast in heaven where "He will gird Himself and have them sit down to eat, and will come and serve them" (Luke 12:37).

Can you imagine the sight? Row after row of food-laden tables. The redeemed of the ages celebrating and singing, and someone asks, "Has anyone seen Jesus?"

"Yes," another person replies. "He's on the other side of the banquet room serving iced tea."

"Christ Himself was like God in everything. But He did not think that being equal with God was something to be used for His own benefit. But He gave up His place with God and made Himself nothing. He was born as a man and became like a servant" (Phil. 2:6–7, NCV).

Jesus was content with the humblest of titles. He was pleased to be called a servant.

It's your turn to serve. Suppose you took that role. Be the family member who offers to wash the dishes after dinner, the church member who supports the pastor with prayer and notes of encouragement, or the neighbor who mows the grass of the elderly couple.

Father God, make us a servant like our Lord
Jesus Christ. In Jesus's name, amen!

_____

_____

_____

_____

No More Excuses!

Rick Warren
Adapted from *The Purpose Driven Life*

Each of us will give a personal account to God.
—ROMANS 14:12, NLT

Service is not optional.

God wants to use you to make a difference in His kingdom. He wants to work through you. What matters is not the *duration* of your life but the *donation* of it. Not *how long* you lived, but *how* you lived.

If you're not involved in any service or ministry, what excuse have you been using?

- Abraham was old.
- Jacob was insecure.
- Leah was unattractive.
- Joseph was abused.
- Moses stuttered.
- Gideon was poor.
- Samson was codependent.
- Rahab was immoral.
- David had an affair and all kinds of family problems.
- Elijah was suicidal.
- Jeremiah was depressed.
- Jonah was reluctant.
- Naomi was a widow.
- John the Baptist was eccentric.
- Peter was impulsive and hot-tempered.
- Martha worried a lot.
- The Samaritan woman had several failed marriages.
- Zacchaeus was unpopular.

- Thomas had doubts.
- Paul had poor health.
- Timothy was timid.

That is quite a variety of misfits, but God used each of them in His service. He will use you, too, if you stop making excuses. What is holding you back from accepting God's call to serve Him?

Father God, let us learn how to love and serve others unselfishly. In Jesus's name, amen!

_____

_____

_____

_____

Serving Our Family
Dean De Castro

...put their religion into practice by caring for their own family.
—1 TIMOTHY 5:4

In the context of laying out the qualifications for a widow to receive material support from the church, the Apostle Paul reveals seven truths concerning the believer's ministry to their own families.

First, believers should *learn* to serve their parents and relatives and meet their needs. Fulfilling such responsibility does not come naturally. Even if it means self-denial, believers must learn this lesson.

Second, our family is a priority. Children should first learn to apply their Christian faith in their family life. The first place for us to serve God is in our families. After Jesus drove the demons from a demon-possessed man, He instructed him to return to his family and share the gospel (Mark 5:19).

Third, genuine godliness is practiced in providing support for aging and needy family members. Caring for parents or grandparents is a reverent action. A failure in piety toward our parents is a failure in piety toward God.

Fourth, filial duty is based on grace and gratitude. It is children repaying their parents as a thankful response for all the sacrifice and tender care they received at their parents' hands. They have to take care of their aging parents.

Fifth, serving the needs of our parents or grandparents is not only a filial duty but also our spiritual duty to God, for this is pleasing to God. When we honor our parents, we honor God in obeying the fifth commandment (Exod. 20:12). Such conduct is acceptable in the sight of God.

Sixth, failure in serving our family is a denial of Christianity (1 Tim. 5:8a). The most fundamental article of the Christian faith is love

(1 Thess. 4:9). Therefore, a child's loving care of aging or destitute parents should express love for them and God.

Seventh, failure to serve our family makes it hard for Christians to witness to unbelievers (v. 8b). They are worse than the pagans who assent in principle to the filial obligation of caring for aging parents. Matthew 5:46–47 suggests that even sinners feel family devotion and responsibility.

Father God, we believe your promise to bless us if we obey your commandment to care for our families. In Jesus's name, amen!

_____

_____

_____

_____

Serving Our Neighbors

Dean De Castro

And who is my neighbor?
—LUKE 10:25–37

An expert in the Mosaic law asked this question to test Jesus and get Him into a debate on the meaning of the word "neighbor." This man knew the answer to his own question.

In *The Parables: Understanding What Jesus Meant,* Gary Inrig explains, "Leviticus 19:18 uses the term 'neighbor' as a synonym for 'brother' or 'people.' So the rabbis taught that one's neighbor was a fellow Israelite."

The teacher of the law and the audience must be greatly shocked when Jesus used a Samaritan man as the hero in His story, widely known as the parable of the Good Samaritan. This famous story teaches us three main concepts that are relevant to our responsibility to love our neighbors.

Character. Our Lord did not directly answer the question "Who is my neighbor?" Instead, He asked the expert, "Which of these three [a priest, a Levite, and a Samaritan] do you think was a neighbor to the man who fell into the hands of robbers?" (Luke 10:36). That is, the right question to ask is "How can I be a good neighbor to the people around me?"

Both the priest and the Levite failed to love and serve their neighbors because they lacked the strength of character to leave their comfort zone.

Compassion. The good Samaritan did not allow the usual hostility between Jews and Samaritans to become an excuse to do nothing. Rather, "he took pity on him" (Luke 10:33). His compassion motivated him to serve the wounded Jewish man and not think of himself.

Compassion describes the way God feels about us. When we show mercy to others, we treat them how God has treated us. Love for people is the overflow of our love for God (see 1 John 3:17).

Care. John Maxwell writes, "People don't care how much you know until they know how much you care." Notice the seven steps the good Samaritan took to care for the needs of the victim: He approached the man, cleansed his wounds with wine and oil, bound the wounds, put the man on his donkey, took the man to the inn, stayed with him for a night, paid the bill, and promised to come back and pay the remaining expenses.

Father God, help us be good neighbors to
everyone. In Jesus's name, amen!

The Two-Story View of Work

Doug Sherman and William Hendricks
Adapted from *Your Work Matters to God*

My Father is always at His work to this very day.
—JOHN 5:17A

Too many believers have bought into what we call a two-story view of work. It wrongly divides life into *sacred* and *secular* categories.

In this way of thinking, Sacred activities, such as church attendance, Bible reading, prayer, and the like, are spiritually valuable and count before God. They last in eternity. According to this view, work that matters to God is ministry, evangelism, and missions.

By default, *secular categories* are things that God is presumably disinterested in: hobbies, yard work, politics, sports, entertainment, and of course, everyday work.

According to this view, if you drive a truck, program computers, sell insurance, or work in the financial services industry, your job doesn't count before God. In His eyes, you're a second-class citizen.

Is this a biblical view of work? Does it accurately represent God's perspectives? *Absolutely not!* While it may sound spiritual and Christian, it distorts the truth.

Scripture shows us that work has *intrinsic* value because God Himself is a Worker and has created humans in His image to be workers and coworkers. Work is a gift from God, given to us at creation, before the world knew sin and evil.

Furthermore, work has *instrumental* value in that it serves at least five general purposes according to the Bible:

- Through work, we help other people and meet their needs.
- Through work, we meet our own needs.
- Through work, we meet the needs of our families.

- Through work, we earn money to help the poor and those in Christian vocations.
- Through work, we express our love for God.

Your work matters to God! It matters to Him as much as the work of your pastor. You do not have to quit your job and go into the ministry to do something significant for God.

God wants you to stay where you are and glorify Him in the workplace. Develop a godly work style so striking and authentic that your coworkers will be itching to learn your secrets.

Father God, let us be the light and salt in our workplaces to bring our coworkers to Christ. In Jesus's name, amen!

_____

_____

_____

_____

How Helping Others Helps You

Dr. Carol Tanksley

Adapted from drcarolministries.com

We must help the weak.
—ACTS 20:35

God created you but not for yourself alone. There comes a time when focusing inwardly becomes seriously destructive. A life dedicated to self-service is always miserable.

Focusing outward and finding people you can help by improving their lives will lift your spirits as little else can. Helping others helps you.

But how do you know who you're supposed to help? Here are a few questions to consider.

Who is nearby you right now? How can you encourage your spouse and children? Who are the coworkers, neighbors, church acquaintances, colleagues, friends, etc. that you interact with regularly? Who among them is struggling? How can you make their lives better in some way?

Ask God to help you be more aware of people around you who you can lift in some way. Pay close attention, and notice who is having a tough time. Then determine to do something about it, and quietly follow through.

Whose pain do you feel? Your struggles may have made you more sensitive to others who are struggling similarly. Perhaps your past or life experiences have made you aware of those facing the same problems you have.

Perhaps there's a group of people, or one particular person, who you can't get out of your mind. That's a massive clue about what God may be asking you to do. Find that one person or ten people who get "under your skin" and then find a way to make things better for them.

Where are you most gifted? You have unique gifts or resources of some kind. God does not ask you to give what you don't have. Instead, He grants talents and skills to equip you to bless others. Don't waste His gifts on yourself only.

So, if you're stuck in a negative swirl of navel-gazing—stop. It's not all about you! If you have a home, a bank account, a healthy body, a little time to listen, and know how to read, there is someone who can use your help.

And your emotions will be transformed quicker than you expect. Helping others helps you.

Father God, save us from selfishness by using our talents
and gifts to serve others. In Jesus's name, amen!

_____

_____

_____

_____

Will We Work in Heaven?

Randy Alcorn
Adapted from *Heaven*

*My Father is always at His work to this
very day, and I too am working.*
—JOHN 5:17

The idea of working in heaven is foreign to many people. Yet Scripture teaches it.

God works. God Himself is a worker. Jesus says, "My Father is always at His work to this very day, and I, too, am working" (John 5:17). As God's image-bearers, we're made to work. When God created Adam, work was part of the original Eden (Gen. 2:15). It was part of a perfect human life.

Only after man sinned did work become a curse. The curse made work menial, tedious, and frustrating (Gen. 3:17–19).

Humans work. Since work began before sin and the curse, we should assume human beings will work on the new earth. Thus, we should think we'll be able to resume the work started by Adam and Eve, exercising godly dominion over the earth and ruling it for God's glory.

On the new earth, work will be redeemed and transformed into what God intended: "No longer will there be any curse...and His servants will serve Him" (Rev. 22:3).

When the faithful servant enters heaven, he is offered not retirement but this: "Well done, good and faithful servant; you have been faithful over a few things, I will make you ruler over many things. Enter into the joy of your Lord" (Matt. 25:23, NLT).

Works in heaven. What kind of work will we do in heaven? Maybe you'll build a cabinet with Joseph of Nazareth. Or with Jesus. Perhaps you'll tend sheep with David, discuss medicine with Luke, sew with

Dorcas, make clothes with Lydia, design a new tent with Paul or Priscilla, or ride horses with John Wesley.

The night before Jesus died, He said to His Father, "I brought glory to you here on earth by doing everything you told me to do" (John 17:4, NLT). What will we do for eternity to glorify God? By doing everything that He tells us to do. We'll exercise dominion over the new earth, demonstrating God's creativity and ingenuity as His image-bearers, producing Christlike culture.

Father God, let us celebrate the sanctity of work both here on earth and in heaven in the future. In Jesus's name, amen!

_____

_____

_____

_____

The Right to Rule in Heaven

Bruce Wilkinson

Adapted from *A Life God Rewards*

Take charge of ten cities.
—LUKE 19:17

When you get there, what do you think your strongest desire in heaven will be?

When we see our Savior, we will realize that worship and praise won't be enough. We will want to do something for Him. In heaven, we will desperately crave to serve Him in response to His love for us.

In the parable of the faithful stewards, our Lord rewarded the faithful believers with authority to rule over ten cities (Luke 19:17).

Serve faithfully here on earth. As a steward, you have been commissioned to manage an asset for Your Master. Your asset is your life—the sum of your talents, strengths, personality, and interests. Your opportunity is to manage your life in such a way that you significantly increase your Master's kingdom.

Are you a seamstress or the leader of a nation? A factory worker or a young mother? A village pastor or a builder? Every disciple has the same opportunity for productivity now and the same chance for a great reward later in heaven.

Rule perfectly there in heaven. It's not biblical to assume that all Christians will reign together with Christ in His eternal kingdom despite how we live here on earth.

A careful study of Revelation and the prophetical books in the Old Testament shows that believers will have different positions and responsibilities in the future kingdom.

Ruling in heaven will have nothing in common with the corruption and manipulation we're so used to seeing in displays of power on earth! When the curse of sin is removed and you and I are restored to our creation purpose (Gen. 1:28), we will be free to rule for God to our most total powers while bringing only the highest good to ourselves and others.

Don't waste another day living for less. Instead, seize the opportunity that is right in front of you. Your chance is now. Serve Him faithfully on earth, and you will be perfectly prepared to do what you will desperately crave to do in heaven.

Father God, let us faithfully serve You on earth so we
can reign with You in heaven. In Jesus's name, amen!

_____

_____

_____

_____

The Believer's Judgment

Bruce Wilkinson

Adapted from *A Life God Rewards*

For we must all appear before the judgment seat of Christ.
—2 CORINTHIANS 5:10

Revelation 20:11 tells us that unbelievers will stand at a great white throne. However, today's verse reveals that every Christian will stand before the judgment seat of Christ, give an account, and receive compensation from God based on their works.

The platform. The phrase "judgment seat" in Greek is *bema*. It is a raised marble platform where officials sit at athletic contests. The *bema* represented authority, justice, and reward (John 19:13; Acts 25:10–12).

We will all face and stand alone at the *bema*, and our judge will be Jesus Christ Himself (John 5:22). He will be the best judge who understands justice from heaven's perspective and knows what it feels like to be tempted in all points, yet without sin (Heb. 4:15).

The purpose. When Paul mentions "things done in the body," he is referring to things you did while alive on earth. Therefore, everything we do for God here on earth will be judged at the *bema*.

No deed for God will be overlooked or unappreciated. God will not only repay you for grand acts of personal sacrifice; He will even reward you for giving one cup of water in Jesus's name (Mark 9:41).

It's important to note that it is not your beliefs that God will judge but your works. Your faith in Christ determines your eternal destination; however, what you have done for Christ will determine your experience in eternity.

The promise. In 1 Corinthians 3:15, Paul tells us when we stand before the *bema* of Jesus, we may suffer loss, "but he himself will be saved, yet so as through fire." We could suffer loss in heaven whenever we do good deeds without the motivation of true love (see 1 Cor. 13:3).

However, regardless of what happens at the *bema*, "God will wipe away every tear from their eyes" (Rev. 21:4). Therefore, irrespective of what happens at the *bema*, Jesus will not love you any less or any more for all eternity than He loved you when He purchased your life with His blood.

> *Father God, let us do good works motivated*
> *by Your love. In Jesus's name, amen!*

God Is A Rewarder

Bruce Wilkinson

Adapted from *A Life God Rewards*

[God] is a rewarder.
—HEBREWS 11:6, KJV

Many Christians agree that God rewards people for the good they do in this life. However, they overlook God's promises to repay them in the next life. In Luke 14:13–14, Jesus tells His Pharisee host to invite people who cannot pay him back because God will compensate him after he dies.

The reality. Nowhere does Jesus give us an exhaustive list of what actions He will reward. However, below is a short list of the measures God rewards:

- God will reward you for seeking Him through spiritual acts, such as fasting and praying (Matt. 6:6).
- God will reward you for submitting to your employer as a faithful steward (Eph. 6:8).
- God will reward you for self-denial in His service (Matt. 16:24–27).
- God will serve you for serving those in need in His name (Mark 9:41).
- God will reward you for suffering in His name (Luke 6:22–23).
- God will reward you for the sacrifices you make for Him (Luke 6:35; Matt. 19:29).
- God will reward you for sharing your time, talent, and treasure to further His kingdom (Matt. 6:3–4; 1 Tim. 6:18–19).

The rewarder. I'd been happily working for God for years. However, I couldn't believe that God would want to reward me for what I was already willingly doing for Him. After all, Jesus died for me. Serving Him was the least I could do!

Then one day, I remembered Hebrews 11:6, which changed my thinking on this matter once and for all. The Bible says that if we want to please God, we must also believe that God is a rewarder. God chooses to reward because it expresses His generous, faithful, and just nature.

The Bible also says that if we want to please God, we must live by faith. Without faith, we could never see or even imagine our true destination.

Hence, the issue is this: Will you live with what you can see, knowing it will soon disappear? Or will you look forward to eternity and live today for God's pleasure?

Father God, let us believe Your promise to reward
us in eternity. In Jesus's name, amen!

_____

_____

_____

_____

The Rewards of Serving

Charles Swindoll
Adapted from *Improving Your Serve*

[God] rewards.
—HEBREWS 11:6

Serving God has numerous rewards. When we think about them, they motivate us to keep going. In 1 Corinthians 3:10–14, I find three primary facts about rewards.

First, most rewards are received in heaven, not on earth. There are earthly rewards, though. But when it comes to servanthood, God reserves special honor for that day when "each man's work will become evident" and "he shall receive a reward" (3:13–14).

Second, all rewards are based on quality, not quantity. "The fire itself will test the quality of each man's work." God's eyes are always on motive, authenticity, and the absolute truth beneath the surface— never the external splash.

Third, no reward that is postponed will be forgotten. You can be a "nobody" in the eyes of this world, and your faithful God will, someday, reward your every act of servanthood.

The Bible mentions at least five eternal "crowns" for those who faithfully serve God.

- The imperishable crown (1 Cor. 9:24–27). This reward is promised to those who victoriously run the race of life. It will be awarded to those believers who consistently bring their bodies under the Holy Spirit's control (vv. 26–27).
- The crown of exultation (Phil. 4:1; 1 Thess. 2:19–20). This is the "soul-winners crown." Our Lord will distribute this crown to those who are faithful in leading souls to Christ and building them up in Him.

Dean De Castro   473

- The crown of righteousness (2 Tim. 4:7–8). This crown will be awarded to those who live each day loving and anticipating Christ's imminent return, those who conduct their earthly lives with eternity's value in view.
- The crown of life (James 1:12). This crown is not promised simply to those who endure suffering and trials but to those who survive their difficulties, loving the Savior all the way.
- The crown of glory (1 Pet. 5:1–4). This reward is promised to those who faithfully "shepherd the flock" with sacrificial dedication, humility, and exemplary life.

According to Revelation 4:9–11, those who have received these crowns will cast them before the only One deserving of praise—the Lord God!

*Father God, You are a just God who loves to
reward faithfulness. In Jesus's name, amen!*

_____

_____

_____

_____

Dedicated Serving

Stephen Olford
Adapted from *Basics for Believers*

Not slothful in business; fervent in spirit; serving the Lord.
—ROMANS 12:11, KJV

Dedicated service touches every department of our lives. For example, a housewife doing her task in the home serves the Lord just as much as a preacher in the pulpit or a missionary on the foreign field if she does her job in the power of the Holy Spirit.

There are three aspects of dedicated service that I want to draw your attention to:

Determined service. "Not slothful in business" (KJV). A better rendering is "Never let your zeal flag."

Enthusiastic determination. Whatever our Master did, He did it enthusiastically and fervently, whether serving as a carpenter or carrying through His redemptive task on the way to Calvary. In Titus 2:14, Paul describes Christians as those who are "zealous for good works," who share the zeal of Christ in their service for God.

Enduring determination. When Mary confronted Jesus concerning His absence from them for three days, Jesus said, "Did you know that I must be about my Father's business?" (Luke 2:49). Is there a "must" in your life? That's the acid test of faithful service.

Dynamic service. "Fervent in spirit" (NKJV). The word "fervent" means "boiling" or "seething." We are to allow the Holy Spirit to keep us passionate and dynamic in our service all the time. Fervency is to be expressed in several realms:

The believer's spirit. We must always be boiling hot for God and not lukewarm (Rev. 3:15–16).

The believer's speech. In Acts 18:25, we read of Apollos, who was "fervent in spirit [and] spoke" with sincerity, earnestness, and zeal.

Devoted service. "Serving the Lord" (NKJV). The word "serving" conveys the idea of a "bondslave." It reminds us of the slave in Exodus 21 who refused to leave his master even with the freedom allowed by the law of Moses. He was devoted to several kinds of service:

Lowly service. "He shall serve," however humble the service (Exod. 21:6).

Loving service. "I love my master" (Exod. 21:5).

Loyal service. "I will not go out free" (Exod. 21:5).

Lasting service. "He shall serve him forever" (Exod. 21:5).

Are you willing to serve God as His bondslave?

Father God, let us serve you with determination,
drive, and devotion. In Jesus's name, amen!

_____

_____

_____

_____

Habits of Diligence

David Jeremiah

Adapted from *Everything You Need*

Whatever you do, work at it with all your heart, as
working for the Lord, not for human masters, since you
know that you will receive an inheritance from the Lord
as a reward. It is the Lord Christ you are serving.
—COLOSSIANS 3:23–24

In my first tour of duty as a pastor, the Lord gave me Colossians 3:23–24 as my life verse. Let me share the four habits of diligence I try to practice every day.

Look around. "Whatever you do." This means that nothing falls outside of this instruction to the believer. That includes everything from fixing a leaky faucet, changing diapers, and paying bills to resolving conflicts between loved ones, finding a job, and making our marriages stronger—you name it.

Look within. "Do it heartily." This means that diligence is strenuous. In *Grit*, author Angela Duckworth tells how Olympic swimmer Rowdy Gaines prepared himself to win an Olympic gold medal. In the eight years leading up to the 1984 games, he swam, in increments of fifty laps, at least twenty thousand miles.

Gaines says, "I swam around the world for a race that lasted forty-nine seconds." If diligence would drive a man to swim around the world to prepare for a forty-nine-second race, what kind of diligence should we be striving for with eternity as our goal?

Look above. "As to the Lord." We must put our best efforts into all we do because, ultimately, we're not working for a human employer to earn money or for a human corporation to make profits or even for ourselves to build success. Instead, we are serving Christ to please Him.

Look ahead. "You will receive the reward." All of us who do whatever we do diligently unto the Lord will receive our reward of an eternal inheritance with Him. There will be no end to the hallelujahs! No end to the joy! There is no end to our passion and purpose, for even in heaven, His servants will serve Him.

Father God, let us do everything with excellence and diligence and all for Your glory. In Jesus's name, amen!

_____

_____

_____

_____

The Difference Between Mediocrity and Excellence

Brandon A. Cox
Adapted from brandonacox.com

An excellent spirit was in him [Daniel].
—DANIEL 6:3, KJV

Mediocrity is a Dad tucking his kids into bed. Excellence is intentionally reminding them of our love, reading them a story, and praying with them. Mediocrity is performing the minimum requirements of our job. Excellence is going above and beyond what is required to serve our supervisors in unexpected ways.

A quote I picked up somewhere and wrote inside the front cover of my Bible says, "The difference between mediocrity and excellence is midnight oil, elbow grease, and the power of God." According to this, three tools help us achieve excellence instead of settling for mediocrity.

Midnight oil. We can't achieve a life of excellence in an eight-to-five window. This isn't a call to workaholism but rather a challenge to realize that dreamers and doers who change the world put in extra hours thinking, planning, and working toward their goals.

Our minds and bodies need an appropriate amount of rest, but our spirits need time to cultivate a vision for excellence.

Elbow grease. Practice makes perfect, right? Maybe close. The point is people who do things well usually spend a lot of time doing those things poorly, learning and improving. This takes time. It takes years.

Excellence is only possible when we're willing to transition from dreaming to doing. We have to be ready to devote time, energy, and resources toward our big goals.

The power of God. Even nonbelievers, who have no real access to God's supernatural power, can build nations, businesses, and legacies.

But I'm a follower of Jesus, so my aims and pursuits should be oriented around God's kingdom.

When it comes to seeking the kingdom first, excellence is only possible with the power of God working within and around us. And that requires humbling ourselves, yielding to His plan, and depending on His enabling.

Every day is a new opportunity to reject passivity and mediocrity and choose intentionality and excellence. So, what does the future look like when we decide to take the hard road and do the hard work of accomplishing exceptional things for God?

Father God, help us develop the spirit of excellence and reject our bias toward mediocrity. In Jesus's name, amen!

_____

_____

_____

_____

The Ministry of John the Baptist

Vaneetha Rendall Risner

Adapted from desiringGod.org

He must increase, but I must decrease.
—JOHN 3:30, KJV

John the Baptist's life began with great promise (Isa. 40:3; Mal. 3:1), an angelic proclamation (Luke 1:15–17), a call from God, a thriving ministry. With such a background, how could John the Baptist not be successful?

The success of John. At first, John achieved great success. John preached with great power, like Elijah. As a result, crowds flocked to him during his short public ministry, which scholars say may have lasted less than a year.

John was the only prophet who had the privilege of seeing the Messiah in the flesh. John even baptized Jesus, saw the Spirit descend on Him, and heard God say, "This is my beloved Son, with whom I am well pleased" (Matt. 3:17).

He undoubtedly would have been excited about what God was doing. The long-awaited Messiah had come, and John might have assumed that he, the Messiah's herald, would minister and succeed at His side.

The failure of John. John was imprisoned just a few months after Jesus began His public ministry. After that, his life kept diminishing and fading away. Once Jesus emerged, the masses paid less and less attention to John. Some of his disciples, like Andrew, left him to follow Jesus.

From a worldly perspective, John probably looked like a failure. He was never prosperous, and his ministry quickly evaporated. John didn't even have a glorious death. He died at the whim of a foolish girl, her vengeful mother, and a wicked and weak king.

True success. Yet John the Baptist was wildly successful in God's eyes. He had served a crucial purpose in the kingdom, faithfully preparing the way for Christ. Jesus had nothing but praise for John. He said he was the greatest man who had ever lived up to that time (Matt. 11:11).

Are you judging your worth by the standard of worldly success? Remember what God values. He is after our hearts and our willingness to be used by Him. Our goal on this earth is to glorify God's name, not our own.

> *Father God, let us focus on being faithful in what You*
> *have called us to do. In Jesus's name, amen!*

Seven Lessons for Productivity

John Piper
Adapted from desiringGod.org

I worked harder than any of them, though it was
not I, but the grace of God that is with me.
—1 CORINTHIANS 15:10, ESV

Here are the seven lessons I learned for my productivity in the ministry:

Know why you are here. My mission statement reads: *You exist to spread a passion for the supremacy of God in all things for the joy of all peoples.* I wrote it on paper and carried it around in my wallet, lest I forget the reason why I exist here on earth.

Embrace your role as a sub-creator. God is the great Creator-Maker, and He created humans in His image as secondary creator-makers (Gen. 2:15). So, we are all creators, makers, in some sense. Every time we act, every time we do anything, we make something into something else.

Discover the difference between sloth and rest. We need to discover and embrace, with zeal, the difference between sloth and rest, laziness and leisure.

Make peace with imperfection. Decades ago, I made peace with imperfection and finitude. I have no illusions that I will say the last word about anything. My job, while I live, is to speak the truth as I see it in God's Word as well as I can say it and let God do what He wants to with that imperfection.

Act promptly. Act promptly, as soon as you feel your mind is ripe for taking action. In other words, seminal ideas, far-reaching fruitful thoughts, come to us at night while we're reading, meditating, praying, walking, or playing, and if you don't capture those in some way, in writing, you'll undoubtedly lose them.

Chop a little each day. Steady, small chops with a good, sharp axe will certainly bring down a massive tree after a few hundred blows. Just keep chopping at whatever worthy task you have.

Get excited for what's ahead. Let your motto be the principle of the Apostle Paul: forgetting what lies behind, pressing forward to the goal (Phil. 3:13–14). Don't be content with what you have already done. Instead, be excited about what you can accomplish in the future.

Father God, make the next season of our lives the
most fruitful ever. In Jesus's name, amen!

_____

_____

_____

_____

A Biblical Picture of Success

Dean De Castro

Then you will be prosperous and successful.
—JOSHUA 1:8B

Is God interested in your success?

Our heavenly Father wants all His children to succeed, just as all parents want their children to be successful. When God created Adam and Eve, He wanted them to succeed in managing the earth He made for humankind to enjoy (Gen. 1:28).

In Psalm 128, we see a picture of success that came from following God's way. It describes a godly man who is successful in every area of his life. We can at least extract seven principles of success from this passage.

First, God is interested in your success, provided your definition of success is biblical.

Second, from God's standpoint, success means walking in His ways. "Blessed are all who fear the Lord, who walk in His ways" (v. 1).

Third, a God-fearing person is successful in his personal life. He has a right and healthy relationship with God. He fears God—not because He is afraid of His punishment, but because he is scared of disappointing God. His goal in life is to please God and put a smile on His face.

Fourth, the successful person earns a decent salary, enough to feed his family and enjoy some of the niceties of life (v. 2).

Fifth, the blessed man is successful in his family life. He has a wife who is successful in managing her household ("fruitful vine within your house") and children who love to communicate with their parents ("olive shoots around the table") (v. 3). A person can succeed in the marketplace and fail in their domestic life.

Sixth, a successful person is actively involved in the life and service of the church. In verse 5, the city of Zion symbolizes the local church God uses to bless His children. God incredibly blesses him as he lovingly and generously shares his time, talent, and treasure to bless other people.

Finally, a godly and prosperous person is blessed to see their grandchildren live in a peaceful community ("Jerusalem" in vv. 5b–6a) where they can faithfully pray for its safety and prosperity ("peace be upon Israel" in v. 6b; see also 1 Tim. 2:1–3).

> *Father God, thank You for writing a book that reveals the*
> *meaning of true success in life. In Jesus's name, amen!*

A New Body

Dean De Castro

...so that the body ruled by sin might be done away with...
—ROMANS 6:6B

Through Christ's death on the cross (Rom. 6:6a), God changed the body's status and function. The body is now unemployed in serving sin (Rom. 6:6b). It is no longer the slave of sin (Rom. 6:6c). Instead, it is the slave to God (Rom. 6:22) and righteousness (Rom. 6:18).

In Romans 12:1, Paul uses three words to describe the body that desires to serve God: "holy, acceptable," and "reasonable" (KJV).

Holy. The word "holy" in the Old and New Testaments means to be set apart exclusively for the Lord and His purposes. In 1 Corinthians 6:19, Paul calls the body the temple of the Holy Spirit, where God dwells.

When confronting the Corinthian believers to abstain from sexual immorality, Paul equated their sins with defiling the temple of God. "Flee from sexual immorality...Do you not know that your body is the temple of Holy Spirit?" (1 Cor. 6:18–19).

Acceptable. Many believers today feel self-conscious about their bodies. They have a body image issue. They know that God loves them, but they think their bodies are not acceptable and pleasing to God.

The fact that God wants us to offer our bodies to Him as living sacrifices proves that He likes our bodies and wants to use them. "May the words of my *mouth* and the meditation of my *heart* be pleasing in Your sight" (Ps. 19:14).

Reasonable. The Greek word translated as "reasonable" is *logikos,* which is the source of our word "logic." Although it describes serving God as a logical and rational response to God's mercies, it could also refer to the new body that understands God's will and is willing to obey the Holy Spirit's desires.

Through the death and resurrection of Christ, every born-again believer can "beat my body and make it my slave" (1 Cor. 9:27).

The disciples justified taking a colt for Jesus to ride during His triumphal entry into Jerusalem because "the Lord needs it" (Mark 11:3). Likewise, the Lord needs our bodies to glorify Him and serve others.

Father God, I have a body You prepared for me. Here I am to do Your will (Heb. 10:5–9). In Jesus's name, amen!

A Brief Theology of the Body

Dr. Carol Peters-Tanksley
Adapted from drcarolministries.com

Your bodies are temples of the Holy Spirit.
—1 CORINTHIANS 6:19

Let's briefly look at the range of the Bible's views on your physical body.

God Himself created our physical bodies (Gen. 2:7). God formed humanity with His own hands! And He called His creation "very good."

Jesus cared for and healed physical bodies (Luke 6:19). Caring and ministering to physical bodies was a critical element of Jesus's earthly ministry.

Jesus came in a physical body and was resurrected with a physical body (Heb. 10:5; Acts 2:31). God values the body enough to take on a human body Himself—not only during His time on earth but for eternity!

The Holy Spirit dwells in our physical body (1 Cor. 6:19–20). Jesus paid dearly—"with a price"— so that God the Holy Spirit can make us His home!

How you care for your body can glorify God—or not (1 Cor. 6:20). What you choose to take into your body, in terms of food or other substances, honors God—or not.

Your body impacts your usefulness in God's kingdom (Rom. 12:1). You are a steward of your physical body, entrusted by God with caring for it and using it for the benefit of His kingdom.

Our physical body is integrated with our whole human nature (Rom. 12:2). The renewal of our minds and our relationship with God is connected with presenting our bodies. Every part of us impacts every other function as well.

Our physical body is not ultimately the most important thing (Matt. 10:28). A body impacted by disease says nothing about your value or whether or not God loves you.

Our physical body here is temporary and finite (2 Cor. 5:6–8). Keeping our eyes on eternity helps us navigate disappointments when we do not experience physical healing now and assures us of future bodily resurrection (2 Cor. 4:17).

Our resurrected body will be different but still a body (1 Cor. 15:53–55). The body God has for us in eternity will be far beyond anything we are experiencing now. It will be worth the wait.

Father God, help us take care of our
bodies. In Jesus's name, amen!

_____

_____

_____

_____

Glorify God in Your Body
Dean De Castro

Your body is the temple of the Holy Spirit....
Therefore bring glory to God...in your body
—1 CORINTHIANS 6:19–20, PHILLIPS

The body is significant because the Holy Spirit has made it His home. Therefore, as devoted disciples of Jesus Christ, we must acknowledge the lordship of Christ by faithfully taking good care of our bodies to glorify God and serve people.

God owns our bodies by the right of creation and redemption. Our bodies are loaned to us for a short time so that the Holy Spirit might manifest the life of Christ to the world. The body is like a lighthouse that shines the light of God's truth into dark lives.

According to Paul, there are three ways we can glorify God in our bodies:

Eating and drinking. "Whether you eat or drink, or whatever you do, do all to the glory of God" (1 Cor. 10:31).

Can we honestly say we glorify God if we excessively overeat and lose control of our appetites? On the other hand, how can we honor God if we are flabby and out of shape?

Flee sexual immorality. You glorify God in your body with the way you handle your sexuality.

Paul argues in 1 Corinthians 6:18–20 that "the sexually immoral person sins against his own body." However, it is no longer his own body but the temple of the Holy Spirit, since the Holy Spirit lives in him.

Therefore, we defile God's temple and dishonor God's name by committing sexual sins in God's sanctuary, our own bodies.

Death and dying. Paul and Silas were persecuted for preaching the gospel of God's grace. They were almost stoned to death and later put into prison. Despite facing death, Paul and Silas glorified God in their bodies by worshipping Him.

"About midnight Paul and Silas were praying and singing hymns to God, and the other prisoners were listening to them" (Acts 16:25). The prisoners were so touched by the bold testimony of God's servants that when a violent earthquake shook the jail and loosened the chains of all the prisoners, they didn't try to escape (v. 26).

Father God, may the light of Your truth shine through
our bodies to those in the dark. In Jesus's name, amen!

_____

_____

_____

_____

Dedicate Our Bodies to God
Dean De Castro

Present yourselves to God as those who are alive from the dead,
and your body's parts as instruments of righteousness for God.
—ROMANS 6:13B, NASB

If we have accepted Christ to be the Lord of our life, it is reasonable to offer every part of our being, including the members of our body, to the will of God, to be and to do whatever He requires. As the famous saying goes, "If God is not the Lord of all, He is not the Lord at all."

Eyes
"I made a covenant with my eyes not to look lustfully at a girl" (Job 31:1).

"I will not set before my eyes anything that is worthless" (Ps. 101:3).

"Let us fix our eyes on Jesus, the author, and perfecter of our faith" (Heb. 12:2).

Ears
"An evildoer listens to wicked lips, and a liar gives ear to a mischievous tongue" (Prov. 17:4, ESV).

"He who has an ear, let him hear what the Spirit says to the churches" (Rev. 2:11a).

Mouth and tongue
"Death and life are in the power of the tongue, and those who love it will eat its fruits" (Prov. 18:21, ESV).

"Whoever keeps his mouth and his tongue keeps himself out of trouble" (Prov. 21:23).

"There is one whose rash words are like sword thrusts, but the tongue of the wise brings healing" (Prov. 12:18, NRSV).

"Set a guard, O Lord, over my mouth; keep watch over the door of my lips" (Ps. 141:3).

Hands

"Lazy hands make a man poor, but diligent hands bring wealth" (Prov. 10:4).

"You yourselves know that these hands of mine have supplied my own needs and the needs of my companions" (Acts 20:34).

Feet

"How beautiful are the feet of those who bring good news!" (Rom. 10:15).

"Give careful thought to the paths on your feet....Do not turn to the right or the left; keep your foot from evil" (Prov. 4:26–27).

Father God, take our lives and let them be consecrated,
Lord, to Thee. In Jesus's name, amen!

Body as an Earthen Vessel

D. G. Kehl

Adapted from *Control Yourself!*

First clean the inside of the cup.
—MATTHEW 23:26

Today's Scripture depicts the body as an earthen vessel to be sanctified. Jesus told the Pharisees to clean first within the cup so that its outside may also be clean. The point is that we are to have a pure heart in a pure body.

Holy vessel. In his admonition to Timothy, Paul likens our bodies as holy vessels to be used for God's noble purposes. "In any large house there are articles not only of gold and silver but also of wood and clay; some for noble purposes and some for ignoble" (2 Tim. 2:20).

The noble vessels are gold and silver platters and goblets for royal weddings and state banquets, whereas the lowly ones are those like commonplace clay water jars.

Both sets are functional, each serving a useful purpose on the right occasion. Ultimately, the outward appearance is not all-important; it's what's inside the vessel that counts.

In verse 21, Paul warns Timothy, "If a man cleanses himself from the latter [both the contamination and the contaminated vessels], he will be an instrument for noble purposes, made holy, useful to the Master and prepared to do any good work."

Unholy vessel. In 1 Thessalonians 4:4–5, Paul again uses the metaphor of an earthen vessel as a body: "Every one of you should learn to control his body, keeping it pure and treating it with respect, and never regarding it as an instrument for self-gratification, as do pagans with no knowledge of God" (Phillips).

How can we learn to master our bodies in holiness and honor rather than gratification from our passion? Again, Paul gives the secret in the same passage (1 Thess. 4). It is God's will that we become holy (v. 3). God has *called* us unto holiness (v. 7) and has given us His Spirit, who is holy (v. 8).

The same two philosophies or lifestyles are still present today. One says: "If it *feels* good, *do* it! Do what comes naturally!" The other says: "Deny yourself! Practice restraint!" Which lifestyle is yours?

Father God, we present to You our bodies as instruments
of righteousness and holiness. In Jesus's name, amen!

_____

_____

_____

_____

Borrowed Property

Dr. Alfred L. Heller
Adapted from *Your Body, His Temple*

If anyone destroys the temple of God,
God will destroy that person.
—1 CORINTHIANS 3:16–17

Today's Scripture reminds us that each of us is an individual temple that houses God's Spirit.

Verse 17 also warns us in no uncertain terms that God cares about our health. If a person destroys the temple of God, which is our bodies, God will destroy him. The Message translation says, "No one will get by with vandalizing God's temple."

Maintain God's property. If you were to borrow your father's brand-new car for a few days, would you take care of it? You probably would be more careful with a borrowed automobile than with a vehicle you owned.

And 1 Corinthians 6:20 tells us that our bodies are on loan to us. They are borrowed in the sense that they are someone else's property. The sacrifice of Jesus Christ bought our bodies at a great price. Thus, we are to glorify God through our bodies. Are you proud of your body? Do you take care of it as God's faithful stewards?

Destroy God's property. Paul teaches that those who worship their appetites are enemies of the cross of Christ whose end is destruction (Phil. 3:18–19). The Bible tells us that we must control our sensual drives. This includes things like sleep, sex, food, or other areas of our lives that keep us from being a healthy temple of God when misused.

Dr. Thomas Bassler, a pathologist, tells us that two out of every three deaths are premature based on the many autopsies he has performed. He believes these deaths are the result of "smoker's lung," "loafer's heart," and "drinker's liver."

A smoker's lung is a result of the daily pollution of the lungs with cigarettes. Loafer's heart results from spending more time in front of the TV set than walking. A drinker's liver results from polluting that organ with alcohol until it is incapable of operating normally.

Are you physically what God planned for you to be? We must restore the value and sacred respect we have lost for our bodies.

Father God, help us respect our bodies as borrowed properties
to be maintained carefully. In Jesus's name, amen!

_____

_____

_____

_____

The Holy Spirit and the Body

Watchman Nee
Adapted from *The Spiritual Man*, vol. 3

*But if by the Holy Spirit you put to death
the deeds of the body, you will live.*
—ROMANS 8:13B

The body is essential; otherwise, God would not have given man a body. Through the incarnation, the Son of God took on a body of flesh and blood. And through the resurrection, our Lord still has this glorious body for all eternity.

In Romans 8, we see the relationship between the Holy Spirit's provision and the believer's obligation in living a healthy life.

God's provision. "He...will also give life to your mortal bodies through the Holy Spirit" (Rom. 8:11).

This verse means that if our body has an illness, the Holy Spirit can cause it to heal, and if our body does not have a disease, He will keep us from getting sick.

In short, the Holy Spirit wants to make our body healthy to meet all the requirements to serve God and live for Him. Therefore, neither our present life nor the kingdom of God will suffer any damage because of the weakness of the body.

The believer's obligation. "By the Spirit put to death the deeds of the body" (Rom. 8:13).

Formerly, we were debtors to the flesh (Rom. 8:12). We had no way to stop sinning. However, through the Holy Spirit, we now have the power to break the body's evil practices (habits). The flesh cannot force us to do anything, and even its weakness, disease, and pain can no longer control us.

As born-again Christians, our spiritual obligation is to stop fulfilling the evil desires of the flesh. Instead, we must constantly put to death the misdeeds of the body.

And if we do live according to the flesh, it will speed up the body's aging process and bring death faster. But if we depend on the Holy Spirit's mortifying power, we can enjoy longer, healthy, productive, and holy lives.

Father God, thank You for the gifts of health and holiness through the Holy Spirit. In Jesus's name, amen!

Owe No Debts to the Flesh

Watchman Nee
Adapted from *The Spiritual Man*, vol. 3

Therefore, brethren, we are debtors, not
to the flesh, to live after the flesh.
—ROMANS 8:12, NKJV

Many people think that the flesh (body) has its lawful desires and cravings, and we should fulfill them. But the Apostle Paul tells us that we do not owe the flesh anything since "we are debtors not to the flesh." Beyond keeping the flesh in a proper condition as a vessel for God, we do not owe it any debt.

Of course, the Bible does not forbid from taking care of the body. Of course, it will require more attention when illness occurs. Clothing, food, and dwelling are all needed. Sometimes, rest is indispensable. We must eat when hungry, drink when thirsty, rest when tired, and put on clothing when cold.

But we should not focus on these things. These physical appetites must not preoccupy our hearts or become the focal points of our daily lives.

We should not crave these things. They should come and go according to *needs*; they should never linger inside us for a long time. It is detrimental to our spiritual growth if they become our passions.

At times, the body does have these legitimate needs. Yet because God's work or some essential tasks are more important, we should discipline ourselves and not allow the body to rule over us.

For example, in the garden of Gethsemane, our Lord told the disciples to pray and not give in to their sleepiness, lest they fall into Satan's temptation. The endurance of hunger by Jesus at the well of Sychar demonstrated the need to overcome even lawful desires. Our

Lord denied Himself rest and food to finish the work of leading the Samaritan woman to God.

We owe no debts to the flesh. Therefore, we should not sin by indulging in the lust of the flesh and reducing our ministry because of the body's weakness, disease, and pain. The flesh and its appetites should no longer control us.

Father God, help us subject our bodies' legitimate needs
and desires to Your will. In Jesus's name, amen!

_____

_____

_____

_____

Biblical Teachings on Physical Health

Megan Bailey
Adapted from beliefnet.com

I pray that you may enjoy good health.
—3 JOHN 1:2

Today's verse reveals that God cares about our spiritual and physical health.

The Bible is the best place to learn how to care for ourselves. As our Creator, God knows what's best for us. Therefore, when we obey His instructions and commands, we will be in the best health possible (Prov. 3:1–2, 8; Eccl. 12:13).

Exercise and diet. God gave us our human bodies on earth, and He wants us to care for them. That means providing ourselves with food that is nourishing and getting ample exercise. Neglecting our bodies can be considered a sin.

But God has also given a specific plan for how He wants us to use our bodies for His greater purpose. If we are trashing our bodies with poor food, we won't have the energy to spread His Word and do His work that is ready for us here on earth (Eph. 2:10).

The Old Testament warns us of foods that may be harmful. It also speaks about how alcohol negatively affects our bodies and minds (Prov. 23:29–35) and should only be consumed in certain situations (Prov. 31:6).

Disease and sickness. Exodus 15:26 says: "If you listen carefully to the voice of the Lord your God and do what is right in His eyes, if you pay attention to His commands and keep all His decrees, I will not bring on you any of the diseases I brought on the Egyptians, for I am the Lord who heals you."

The ancient Egyptians suffered from many diseases because they did not understand the health principles God gave to Moses. Due to this ignorance, they suffered illnesses such as tuberculosis, bladder stones, smallpox, and arthritis.

The Bible gave us instructions regarding physical health long before scientists developed the relevant technology. God is all-knowing regarding our health; therefore, all modern medical discoveries originate from Him.

However, this doesn't mean we should abandon modern medicine. On the contrary, God can work through doctors and other health care providers to improve people's lives.

Father God, let us cherish our earthly bodies to
glorify Your name. In Jesus's name, amen!

_____

_____

_____

_____

Seven Keys to a Higher-Energy Lifestyle

Tommy Newberry
Adapted from *Success Is Not an Accident*

I pray that you may enjoy good health.
—3 JOHN 1:2

When you manage your body wisely, you will have better health and more energy to accomplish God's purpose and plan for your life. Consider these seven principles:

Set a goal for how long you want to live (Prov. 29:11). Set a goal to live at least ninety years. Then begin to organize your lifestyle around health habits that are consistent with that goal.

Maintain a positive attitude (1 Thess. 5:18–20). The more positive you are, the more energy you will have. You become positive by deciding in advance that you will always choose the most resourceful response to any given circumstances. Make harmful, limiting thoughts unwelcome in your mind.

Control stress (Ps. 94:19). The way you interpret your circumstances can trigger a stress response. Finding a positive angle on a negative situation goes a long way toward minimizing stress.

Exercise effectively (Prov. 31:17). Combine aerobic, strength, and flexibility exercises. Work out aerobically for at least forty-five minutes, four to six times a week. Proper strength training improves muscle tone, burns extra fat, and avoids injuries. Add some types of martial arts to your overall fitness plan to achieve a flexible and resilient body.

Eat for maximum energy (Gen. 9:3). Focus on balanced nutrition by eating low-fat or nonfat foods, balanced meals and snacks, and seven or more servings of fiber-rich fresh fruits and vegetables daily. Limit the white poisons: sugar, salt, and bleached flour. Drink lots of water, and supplement your diet with an all-natural vitamin and mineral formula.

Sleep for success (Ps. 127:2b). Develop a calming bedtime routine. Applying relaxation techniques, listening to classical music or nature sounds, praying, or reading inspirational material contributes to optimal sleep.

Take time for rejuvenation (Mark 6:31). No skill is as valuable to your overall well-being as learning to disengage from the compulsion toward constant busyness.

Take frequent five-minute breaks during the day, a day per week, a four-day vacation every quarter, and at least two weeks of leave each year to redirect your thinking to something fun and undemanding.

Father God, help us increase the energy levels of our
minds, bodies, and spirits. In Jesus's name, amen!

_____

_____

_____

_____

NEW START
Dean De Castro

*For we must all appear before the judgment seat of
Christ, that each may receive what is due him for the
things done while in the body, whether good or bad.*
—2 CORINTHIANS 5:10

Taking care of our bodies is a sacred task and has eternal consequences. For us to become good and faithful stewards of the body
(temple) God has temporarily leased to us here on earth, we need to
have a **NEW START**, which consists of the following elements:

N—Nutrition
"And you are free to eat from any tree in the garden" (Gen. 2:16).

E—Exercise
"For physical training is of some value" (1 Tim. 4:8).
"We went on ahead to the ship and sailed for Assos, where we are
going to take Paul aboard. He had made this arrangement because
he was going there on foot" (Acts 20:13).

W—Water
"She replied, 'Since you have given me land in the Negev, give me also
springs of water.' Then Caleb gave her the upper and lower springs"
(Judg. 1:15).

S—Sunshine
"He causes His sun to rise on the evil and the good" (Matt. 5:45).

T—Temperance
"Resentment kills a fool, and envy slays the simple" (Job 5:2).

A—Air

"Then the man and his wife heard the sound of the Lord God as He was walking in the garden in the cool of the day" (Gen. 3:8a).

R—Rest

"He said to them, 'Come with me by yourselves to a quiet place and get some rest'" (Mark 6:31).

T—Trust

"Do not be anxious about anything, but in everything, by prayer and petition, with thanksgiving, present your requests to God. And the peace of God, which transcends all understanding, will guard your hearts and your minds in Christ Jesus" (Phil. 4:6–7).

Father God, let us keep our bodies in a proper condition as useful vessels for You. In Jesus's name, amen!

_____

_____

_____

_____

The Sin of Gluttony

D. G. Kehl

Adapted from *Control Yourself!*

Their god is their stomach.
—PHILIPPIANS 3:19

Preachers in evangelical churches today seldom preach about the sin of gluttony.

Gluttony is perhaps the chief among the seven deadly sins (envy, pride, covetousness, anger, lust, and sloth) in exacting the heaviest penalties on this side of the grave.

Someone has mentioned five ways of sinning by gluttony: overeating, too often, too greedily, too expensively, and too much fuss.

Physical dimension of eating. Eating is not an end in itself but rather a means to other ends: gratifying our God-given appetite for food, satisfying our hunger, and nourishing our bodies. God indeed expects us to enjoy, with moderation, this sensual experience. After all, He gave us our taste buds!

Paul tells the Corinthians, "Foods are intended for the stomach and the stomach for foods" (1 Cor. 6:13). However, In the church at Philippi, some church members made their bellies their god or supreme object of concern (Phil. 3:19; see Rom. 16:18).

Like the early churches, many believers today live to eat rather than eat to live—for Christ. How pathetic to be a slave of one's midsection!

Spiritual dimension of eating. It is a perfect symbol of fellowship. Jesus often ate with His disciples and others, like when He multiplied the loaves and fishes and prepared breakfast on the shore after the Resurrection. He offers to feast with anyone who will open the door to Him (Rev. 3:20).

Jesus always put eating in its rightful place. When the disciples returned with food after His conversation with the Samaritan woman at the well, He told them, "I have food to eat that you know nothing about...My food is to do the will of Him who sent me and to finish His work" (John 4:32, 34).

After fasting for forty days and nights, Jesus did not turn stones into bread to satisfy His legitimate hunger. Instead, He said no to food because it was at the suggestion of Satan.

Jesus could say no to food. Can you? If we are physically out of condition, maybe it's time to practice some girth-control!

Father God, let us not misuse or abuse food for
our sinful pleasures. In Jesus's name, amen!

_____

_____

_____

_____

Appetite for Excess Food

Dr. Alfred L. Heller

Adapted from *Your Body, His Temple*

And they shall say to the elders, "This son of ours is stubborn and rebellious. He will not obey us. He is a glutton and a drunkard."
—DEUTERONOMY 21:20

In *More of Jesus, Less of Me*, Joan Cavanaugh makes an interesting observation. Notice that the elders do not say the problem is gluttony or drunkenness. Those are only *symptoms* of the real issues of stubbornness and rebelliousness.

Perhaps our problem with diets has been that we have not obeyed the voice of the Holy Spirit, that we have eaten at the suggestion of the world, the flesh, and the devil—all of them trying to bring defeat to us through our eating.

Have you ever asked God to remove your desire for certain junk foods, like candy, ice cream, or pie? Do you have a weakness for a particular food? God can deliver us from junk food diets if only we would call on Him. Only with God's help can we overcome eating the junky foods that contaminate our temples.

What foods do you eat that you know are bad for you? Do you eat them but feel unsatisfied? Are you overweight? Overeating is just like swearing, cheating, or lying.

Pray that God will remove your appetite for these harmful foods that Satan uses to defile your body. Also pray that God will allow you to learn more about nutrition to know what is best for your temple.

After I seriously asked God to change my desire to overeat ice cream, my craving for it ultimately left me. I did not even want to taste it even though it was offered to me several times after my commitment. God can and will remove your desire for certain foods!

Why don't you take a piece of paper right now, list those foods that are bad for your temple, and think about how to ask God for help.

Father God, please remove our desire for foods that are bad for our health. In Jesus's name, amen!

The Discipline of Fasting

Donald S. Whitney

Adapted from *Spiritual Disciplines for the Christian Life*

When you fast...
—MATTHEW 6:16–17

A biblical definition of fasting is a Christian's voluntary abstinence from food for spiritual purposes. Without a spiritual meaning for your fast, it's just a weight-loss attempt.

Here are some of the several reasons for fasting given in Scripture.

To strengthen prayer. The most important aspect of this discipline is its influence on prayer. You'll notice that all the other biblical purposes of fasting relate to prayer in one way or another.

It wasn't until after "they had fasted and prayed" that the church in Antioch "placed their hands" on Barnabas and Saul of Tarsus and "sent them off" on their first missionary journey (Acts 13:3).

To seek God's guidance. According to Acts 14:23, before Paul and Barnabas appointed elders in the churches they founded, they first prayed with fasting to receive God's guidance.

Fasting does not *ensure* the certainty of receiving clear guidance from God. Rightly practiced, however, it does make us more receptive to the One who loves to guide us.

To seek deliverance or protection. One of the most common fasts in biblical times was done while seeking salvation from enemies or circumstances. For example, in Esther 4:16, Queen Esther calls a corporate fast to appeal to God for protection from Xerxes' wrath.

When faced with persecution because of our faith, it's tempting to strike back with counteraccusations or even legal action. But instead of imitating the worldly tactics of our enemies, we should appeal to God with fasting for protection and deliverance.

To overcome temptation and dedicate yourself to God. Our Lord fasted to overcome a direct onslaught of temptation from Satan himself. During that fast, He privately dedicated Himself to the Father for His future public ministry (Matt. 4:1–11).

At the start of a new job or ministry, it may seem appropriate to dedicate ourselves anew to the Lord. Often, we face decisions that place unusual temptations before us. For example, do we take a new job that will mean much more money but less time with the family?

Fasting to overcome temptation and renew our dedication to God is a Christlike response.

Father God, guide us through Your Spirit to practice
the discipline of fasting. In Jesus's name, amen!

How Exercise Serves the Christian Life

David Mathis
Adapted from desiringGod.org

...zealous for good works...
—TITUS 2:14, NKJV

God did not build our bodies to be liabilities. He crafted and sustained them to enable us to live and *do good* for His glory (Matt. 5:16).

God gave His own Son a human body as a vessel for doing His will in the world (Heb. 10:5–7). So we, too, have bodies, prepared for us by our Father, to carry out His will in the world, to use them to advance Christ's kingdom.

Present your body. We are to present our bodies as a living sacrifice (Rom. 12:1). Will that be active or sedentary? Most likely, it will take at least some effort, exertion, and action—sometimes vigorous action.

Will we be "conformed to this world" and its sedentary defaults and let it flatten our faith and calling? Or will we be "transformed by the renewal of your mind" so that we will be not only able to "discern what is the will of God" (Rom. 12:2) but also be ready and able to present our bodies to do it?

Will I be ready and willing to make use of this body God gave me, or have I imbibed the pattern of the age to keep it on the shelf and use it as little as humanly possible?

Move your body. Our bodies are not just for us to look at in photos or on stages but for doing something, moving, taking actions, and accomplishing tasks in the world.

Although we welcome the charges to meditate, study, and be still in God's presence, we also want to be ready to move and display God in His world.

When love calls, will our bodies be ready to move, with hands and arms not too bulky and flabby, that can reach, lift, pull, and push? Will we be prepared with feet and legs that feel life and energy as they move rather than sitting motionless and heavy?

Unlike our world and its extremes, we have a higher calling, flowing from the very purpose of God Himself, putting our bodies to work in the service of love to the glory of God.

Father God, let us exercise our bodies to be vital in the service of love and to Your glory. In Jesus's name, amen!

_____

_____

_____

_____

Fit for His Service

Dr. A. L. Heller

Adapted from *Your Body, His Temple*

—

Dear friend, I pray that you may enjoy good health.
—3 JOHN 2

Without wanting to press the issue too far, some intriguing situations in the Scriptures show that our forbearers in the faith were, by and large, people who were in shape. Let's look at some of the saints and prophets of the Old and New Testaments.

Genesis 37:13–17 tells us that Joseph had to walk fifty miles to get to his brothers, and he was only a teenager at the time.

Exodus 5:17–19 tells us that God brought circumstances to the Hebrews held captive in Egypt that caused them to do physical labor for long hours. Being in good condition, they were prepared for the long and strenuous walk into the Promised Land.

Deuteronomy 34:1 tells us that Moses, God's chosen man to lead the Jews out of captivity, was still able to climb Pisgah Peak on Mount Nebo at the age of 120 years old. Likewise, Deuteronomy 34:7 tells us that "although Moses was 120 years old when he died, his eye was not dim, nor his vigor abated."

We read in Kings 18:46 and 19:1–5 that Elijah ran about twenty miles, then fled another ninety miles as he ran for his life (1 Kings 19:3). He then left his servant and ran for a day into the wilderness.

Matthew 15:21 tells us that Jesus walked to the districts of Tyre and Sidon, which were some fifty miles away from him.

John 21:7–8 says Peter swam about one hundred yards to Jesus, who was standing on the shore.

John 20:1–2 shows that Mary Magdalene went to the tomb while it was still dark. Seeing the stone had already been taken away, she ran to Jerusalem to tell Peter and John (a trip of approximately three miles).

Luke 24:13–24 tells us that two disciples walked from Jerusalem to Emmaus, ate supper, and hurried back to Jerusalem, which was a round trip of about fifteen miles. That is quite a long distance to travel for supper. Nevertheless, they must have walked briskly because it was late afternoon before they left Jerusalem.

Father God, let us move our bodies more often to help us sustain our health for Your service. In Jesus's name, amen!

Relax with Jesus

Bill and Kristi Gaultiere
Adapted from soulshepherding.org

Learn from me...and you will find rest for your souls.
—MATTHEW 11:29

I struggled with anxiety for most of my life until about the age of forty. During that time, my mind frequently circled with worries, my stomach churned, and my bowels were irritated.

One of my favorite qualities of Jesus is that He is relaxed. Jesus has a patient, acutely aware, and nonreactive mode of being. Everywhere He goes, Jesus brings a calm presence. He ministers the fullness of God's peace to us.

Consider a few examples from the Gospels of how Jesus is relaxed as He deals with some very stressful situations:

- While it must have been very tempting to launch His public ministry as a young and ambitious man, He chose to be content to grow in grace, care for His family, and work as a blue-collar worker for eighteen years until the Father released Him (Luke 2:52).
- When it's time to launch His public ministry, He's unhurried and goes to the desert to pray for forty days (Mark 1:12–13).
- When His family tries to manipulate Him in front of a crowd, He calmly sets a boundary (Mark 3:34–35).
- When He's in a fishing boat at sea and caught in a life-threatening storm, He naps (Mark 4:37–38).
- When mobs try to kill Him, He coolly walks away (Luke 4:29–30; John 10:31, 39).
- While being tortured to death, He lovingly ministers to everyone around him, even His enemies (Luke 23:34, 43).

In all these situations, Jesus is relaxed. Indeed, Jesus does have some unrelaxed emotions. He experienced anger when He cleansed the temple of thieves, for example. In the garden, He experienced grief when He sweated drops of blood. And he experienced excruciating pain on the cross and overwhelming pressure when confronting the Pharisees.

These are emotions that work against feeling relaxed. But Jesus shows us that a mature person can flow with divine love, joy, and peace even in emotional stress and pain.

The few times you see Jesus experiencing anxiety are because it's natural and healthy to feel a kind of fearful and worrisome turmoil during the stressful and traumatic crises that He experienced.

Father God, help us relax with the Prince of Peace
during the storms of life. In Jesus's name, amen!

God's Perfect Peace

Rick Warren

Adapted from *The Power to Change Your Life*

My peace I give you...Do not let your hearts be troubled.
—JOHN 14:27

Before our Lord went to the cross, He promised us in John 14:27 that the peace He gives us is not a trouble-free life; it's a sense of calm amid life's storms. So how do we get this peace? Following are the five keys to acquiring God's perfect peace.

Obey God's principles. The psalmist says, "Great peace have they who love your law" (Ps. 119:165). Just as a car runs more smoothly when you operate it according to its design, your life runs smoothly if you live it according to God's design as presented in His Word.

Accept God's pardon. Guilt is the number one destroyer of peace for most people. The only way to have peace of mind is to have a clear conscience and be free from guilt. And only God can give that (Mic. 7:18; 1 John 1:9).

Focus on God's presence. Isaiah 26:3 reminds us to fix our gaze on God: "You will keep in perfect peace him whose mind is steadfast because he trusts in you."

It's what you concentrate on that determines your level of personal peace. If you look at the world, you'll be distressed; if you look within, you'll be depressed. But if you look at Christ, you'll be at rest.

Trust God's purpose. Even when things don't make sense, we must trust God's purpose (Prov. 3:5–6, NKJV).

Stop leaning on your understanding to figure out why, how, or when God does what He does. He even uses the problems and heartaches you bring upon yourself to work out His purpose in your life. When we believe in the Lord, He directs our paths and makes them straight, not stressful.

Dean De Castro   521

Ask for God's peace. In Philippians 4:6, Paul tells us not to worry but to pray. Worry is the opposite of peace; they cannot coexist. Prayer is a tremendous stress reliever. When the pressure builds up within you, turn your cares into prayers.

Father God, grant us the serenity to accept the things we cannot change, the courage to change the things we can, and the wisdom to know the difference. In Jesus's name, amen!

_____

_____

_____

_____

The Essentials of the Daniel Plan

Rick Warren

Adapted from *The Daniel Plan*

Love the Lord your God with all your
heart...soul...strength and...mind.
—LUKE 10:27

The Daniel Plan is based on the five essentials: faith, food, fitness, focus, and friends. Integrating these essentials can lead to a whole, healthy life that helps you love fully, serve joyfully, and live out your calling at your best.

Faith. The Daniel Plan starts with faith because health is about more than a physical fitness program. It comes from recognizing and using God's power in your life to take care of your body and mind.

When you look in a mirror, faith means you believe that, with God's help, you'll get healthy even though the person staring back at you is exhausted, stressed, out of shape, or overweight (Heb. 11:1).

Food. The Daniel Plan believes that food is the most potent drug on the planet. It can cure most chronic diseases, and it works faster, better, and cheaper than any drug—and all the side effects are good ones.

The Daniel Plan is rooted in a simple principle: Take the junk out and let the abundance in. Our philosophy is that if it is grown on a plant, eat it. If it was made in a plant, leave it on the plate.

Fitness. The American College of Sports Medicine has discovered that moving your body regularly, even just a little bit, impacts your physical, intellectual, emotional, social, financial, and spiritual health.

The prophet Daniel was a strong man. Whether he found himself in the comfort of the king's court or the darkness of a lion's den, Daniel was fit to serve whenever, wherever, under extreme difficulty, and in any circumstances.

Focus. Part of staying focused is developing mastery over the quality of your thoughts (Phil. 4:8). Unfortunately, your uninvestigated thoughts often drive depression, anxiety, fear, and overeating. These thoughts derail progress toward better health.

Friends. The prophet Daniel didn't make his commitment to healthy choices by himself. Instead, he did it with three friends. When you surround yourself with people who share the same health goals, you are going to progress farther than you could on your own (Eccl. 4:9).

Father God, may these essentials teach us how to have a whole and healthy life in Your ways. In Jesus's name, amen!

_____

_____

_____

_____

The DIET Plan

Steve Reynolds
Adapted from *BOD4GOD*

Whoever loses their life for me will find it.
—MATTHEW 16:24–25

When we think about the word "diet," we think about some crash plan or weight-loss program. The Bod4God Losing to Live plan is not a "diet" plan. It is a "live-it" plan! The program uses the DIET acrostic.

D—Dedication: Honoring God with my body. Romans 12:1 teaches us to present our bodies as "living sacrifices." If we are going to dedicate our bodies to God, we will have to listen to the Holy Spirit's promptings every time we approach food. I had to realize that my body was not made for the gratification of self but the glorification of God (see Phil. 1:20).

I—Inspiration: Motivating myself for change. You will have to recognize that keeping yourself healthy will be a fight. You will get hungry. You will get lazy. You will want to give up. You need to find inspiration to keep your commitment to God.

For me, Matthew 16:24–25 was a massive inspiration for change. I realized that I had to lose myself so that I could live. I had to give up overindulgence with food to find a better quality and quantity of life.

E—Eat and exercise: Managing my habits. The secret to weight loss is to eat less and exercise more. You must face this reality and quit looking for a pill or potion to solve your weight loss needs.

The Word of God teaches two basic things about managing our habits of eating and exercising. First, eat in moderation (see Prov. 23:2), and make healthier eating choices. Then, get the right amount of exercise (see Gen. 2:15) to get your metabolism going.

T—Team: Building my circle of support. Enlist people who could support you to move toward better health (Prov. 27:17). Allow health experts to impact you through books, one-on-one encounters, and group meetings.

Even if you don't have a person or a group for encouragement, you can still be a team of one and ask God to join you. He will bring resources to you that you have never dreamed of.

Father God, help us keep a better body for
Your glory. In Jesus's name, amen!

_____

_____

_____

_____

The Mirth Diet

Joyce Myer
Adapted from *Overload*

A cheerful heart is good medicine.
—PROVERBS 17:22

The Bible says that a happy heart is good medicine. And it costs nothing. You've got a God-given weapon against stress that is free of charge and that you can use at any time, day or night.

The medical benefits of laughter. Laughter has been shown to boost your immune system, act as a natural painkiller, lessen depression, and increase personal satisfaction. In addition, it can discontinue the pain-spasm cycle seen in muscle disorders and even benefit people experiencing chronic depression.

Learn to laugh at yourself. Try to do your best, but you can't undo a mistake once you make it. So, instead, use it to your advantage. Laugh about the silliness of it, learn from it, and move on.

One of the reasons people refuse to laugh at themselves is insecurity and a low self-worth. Instead, they find their worth in what they do or what others think about them.

But if you're confident in who you are in Christ—knowing that you find your worth in Him and His love for you—no mistake or opinion of another person can keep you from confidently being able to laugh at yourself once in a while.

I laugh at myself often. For example, I have caught myself looking frantically for my phone while talking on it. I have called someone, promptly forgotten whom I called, and then had to ask, "Who am I talking to?"

Smile more often. Some Christians are so sour-faced they look as if they were baptized in lemon juice. Yet the Word of God says that we are the light of the world (Matt. 5:14). Imagine that your smile is the switch to turn that light on.

I pray that you'll have a smile on your face no matter how intimidating the incident, how stressful the situation, or how discouraging the dilemma. We don't laugh about our problems, but thankfully we can laugh as we trust God to care for them.

Father God, may our mouths be filled with laughter and our tongues with songs of joy because you have done great things for us (Ps. 126:2). In Jesus's name, amen!

———————————————————————————

———————————————————————————

———————————————————————————

———————————————————————————

Get God's Help

Joyce Meyer
Adapted from *Good Health, Good Life*

Not by might nor by power, but by My Spirit...
—ZECHARIAH 4:6, NKJV

Most of us want to look great and feel great. We want to be in good health and enjoy our lives. But when we try to lose weight and our attempts to be healthy fail, we feel guilty. We criticize ourselves for lack of willpower.

God's power is better than willpower. So let me tell you a little secret about willpower: Willpower is your best friend when things are going well, but when you begin to get weary or stressed, it will run out on you.

The Bible says we are not to be willpower-led; we are to be Spirit-led. Willpower and determination may get us started on the right path to some worthy goal, but they have a reputation for quitting in the middle. On the other hand, the Spirit of God always brings us across the finish line to victory (see Zech. 4:6).

Breaking bondage. In Christ, everyone can break free from old destructive habits and start living the new and exciting life of freedom God has for us. But if we have fallen into bondage over time, the thought of freedom can be scary. We may prefer the comfort and ease of our familiar bonds.

Some people would rather endure poor diets, low energy, compromised health, self-neglect, and exhaustion than do what is necessary to taste freedom and develop a liberty lifestyle.

However, facing the truth about ourselves and our habits is the key to being set free to live a better and healthier life (see John 8:32).

Let God bear the burden. Sometimes, the journey toward long-term good health can seem unbearable. Soul-searching, facing the truth, and making necessary changes will indeed be painful if you try to bear them alone.

Only God is strong enough to accomplish what needs to be done in your life. If you turn things over to Him, you will find the power you need to break free. God is ready and eager to help you become a stronger, healthier person. So let Him do the heavy lifting for you (see Isa. 40:31).

Father God, we believe more in Your limitless power
than our limited willpower. In Jesus's name, amen!

_____

_____

_____

_____

Sin Leads to Diseases

Brenda Polk
Adapted from lifeway.com

For the wages of sin is death.
—ROMANS 6:23

When we sin, consequences follow—disappointment, disillusionment, and even despair. Sin's consequences can also include sickness and disease. While not all disease results from sin, some dangerous and harmful behaviors can result in severe illness and loss of health.

Promiscuous lifestyle. A sexually promiscuous lifestyle dramatically increases the odds of contracting sexually transmitted diseases (STD) and AIDS. STDs can lead to painful sores, certain types of cancer, infertility, and nervous system disorders. AIDS can impact the innocent through infected blood.

Substance abuse. Illegal drug abuse, smoking, and alcohol consumption produce lifelong harmful consequences. All are addictive, mind-altering, body-damaging substances that may shorten life, affect the quality of life, and thus potentially limit opportunities to serve God.

Some long-term damage of drug abuse includes nervous system disorders, loss of brain cells and memory, heart damage, and seizures. In addition, smoking has been proven to cause emphysema and lung, mouth, and throat cancers.

Drinking alcohol can lead to a dulling of the senses, malnutrition, loss of brain cells, liver disease, accidents, and heart disease. These behaviors cause short-term and lifelong harm to the body, and none of them honor God.

Gluttony and sloth. These two behaviors are two of the seven deadly sins according to sixth-century religious teachings. While the

Bible doesn't list these sins in a specific passage, the Apostle Paul and Proverbs teach the hazards of overindulgence and inactivity.

Overeating while remaining inactive is a deadly combination that leads to weight gain, obesity, heart disease, diabetes, loss of strength, and body breakdown. While God gives us direction and laws for what was right and wrong, He does not force legalism on us but to set us free from the consequences of sin.

God designed the human body and knows what would be best for us. Therefore, He outlines the best choices for us. When we follow God's guidelines and remain sexually pure, avoid substance abuse, eat healthfully, and use our bodies as God intended, we can prevent diseases and a litany of other negative consequences.

Father God, thank You for protecting us from
the painful consequences of sin by following
Your guidelines. In Jesus's name, amen!

A Biblical Prescription for Healing

Richard Mayhue

Adapted from *The Healing Promise*

It is I who heal.
—DEUTERONOMY 32:39, NASB

Once, God allowed me to experience a serious illness. Eventually, after a five-hour glucose tolerance test, a doctor diagnosed hypoglycemia as the source of my problem. After that, the Lord generously restored my whole health. But during those dark days, my only sustaining help came from applying the truths I now share with you.

First, acknowledge that God sovereignly rules life, and then rest in that unshakable truth. God controls our every moment, whether in sickness or health. "I have wounded and it is I who heal" (Deut. 32:39, NASB).

Second, remind yourself of the biblical reasons for sickness. Think about those purposes that God can accomplish through your time of illness. Pray that God will use you in weakness to display His strength.

Third, determine if your sickness results from continued sin in your life. Is God using your illness as a chastisement? And if your answer is yes, confess your sin (1 John 1:9).

Fourth, commit the entire matter to the Lord by faith. Pray for God's will to be done, seek His glory, and wait patiently for His response.

Fifth, never disregard God's ordinary means of restoring health through medical experts. But on the other hand, do not be presumptuous about God's actions and wait too long or ignore your doctor altogether.

Sixth, recognize it might not be God's will for you to recover fully. Many of God's great servants were sick— Job, Paul, and Epaphroditus.

Seventh, thank God for the circumstances in which He has placed you (Eph. 5:20; 1 Thess. 5:18). You are not thanking God that you hurt but instead that He is who He is and that He will work His will through your circumstances.

Eight, as you pray, ask God for the faith and patience to endure and the wisdom to understand why (James 1:2–5).

Finally, pray that your circumstances would bring glory to God (1 Cor. 10:31) and that Christ will have preeminence in all of your life.

Father God, we pray for healing until You grant
it or unless or until You make it plain that it is
not Your will. In Jesus's name, amen!

_____

_____

_____

_____

Growing Older Gracefully

Selwyn Hughes
Adapted from *Daily Walk with Jesus* (1998 ed.)

The righteous...will still bear fruit in old
age, they will still stay fresh and green.
—PSALM 92:12, 14

Each stage of life is crammed with possibilities—even in older years. So don't fight the fact you are getting old; accept it and use the experience you have gained.

Nowadays, it is not regarded politically correct to refer to people as "old." On the contrary, using this word is viewed as insensitive. We are told a better term is "older adults." But at what stage of life are we called older adults?

When I was forty, I regarded sixty and over as older adults. When I was sixty, older adults to me were upwards of seventy. Now that I am seventy, an older adult is upwards of eighty! I have asked several people when they think people become more senior adults, and the consensus is from seventy upwards.

Many older people become irritable and fussy. Check on yourself to see if this is so. Be courageous enough to ask a friend or relative, "Do you find me grumpy? Are there things about me or things I say or do that hurt you or concern you?"

Develop your mind for as long as you can. We are told the mind never grows. The brain grows old, but the mind can help prolong the brain's power by refusing to sag. Read some portion of a good book each day. Engage in activities that compel your mind to function.

If you have retired and are still healthy, don't stop working. The human personality is made for creativity, and when it ceases to create, it creaks, cracks, and crashes. You may not develop and produce things as vigorously as you did before, but do something; otherwise, you will grow tired of doing nothing.

On the physical level, keep your body moving. Exercise regularly. Not strenuously, but regularly.

And above all, fill your mind with thoughts from the Bible. Nothing is more beautiful than watching an older person grow old gracefully and come to maturity majestically. Constant companionship with Jesus Christ will help you do this.

Father God, help us adjust to all change, knowing
that the best is yet to be. In Jesus's name, amen!

Fear Factors in Facing Death

Adapted from gotquestions.org

Even though I walk through the valley of the
shadow of death, I will fear no evil.
—PSALM 23:4A, ESV

Even the most secure, devoted believer can have occasions when he fears death. Several aspects of death could potentially cause fear.

Fear of the unknown. What exactly does it feel like when you die? No one knows for sure, but the Bible does describe what happens.

The Bible says when we leave our bodies, we will be at home with the Lord (2 Cor. 5:6–8; Phil. 1:23). We will stay in this state until Christ comes and resurrects believers with a new, glorified body (2 Cor. 5:6–8; Phil. 1:23).

Fear of loss of control. Some people are so insecure that they need to manipulate their surroundings and control the people around them to their benefit. How much more they must fear the loss of control upon their deaths.

Directly after Jesus described how Peter would die, he reacted by demanding to know how John would die (John 21:18–20). But when Peter received the Holy Spirit, God changed him to release his need to control his surroundings and empowered him to face whatever challenges he might encounter (Acts 5:17–42).

Fear for those left behind. Physical death will separate us from our loved ones on earth for a time. But if they are also Christians, we know that the separation will be a short blink of an eye compared to the eternity we'll spend with them in heaven.

If they are not Christians, we have to talk to them about where they will go when they die. Ultimately, however, the decision rests with them. Just as God gives them the room to choose, we must also.

Dean De Castro   537

Fear of the acts of dying. Few of us know how we will die. Quick and painless, in our sleep, a long, drawn-out illness—the mystery of it, the inability to prepare can be frightening. But it is only a moment. And when that moment is over, we can claim the promise in Philippians 3:20–21 that when our Lord comes back, He will transform our lowly bodies to be like His glorious body.

Father God, as You are with us, take away our
fear of death. In Jesus's name, amen!

Steps to Overcome the Fear of Death

Adapted from gotquestions.org

Prepare to meet your God.
—AMOS 4:12

How can we overcome the fear of death? Often, being informed and actively participating can help assuage fear. You can take steps to prepare yourself and those around you.

Practical steps. Many people believe they shouldn't die because they have responsibilities and unfinished business that nobody can take care of if they were gone. But having people and things you are responsible for won't keep you from dying if it's your time. But doing what you can to make sure you've done your best to take care of your responsibilities can alleviate fear.

If you have a business or children or other dependents, consider their care. Decide who will take over your role and work with that person to come up with a plan. Look into a will or trust. Make sure all of your necessary paperwork is organized and easy to find.

Reconcile broken relationships before you're unable to do so.

Physical steps. If you have strong feelings about what you want to happen to you should you become incapacitated, express them now. You may lose control over the situation during an illness or injury and be unable to make your wishes known.

Get a living will, and then choose someone you trust to be authorized to make decisions for you should you become unable.

Spiritual steps. These are steps to keep up responsibilities or maintain a measure of control in the worldly realm, but they don't get to the meat of the matter.

The most important thing to remember regarding death is the truth about life. You love your family and care for them, but God loves them more. You may worry about your earthly legacy, but God is more concerned with a kingdom perspective.

All the paperwork in the world won't bring the peace of mind of a straightforward action: abide. Abiding in Christ (1 John 2:24) means staying in the truth of His Word. Believing what He says about us and the world around us will give us the proper perspective regarding this life and the one we will receive when the time comes.

Father God, let our fearless attitude towards death
make the world see that we truly belong to You as Your
children (1 John 3:1–2). In Jesus's name, amen!

_____

_____

_____

_____

Our Resurrection Bodies

Randy Alcorn

Adapted from *Heaven*

And we eagerly await a Savior from there, the Lord
Jesus Christ, who...will transform our lowly bodies
so that they will be like His glorious body.
—PHILIPPIANS 3:20–21

This Scripture assures us that Christ's resurrection body is the model for ours. Our resurrection bodies will be like His. They are the same bodies God created for us here on earth, but God will raise them to greater perfection than we ever could have imagined.

Jesus is not a ghost. When Jesus appeared to His disciples in His resurrected body, He proclaimed, "I am not a ghost" (Luke 24:39, NLT).

The risen Jesus walked and talked with two disciples on the road to Emmaus (Luke 24:13–35). They saw the resurrected Jesus as a normal human being. The soles of His feet didn't hover above the road. No one saw bread going down a transparent esophagus when He ate with them.

The times Jesus spent with His disciples after His resurrection was remarkably normal. Early one morning, He "stood on the shore" at a distance (John 21:4). He didn't hover or float—or even walk on water, though He could have.

He stood, then called to the disciples (v. 5). His voice sounded human as it traveled across the water, and the disciples didn't suspect it was anyone or anything but a human. It didn't sound like the deep, otherworldly voices that movies assign to God or angels.

Jesus started a fire, and He was already cooking fish that He'd presumably caught Himself. He cooked them, which means He didn't just snap His finger and materialize a finished meal. Instead, He invited them to add their fish to His and said, "Come and have breakfast" (John 21:12).

Christ's resurrection body seamlessly interacted with the disciples' normal bodies (John 20:19–23). Nothing indicated that His clothes were strange or that there was a halo over His head. Instead, He drew close enough to breathe on them (v. 22).

Inside your failing body is the blueprint for your resurrection body. With it, you'll be better able to enjoy an eternity of wonders God has prepared for you.

Father God, we look forward to the glorious body You have prepared for us. In Jesus's name, amen!

———————————————————————————————

———————————————————————————————

———————————————————————————————

———————————————————————————————

God Wants You Whole

Dale Fletcher
Adapted from ourjourneyofhope.com

May your whole spirit, soul, and body be kept blameless.
—1 THESSALONIANS 5:22–23

God marvelously made us with a spirit, a soul, and a body. God wants us to be whole. To have the full life God wants us to enjoy, we must attend to our spirit, soul, and body.

Spirit. God wants you to have a solid personal relationship with Him—a deep connection that frees you from any chains that keep you from being completely whole.

Do you believe in your heart that God sent His Son Jesus to die for you and give you abundant life here on this earth and for eternity (John 3:16)?

One way to assess our spiritual wholeness is to gauge the degree to which we are experiencing the "fruit of the Spirit" in our lives (Gal. 5:22–23). For example, how prevalent are love, joy, peace, patience, kindness, meekness, faithfulness, gentleness, and self-control in your life?

Soul. Our souls are where we have our will, mind, and emotions. It's where we make our choices, do our thinking, and have our feelings.

Your soul may be wounded from experiencing major disappointments and hurts from people and life circumstances. You need to mend these wounds by deeply receiving the loving balm that God has for us through His Son, Jesus.

Perhaps your pride has caused your will to choose to depend on yourself, not on Jesus. Therefore, you need to relinquish control of your life to God so you can enjoy the deep inner peace and wholeness that comes from Him.

Body. Research has shown that all the unresolved thoughts and the negativity we hold on to show up in the body and make us sick. These negative thoughts and toxic emotions, like fears, guilt, and anger, cause harmful chemicals to be released into our bodies. As a result, our bodies develop stress-related problems.

Science shows that the body, mind, and spirit are interconnected. Therefore, our deep beliefs, emotions, and habits could affect our emotional, spiritual, and physical health. Let us take care of our inner soul and spirit, and then God will keep our bodies strong and healthy.

Father God, let our spirit, soul, and body be
whole and healthy. In Jesus's name, amen!

_____

_____

_____

_____

Love Life

Dean De Castro

Whoever of you loves life and desires to see many good days...
—PSALMS 34:12–14

This passage shows us how to be healthy and live long. David lists four things we should do.

Tame your tongue. "Keep your tongue from evil and your lips from speaking lies" (Ps. 34:13). If you want to see good days in your life, use your tongue wisely. Speaking lies and nasty words about people can cost us our relationships and destiny.

Joel Osteen wisely observes, "Be careful what you say. You can say something hurtful in ten seconds, but ten years later, the wounds are still there."

On the other hand, "Pleasant words are a honeycomb, sweet to the soul and healing to the bones" (Prov. 16:24). "The tongue that brings healing is a tree of life, but a deceitful tongue crushes the spirit" (Prov. 15:4).

Tame your tongue, only using words that benefit those who hear them (Eph. 4:29). And then watch your life unfolds with blessings, success, peace, and happiness.

Turn from evil (Ps. 34:14a). We are free to sin, but we are not exempt from the consequences of our sins. When people ask me if Christians can smoke, I jokingly respond, "Believers who smoke can still go to heaven, but they get there sooner than others."

Moreover, the sins of overeating and laziness can lead to weight gain, obesity, heart disease, diabetes, and a body breakdown.

Do good (Ps. 34:14b). Doing good does good for the doer (see Acts 20:35). Research shows when volunteers were put in an MRI scanner and told they would give some of their money to charity, the areas of their brains associated with pleasures like food and sex lit up like Christmas trees. Likewise, offering to help others triggers dopamine—the happiness hormone released by the brain.

Pursue peace (Ps. 34:14c). In 1 Peter 3:8–12, Peter quotes Psalm 34 as the backdrop against which he instructs his readers how to treat people. You can't enjoy life until you are at peace with the people around you.

"That you may inherit a blessing..." (1 Pet. 3:9b). The blessing here refers to the long life promised in verse 10, which is built on peaceful and harmonious relationships (1 Pet. 3:8–9a).

Father God, help us follow Your guidelines for living
healthy and happy lives. In Jesus's name, amen!

_____

_____

_____

_____

The Discipline of Witnessing
Dean De Castro

You will be my witnesses.
—ACTS 1:8

Many of us don't witness Christ to the unbelieving world because we lack the discipline or motivation to do it.

The discipline of commitment. Once the Holy Spirit indwells us when we believe in Christ, He calls and empowers us to witness for Him (Acts 1:8). Evangelism is the responsibility of every born-again Christian.

Paul says that God chose us "to do His work and speak out for Him, to tell others of the night-and-day difference He made for you" (1 Pet. 2:9, MSG). This is the essence of witnessing—sharing your personal experience regarding the Lord.

In a courtroom, a witness isn't expected to argue the case, prove the truth, or press for a verdict; that is the attorneys' job. Instead, witnesses only report what happened to them or what they saw (1 John 1:1–3).

The discipline of prayer. Jesus taught us to pray, "Thy kingdom comes" (Matt. 6:10). It is an evangelistic prayer. God's kingdom is brought to this earth every time a new person is introduced to Jesus.

Isaiah 53:12 tells us that Jesus, the Messiah, would intercede for transgressors, which He did. Remember His first words from the cross: "Father, forgive them, for they do not know what they do" (Luke 23:34). As a result, the thief who was being crucified next to Him believed.

We have to pray for our unbelieving friends and relatives because it is God's will for "all men to be saved and to come to a knowledge of the truth" (1 Tim. 2:4). Therefore, we need to press forward in our prayers, seek God's face, and not back down (see Matt. 7:7).

The discipline of love. Confidence in evangelism begins with God's love. One of the reasons we hesitate to tell others about Jesus is that we forget how deeply and unconditionally He loves us. What's missing most in our evangelism is a disciplined passion for the Lord.

We need to rekindle within us a sense of God's love for us; in doing so, sharing the gospel with unbelievers will become easier and more natural as time goes by.

Father God, let your love motivate us to share Your
love with unbelievers. In Jesus's name, amen!

_____

_____

_____

_____

God's Power to Save

Donald Whitney
Adapted from *Spiritual Disciplines for the Christian Life*

But you will receive power...and...be my witnesses.
—ACTS 1:8

God expects every Christian to witness for Christ because He has empowered them to do so. He has provided the power to evangelize through the following means:

The power of the Holy Spirit. The power that saved your life is the same power that enables you to witness for Christ. This means that in ways and methods compatible with your personality, temperament, spiritual gift, opportunities, etc., you have the power of the Holy Spirit to share the gospel with others.

It also means that God will empower your life and words in sharing the gospel in ways you will often not perceive. The Holy Spirit may grant much power to your witness in an evangelistic encounter without giving you any feeling or sense of control.

The power of the gospel message. The gospel itself carries with it the power of the Holy Spirit (Rom. 1:16). That's why God can convert people whether they hear the gospel from a teenage teacher of a vacation Bible school class or a seminary-trained evangelist with a PhD, whether they read it in a book by an Oxford scholar like C. S. Lewis or a simple tract. It is the *gospel* God blesses like no other words.

The gospel message rests on the power of God to save people and not our powers of eloquence or persuasiveness. The ability for people to be made right with God comes through the message of His Son. That's why we can be confident that some will believe if we faithfully and tenaciously share the gospel (Rom. 10:17).

The power of a transformed life. There is also a power for evangelism in people living a sincere Christian life. The most powerful ongoing Christian witness has always been the *speaking* of God's word by one *living* God's Word.

The Lord empowers the *life* and *words* of the faithful believer with the power of spiritual attraction. It is like the power of a fragrant aroma (2 Cor. 2:14–17) that God uses to attract people to the message of His Son.

> *Father God, let the fragrant aroma of your*
> *presence in our lives attract the unbelievers*
> *around us to Christ. In Jesus's name, amen!*

Easy Believism

Dean De Castro

*I am not ashamed of the gospel because it is the power
of God that brings salvation to everyone who believes.*
—ROMANS 1:16

Paul describes the gospel of God's grace in Jesus Christ as His power to change people's lives.

If the message of Christ's death, burial, resurrection, and ascension to heaven is the glimmer of hope for this dark and chaotic world, why are many Christians ashamed to share the gospel and witness for Christ?

Moreover, the gospel promises that God's love manifested on the Cross is the panacea to people's emotional problems. If it's true, why do many unbelievers refuse to come to Christ personally and be reconciled with God?

I firmly believe that the main reason for the church's failure to impact the unbelieving world with the power of the gospel is because of the unbalanced understanding of the gospel message.

To increase church attendance, many pastors have watered down the gospel's message to suit the unbeliever's selfish interest. Many preachers aim at making the gospel sound as comfortable and appealing as possible. This unbalanced gospel is often called *easy believism.*

Simply put, the idea is that if you believe in Jesus, everything will be all right. You don't have to change anything, for God loves you just the way you are. Jesus is a kind Savior who offers eternal life—no strings attached—in exchange for any person's decision to do so.

In *Why Am I Afraid to Tell You I'm A Christian*, Don Posterski keenly observes that many teachings on evangelism today are frequently result-oriented. Faithful witnessing equals positive results.

Christians measure their success by counting converts. Eventually, many believers stop witnessing due to unrealistic expectations and guilt.

According to these success criteria, Jesus failed with the rich ruler because he finally left Jesus and followed money instead (Mark 10:22). In actuality, Jesus's witness with the rich ruler was successful because it was truthful. Jesus communicated the truth, and the rich ruler understood it.

We are faithful witnesses when we present God's message clearly and completely—just like Jesus did.

*Father God, let us faithfully communicate the gospel
truth just like our Lord did. In Jesus's name, amen!*

_____

_____

_____

_____

The Feel-Good Gospel

Greg Morse
Adapted from desiringGod.org

Come to Me those who are weary and burdened.
—MATTHEW 11:28

Jesus invites the dissatisfied, the thirsty, the unhappy to find joy in Him,.

But Jesus came to address more than our felt needs of the moment. He came to save us from sin, death, and God's wrath through His substitutionary death and subsequent resurrection.

Comfort first. The feel-good gospel promises that Jesus came into the world to save people from erratic human psychologies. The center of the new gospel is the man and the help God gives him to live a better life.

The feel-good gospel loves the *effect* of the Christian faith while tragically forgetting its God and the true gospel message. The comfort of man—not the worship of God—has become the main goal. The good news that man can be happier—not that Jesus died for sinners—is the gospel. Man comforted—not Christ crucified—is the heart of the system.

In this modern gospel, the chief problem with sin is *it doesn't work*—not that it offends a holy God. It denounces evils, but for very different reasons. It encourages us to fight anxiety because it isn't helping us sleep at night.

It sends us to God to fix our present inconvenience, not to forgive or transform us. It beckons us to settle for rejuvenation, not regeneration; being burped and fed, not born again.

Comfort follows. The paradox stands that emotional health is caught when indirectly sought. The emotional help that God provides His people is unparalleled. His promises and who He is give us reason to rejoice always. But this stability is often attained *accidentally* as we "seek first the kingdom of God" (Matt. 6:33).

Emotional health in the Christian life comes first from looking outside ourselves: Hate sin, love Christ, believe in His power to save, seek to live for His glory, and mature in emotional health. We seek first for God, and in finding Him, we gain complete joy and heaven is thrown in.

Well-being will come through authentic worship. However, if you seek comfort for comfort's sake and relegate God to the background, you'll get neither. But if we set our minds on Christ, He will, in His perfect time, keep us in perfect peace (Isa. 26:3).

Lord Jesus, let us take Your yoke upon us and enjoy
Your peace in our souls. In Your name, amen!

_____

_____

_____

_____

The Gospel Reveals God's Character
Dean De Castro

For in the gospel the righteousness of God is revealed.
—ROMANS 1:17

In Romans 1:16–17, the gospel of God's grace reveals four things about God's character.

God's power. "The gospel...is the power of God that brings salvation" (v. 16). It is not our eloquence or persuasiveness that saves people. It is the message of the cross through which the power of God saves those who believe.

Through Christ's death and resurrection, God saves us from the penalty of sin (Rom. 3:23), the power of sin (Rom. 6:14), and the presence of sin (Rom. 8:22–25). The challenge for the church today is to preach the *whole* gospel, as Paul brilliantly argues in the book of Romans.

God's faithfulness. "Of everyone who believes" (v. 16). God is faithful to save those who "confess with your mouth, 'Jesus is Lord,' and believe in your heart that God raised Him from the dead" (Rom. 10:9).

God is no respecter of people. He is faithful to save the worst sinner, like the thief on the cross, and the most educated and religious person, like Paul.

God's compassion. "First for the Jews, then for the Gentile" (v. 16). Both Jesus (Matt. 24:37) and Paul (Rom. 9:2–4a) were compassionate regarding the salvation of God's chosen people. God never forgets His covenant with Abraham and will fulfill His promises to restore the nation of Israel in the future millennial kingdom (Gen. 17:7–8; see Rom. 9–11).

I believe that there will be more people in heaven than in hell (Rev. 5:9). You'll be surprised to see some people who you don't expect to be there. Indeed, God works in mysterious ways that are beyond the comprehension of our finite minds (Rom. 11:33–36).

God's righteousness. "For in the gospel a righteousness from God is revealed" (v. 17). The only righteousness that God accepts is the righteousness from Him that He credits to those who put their faith in Christ (Rom. 3:22).

The message of the gospel is that our sins are forgiven in Christ; His righteousness is on us. This great exchange becomes ours not by works but by faith alone (Eph. 2:8–9).

Father God, let us share the good news so that we
may know You better. In Jesus's name, amen!

The Core Messages of the Gospel
Dean De Castro

[The Holy Spirit] will prove the world to be in the
wrong about sin and righteousness and judgment.
—JOHN 16:8

One of the Holy Spirit's ministries is to convince the unbelieving world of their need to believe in Jesus Christ as their Lord and Savior. And "whoever believes in Him is not condemned" (John 3:18a), "but whoever rejects the Son will not see life, for God's wrath remains in him" (John 3:36b).

The Holy Spirit will convict the fallen world in three areas: sin, righteousness, and judgment. In John 16:9–11, Jesus gives the reasons for each sentence.

Sin. The Holy Spirit convicts the world of one particular sin: the sin of not believing in Jesus (v. 9). John MacArthur writes, "Though all men are depraved, caused by their violation of God's law and sinful by nature, what ultimately damns them to hell is their unwillingness to believe in the Lord Jesus Christ as Savior."

Unless sinners see sin for what it is and stands for—a rebellion against God, breaking His law and despising of His authority—they will never experience true conversion.

Righteousness. The Holy Spirit also convicts the world because it fails to accept the standard of righteousness that God approves. God's standard of righteousness is the absolute morality of Jesus Christ—the perfect Lamb of God.

And the proof that Christ's righteousness was acceptable to God would be His return to the Father through resurrection, ascension, and exaltation (v. 10).

Paul was genuinely converted because the Holy Spirit had convicted him of the sin of self-righteousness. He then became a fierce advocate of the divine grace given to those who accept the righteousness of God that is found only in Jesus Christ (2 Cor. 5:21).

Judgment. The Holy Spirit finally convicts the world of its liability for judgment. Christ's death defeated Satan, the prince of this world (John 16:11; see John 12:31; Col. 2:15).

Yet, though defeated at the cross, Satan is still active (1 Pet. 5:8). But, like a condemned criminal, his "execution" is coming (Rev. 20:2, 7–10). Hence, all who follow Satan will also be judged (Matt. 25:41).

Any gospel presentation that does not contain these fundamental spiritual realities is impotent to save and transform people's lives.

Father God, let us present the true gospel empowered
by the Holy Spirit. In Jesus's name, amen!

_____

_____

_____

_____

The Whole Gospel

Dean De Castro

The whole counsel of God...
—ACTS 20:27, NKJV

Any presentation of the gospel must have its message based on the whole counsel of God. The Bible teaches that God's salvation has three aspects:

Past salvation: Justification by faith. The good news is that Christ died to pay the penalty for our sins. As a result, God pronounced us not guilty in the court of Heaven and declared us righteous in His sight (2 Cor. 5:21).

However, there is still more good news. The gospel of God's grace also provides salvation from the present power of sin and future deliverance from the presence of sin.

Present salvation: Entire sanctification. Sanctification is the process whereby the Holy Spirit transforms believers to become Christlike and sin less and less. According to 1 Thessalonians 5:22–23, God will sanctify our entire being-spirit, soul, and body and faithfully work on us and in the world until the second coming of our Lord Jesus Christ.

Strong Spirit. The Holy Spirit strengthens our new born-again spirits by assuring us that we are God's children (Rom. 8:16). It is this assurance of God's filial love and protection that we can, by the power of the Holy Spirit, say no to sin and say yes to God (Rom. 8:13).

Moreover, our spirits need to be strong in the Lord and His mighty power to overcome all of Satan's temptations and evil schemes (Eph. 6:10–11).

Submissive soul. Paul argues that since we have offered ourselves to obey God as His slaves at our conversion (Rom. 6:16–17), God will certainly allow trials and temptations to test our commitment to obedience.

Sound soma *(body).* When believers learn to avoid evil, God promises to give vibrant energy to our mortal bodies (Rom. 8:11) and thus enjoy good health and long life (1 Pet. 3:10–11).

Future salvation: Resurrection of the body. Through His death on the cross, Christ has redeemed our bodies from the ownership of Satan (Rom. 6:13). But the complete "redemption of the body" (Rom. 8:23) awaits Jesus's return (Phil. 3:20–21). This hope of future glory with Christ purifies us to live holy lives today (Rom. 13:11–14).

Father God, let us faithfully proclaim the whole gospel—
nothing more, nothing less. In Jesus's name, amen!

_____

_____

_____

_____

Half-Baked Gospel

Andrew Farley
Adapted from *The Naked Gospel*

For we know that our old self was crucified with Him.
—ROMANS 6:6

If you're in Christ, your old self is no longer within you. God had crucified and buried it together with Christ on the cross.

The spiritual person you used to be in Adam has been obliterated. The new you had been raised and seated with Christ. You're an entirely new creation. There was an exchange of the old self for the new self that took place at salvation. And there's nothing sinful about the core of your being.

At conversion, God gives us a new heart (see Ezek. 36:26–27). We are new creations, with God's desires stamped on our new hearts and minds. It is more characteristic, more fitting, and more like us to display the fruit of the Spirit than to display sin.

Now, if the old self is dead and gone, why do we still sin? The Apostle Paul provides us with some solid reasons: We sin because of the continuous pressure of sin's power, hooking us in various ways through the flesh.

It does this through the presence of sin, a power that lives in us but is not us. The power of sin is not the old self. It *controlled* the old self. The old self was a slave to sin, while the new self is not. Likewise, the flesh is not the old self either.

The flesh is all of the programming (mindsets, attitudes, reactions) that builds up over time as a person allows sin to operate in their life.

When we're made new in Christ, those memories of coping with life are still in the brain. We can even resort to living according to the outmoded programming of the old self.

But God calls us to hold to the truth of His explanation of our ongoing struggle with sin. Why? Because if we don't, we're living under the delusion that we're no different from unbelievers. We are believing the lie that sinning is the most natural thing for us to do. And that's a pitiful, half-baked gospel!

Father God, thank You for the whole gospel,
which shows us the reason for and solution to
our sin problem. In Jesus's name, amen!

The Fear of Witnessing (1)

Dean De Castro

So do not be ashamed of the testimony about our Lord.
—2 TIMOTHY 1:8

If God calls and empowers every Christian to witness for Christ, why do almost all Christians seem to be afraid to share the gospel?

There are many possible reasons why Christians fail to evangelize. However, I will offer two of the primary explanations here.

Fear of failure. How do you define success in evangelism? If success means every person you witness to comes to Christ, then Jesus was an evangelistic failure because the rich young ruler turned away from Him and His message (Matt. 19:16–23).

We need to learn that success in evangelism is not measured by the positive response of the recipient but by the careful and accurate delivery of the message. In this regard, we are like the Postal Service.

If our efforts do not yield results, we must examine whether we have faithfully delivered the core message of the gospel, which includes sin, righteousness, and judgment (John 16:8).

On the other hand, if we are sure we are doing everything God expects of us, then we leave the matter with Him and carry on witnessing whether we see results or not.

Fear of incompetency. Many Christians are afraid to engage in spiritual conversations because they fear being asked a question they can't answer.

Think about it. What if the formerly blind man that Jesus healed in John 9 had thought that way? Would he even have felt ready to witness to the scholarly, critical Pharisees? And yet, with hours, perhaps minutes, of meeting with Jesus, he bravely told them what he knew about Jesus.

The formerly blind man had a story to tell: "I was blind, but now I see!" (John 9:25). We all have a life story to share. Our personal experience with the Savior is the most exciting story we can tell.

Learn how to craft your conversion testimony and practice sharing it with other Christians, then share it with your unsaved friends and relatives. Be prepared to share your testimony because God is ready to send someone who is open-minded and ready to hear the gospel from you (1 Pet. 3:15).

Father God, grant us the boldness to witness and faith
to entrust the result to You. In Jesus's name, amen!

The Fear of Witnessing (2)
Dean De Castro

So do not be ashamed to testify about our Lord.
—2 TIMOTHY 1:8

Timothy had served with the great evangelist Paul for many years, preaching the gospel. Yet he still struggled with witnessing for the Lord.

Here are some more reasons why doing evangelism is difficult.

Spiritual warfare. Reaching out to the lost with the good news of Jesus is a declaration of war against Satan. When a church equips believers to engage in evangelism, all hell breaks loose. As a result, many churches stop doing intentional evangelism and don't even know why in most cases.

Paul commands the church to take the armor of Christ, which includes the shoes of the gospel (Eph. 6:15). Satan has declared war, but you and I are ambassadors of peace (2 Cor. 5:18–21), and as such, we take the gospel of peace wherever we go.

Any soul rescued for God constitutes a violent attack on the kingdom of darkness. As Warren Wiersbe tells us, "The most victorious Christian is a witnessing Christian."

Personal problems. Another reason why some Christians fail to witness is the weight of their emotional problems. They argue, "I would feel a hypocrite of telling others that Christ is the answer to all their problems while I still struggle with so many problems of my own."

We successfully lead people to Christ not because of our holiness but because of God's grace. Even unbelievers know that we are not perfect, and if we pretend we have no problems when we in fact do, they will soon find out about our dishonesty.

Coming to Christ does not mean that we are exempt from facing problems. However, it does mean that we have Someone to grant us wisdom, comfort, and help.

Wrong temperament. A further reason why some Christians are reluctant to witness is that they don't have the right temperament. They are introverts and don't know how to talk to strangers.

When God called Jeremiah to be His prophet, he pleaded, "I do not know how to speak; I am only a child" (Jer. 1:6). But when he finally obeyed God's bidding, he became a mighty spokesman for God.

Father God, let us share the gospel even if we are afraid. In Jesus's name, amen!

How Can We Overcome Our Fear of Evangelism?

Jerry Root
Adapted from christianitytoday.com

Perfect love drives out fear.
—1 JOHN 4:18

What keeps believers from telling nonbelievers that God loves them and wants to forgive their sins? Mostly, they are afraid of what people might think of them.

If I am looking to anyone other than God as the primary source of love, I am setting myself up to be afraid and insecure, especially when sharing the gospel. Being more concerned about what others think of us than what Jesus thinks of us will freeze us in our tracks.

1 John 4:18 says, "Perfect love casts out fear." Confidence in evangelism begins in the love of God.

One of the reasons we're hesitant to tell others about Jesus is that we've forgotten how deeply and unconditionally He loves us. What's missing most in our evangelism is a passion for the Lord Jesus.

We need to rekindle within us a sense of God's love for us; in doing this, sharing the gospel with others will become easier and more natural as time goes by.

Anyone can talk freely about what they love. Most of us, for example, know or are ourselves big fans of a sports team, knowing all there is to know about the team, wearing their favorite player's jersey, and talking incessantly about the big win the night before.

Furthermore, those who love to play a particular sport likely did not exhibit skill in the game after the first attempt at playing. If they had a love of the sport and if that love began to grow, they would be willing to invest further time and energy in the hopes of acquiring proficiency.

So too, an interest in Jesus and a desire to tell others about Him develop in direct proportion to one's growing love for Him.

The moon has no natural light of its own; nevertheless, it keeps on shining by staying in the sun's light. Similarly, we reflect on others, naturally and efficiently, the love we receive from the Son's light shining on us.

Remember, God loves you. With this in mind, tell others He loves them just as He loves you.

Father God, save us from the idolatry of seeking
people's approval. In Jesus's name, amen!

_____

_____

_____

_____

Seven Motives in Evangelism
Michael Green
Adapted from *Evangelism: Now and Then*

For Christ's love compels us...
—2 CORINTHIANS 5:14

We need powerful motives if we are to do evangelism and not give up. Here are seven reasons that motivate more recent believers to witness for Christ.

God's love. God so loved the world that He gave His only Son. God's love became implanted in the believers' hearts (Rom. 5:5) such that they began to share the heavenly Father's attitude toward the lost.

Christ's command. We treat the last wishes of those we love very seriously. So did the early Christians. To go into the world and make disciples was Christ's farewell words to His disciples (Matt. 28:18–20).

The Holy Spirit's thrust. It was inconceivable to the early Christians that anyone could receive God's Holy Spirit without thereby being fired up and equipped to speak for the Lord whenever opportunity knocked (Acts 1:8).

The Christian's responsibility. In 2 Corinthians 5:20, Paul speaks of the Christian as Christ's ambassador who beseeches people on behalf of Christ to be reconciled with God. We are debtors, says Paul, both to the Greek and the Jew (Rom. 1:14).

The Christian's great privilege. In 2 Corinthians 4:1, Paul tells us why he did not lose heart in proclaiming the good news. It never ceased to amaze Paul that the right of representing the Lord had been entrusted not to the angels, kings, and high politicians but forgiven sinners like him.

People's need for salvation. Paul and the other early missionaries had a clear recognition of the appalling condition of those who were out of touch with God (Eph. 2:1).

Paul also believed there was a great "outside hindrance" to evangelism. Satan blinded people's minds both to their needs and to what Christ could do (2 Cor. 4:4). We will not be of much use in evangelism unless we acknowledged this satanic opposition.

Witnessing brought joy. "For what is our joy? Is it not you?" (1 Thess. 2:19). Recently, I had the chance to meet a Ghanaian individual in Toronto and a Chinese person in Vancouver that I enjoyed introducing to the Lord. It was a tremendous joy for all of us. There is no joy like it.

Father God, grant us the joy of leading people
to Christ. In Jesus's name, amen!

Principles of Evangelism (1)

Walter Henrichsen
Adapted from *Disciples Are Made Not Born*

Many...believed in Him because of the woman's testimony.
—JOHN 4:39

In John 4, we can learn eight principles that enabled our Lord to lead the Samaritan woman to put her trust in Him.

Open the opportunity by asking for a favor. Jesus requests, "Give Me a drink" (v. 7 NASB). By asking her for water, Jesus made the Samaritan woman feel needed and important. Likewise, a home-maker can use the same approach with her neighbor by asking to borrow a recipe, a cup of flour, or some other supplies.

Tailor the approach to the person. "Jesus answered...'If you knew... who it is who says to you, 'Give Me a drink,' you would have asked Him, and He would have given you living water'" (v. 10, NASB)

The Lord Jesus was a master at using the right approach for the right person. With the Samaritan woman, Jesus offered her a gift and aroused her curiosity. However, with the religious leader Nicodemus, Jesus's approach was theological: "You must be born again" (John 3).

Choose the questions you want to answer and ignore the others. The Samaritan woman said to Jesus, "The Jews have no dealings with the Samaritan" (v. 9). Jesus chose to ignore her point.

She again brought up a point of contention, this time about the place where people ought to worship God (v. 20). Now she was striking at a critical issue, and Jesus chose to respond.

Strike for the "open nerve" that causes the person to expose his need. At one point, the Samaritan woman mentioned that she had no husband. Jesus confronted her, "You have well said, 'I have no husband,' for you have had five husbands, and the one whom you now have is not your husband" (vv. 17–18, NASB).

Dean De Castro   571

I once spoke to a young woman who wanted to become a social worker. I asked her what she felt were the real needs people faced. It triggered off a deep, spiritual conversation during which I was able to share the gospel.

Father God, may the example of our Lord encourage us
to do the work of evangelism. In Jesus's name, amen!

_____

_____

_____

_____

Principles of Evangelism (2)

Walter Henrichsen

Adapted from *Disciples Are Made Not Born*

Many...believed in Him because of the woman's testimony.
—JOHN 4:49

Here are more principles to ponder:

Tell the truth even if it hurts. Jesus's statement that "salvation is from the Jews" (v. 22 NASB) was offensive to the Samaritans. Yet our Lord said it anyway

When unbelievers ask you, "Do men go to hell if they don't believe in Jesus Christ?" Do you change the topic or tell them the truth? If we hedge on things we know to be accurate, our listeners will doubt our integrity.

Agree with the person as much as possible. Agreeing partly with the Samaritan woman, Jesus replied, "Well, you are partly right. The issue is not between Jerusalem and this mountain. God is a Spirit. You worship Him in spirit and truth" (vv. 20–24).

My buddy witnessed to a friend who retorted, "I'm a Catholic, and you're a Protestant."

My friend replied, "Well, that's interesting. I have more in common with my Catholic friends than I do with many Protestant friends." That simple statement was enough to prevent a potential argument and allow the conversation to continue.

Don't allow the conversation to get off the subject. When Jesus revealed the man the Samaritan woman was now living with was not her husband, she tried to avoid the moral issue by asking a theological question about the proper place to worship God.

Similarly, when confronted with personal issues, some unbelieves might counter with, "What about those people in non-Christian countries who have never heard the gospel?" It would be loving to point out the real issue: "What will you do with Jesus Christ now that you have heard?"

Be sensitive to how the Holy Spirit is working in the person's life. When you witness for Christ, you can often tell where people are spiritually by changes in their view of who He is.

Note the Samaritan's woman's response to Christ. *First,* she calls Him a Jew (v. 9). *Next,* she addresses Him as Sir (v. 11). *Then,* she calls Him a prophet (v. 19). *Finally,* she confesses Him as the Christ (v. 29).

Jesus guided the woman to want salvation for herself. He did not push it to her.

> *Father God, teach us to follow our Lord's*
> *evangelism style. In Jesus's name, amen!*

Two Styles of Evangelism
Donald Whitney
Adapted from Spiritual Disciplines for the Christian Life

If anyone speaks...If anyone serves...
—1 PETER 4:10–11

Many Christians are afraid to share the gospel. They may have a picture of specific methods of evangelism that seem terrifying to them. But the preconceived style of evangelism you may fear is not necessarily the best way for you to lead people to Christ.

Peter divides all spiritual gifts into the two broad categories of serving gifts and speaking gifts. Some find that they evangelize more through serving, others more through speaking.

Evangelistic serving. I heard that every family averages a "crisis" once every six months. During that time of illness, job loss, birth, death, etc., being a Christlike servant to that family demonstrates the reality of your faith in a way that piques their interest. Through serving, you may have a chance to give evangelistic literature or witness in more creative ways.

An evangelistic serving might involve inviting neighbors, coworkers, and friends into your home for the expressed purpose of hearing a guest speaker talk about Jesus Christ and answering their questions about Christianity and the Bible.

Evangelistic speaking. On the other hand, some are more adept at communicating the gospel directly. Suppose you are better at speaking than serving. In that case, you may be able to work with someone who specializes in evangelistic serving in ways that will provide more witnessing opportunities than you've had before.

However, just as servers may need to serve to open a door for *speaking* the gospel themselves, those whose strength is speaking may need to discipline themselves to *help* more people to have chances to speak.

In short, believers with the gift of speaking need to serve so they can share the gospel, while those who have the gift of serving must verbally communicate the gospel eventually.

No matter how well we live the gospel, sooner or later, we must communicate the gospel's *content* before a person can become a disciple of Christ. In 1 Corinthians 1:21, Paul tells us that it is the message of the Cross through which the power of God saves those who believe its content.

Father God, help us demonstrate and communicate
the message of the gospel. In Jesus's name, amen!

The Evangelism Style of Jesus

Don Posterski

Adapted from *Why Am I Afraid to Tell You I'm a Christian?*

He went away sad, because he had great wealth.
—MATTHEW 19:22B

We are not left guessing about Jesus's style of evangelism. Jesus practiced personal evangelism and dealt with no two people in the same way. Without compromising the truth, He personalized the message. He stated facts that were tailored to His specific audience. He conveyed the message that was appropriate for the occasion.

Jesus's evangelism. The biblical record shows that Jesus had something different to say to each person. It was only to Nicodemus, a rabbi, that Jesus said, "You must be born again" (John 3:7). We have no basis for contending that Jesus offered that particular directive to anyone else.

Likewise, His dealings with Zacchaeus (Luke 19:1–10) were radically different from His decree to the rich young ruler (Mark 10:17–22) even though money was the core issue in both instances. Furthermore, His approach to the Samaritan woman and her many husbands (John 4:1–30) was distinct from His handling of the woman caught committing adultery (John 8:1–11).

Jesus's approach was so sensitive and personal that even those who had the same condition of blindness were treated differently (see Matt. 9:27–28; Mark 8:22–23).

Today's evangelism. Teaching evangelism today is frequently result-oriented: Faithful witnessing is equated with positive results. Sowing is successful if there is reaping. This emphasis pressures followers of Jesus to measure their success by counting converts.

Guilt results when production figures fall below the target quotas. People are viewed as projects rather than full-fledged persons.

Friendships are seen only as opportunities to share one's faith. Eventually, the motivation to witness is replaced by discouragement.

Teaching that focuses on results is also an indictment against Jesus. According to these success criteria, Jesus failed with the rich ruler. He ultimately left Jesus and followed money instead (Mark 10:22).

We must reject this emphasis on results. Jesus's witness is the standard for successful evangelism. His witness with the rich ruler was successful because He clearly and accurately communicated the gospel truth. Likewise, we evangelize successfully when we make God's message clear—just like Jesus did.

Father God, let us present the gospel in a way
suitable to the needs of the lost people You bring
into our lives. In Jesus's name, amen!

_____

_____

_____

_____

How to Witness to a Stranger

Dean De Castro

Let your conversations be always full of grace.
—COLOSSIANS 4:6

The best approach to sharing the gospel with a stranger is to start with common ground. Jesus used this strategy to lead people to their conversions.

He discussed with the Pharisee Nicodemus the theology of rebirth in the Old Testament. While resting at the well, Jesus asked the Samaritan woman for a drink. To give the invalid man hope, our Lord asked him if he wanted to get well.

As God gives us opportunities to witness to strangers, we can learn to ask good questions about the personal side of their lives. We'll discover their felt needs and hopefully explore their most profound need—the need for Christ.

Pastor Rick Warren uses the acronym SPEAK to ask great questions that lead to great conversations. Hopefully, that will open up the door of opportunity to share the gospel.

Story: "What is your story?" This is an open-ended question that gets people started. Most people like to talk about their own stories because being known is a basic need we all have.

Passion: "What motivates you?" You make a significant connection when you take an interest in what others care about. When you get people to talk about what they love, you'll gain perspectives about their unique personality.

Encouragement: "Do you know what you'd be good at?" Once you know the person's story and passions, it's natural to encourage them to do something they could do well. You can encourage them to take the next step.

Assistance: *"How can I help you?"* When you ask this kind of question, you are like Jesus. He often asked, "What do you want me to do for you?" You may be in a person's life so you can give them the help they need to fulfill God's purpose for their life.

Knowledge: *"What do you know that I need to know?"* You gain wisdom by learning from other people's experiences. Moreover, you make the person feel important. They will then be willing to engage in more meaningful conversations with you.

> *Father God, help us talk to make a difference*
> *in people's lives. In Jesus's name, amen!*

A Three-Word Testimony
Chuck Barber

You're the message!
—1 THESSALONIANS 1:8, MSG

One of the messages you can share with unbelievers is your own conversion testimony. It's the story about how you came to know Jesus personally and the difference He has made in your life.

Chuck Barber, the discipleship pastor at Hill County Bible Church in Austin, Texas, had developed a format to distill your testimony into three words, then into two or four simple explanatory sentences relating to each word.

The process. *First word.* What were you like before you placed your faith in Christ? Focus on your spiritual condition, not your behavior. Examples of words people have used: hopeless, empty, miserable, addicted, aimless, insecure, ambiguous.

Second word. How did you come to place your faith in Christ? Also, include a short and clear statement of the gospel. Examples of words people have used: friend, trouble, church, spouse, awakened.

Third word. What has trusting Christ helped you become or overcome? Describe your life, feelings, or thoughts now that you have placed your faith in Christ. Examples of words people have used: peaceful, purpose, confident, loving, assured.

Share your testimony in no more than three or four minutes using these sentences and keep them concise. Then alter them to your audience as needed.

An example. *First word.* Ambiguous. Although I believed in the existence of a God and even knew the story of Jesus, I didn't fully understand how it all fits together. As a result, I had *ambiguous* ideas about Jesus being God and how He has provided a way to reconcile me to the Creator of the universe!

Second word. Awakened. Through a series of conversations with new Christian friends in college and exposure to some Christian music with meaningful lyrics, I came to understand Jesus as Savior. I was *awakened* to the reality that Christ died for my sins and rose from the dead.

Third word. Assured. Now I am *assured* that through my faith in Jesus Christ, I have an unbroken relationship with God, my Creator. Furthermore, this relationship is for eternity, and my life with Him will not end when my time on earth does.

Father God, let us always be prepared to
share our conversion testimony when the right
opportunity comes. In Jesus's name, amen!

_____

_____

_____

_____

How to Pray for Unbelievers
Dean De Castro

My heart's desire and prayer to God for the
Israelites is that they may be saved.
—ROMANS 10:1

Paul understood the importance of prayer as it relates to evangelism. His passion for the salvation of his own people moved him to pray day and night that his fellow Jews would recognize and accept Jesus Christ as their long-awaited Messiah.

Below is a guideline for praying for the people you feel led to witness to and share the gospel with. Each request is based on the truths of God's Word.

Lord, I pray that you draw _____ to yourself. "No one can come to me unless the Father who sent me draws him" (John 6:44).

I pray that _____ seeks to know you. "God did this so that men would seek Him" (Acts 17:27).

I pray that _____ hear and believe the Word of God for what it really is. "When you receive the word of God...you accepted it as it actually is...the word of God" (1 Thess. 2:13).

I ask You, Lord, to prevent Satan from blinding _____ to the truth. "The god of this age has blinded the minds of unbelievers" (2 Cor. 4:4).

Holy Spirit, I ask you to convict _____ of their sin and need for Christ's redemption. "When He comes, He will convict the world" (John 16:8).

I ask that you send someone who will share the gospel with _____ .
"Ask the Lord of the harvest, therefore, to send out workers"
(Matt. 9:38).

*I ask that you give me the opportunity and courage to share the truth
with* _____ . "Pray...that I will fearlessly make known the mystery of
the gospel" (Eph. 6:19).

I pray that _____ *turn from their sin and follow Christ.* "He commands all people everywhere to repent" (Acts 17:30).

I pray that _____ *would put all of their trust in Christ.* "Whoever
hears My word and believes Him who sent me has eternal life"
(John 5:24).

I pray that _____ *confess Christ as Lord, take root and grow in faith,
and bear much fruit for your glory.* "If you confess with your mouth,
Jesus as Lord..." (Rom. 10:9–10; Col. 2:6–7).

*Father God, we believe in the power of prayer to
save those who believe. In Jesus's name, amen!*

_____

_____

_____

_____

Lifestyle Evangelism

Warren Wiersbe

Adapted from *The Bible Exposition Commentary*

Having your conduct honorable among the Gentiles, that when they speak against you as evildoers, they may by your good works which they observe, glorify God in the day of visitation.
—1 PETER 2:12, NKJV

Somebody's watching you!

As Christians, we must constantly remind ourselves who we are. Peter reminds us that we are witnesses to the unbelievers (Gentiles) around us. Unsaved people are watching us, speaking against us, and looking for excuses to reject the gospel.

Live honest lives. In verse 12, Peter reminds us that we are witnesses to the lost around us. If we are going to witness to the lost people around us, we must live honest lives. This word implies much more than telling the truth and doing right. It carries the idea of beauty, comeliness, admirableness, and honorableness.

We do not witness only with our lips; we must back up our talk with our walk. Nothing in our conduct should give the unsaved ammunition to attack Christ and the gospel. Our good works must back up our good words.

During my many years of ministry, I have seen the powerful impact Christians can make on the lost when they combine a godly life with a loving witness. I remember many instances of wonderful conversions because Christians let their lights shine.

On the other hand, I recall with grief some lost persons who rejected the Word because of its apparent inconsistencies with the lives of professed believers.

The day of visitation. Peter encouraged his readers to bear witness to the lost, by word and deed, so that God might visit them and save them one day.

"The day of visitation" could mean that day when Christ returns and every tongue confesses that He is Lord. But I think the visitation Peter mentioned here is the time when God visits lost sinners and saves them by His grace. The word is used in this sense in Luke 19:44.

When these people trust Christ, they will glorify God and give thanks to Him because we were faithful to witness to them even when they made life difficult for us.

> *Father God, let us witness by our good words and*
> *consistent deeds. In Jesus's name, amen!*

Relationship Evangelism

Tom Stebbins

Adapted from *Friendship Evangelism by the Book*

Go home to your friends and tell them how
much the Lord has done for you.
—MARK 5:19

In Mark 5:1–5, Jesus and His disciples had gone by boat southeast across the Sea of Galilee to an area called the Decapolis, or ten cities. These cities were essentially Greek but subject to Roman taxation and military service.

The conversion of a demon-possessed man. A deranged and demon-possessed man lived in one of the ten cities called Gadera. He came to Jesus and was miraculously delivered from demonic forces. After being rescued from the demons, the formerly demented man wanted to join Jesus's entourage.

However, Jesus denied his request. Instead, He sent him back home to tell his family and friends what great things the Lord had done for him.

In Mark 7:31–8:10, we see that the converted demoniac shared his testimony because we're told that all the people in Decapolis were amazed. After six weeks of ministry in Galilee, which took Him as far northwest as Tyre and Sidon, Jesus returned to the ten cities.

The restored demoniac had been testifying to his network of relationships. The testimony of his conversion made quite an impact! When word came that Jesus was again in their area, the people poured out eagerly to meet Jesus. As a result, Jesus encountered a multitude, preached to them, healed a deaf-mute, and fed four thousand people.

Relationships work. This scriptural account in Mark's Gospel attests that the web of influence principle works: having people focus their witness within their networks of relationships. The gospel spreads most effectively across an existing network of trust.

If, over the years, you have been "lifted" out of non-Christian relationships, try to build new webs of influence across which you can share the good news. You may want to explore natural bridges—anything about you similar to the non-Christians that you want to reach for Christ. These things might be hobbies, interests, occupations, or backgrounds.

Try to find a need and meet it; find a hurt and heal it. Believe that there are people whom God will draw unto Himself through you.

Father God, let us be sensitive to the needs and hurts of our family, friends, and neighbors. In Jesus's name, amen!

Seven Thoughts On Introverts And Evangelism

Chuck Lawless
Adapted from chucklawless.com

*For the Spirit God gave us does not make us timid...So
do not be ashamed of the testimony about our Lord.*
—2 TIMOTHY 1:7–8

I'm an introvert. I'm also a professor of evangelism and missions at Southeastern Seminary.

I'm convinced, though, that introverts can do well in ministry, including doing evangelism. Here are some steps that have helped me in evangelism:

Refuse to allow your introverted nature to excuse you from doing evangelism. I'm not going to be the "life of the party" at the office gathering. I'm generally quiet in crowds. None of these tendencies, though, permit me not to tell others about Jesus.

Be motivated by the reality of lostness, judgment, and God's grace through Christ. That is, it's my theology that compels me to get outside my introversion and reach out to people.

Make yourself see people not as intruders on your space but as sheep without a shepherd. I like my alone time and fight to get it some days. Anytime I feel overwhelmed by people, though, I try to see them as Jesus did (Matt. 9:36).

Focus on a few people at a time. I have fewer deep relationships, but that helps me focus on evangelism. I want to be ready at any time to name the nonbelievers for whom I'm praying, with whom I'm developing relationships, and with whom I've shared the gospel.

Pray for daily opportunities to share the gospel. For example, the Apostle Paul requested the Ephesians and the Colossians (Eph. 6:18–20; Col. 4:2–4) pray that he would have the opportunity, boldness, and clarity to tell the good news. Praying like this forces me to keep my eyes and ears open for opportunities.

Listen well to others. Inviting someone to tell their own story—and then genuinely listening with intentionality—often says, "I care about who you are and where you've been." That kind of care can open the door to sharing the gospel.

Ask for an opportunity to share the gospel with someone. I avoid sliding the gospel in the side door of a conversation. If my hearer grants me space for telling my story, I'm ready to go.

Father God, let us overcome our timidity to share
Your good news. In Jesus's name, amen!

The Gospel and Repentance
John MacArthur
Adapted from *The Gospel According to Jesus*

...demonstrate their repentance by their deeds.
—ACTS 26:20

Repentance has always been the foundation of the New Testament call to salvation. It is a critical element of genuine conversion.

From His first message to His last, the Savior's theme was calling sinners to repentance. The gospel He wants us to preach is the same: "repentance for the forgiveness of sins" (Luke 24:47).

When Peter gave the gospel invitation at Pentecost, repentance was at the heart of it (Acts 2:38). Paul's message to King Agrippa shows that true repentance also involves a change in one's conduct: "performing deeds appropriate to repentance" (Acts 26:20).

Genuine repentance involves intellect, emotions, and will.

Intellectually, repentance begins with a recognition of sin—the understanding that we are sinners, that our sin is an insult to a holy God. More precisely, we are personally responsible for our guilt.

The repentance that leads to salvation must also include a recognition of who Christ is and an understanding of His right to govern people's lives.

Emotionally, genuine repentance often accompanies an overwhelming sense of sorrow. This sorrow, in and of itself, is not repentance; one can be sorry or ashamed without truly being repentant. Judas, for example, felt remorse (Matt. 27:3), but he was not repentant.

Nevertheless, sorrow can lead to genuine repentance. Second Corinthians 7:10 says, "The sorrow that is according to the will of God produces a repentance without regret."

It is difficult to imagine genuine repentance that does not include at least an element of contrition—not sorrow for getting caught, nor sadness because of the consequences, but a sense of anguish at having sinned against God.

Volitionally, repentance involves a change of direction, a transformation of the will, and behavior change. The behavior change is not itself repentance, but it is the fruit repentance will undoubtedly bear. If there is no observable difference in conduct, there can be no confidence that repentance has taken place (see Matt. 3:8; see 1 John 2:3–6; 3:17).

No message that eliminates repentance can properly be called the gospel, for sinners cannot come to Jesus Christ apart from a radical change of heart, mind, and will.

> *Father God, let us have repentant hearts that renounce*
> *sin and embrace righteousness. In Jesus's name, amen!*

_____

_____

_____

_____

Baptism and Evangelism

Dean De Castro

Make disciples all nations, baptizing them.
—MATTHEW 28:19

I sincerely believe that true evangelism is not complete until we encourage a repentant sinner to obey the command of the Lord Jesus Christ to be baptized (Matt. 28:19).

Baptism is the outward public confession that true repentance in the heart has occurred.

Repentance and baptism. After Peter preached a powerful and convicting message on the day of Pentecost, his audience asked him and the rest of the disciples, "Brothers, what shall we do?" To which Peter replied, "Repent and be baptized, every one of you, in the name of Jesus Christ" (Acts 2:38).

Repentance in Greek means a change of mind. Peter urged his listeners to change their minds about the person of Jesus of Nazareth. "God has made this Jesus, whom you crucified, both Lord and Christ" (Acts 2:36).

Genuinely repentant people not only believe Jesus as their Lord and Savior, but they also change their attitude towards sin and their sinful ways. In Acts 2:40, before Peter baptized around three thousand people, he first warned them, "Save yourselves from this corrupt generation."

Baptismal class. We don't know how long Peter preached nor the details of his teaching. Acts 2:40a states, "With many other words he warned them, and he pleaded with them." But there's one thing we can be sure of: Before baptizing people, Peter presented to them the importance of forsaking their sinful ways and keeping themselves pure and holy in the midst of this wicked and corrupt world.

Serving several churches for these many years, I realize that our traditional baptismal class only teaches the baptismal candidates correct doctrines. We falsely assume they are qualified to be baptized if they know all the central biblical doctrines.

No wonder many churches today are filled with nominal Christians or weak Christians who don't have the kind of changed life that can convince unbelievers to put their trust in Jesus. This may be the real reason why many Christians are hesitant about witnessing to their unsaved friends and relatives.

May churches today see the importance of baptism and preach the whole gospel: Jesus is not only our Savior who saved us from the penalty of sin but also continually saves us from the power of sin.

Father God, we have decided to follow Jesus. No turning back, no turning back. In Jesus's name, amen!

A Sample Baptismal Vow

Dean De Castro

Baptism...the pledge of a clear conscience toward God...
—1 PETER 3:21

We make marriage vows during the wedding ceremony. We recite the Pledge of Allegiance when we go through the naturalization ceremony. As a pastor, I ask parents and the congregation to commit to praying and taking care of the spiritual well-being of the minor children before I dedicate them to God.

However, it never dawned on me to challenge the baptismal candidates to make a vow to forsake all their sins and follow Christ as their Lord.

If baptism is such a sacred and solemn ceremony that centers on acknowledging Christ as Lord, shouldn't we have some vow to declare in front of God, people, angels, and Satan our commitment to love and serve Christ?

Thankfully, I found a covenant that serves as an excellent guideline for crafting a baptismal vow. I have taken the liberty to change some words for easier reading. It reads, in part,

> This day, I surrender myself to You with the utmost solemnity.
> I renounce all former idols that have had dominion over me.
> I consecrate to You all that I have: the faculties of my mind, the members of my body, my worldly possessions, my time, and my influence over others.
> I vow to use all of these entirely for Your glory and resolutely employ them in obedience to Your commands, as long as you allow Me to live.
> I ardently desire and humbly resolve to continue loving You through all the ages of eternity.

I ever hold myself to observe, with zeal and joy, to the execution of Your will.

I resign myself to follow Your direction and all that I am and have, be disposed of by You according to Your wisdom, and serve the highest purpose of glorifying You.

To You, I leave the management of all events and say without reserve, "Not my will, but Your will, be done."

I suggest that all baptismal candidates read this covenant before they are baptized. I also recommend renewing this vow as often as you can.

Remember your holy vow and your loving Lord whenever you are tempted to sin.

Father God, Christ is our Savior, and we pledge
allegiance to Him as Lord. In Jesus's name, amen!

_____

_____

_____

_____

Focus on Planting, Not Harvesting

Steve Sjogren
Adapted from *Conspiracy of Kindness*

I have planted, Apollos watered; but God gave the increase.
—1 CORINTHIANS 3:6–7, KJV

In this passage, Paul understands that evangelism is a process.

When we talk about evangelism, we aren't talking about the plant-ing-watering-harvesting cycle that Paul describes in 1 Corinthians 3:6–7. Instead, we usually mean the results—the harvest alone.

We have become so completely preoccupied with this last phase of the evangelism process that it has tainted our approach to bringing people to Christ.

When I would pray with someone to accept Christ, I used to say that "I led the person to the Lord." I no longer use that phrase because it is inaccurate. We need to understand that we are incapable of leading anyone to Christ if the Holy Spirit is not already drawing them in.

Evangelism is a process. It begins with planting the seed of the gospel as Paul did in the city of Corinth. After that, some would listen, some wouldn't.

The process continued with people like Apollos, who watered and nurtured the already planted seed. At some point, God Himself would eventually reap a harvest as someone came to faith in Jesus Christ. This process flies in the face of our cultural emphasis on imme-diate results.

Cultural values. Our houses are full of products that give testi-mony to our demand for immediacy and convenience: microwave ovens, remote controls to cable TV with umpteen channels, instant glue that forms a permanent bond in less than a minute.

I fear our cultural values of instant response and the bottom line have produced a distinctly American form of evangelism. Our evangelistic efforts are too often met with the question, "So, how many people prayed to accept Christ?" If the number is low, we automatically feel disappointed and mutter, "Oh well, I tried."

Am I disappointed when people don't respond? Hardly ever, because I know from lots of experiences that each person I meet is being worked on by the drawing power of the Holy Spirit. My joyful task is to nudge them forward an inch or two through acts of love and service.

Father God, let us faithfully plant the seed of the gospel through our words and acts of kindness. In Jesus's name, amen!

Beholding Christ in the Gospel of Grace
Dean De Castro

But we all, with unveiled faces, looking as in a mirror the
glory of the Lord, are being transformed into the same
image from glory to glory, just as from the Lord, the Spirit.
—2 CORINTHIANS 3:18, NASB

In 2 Corinthians 3, Paul contrasts the glory of the law given by Moses with the far-surpassing glory of the gospel (2 Cor. 3:7–11). In 2 Corinthians 4:4, the gospel is called the "gospel of the glory of God."

In other words, the mirror in 2 Corinthians 3:18 represents the gospel truths. The glory that has a transforming effect on us is the glory of Christ as revealed in the gospel.

In the book of Romans, Paul presents us with the complete truths of the gospel. They involve the blood of Jesus that forgives our sins and the body of Jesus that sets us free from the power of sin.

The blood of Jesus. Romans 5:9 tells us that the blood of Jesus reminds us that we are now saved from the wrath of God. God has forgiven all our sins, and we are no longer His enemies.

The blood of Jesus not only forgives our sins; it also cleanses our conscience from guilt (Heb. 9:14). We cannot serve God or pursue holiness with any vigor at all if we are dealing with an evil and guilty conscience.

The body of Christ. Romans 6:6 states that our old self was crucified with Christ. The blood of Jesus dealt with the fruits—sins—while the body of Christ dealt with the root—sin. So, God had to cut off the old man at the root or he would continue to produce his sinful fruit.

Before we received Christ, we were slaves to sin. But because of Christ's death on the cross, sin's power over us had been broken. "It was for freedom from sin that Christ set us free" (Gal. 5:1a).

The gospel of grace is the mirror through which we now behold the beauty of Christ. As we understand and appropriate the total truths of the gospel, we are increasingly changed to become more like Christ.

Father God, save us from the ignorance of not knowing the gospel's message in its totality. In Jesus's name, amen!

_____

_____

_____

_____

Preach the Gospel to Yourself
Dean De Castro

My only aim is to finish...the task of testifying
to the good news of God's grace.
—ACTS 20:24

The gospel of God's grace is not only for unbelievers; it is also for believers.

In *The Discipline of Grace*, Jerry Bridges suggests that every follower of Christ preach the gospel to themself every day.

I like the acronym GRACE, which means **G**od's **r**esources **at** Christ's **e**xpense. I want to highlight three attributes of God's character that can remind us often of the riches of His grace in Christ Jesus (Eph. 1:7).

God's mercy. Ephesians 2:3 states that we were by nature objects of God's wrath. We deserved hell, but due to His mercy, we received eternal life. The blood of Jesus appeased and turned God's just and holy wrath away from us (Rom. 3:25).

God is not angry with us because we still sin. God is not mad at us; He is madly in love with us. His mercy and compassion endure forever at the expense of Christ (Ps. 103:8–14).

God's forgiveness. God's grace includes His forgiveness of *all* our sins (1 John 1:7; Col. 2:13). The blood of Christ cleanses our consciences from the defilement of sin (Heb. 9:14).

Bridges writes, "Few things cut the nerve of desire and earnest effort to change like a sense of guilt. On the contrary, freedom from guilt through the realization of forgiveness in Christ usually strengthens a person's desire to lead a more disciplined and holy life."

God's blessings. God's blessings do not depend on our obedience or performance. God "has blessed us in the heavenly realms with every spiritual blessing in Christ" (Eph. 1:3).

Many Christians don't share the gospel because they think they are not spiritual enough for God to use them. They falsely believe that some Christians are highly effective in evangelism because they are good Christians and deserve it.

Every blessing we receive is of God's grace. We don't deserve it. Paul realized that he didn't deserve to be called an apostle and yet led many people to Christ. "But by the grace of God, I am what I am" (1 Cor. 15:10).

Father God, we praise You for Your glorious grace given to us in the Son You love (Eph. 1:6). In Jesus's name, amen!

The Corporate Witness of the Church
John MacArthur
Adapted from *The Body Dynamic*

And in Him you [plural] too are being built together to
become a dwelling in which God lives by His Spirit.
—EPHESIANS 2:22

The entire Church, the Body of Christ, is the temple of the Holy Spirit, just as the individual member is. Therefore, the Holy Spirit indwells the total body to witness Christ in the world.

As a body, believers are called together to be mature and edified, taught and built up that they can manifest the mighty victorious power of Christ to the world. What a demonstration of God's power in love!

How can the Body witness in a collective, single testimony? There are two ways:

The unity of the church. The Body witnesses by its visible oneness. Jesus prays "that they also may be one in Us; that the world may believe that You have sent Me" (John 17:20–21).

I don't mean an ecumenical church where everybody kisses doctrine goodbye, throws their arms around each other, and marches off to battle over the latest social issue. The Body of Christ comprised of true believers needs to be one. But sadly, it is not.

Today, this Body witness is not from a unified body. We are fragmented, each group trying to protect its own ideas. We haven't begun to see what God can do through a united testimony to Jesus in the church. What an impact we could make if only the world could see us as one.

The love in the church. The second way the Body witnesses is by love. "By this shall all men know that you are My disciples if you have love one to another" (John 13:33–35).

Christians love one another when they don't judge one another, they don't bite and devour each other, they don't provoke, envy, lie, speak evil, or grumble about one another.

Since true love builds up, Christians receive one another and are kind and compassionate; they forbear and forgive one another, serve one another, practice hospitality ungrudgingly, admonish, instruct, submit, and comfort one another.

Christians would have a powerful effect on this world if they showed love for one another.

Father God, may the world know we are Christians
by our love. In Jesus's name, amen!

_____

_____

_____

_____

The Goal of the Gospel

Watchman Nee

Adapted from *The Normal Christian Life*

Truly I tell you, wherever the gospel is preached throughout the world, what she has done will also be told, in memory of her.
—MARK 14:9

The Lord ordained that the story of Mary anointing Him with that costly ointment should always accompany the preaching of the gospel. But why?

Our Lord intends that the preaching of the gospel should win committed believers, like Mary, who are willing to give their lives to Jesus and seek to please Him.

There are three types of converts represented in the story:

False followers. Judas represents those who claim to be Christians but never know Jesus as Lord of their lives. Judas stands for the world. His assessment of Mary's action reflects the worldly view that giving one's life to Jesus is a waste of useful life.

In essence, Judas was saying, "We could manage better with the money by using it in some other way. Why not use the money to help the poor in some practical way? Why pour it out at the feet of Jesus?" (see John 12:4-6)

That is always the way the world reasons: "Can you not do something better with yourself than serving Jesus? Is it going a bit too far to give yourself altogether to the Lord?"

Uncommitted followers. The other eleven disciples responded the same way as Judas. They said the same thing with anger (Matt. 26:8–9). They wanted to do ministry instead of pleasing the Lord.

Our work for the Lord must spring out of our ministering to Him. God forbid that I should preach inactivity or seek to justify a complacent attitude to the world's need. Our Lord's concern is with our position at His feet and our anointing of His head.

Devoted followers. Mary represents the ultimate spiritual believers who seek to satisfy the heart of God. Dedicated believers, like Mary, are willing to give up everything, even their treasured "alabaster box," at the feet of Jesus.

The goal of the gospel is to bring each sinner to a proper estimate of who Jesus is: worthy to waste one's precious life to serve and please Him.

Father God, let us make it our goal to please You,
for You are worth it. In Jesus's name, amen!

_____

_____

_____

_____

Evangelism and Discipleship
Dean De Castro

Make disciples of all nations.
—MATTHEW 28:18–20

The ultimate goal of all biblical evangelism is to turn converts into disciples. This is based on the Great Commission passage in Matthew 28:19–20: "Make disciples of all nations."

Evangelism and discipleship are not two separate events. They are the two sides of the same coin. True evangelism is not complete until converts are trained to become obedient followers of Jesus Christ.

In *Out of the Saltshaker and into the World*, Rebecca Pippert tells the story of Lois, who faced difficult relationship decisions when confronted with the gospel. She lived in an apartment with her boyfriend when she first joined Becky's dorm Bible study.

The next day, Becky asked Lois whether there was any reason why she couldn't become a Christian. "No," she replied.

As they talked about being a Christian, Becky pointed out that Christianity is not a religion but a relationship. It's a personal commitment to the lordship of Christ in one's life. It affects every area of life, like values, lifestyle, and sexuality.

Becky lovingly pointed out Lois' relationship with her live-in boyfriend, Phil. After repenting of her past sins, Lois finally asked Christ to come into her life as Lord.

Immediately, Lois wrestled with a new dilemma: finding another place to live. Miraculously, a space opened up in the dorm the next day, so she moved in. Lois's conversion had tremendous implications not just for her but also for her friends.

Lois witnessed to three girls in the dorm, and they decided to get right with Christ. Phil, at first, was furious when Lois moved out. But three months later, he accepted Christ as well. He later credited Lois' obedience to Christ for affecting his own decision to follow Him.

The example of Becky's approach to evangelism serves as a good model for obeying Christ's Great Commission. We are not to be content with simply seeing people come to Christ. Our solemn duty and obligation is to nurture their faith until they learn to share it with others and their lives reflect the glory of God and the character of Jesus Christ.

Father God, help us not only save a soul but
make a disciple. In Jesus's name, amen!

_____

_____

_____

_____

The Discipline of Reproduction
Dean De Castro

Be fruitful and increase in number.
—GENESIS 1:28

Just as God planned for everything to reproduce itself physically, He also commanded us and designed us to multiply spiritually. The plan for spiritual reproduction is clearly stated in the Great Commission passage: "Therefore go and make disciples of all nations, baptizing them in the name of the Father and of the Son and of the Holy Spirit and teaching them to obey everything I have commanded you" (Matt. 28:19–20).

In the Greek text, this verse has one main verb—"make disciples"—and three participles— "going," "baptizing," and "teaching." These are the three means to make disciples.

Make disciples. This is the core of Christ's command to convert sinners to be followers of Christ who will reproduce their faith in the lives of their future disciples who then will win others who, in turn, will win even more others for Christ.

Going. A more precise translation of the key phrase here would be "As you are going, make disciples." This assumes believers take the initiative to witness Christ as they live their ordinary lives, interacting with their relatives, friends, coworkers, and neighbors.

Many people (including preachers) believe this word is a regular verb, not a participle, and wrongly teach that the Great Commission is primarily about evangelism. But evangelism is not actually the goal; it is only a means in the disciple-making process.

Baptizing. Jesus says to baptize new disciples "in the name of the Father and of the Son and of the Holy Spirit." Thus, when a person undergoes water baptism, they openly and unashamedly proclaim that they are followers of Christ.

In the early days of the church, water baptism was a high price to pay. This act could lead to martyrdom. And, unfortunately, that is still happening today in many parts of the world.

The disciple-makers are responsible for incorporating recent converts into a local church for protection, instruction, and ministry to grow and be strong in faith.

Teaching. Jesus says these new converts must be taught to obey Him in everything. Notice that Jesus did not say "teaching them to _know_" but rather " teaching them to _observe_ all that I commanded you."

The discipler's main job is to train the disciple in the practical outworking of Christ's commands, which include making disciples. Therefore, disciple-making is a mark of every Christian.

Father God, help us win others to be disciple-makers. In Jesus's name, amen!

_____

_____

_____

_____

Born to Reproduce

David Platt

Adapted from *Follow Me*

Follow Me, and I will make you fishers of men.
—MATTHEW 4:19, KJV

By God's design, He has wired His children for spiritual reproduction. He has woven into the fabric of every single Christian's DNA a desire and ability to reproduce. All who know the love of Christ yearn to multiply the life of Christ in them. God has even filled Christians with His own Spirit for this very purpose (Acts 1:8).

The call of Jesus. To be a disciple of Jesus is to make disciples of Jesus. Therefore, Jesus calls every one of His disciples to make disciples who make disciples until the gospel penetrates every group of people in the world. There are no spectators; we are all born to reproduce.

Two thousand years ago, Jesus initiated a revolution, but His revolution didn't revolve around the masses or multitudes. It revolved around a select few. These few disciples would learn to think like Him, love like Him, and serve like Him.

As Jesus transformed their lives, they became fishers of men, and you and I have the gospel today because they were faithful in becoming and creating disciple-makers. So, let us be faithful in doing the same.

Examine your heart. If, deep down inside of you, you didn't desire for the life of Christ *in* you be multiplied *through* you, allow me to encourage you to search your heart and examine your faith (2 Cor. 13:5).

Is Christ in you? Do you believe God's Word claims that Christ alone can save sinners, that God alone is worthy of worship, and that all who do not receive God's grace in Christ will spend eternity in hell?

Do you delight in knowing Christ and desire to proclaim Him to the people around you? Do you abandon yourself to His will for you to be His witness in the world?

So, are you reproducing? To quote Dawson Trotman, "Men, where is your man? Women, where is you woman? Where is the one whom you led to Christ and who is now going on with Him?...Do you know by name today who were won to Christ by you and now living for Him?"

Father God, let us make disciples who make disciples
fulfill the Great Commission. In Jesus's name, amen!

_____

_____

_____

_____

Fishers of Men

Steven Collins

Adapted from *Christian Discipleship*

Follow Me, and I will make you fishers of men.
—MATTHEW 4:19, KJV

After His resurrection, Jesus powerfully reemphasized His demand that the disciples become fishers of men (John 21:1–19). In verses 15–17, Jesus reminds Peter that people, not fish, are the calling of his life.

There's a powerful lesson here for all disciple-makers: Although they had caught nothing prior to His arrival, when Peter and his companions followed Jesus's instructions to cast their nets on the right side of the boat, they caught 153 large fish—too many to even haul into the boat.

Fishers of men. The Master's implication was obvious. In the three years that the disciples spent with Him, Jesus had made them into fishers of men. Soon He would be casting them forth into the world with the Great Commission, and He wanted them to remember that they were no longer fishermen but fishers of men.

How is the net of discipleship made? The net is made one strand at a time by applying the discipleship methodology in the lives of those brought to Christ. Thus, the net of discipleship grows by spiritual reproduction.

Spiritual reproduction is a process by which the Holy Spirit multiplies the number of believers using the vehicle of disciple-making. At every juncture, new believers are not allowed to become lost in the shuffle or overlooked. Instead, each one is thoroughly discipled and becomes a discipler, and the process continues on and on.

How is the net cast? The net is cast every time a body of believers departs after gathering together. The body disperses, as disciple-makers, into the community, penetrating every niche of society. Each disciple-maker is sensitive to the Spirit's leading and the needs of others.

How is the net drawn in? The catch is drawn in as disciple-makers train new believers and help them become integrated into the local church body as functioning members. After each new believer has taken up their symbiotic relationship within the church body, they become part of the network of disciple-makers who are cast back into the world to be future disciple-makers.

Remember that evangelism alone isn't enough to fulfill the Great Commission. There is only one way to be obedient to the Great Commission: MAKE DISCIPLES!

Father God, let us obey the Great Commission by
becoming disciple-makers. In Jesus's name, amen!

The Making of a Disciple

Greg Ogden
Adapted from *Discipleship Essentials*

Make disciples of all nations.
—MATTHEW 28:19

We will not make disciples through the methods of mass production, which are always looking for shortcuts to maturity.

Though adult education programs and small group ministries are good tools to produce maturity, a solid foundation of spiritual growth is challenging to build without the focus provided by small discipling units, usually of three or four people each.

Keith Phillips's chart compares the numeric difference between one person a day coming to Christ and one person a year being discipled to maturity:

Year	Evangelist	Discipler
1	365	2
2	730	4
3	1,095	8
4	1,460	16
5	1,825	32
6	2,190	64
7	2,555	128
8	2,920	256
9	3,285	512
10	3.650	1,024
11	4.015	2,048
12	4,830	4,096
13	4,745	8,192

14	5,110	16,384
15	5,475	32,768
16	5,840	65,536

As you can see, when people are empowered as disciples to make yet more disciples themselves, the results quickly far surpass the more centralized model of evangelism.

If the principle of disciple-making (spiritual reproduction) continues as the only method of evangelism, then it would only take a few centuries to reach the whole world for Christ. Unfortunately, as this has not happened over the last twenty centuries, somebody must have dropped the baton of discipleship.

Robert Coleman, author of *The Master Plan of Evangelism*, writes, "One must decide where he wants his ministry to count—in the momentary applause of popular recognition or the reproduction of his life in a few chosen men who will carry on his work after he has gone."

Father God, raise more disciple-making churches
that change people's lives. In Jesus's name, amen!

_____

_____

_____

_____

The Business of Making Disciples
Charles Swindoll

I must be about my Father's business.
—LUKE 2:49, KJV

A pastor boarded a plane and sat next to a businessman. The pastor asked him what he did for a living.

"I am in the figure salon business. We can change a woman's self-concept by changing her body." Then the man asked, "What do you do?"

The pastor said, "It is interesting that we have similar business interests. You are in the body-changing business, and I am in the personality-changing business."

Intrigued, the man asked, "How do you do that?"

The pastor replied, "We apply basic theocentric principles to accomplish meaningful personality modification."

The man then asked, "Do you have an office here in the city?"

"Oh, we have many offices," said the pastor. "We've gone international, and management has a plan to put at least one office in every country of the world."

"How do they make it work?"

The pastor replied, "Well, it's a family business. There is a Father and a Son, and they run everything."

"It must take a lot of capital to run this business," the businessman observed.

"I don't know how much it takes totally, but we never worry because the Boss always seems to have enough. So, every time you need the money, it is just there."

"What about your employees?"

The pastor said, "They have one Spirit that permeates the entire organization. It works like this: The Father and Son love each other so much that their love filters down through the organization so that we all find ourselves loving one another too."

"Why haven't I heard about it before now?" the man asked.

The pastor said, "That is a good question because our company has a two-thousand-year-old tradition, and we have a manual that is at least three thousand years old."

The man said, "What is the name of your business, and who is your boss?"

With a big smile, the pastor answered, "My business is the church, and my boss is Jesus Christ. Would you like to sign up?"

Father God, may every church be in the business of
making disciples who make disciples, expanding
Your kingdom. In Jesus's name, amen!

_____

_____

_____

_____

The Principle of Multiplication

Walter Henrichsen

Adapted from *Disciples Are Made Not Born*

If [a grain of wheat] dies, it bears much fruit.
—JOHN 12:24, NASB

Multiplication is one of the foundational laws of the universe.

Jesus says in John 12:24 that if a grain of wheat dies, it bears much fruit. Grain dies in order to reproduce. Multiplication is initially slower than the process of addition. This fact is crucial to keep in mind as we think about and undertake the Great Commission.

Let's say, for example, that a gifted evangelist can lead one thousand people to Christ every day. Each year, he will have reached 365,000 people, a phenomenal ministry indeed.

Let's compare him with a disciple who leads not one thousand people a day to Christ but only one person a year. At the end of one year, the disciple has one convert; the evangelist, 365,000.

But suppose the disciple has not only led another person to Christ but also has discipled them—he has prayed with them, taught them how to feed themselves from the Word of God, gotten them into fellowship with like-minded believers, and shown them how to present the gospel to other people. At the end of that first year, this new convert can lead another man to Christ and continue to build him up.

At the start of the second year, the disciple has doubled his ministry—the one has become two. And during that second year, each person leads not one thousand people per day to Christ but one person per year. At the end of the second year, we have four people. You can see how slow our process is.

But also note that we do not have only converts but disciples who can reproduce themselves. At this rate of doubling every year, the disciple, leading one man per year to Christ, will overtake the evangelist numerically early in the twenty-fourth year. From then on, the disciple and his multiplying ministry will be propagating faster than the combined effort of dozens of gifted evangelists.

Multiplication may be costly and, in the initial stages, much slower than addition. But in the long run, it's not just the most effective way of accomplishing Christ's Great Commission—it is the only way.

Father God, help us become multiplying
disciple-makers. In Jesus's name, amen!

_____

_____

_____

_____

Biblical Illustrations of Multiplication

Walter Henrichsen

Adapted from *Disciples Are Made Not Born*

The Israelites...multiplied.
—EXODUS 1:7

Twelve sons were born to the patriarch Jacob. The Bible tells us that they multiplied and filled the land of Egypt (Exod. 1:7).

Jesus's example. Jesus likewise chose twelve men to become His "spiritual children." He invested three years of His life in them and told them to become fruitful, multiply, and spread the gospel to every creature.

You and I are Christians today because these men (excluding Judas) took on Jesus's vision and did as He commanded. Spiritual reproduction works!

Paul's example. Paul desired to preach the gospel throughout the Roman province of Asia (part of modern-day Turkey) on his second missionary journey. However, Acts 16:6–11 tells us that the Holy Spirit held back his plans and then boxed him into the city of Troas. After that, Paul received a vision that urged him to go to Macedonia and preach the gospel.

So, being forbidden by the Holy Spirit to preach the gospel in Asia, Paul and his team left and went to Europe. Notice what happens on Paul's third missionary journey, recorded in Acts 19. Paul is back in Asia once again, this time in the city of Ephesus. Acts 19:8–10 tells us that Paul spoke in the synagogue in Ephesus for three months, and some hardened their hearts and refused the gospel. Paul then took the believers and taught them daily in the school of Tyrannus. As a result, many people believed.

This is a beautiful illustration of spiritual multiplication. Because of Paul's discipling ministry in the school of Tyrannus, everyone in the province of Asia heard the Word of the Lord Jesus. To make this point clear, Luke adds that "both Jews and Greeks" heard the Word.

No excuses. So often, I have heard the excuse that "I just don't have the gift to do this kind of ministry" or "God just hasn't called me to this kind of ministry."

However, the Great Commission was not given to a select few people but all believers. Therefore, irrespective of our gifts and calling, all men and women should be disciple-makers. You may be a teacher, a housewife, or an engineer, but regardless of your vocation, you are also a disciple-maker.

> *Father God, help us fulfill our calling as disciple-makers. In Jesus's name, amen!*

_____

_____

_____

_____

Quality Is the Key to Multiplication

Walter Henrichsen

Adapted from *Disciples Are Made Not Born*

And the things which you have heard from me...entrust
these to faithful people...to teach others also.
—2 TIMOTHY 2:2, NASB

Note the four generations mentioned by the Apostle Paul to Timothy, his son in the faith, in 2 Timothy 2:2: Paul, Timothy, faithful men, and others.

The key to success in the multiplying process is training the disciple in depth. Multiplication occurs when the proper training of faithful people can carry the training process into succeeding generations.

Paul discipling Titus. When Paul came to Troas, not only did the Lord provide an opportunity to preach the gospel but also people who were ready to listen. But Paul turned down the opportunity to reach the whole city of Troas and left in search of his brother Titus (2 Cor. 2:12–13).

But why? Perhaps finding Titus was more important than preaching to the whole city of Troas just then. Because if Paul reached Titus and trained him, he would double the effectiveness of his ministry, and together they could turn around and preach in two cities like Troas instead of just one.

Philip discipling the Ethiopian eunuch. In Acts 8, Philip went to the city of Samaria and preached the gospel (v. 6). Then, right in the middle of his great evangelistic effort, the Spirit of God called Philip and sent him down to the Gaza desert to talk to one man—an Ethiopian eunuch (vv. 26–27).

If Philip could multiply his ministry through the eunuch, this man could become the key to reaching all of his land of Ethiopia.

The importance of reproduction. The training process of sticking with a believer and helping them overcome the obstacles involved in becoming a disciple is a long and arduous task. The ministry of multiplying disciples has never been popular. Everybody likes the results, but few are willing to pay the price necessary to obtain them.

But we can hardly overemphasize the importance of investing in the right kind of person, one of vision and discipline, totally committed to Jesus Christ, willing to pay any price to have the will of God fulfilled in his life.

Father God, let us invest in training future disciple-makers
who faithfully reproduce themselves . In Jesus's name, amen!

_____

_____

_____

_____

The Jesus Model of Discipleship
Josh Erb
Adapted from christiancoachingandmentoringnetwork.org

...that they might be with Him...
—MARK 3:14

The twelve disciples' journey with Jesus falls into five distinct stages. Here are the stages of Jesus's significant and intentional investment in His disciples.

Relational. When Jesus calls His disciples to follow Him, it is an invitation to do life with Him. Unless you have a relationship, you can't have trust, and in a mentoring relationship, trust is the most valuable commodity.

Jesus invited His disciples into an incredible journey of transformation and growth. It started with their yes to come and be with Him.

Teaching. The second stage of discipleship is this whole area of *engagement with truth.* Jesus isn't just lecturing His disciples; He is confronting their worldview with the way of the kingdom. Transformation occurs as believers engage with what they believe about the world with the truth and reality of what Jesus taught.

Heart healing. This is the deep healing work of the Holy Spirit. If we could do Christian discipleship just by following principles, we would not need the Holy Spirit. Life transformation is challenging without the transforming touch of Jesus in our lives.

This stage of the discipleship journey is where we gently, safely, and lovingly face our shame, pain, and hurt and see Jesus minister healing, redemption, and reconciliation.

Mission. Jesus trains His disciples to do the very things that He has been doing. After the disciples have spent some time with Him, He sends them on their first mission trip.

Part of the discipleship journey is creating space for those that we are investing in to have the opportunity to risk while still in a situation where they are covered if they "get it wrong."

Duplication. In Matthew 28, Jesus sends His disciples out to make disciples of all nations. Implicitly, this instruction calls the disciples to do this in the same pattern Jesus employed to engaged with them. They are to go forth and invite others to "come and follow in the way of Jesus."

The kingdom's expansion was to come through multiplication. Each disciple was to disciple others, and in turn, those would go on to disciple yet more others.

Father God, please raise more Christians to be disciple-makers like our Lord. In Jesus's name, amen!

_____

_____

_____

_____

The Original Twelve Disciples of Jesus
Adapted from sermon.com

He appointed twelve of them and called them his apostles.
—MARK 3:14, NLT

To: Jesus, Son of Joseph
Woodcrafter's Carpenter Shop
Nazareth 25922
From: Jordan Management Consultants

Dear Sir:

Thank you for submitting the resumes of the twelve men you have picked for managerial positions in your new organization.

All of them have now taken our battery of tests. We have run the results through our computer and arranged personal interviews with our psychologists and vocational aptitude consultant. The profiles of all tests are included, and you will want to study each of them carefully.

It is the staff's opinion that most of your nominees lack the background, education, and vocational aptitude for the type of enterprise you are undertaking. They do not have the team concept. We recommend that you continue your search for persons of experience in managerial ability and proven capability.

Simon Peter is emotionally unstable and given to fits of temper. Andrew has absolutely no qualities of leadership. The two brothers, James and John, the sons of Zebedee, place personal interest above company loyalty. Thomas demonstrates a questioning attitude that would tend to undermine morale.

We also have to tell you that The Greater Jerusalem Better Business Bureau had blacklisted Matthew. James, the son of Alphaeus, and Thaddaeus have radical leanings.

One of the candidates, however, shows great potential. He is a man of ability and resourcefulness, meets people well, has a keen business mind, and has contacts in high places. He is highly motivated, ambitious, and responsible. We recommend Judas Iscariot as your controller and right-hand man.

All of the profiles of the other candidates are self-explanatory. We wish you every success in your new venture.

Sincerely,
Jordan Management Consultants

> *Father God, use us ordinary people to carry out Your extraordinary purpose. In Jesus's name, amen!*

The Call of a Disciple

Eddie Rasnake

Adapted from *How to Develop a Quiet Time*

And He appointed twelve that they might be with
Him and that He might send them out to preach.
—MARK 3:14

When Jesus called the twelve to follow Him, He called them to a specific purpose.

It wasn't just a general invitation to come and hang out with Him but a particular challenge to follow Him in His mission. In this explanation of Jesus's call to His original twelve disciples (Mk 3:14), we can learn much about what it means for us to be disciples or followers of Jesus today.

With simple reflection, we see that Jesus's call can be divided into two integral components: that the disciples might be with Him and that He might send them out to preach. That is, *Jesus called them to know Him and to make Him known.*

Know Jesus intimately. Jesus appointed these men to be His first disciples, but He invites us to follow Him as well. These aspects of His call are essential to a healthy walk with God. First and foremost, we must develop our relationship with God.

Knowing Jesus means learning from Him and following His example, which automatically leads us to ministry. Jesus says, "Follow Me, and I will make you fishers of men" (Mark 1:17). Following Christ always leads to serving Him. If not, then we are not fully following Him.

Make Jesus known. Jesus spent three years with the twelve disciples and others who chose to follow Him. From the beginning, the invitation was "Come and see" (John 1:39). But, for the first year or so, He expected them to do little else besides build a relationship with Him.

He invited them into His life and let them observe. Toward the end of that time, He began giving them small, manageable tasks. A second invitation follows: "Follow Me" (Mark 1:17). This time, Jesus formalized His relationship with them; He took responsibility for their growth and training.

He continues, "And I will make you fishers of men" (Matt. 4:19). During this next phase, as they continued spending time with Him, He sent them out for ministry, and He desires to do the same with us.

Father God, help us know You intimately and
make You known. In Jesus's name, amen!

_____

_____

_____

_____

The Condition of Discipleship

Dean De Castro

Then He called the crowd along with His disciples and said: "Whoever wants to be my disciple must deny themselves and take up their cross and follow me."
—MARK 8:34

In today's Scripture, we see the condition of discipleship: "Come and die." Dietrich Bonhoeffer, a pastor and theologian executed by the Nazis during World War II, puts it well: "When Christ calls a man, He bids him come and die."

The call to multitudes. Notice that the call to take up one's cross was not only given to the disciples but to all who decided to follow Jesus: "He called the crowd to Him" (Mark 8:34).

Summoning the crowd, our Lord told them bluntly that if they desired to follow Him, then they must be willing to deny themselves and take up their personal cross.

The meaning of self-denial. To take one's cross at the time of Jesus meant to be ultimately executed on that cross. Yet throughout the centuries, many faithful followers of Jesus boldly gave up their lives for the sake of Christ and His gospel.

Our Lord did not intend that all His followers would be martyred for His sake. Instead, He was using the word "cross" in a symbolic sense. Selwyn Hughes helpfully interprets this passage: "Jesus meant that His followers should be prepared to have a death blow delivered to their natural self-interest and live for God's sake."

Sacrifice comes in small packages. For married couples who argue a lot, to take up one's cross means to give up the desire to be right all the time.

Loving people well implies the willingness to sacrifice your time and listen to their concerns. In actuality, giving our lives for Christ means being faithful in surrendering to small sacrifices daily.

The grace of cross-bearing. The next time you need to surrender your rights, leave your comfort zone, and subordinate your self-interests for the interests of others, take heart—under the cross is not only your shoulder but the shoulder of our Lord.

As one preacher, B. D. Johns, puts it, "He who has been on the cross *for us* has promised to be under the cross *with us*" (see Matt. 11:30).

> *Lord Jesus, thank You for helping us lift our cross by*
> *Your sustaining power. In Your Name. Amen!*

———————————————————————

———————————————————————

———————————————————————

———————————————————————

Jesus's Difficult Road Less Traveled

Greg Ogden
Adapted from *Discipleship Essentials*

*Enter through the narrow gate...that leads
to life, and only a few find it.*
—MATTHEW 7:13–14

Jesus promises those who will follow Him abundant life (John 10:10), but He makes it clear from the beginning that to follow Him is difficult and costly. He calls us to follow Him on the road less traveled.

Jesus uses three vivid phrases to describe the narrow road: deny yourself, take up your cross, and lose your life for my sake (Mark 8:34–35).

Deny yourself. Just as Peter denied Jesus by swearing, "I don't know this man you're talking about"(Mark 14:71), to deny yourself is to say, "I don't know me as the lord and god of my life."

To deny yourself means saying no to the god who is me, to reject the demands of the god who is me, and to refuse to obey the claims of the god who is me.

Jesus calls us to say no to ourselves so we can say yes to Him.

Take up your cross. This phrase would evoke the picture of a criminal forced to carry a cross beam and be crucified on it. A criminal picked up his cross only after receiving a death sentence. When a criminal took his cross through the streets, he was a dead man for all practical purposes.

Jesus calls His followers to think of ourselves as already dead, to bury all our earthly hopes and dreams, to bury the plans and agendas we made for ourselves. When we say yes to Christ, we live as though the gods who are us have already died.

Lose your life for my sake. How do we lose ourselves for Jesus's sake? By investing all that we are and have for Him and His gospel.

Those who walk the road of losing everything for Jesus's sake end up gaining everything that finally matters in eternity.

Jim Elliot summarizes it well: "He is no fool who gives what he cannot keep to gain what he cannot lose." The road to resurrection goes through crucifixion. Jesus calls us to walk that road, the road He walked.

Father God, let us walk the narrow path that leads to an abundant and victorious life. In Jesus's name, amen!

_____

_____

_____

_____

The Cost of Following

Chuck Swindoll
Adapted from *Good Morning, Lord...Can We Talk?*

Then he said to the crowd, "If any of you wants
to be My follower, you must give up your own
way, take up your cross daily, and follow Me."
—LUKE 9:23, NLT

Following Christ as His disciple is a costly, unselfish decision.

It calls for a radical examination of our self-centered lives. That's one of those things that is easy to say but tough to carry out.

Let's see if I can break this down into smaller, bite-sized chunks so we don't gag on them.

When you look closely at Jesus's statement, a couple of things seem important.

First, those who desire to follow Him closely must come to terms with *self-denial.*

Second, the decision to give ourselves to others (taking up our cross) must be a *daily* discipline.

That means every day, I bow before the Lord and recommit to the truth that I am *not* the center of my world—that Christ has called me to give myself to meeting the needs of others.

That's costly stuff. Terribly expensive.

If we take His words seriously, then it isn't difficult to see some questions that we must ask and answer ourselves, like

- Am I serious about being a close follower of Jesus Christ?
- Do I think about others to such an extent that self-denial is becoming the rule rather than the exception in my life?
- Am I taking deliberate steps to take up my cross daily?

What is it that keeps you from making such a self-denying commitment to Christ today? A relationship? Your desire to advance your career? A stubborn habit or addiction you can't shake?

Bring whatever it is to Him. He knows where you are. He's been there, done that. Yet He went to the cross for you. Will you take up your cross for Him?

Father God, let us deny ourselves and give up our rights
to meet the needs of others. In Jesus's name, amen!

My Heart, Christ's Home

John MacArthur
Adapted from *The Body Dynamic*

That Christ may dwell in your hearts...
—EPHESIANS 3:17

Notice that Paul doesn't say Christ "comes into your heart"—that is salvation. Instead, he says, "That Christ may dwell in your hearts" (Eph. 3:17).

The difference is between coming initially and dwelling after that. The Greek word used for "dwell" means literally "to settle down." Thus, it carries with it the idea of coming into a home and settling down there. When a Christian is strong within, Christ, who is already there, settles down and feels at home.

In his booklet *My Heart – Christ's Home,* Robert Munger gives a simple but vivid illustration of this spiritual principle. He compares his heart to a home.

Library. This refers to the brain, where all thoughts are, where information is stored. Jesus finds evil and untruth. The man cleans it out. There should be a portrait of Jesus in the library, a reminder that He is at the center of the man's consciousness.

Dining room. It is the room of appetites and desires. Jesus asks the man what he longs for. He wants leeks, garlic, and onions—all the worldly delights. Jesus says, "If you want food that satisfies, seek the will of My Father."

Living room. This represents fellowship, conversation, sharing. Jesus tells the man, "I sit in the living room every morning, and you come right through here so fast you never stop to talk to me."

Workshop. In the workshop, Jesus sees many toys the man has made with his tools. "Is that what you've done with your skills?" He asks. "Use your talents and abilities for the kingdom of God."

Hall closet. Finally, the man and His Savior return upstairs only to encounter a strange odor coming from the hall closet. It represents secret sins. Jesus asks him to open the closet door. The things he didn't want to turn over to Jesus have to come out.

Only when Jesus controls every room is He really at home in our hearts. And we do this when we yield to the Holy Spirit as He extends the lordship of Jesus Christ to every part of the believer's life.

Father God, may our Lord feel at home in
our hearts. In Jesus's name, amen!

_____

_____

_____

_____

True Discipleship: Soldier, Lover, Bond-Slave
Paul Lee Tan
Adapted from tanbible.com

Large crowds were traveling with Jesus...
—LUKE 14:25

The invitation to be saved is for everyone: "Whoever will may come" (Rev. 22:17b). But when it comes to following the Lord as a dedicated disciple, the Lord is not after a crowd but those who mean business.

Here are three pictures of a true disciple from the Bible:

A good soldier. "Endure hardship with us like a good soldier of Christ Jesus" (2 Tim. 2:3).

There are two kinds of soldiers—draftees and enlistees. Statistics say that the most desertions are among the draftees. The enlistees, on the other hand, are potential heroes. The volunteer loves his country, and he loves his commander. Similarly, the disciple of Christ loves his commander and says, "Yes, Sir," to Him all the time.

A true lover. "Simon...do you truly love me more than these?" (John 21:15). Our Lord probably did not point to the breakfast itself, as there was no food on it now. Rather, He likely meant the other disciples.

As Christians, we must not compare and compete with each other over our talents and abilities. But we may compete in our "love for Christ." Do you love Christ more than your friends or even your pastor?

The follower of Jesus is "in love" with Him. He hates what Christ hates, loves what Christ loves. Therefore, we must put Christ first and foremost in our hearts. Anything else—if it comes in between—becomes of no value and is hateful (Luke 14:26).

A bond-slave. "Paul, a servant of Jesus Christ." (Rom. 1:1). In this verse, Paul uses the Greek word *doulos*, which means a bond-slave. In the time of the Roman Empire, slaves had no rights or possessions of their own. They were like things to be used and often abused.

Paul calls himself the bond-slave of Christ. He is a slave who willingly and gladly serves his master. Just like the slave who can go free on the seventh year but decides to stay because he loves his master (Deut. 15:12, 16–17), likewise, a Christian disciple loves and serves Christ not because he has to but because he wants to.

Father God, let us count the cost of following
Christ. In Jesus's name, amen!

_____

_____

_____

_____

Paul's Model of Discipleship

Dennis McCallum and Jessica Lowery
Adapted from *Organic Disciplemaking*

...so that we may present every person complete in Christ.
— Colossians 1:28, nasb

In his roughly thirty years of ministry, Paul used personal discipleship as a conscious strategy for the spiritual formation of his converts and leadership development.

Spiritual formation. Paul says, "We proclaim Him, admonishing every man and teaching every man with all wisdom, so that we may present every person complete in Christ" (Col. 1:28).

This general description of his ministry strategy suggests Paul was not satisfied with gathering a large group of converts. Instead, he was intent on elevating each Christian to a significant level of maturity through a process of warning and teaching.

Churches that disciple large numbers of members have no shortage of volunteers for ministry. As a result, such churches retain more of their new people, and the level of commitment is higher.

In a word, when people in the church are growing spiritually, everyone is happier. Nothing is better for spiritual growth than personal discipleship.

Leadership development. In the New Testament church, where there were no seminaries or graduate schools of theology; the church's leadership was cultivated through the process of personal discipleship.

Paul lived and traveled with numerous young men and at least one married couple (Aquilla and Priscilla). These fellow laborers got the chance to see Paul at work in the field and undoubtedly participated with him in actual ministry.

This kind of field training develops skills and understanding in a way no classroom can. Paul was in a position to see with his own eyes how younger workers ministered, which would naturally lead to the best quality of coaching and feedback.

More than thirty men and women are mentioned by name as fellow workers with Paul. It seems likely that many of these were discipled by Paul, and there may have been others not mentioned.

In 2 Timothy 2:2, Paul instructs his closest disciple to carry on the work of discipleship. Paul was concerned with duplicating disciples down through four generations: himself, Timothy, "reliable men," and "others." He also urged women to disciple other women (Titus 2:3), a practice unknown in Judaism.

> *Father God, revive Your church's strategy for*
> *spiritual formation and leadership through the hard*
> *work of discipleship. In Jesus's name, amen!*

_____

_____

_____

_____

Can You Be a Believer and Not a Disciple?

Peter Scazzero
Adapted from emotionallyhealthy.org

If you hold to my teaching, you are really My disciples.
—JOHN 8:31

Can you be a believer and not a disciple?

I don't know. Only God can judge and sort that out. But I do know that our obsession with getting people to decide for Jesus has led us to a reality where we have large numbers of severely underdeveloped, stunted, nominal Christians filling our churches.

Unlike the witness of the New Testament, this two-tiered American gospel supposes that a person can become a Christian and not follow Jesus. However, the Bible clearly teaches that a genuine disciple follows Jesus, allowing Him to change them for the sake of the world.

A "believer" assents intellectually to what Jesus and Scripture say. But their lives are not directed by Jesus or oriented around Him. A disciple, however, is characterized by the following:

- A first-hand, personal relationship with Jesus
- A commitment to listening to Him for direction
- A love for Scripture
- Self-awareness as reflected in the ability to take their feelings and lay them out before Jesus and themselves
- Silence and stillness
- Community
- An expectation of growing (i.e., knowing)
- Rhythms in their days and weeks (i.e., times with God and Sabbath)
- Regular confession of sin

- A commitment to serve and give

You may add or delete items from this list, but at least one difficult question remains: What percentage of the people in our church are disciples?

Can you be a believer and not a disciple? Again, I am not sure. But I know we must reorient our churches to make disciples by getting people connected and serving. And we must lead them to the uncomfortable places where Jesus can profoundly change them for the sake of the world.

Father God, let us be confident that we are true
disciples of Your Son. In Jesus's name, amen!

_____

_____

_____

_____

Unbiblical Distinction

Greg Ogden

Adapted from *Discipleship Essentials*

The disciples were called Christians first at Antioch.
—ACTS 11:26

Our problem is that we have made peace with an unbiblical distinction.

Many Christian leaders preach that it is alright to be a Christian without being a disciple of Christ. Dietrich Bonhoeffer chided the church two generations ago for what he called "cheap grace." He says that without discipleship, we are practicing a brand of Christianity without a cross.

In his survey of Christian groups, Michael Wilkins discovered that people will readily identify themselves as "Christians" but be quite reluctant to call themselves "disciples."

Being a Christian is easy. The only thing required is that we acknowledge our need for a savior and receive a gift that we cannot earn or deserve. All that is necessary for us is to embrace certain creedal tenets, such as justification by faith alone.

But if I identify myself as a disciple, then I am making a statement about the quality of my followership. Being a Christian is a statement about what Christ has done for me; being a disciple is a statement about what I am doing for Christ.

Today, we are reaping the results of the false notion that we have sown. Christian leaders have acknowledged that we have done a miserable job of making disciples.

George Barna and George Gallup consistently tell us that their polling demonstrates that in terms of moral values and lifestyle choices, there is little distinction between Christians and non-Christians. We are comprised at the core.

We must reaffirm with the Scriptures that there is no distinction between being a disciple and being a Christian; Christian and disciple are used interchangeably in the book of Acts.

In Acts 6:1–2, 7, the followers of Jesus Christ were called disciples. The disciples were later called Christians for the first time in Antioch (Acts 11:26).

In Acts 6:7, after the congregation in Jerusalem chose seven qualified men to take care of the material needs of the neglected widows, a large number of priests became "obedient to the faith." Whether you call yourself Christian or disciple, are you committed to obeying everything Jesus Christ commands you to do?

Father God, remind us to be obedient to the faith that saved us (Rom. 6:17–18). In Jesus's name, amen!

_____

_____

_____

_____

Levels of Growth: Baby

Christopher Adsit

Adapted from *Personal Disciple-Making*

I am writing to you, little children [infants]...
fathers...young men...children
—1 JOHN 2:12–14, NASB

In today's Scripture, the apostle John categorized growing Christians based on different levels of growth: infant, child, adolescent, and adult.

If you want to be a responsible, fruitful disciple-maker, you need to familiarize yourself with the process of spiritual growth. Let's look at the infant stage first.

"I am writing to you, little children [infants], because your sins are forgiven" (1 John 2:12). The New Testament translates three Greek words into the English "baby": *teknia, brephos,* and *nepios.*

As you study where these three words appear in Scripture, you can learn a lot about the characteristics of babies—both physical and spiritual ones—and how to relate to them. Several are listed below. They should give you some good ideas about how to relate better to new Christians.

- They are helpless and need much care and protection (Luke 2:12, 16: Acts 7:19).
- They crave nourishment (1 Pet. 2:2).
- They cannot handle meat and solid food (1 Cor. 3:1–3; Heb. 5:11–14).
- Their speaking, thinking, and reasoning processes are inadequate and must be transformed (1 Cor. 13:11).
- They are easily deceived (Eph. 4:14).
- They should receive proper nourishment, both physical (Acts 7:20) and intellectual (Acts 7:21).

Dean De Castro   647

- They should be gently cherished by their parents (1 Thess. 2:7).
- They should be getting scriptural input (2 Tim. 3:15).
- Their parents are anxious for Christ to be formed in them (Gal. 4:19).
- They should be committed to Jesus by their parents (Luke 18:15).
- They have no authority but are under guardians and managers until they mature (Gal. 4:1–2).
- God reveals extraordinary things to them rather than the (supposedly) wise and intelligent (Matt. 11:25).
- They are innocent concerning evil (1 Cor. 14:20).

Father God, let us put our infantile ways behind us and grow to become children, adolescents, and eventually spiritual fathers and mothers to new Christians. In Jesus's name, amen!

_____

_____

_____

_____

Levels of Growth: Child

Christopher Adsit

Adapted from *Personal Disciple-Making*

I have written to you, children, because you know the Father.
—1 JOHN 2:13B, NASB

The New Testament Greek word *paideuo*, often applied to children, means to "chasten" or "discipline."

Chastening is a big part of relating with our children. Likewise, we should discipline those we are responsible for when they are at the child level. The Bible describes the spiritual child as helpless, inexperienced, and foolish. And Solomon tells us that the "rod of discipline will remove [foolishness] far from him" (Prov. 22:15).

During this phase, he needs to be "at school," learning the fundamentals of walking with the Lord. He may be accumulating a lot of head knowledge that doesn't seem to be seeping down to the heart and hand, but it will in time.

Here are a few more things the Bible says characterize (or should distinguish) the physical child and the relationship between him and his parents. See what parallels you can come up with for the *spiritual* child.

- He is still relatively helpless and needs his parents' protection (Matt. 2:13–16) and provision (2 Cor. 12:14).
- They should grow mentally, physically, socially, and spiritually (Luke 2:52).
- Jesus used a child to demonstrate the kind of spiritual humility necessary to inherit the kingdom of God (Matt. 18:1–4).
- Children were eager to come to Jesus, who had a soft spot for them as well (Mark 10:13, 16).
- A child should obey his parents (Eph. 6:1).

- He should respect his father and the discipline he dishes out (Heb. 12:9–10).
- Servanthood is a prime quality he should have (Phil. 2:22).
- The child can learn and should sit with the adults in heavy teaching sessions (Acts 20:7–12).
- He is sometimes capable of making strategic contributions (John 6:9).
- He is seen as still deficient in spiritual understanding (1 Cor. 14:20).
- God doesn't take kindly to those who would cause a child to stumble (Matt. 18:6).

Father God, may we train our physical and spiritual
children in Your ways. In Jesus's name, amen!

_____

_____

_____

_____

Levels of Growth: Adolescent

Christopher Adsit

Adapted from *Personal Disciple-Making*

I have written to you, young men, because you
are strong, and the word of God remains in
you, and you have overcome the evil one.
—1 JOHN 2:14, NASB

To designate an adolescent, the New Testament uses several words that come from the same root word, *neos*, which is most commonly used to designate people aged from twenty to thirty years old.

One of the primary characteristics of an adolescent is that they are beginning to take on responsibilities. As a result, adolescents start to take their places as movers and shakers in society—some with good results and some with not-so-good results. *Neos* is used to describe the following people:

- The rich young man who came to Jesus asking how to find eternal life (Matt. 19:16–22)
- The young Saul, before whom Stephen's murderers laid their coats (Acts 7:58)
- The young Gospel writer Mark, who fled naked during the commotion when Judas betrayed Jesus (Mark 14:51–52)
- The young men who carried out Ananias and Sapphira after they had lied to the Holy Spirit (Acts 5:6–10)
- The prodigal son, who demanded his share of his father's estate and then squandered it with loose living (Luke 15:11–24)
- Paul's nephew, who overheard the plot on Paul's life and persuaded the centurion commander to take special measures to protect Paul (Acts 23:16–22)

- Sleepy Eutychus who fell out of the rafters while listening to a lengthy exposition from Paul (Acts 20:9–12)
- Timothy, whom Paul urged to set an excellent example for his flock despite his youth (1 Tim. 4:12)
- Younger women, whom older women were to teach to love their husbands and children and be godly wives (Titus 2:4)

In each case, the Scriptures speak of youths taking on adult roles. We need to help our adolescent-level disciples assume responsibilities and authority in the same sense. Not too much yet, but enough to try out their wings a bit.

Father God, help us teach our spiritual adolescents to accept personal responsibility for their lives. In Jesus's name, amen!

_____

_____

_____

_____

Levels of Growth: Adult

Christopher Adsit

Adapted from *Personal Disciple-Making*

I have written to you, fathers, because you know
Him who has been from the beginning.
—1 JOHN 2:14, NASB

Adulthood is our ultimate goal—not only for our disciples but also for ourselves.

If we're ignorant of how an adult is supposed to act, it will be impossible for us to act like one, thus failing to model the Christian life for our disciples' benefit. So, let's look at several characteristics of mature adults found in Scripture:

Grower. A spiritual adult has made their relationship with God their top priority, which results in their continuing growth. John describes the fathers in the group he is writing to as knowing "Him who has been from the beginning" (1 John 2:14). And Paul sees an ultimate goal in individual human development: "a mature man... [grows] up in all aspects into Him" (Eph. 4:13, 16).

Teacher. A spiritual adult teaches younger Christians what they need to learn to enjoy a solid relationship with God.

So, Paul blasted the Christians in Hebrews 5:12 with this indictment: "By now you should be teachers; instead, you're babies! You should be giving, but you're still talking."

Discipliner. Spiritual adults discipline their "children" because they love them, not because they're on some demented power trip (see Prov. 3:12; 13:24; 23:13–14; Heb. 12:4–13).

Sympathizer. On the other hand, a godly parent isn't a tyrant in his disciplining. He knows the difference between a father's firm, loving hand and that of an oppressor or tormentor. Fathers need to find the balance between love and discipline (see 2 Sam. 7:14–16).

Apron string cutter. A good parent has trained his child to be independent. On the other hand, a selfish parent attempts to keep his child forever bound in the proverbial apron strings. The kindest thing would be to prepare the child for separation.

In the same way, we need to keep our disciple's independence as a long-term objective. Train him to feed himself, dig his well, and make his own decisions. Our job as disciple-makers is to help spiritual babies grow into adulthood. It is not an overnight process, and it is not easy. But it's worth it.

Father God, help us grow spiritually to disciple our
earthly and spiritual children to become mature
and responsible adults. In Jesus's name, amen!

_____

_____

_____

_____

Discipling Our Children

Peter and Deonna Tan-Chi
Adapted from *MOTIVATE*

*And Jesus kept increasing in wisdom [mentally]
and stature [physically], and in favor with
God [spiritually], and men [socially].*
—LUKE 2:52

Our children are our first disciples. Our goal in discipling our children is to help them reach their full God-given potential—physically, mentally, socially, and spiritually. And Jesus Christ is the best example of holistic development (Luke 2:52).

Let's look at each aspect of development in which we need to train our children.

Mentally. Avoid too much exposure to television, iPads, cell phones, and other gadgets when they are young. Instead, encourage your children to read books, especially about outstanding men and women who made positive contributions to society.

Wisdom is more important than a good education for success in life. Wisdom is knowing God's Word and principles, being able to weigh and analyze circumstances and situations, and responding and making the right decisions based on and in obedience to God's Word.

Physically. Jesus grew in physical strength and so should our children. They are full of energy and need to exercise regularly and play outdoors as much as possible. In addition, sunlight builds strong bones and helps contribute to positive emotions.

As parents, we train our children to eat healthy and nutritious food. Minimize junk food, like white sugar, fried foods, and soft drinks. These make our children fat. Instead, teach your children to eat many vegetables, fruit, and protein without too much fat.

Socially. We were created for relationships. We need to teach our children to relate socially to others while developing their emotional quotient. They must learn not to be selfish but rather to think of others' needs and relate to others with empathy, genuine interest, and care.

If a child is always on the internet or playing computer games, they will likely become socially awkward. Therefore, we should limit their time with computer games and social media.

Spiritually. Most importantly, we are to nurture our children's spiritual growth by helping them develop an intimate relationship with God through faith in Jesus Christ. Model for them and encourage them to practice the spiritual habits of prayer and reading the Bible daily.

> *Father God, please raise godly parents who*
> *are committed to the holistic development of*
> *their children. In Jesus's name, amen!*

_____

_____

_____

_____

Generational Discipleship

Peter and Deonna Tan-Chi
Adapted from *MOTIVATE*

*He commanded our ancestors to teach their
children...even the children yet to be born.*
—PSALM 78:5–7

We are to be intentionally involved in sharing God's Word with our children and grandchildren so that they can place their faith in God. It is God's vision for us, and He will empower us to do it.

In addition, research reveals that grandparents involved in discipling their grandchildren significantly impact their spiritual lives.

Relay race. In a relay race, the first runner hands off the baton, runs just a few more paces, and then stops. However, when a parent passes the baton to their son or daughter, they do not stop running. Instead, they continue to run alongside their sons and daughters to disciple them *and* their grandchildren.

What a joy to see our adult children disciple their children to raise a godly generation who believes in God and loves and serves Him—an eternal legacy with great reward! This generational discipleship is the real success in parenting! It will have eternal significance.

Personal example. We prayed for our children before they were born, when they were born, and after birth. And we are still praying for them.

We prayed for each of them to have a personal relationship with God through faith in Jesus Christ, to love and obey Him wholeheartedly, and serve Him and others to make a difference in this world for Him. We even prayed for their future spouses. We now desire the same for our grandchildren.

Until we could see fire and passion in their hearts towards the Lord and see them falling in love with our Jesus and living to please Him, we never assumed they knew the Lord.

Thank God all of our five children are dedicated followers of Jesus Christ. They are all happily married to spouses who are also committed to following Jesus.

They are now leading discipleship groups comprised of men and women who are also discipling others. They also practice the biblical principles we have taught them with their children and teach others to do the same.

Father God, change the hearts of our children
and grandchildren to be all that You created
them to be. In Jesus's name, amen!

_____

_____

_____

_____

Discipline and Discipleship

Dean De Castro

No, I beat my body...
—1 CORINTHIANS 9:27

The words "discipline" and "disciple" come from the same root. Hence, a disciple is a disciplined person. He disciplines himself to follow the ways and instructions of another.

As devoted disciples of Jesus Christ, we discipline ourselves to learn and apply all the teachings of Christ, which will result in an ever-deepening commitment to live like Him.

The example of Jesus. Jesus lived a disciplined life. He models for us how to live a disciplined life in this indulgent and pleasure-seeking world. He not only deprived Himself of comfort during His forty days of prayer and fasting in the wilderness and suffered a horrific death on the cross; He also disciplined Himself in everyday affairs.

For example, He missed lunch talking to a woman at the well (John 4:34). His family criticized Him as insane for not eating because of the crowd (Mark 3:20–21). Due to a full schedule of preaching and healing during the day, He deprived Himself of sleep to pray early in the morning (Mark 1:35) and late at night (Luke 6:12).

The example of Paul. In 1 Corinthians 9:25, Paul discusses an athlete's strict training to highlight the importance of self-discipline.

Many who have won medals in the Olympics deprived themselves of the pleasures of life. They have learned to discipline themselves to say no to the myriad distractions that cross their paths. They have clear-cut objectives and have resolved to persevere until they accomplish them.

Paul says it's no different in the Christian life. He disciplined his bodily appetites to be under his control at all times. It is perfectly normal to desire food, sex, sleep, and comfort, but they are to be in subjection and within the bounds prescribed by God.

Paul warns himself of the danger of living an undisciplined life: "I myself will be disqualified for the prize" (1 Cor. 9:27). Paul is not addressing the issue of salvation. He is referring to losing the reward of ruling with Christ in His eternal kingdom (Rev. 2:26–27).

Albert Epp reminds us, "If we allow Christ to rule our hearts in this life, He will share with us His rule in the Age to come."

Father God, help us become disciplined disciples
of Your Son. In Jesus's name, amen!

The Discipline of Obedience

Dean De Castro

Wherefore, my beloved, as ye have always obeyed...
— PHILIPPIANS 2:12–13, KJV

In today's passage, Paul shows the kind of obedience any disciple of Christ should manifest. Here are the seven lessons about obedience from this passage.

The pain of obedience. "Work." Obedience is problematic because it involves suffering, effort, and diligence. It is a type of work rendered to God. It is painful because man has to give up his will and submit to God's will.

The perspective of obedience. "Work out." Paul did not ask the Philippians to work *for* their salvation since they were already saved. Instead, he asked them to work *out* the new life they already received from God. We have the responsibility to work out what God had worked in.

The participation of obedience. "Work out your salvation yourself." God will not do the *obeying* for us. We have to do it ourselves. Our job is to be willing to do God's will, and God's part is to reveal His will and empower us to obey it.

The posture of obedience. "With fear and trembling." As slaves of God, the right attitude for serving and obeying God is fear and trembling (Eph. 6:5). We obey God not because we are afraid of His punishment. Instead, we obey God with all the diligence and seriousness it deserves because we don't want to disappoint Him.

The power of obedience. "For it is God who works in you." When we act, God provides the power. Whatever God asks to do, His power is there and always available. Joyce Meyer says, "Do whatever you can, and God will do what you cannot do."

The process of obedience. "Both to will and to do." The proper sequence of successfully obeying God is to *will*, then to *do*. Before we do any of God's instructions, we must first want it badly. Our commitment will sustain us even when we don't feel like doing it.

The purpose of obedience. "Of His good pleasure." Obedience is not just doing things but doing the *right* things according to God's purpose and for His own benefit and pleasure. It brings glory to His name.

Father God, let us obey You even if it
hurts. In Jesus's name, amen!

_____

_____

_____

_____

The Great Omission: Obedience
Dean De Castro

...teaching them to obey...
—MATTHEW 28:20

I firmly believe that obedience is a significant but common omission in our understanding Christ's final command to His followers.

Please note that Jesus did specifically mention obedience in His Great Commission. He didn't talk about teaching them to *know* but rather "teaching them to obey everything I have commanded you."

Let me share with you how I remind myself to love God by *obeying* Christ in the power of the Holy Spirit, one choice at a time. It is based on the acronym OBEDIENCE.

O—Options. Free will is the greatest gift God has given humanity. We are not victims of our circumstances. There are many options and choices behind any decision we make. God wants us to choose His will over our sinful desires (1 Pet. 4:2).

B—Be. Our *being* must precede our *doing*. We must act according to who we already are in Christ. We obey God because we are His slaves (Rom. 6:16). Christian obedience that's not based on one's identity in Christ is a subtle form of legalism. The result is that man gets the glory.

E—Emotion. Don't let emotions determine your obedience. Feelings are fickle and unreliable. Keep your commitments even if it hurts (Ps. 15:4b).

D—Do. Just do it. You don't need to get it right at first. You just have to get it going. Believe that the Holy Spirit will guide you all along the way (Rom. 8:14).

I—Immediately. "I will hasten and not delay to obey Your commands" (Ps. 119:60).

E—Endure pain. We learn obedience through a process that is no fun at the time. "Although He (Jesus) was a son, He learned obedience from what He suffered" (Heb. 5:8).

N—Never give up. "Let us not become weary in doing good, for at the proper time we will reap a harvest if we don't give up" (Gal. 6:9).

C—Curb cravings. "See that no one is sexually immoral, or is godless like Esau, who for a single meal sold his inheritance rights as the oldest son" (Heb. 12:16).

E—Expect rewards. "Behold, I am coming soon! My reward is with me, and I will give to everyone according to what he has done"(Rev. 22:12; also see Rev. 2:26–27).

> *Father God, we lovingly obey You because we*
> *are Your slaves bought with the precious blood*
> *of Your Son. In Jesus's name, amen!*

_____

_____

_____

_____

Disciplined by Grace

Jerry Bridges
Adapted from *The Discipline of Grace*

For the grace of God that brings salvation...It teaches. . .
—TITUS 2:11–12

The word translated "teaches" in Greek could also be translated as "disciplines" or "trains."

Paul used the same word in Ephesians 6:4 when he charged fathers to bring up their children in the discipline and training of the Lord.

For some Christians, discipline suggests restraint and legalism, rules and regulation, while grace, on the other hand, seems to mean freedom from any constraints, spontaneous and unstructured living.

It's easy for us to practice any spiritual discipline without connecting it with God's grace. The truth is, practicing spiritual disciplines must be based on God's grace and not on one's own performance

Legalism. When somebody introduced me to Christian discipleship, he gave me a list of seven spiritual disciplines I should practice every day—things such as daily quiet time, Bible study, Scripture memorization, and prayer.

While learning those helpful disciplines, I came to believe that my day-to-day relationship with God depended on how faithfully I performed them. I developed a vague but accurate impression that God's smile or frown was turned on based on whether or not I did my spiritual exercises.

My experience is not unusual. A friend who ministers on a university campus told of a student who was exceptionally diligent in keeping his daily quiet time with God. My friend asked the student why he was so rigid in his practice, and the young man responded, "So nothing bad will happen to me."

He was not being disciplined by grace but by legalism.

Dean De Castro   665

Grace. In Titus 2:11–12, Paul teaches us that the very same grace—God's unmerited favor—that brought salvation to us in the first place also disciplines us. It means that all our practices of spiritual disciplines must rest on the knowledge that God relates with us every day based on grace and not on our performance.

It means that we diligently practice every spiritual discipline but not to gain God's favor or try to impress Him with our holy habits. Instead, we allow God to use these spiritual routines as means of growing us in the grace and knowledge of our Lord Jesus Christ (2 Pet. 3:18).

Father God, let Your grace motivate us to diligently
discipline ourselves unto godliness. In Jesus's name, amen!

_____

_____

_____

_____

Great Commission Church

Dean De Castro

...going...baptizing...make disciples...teaching...
—MATTHEW 28:19, GREEK TEXT

By now, I hope we have established the one main verb and the three participles in the Great Commission passage (Matt. 28:19).

Based on the main verb, "make disciples," the primary task of every local church is to be a disciple-making church. Our Lord shows us through the participles the three ways to accomplish this mission.

A Great Commission church is an evangelizing church. The first participle mentioned by our Lord is *going.* Most Bible versions translate this word as a verb, "go," which causes profound misunderstanding. This inaccurate translation might be the reason why many Christians believe that the command of Christ is mainly to evangelize, meaning doing local outreach or becoming missionaries to foreign countries.

However, evangelism is the initial path to fulfilling the Great Commission. But it is not the ultimate goal. The word "go" implies our manner of life. As we go about our daily lives, witnessing should be a lifestyle. It should be intentional and personalized.

I like this definition of evangelism: It is all about you telling others all about Him. Evangelism tells others your personal story of how you came to know Christ and how the gospel has changed you from the inside out.

A Great Commission church is a baptizing church. The second participle is "baptizing." Can a person be a Christian and not get baptized? That's like a man who wants to date a woman and not be committed to marriage.

Just as marriage is a serious commitment, baptism is a pledge to love Jesus and obey His teachings. It is also a commitment to the church of Jesus Christ. It is following the command of Christ to love other Christians and grow together with them.

A Great Commission church is a teaching church. The third participle is "teaching." A disciple-making church faithfully teaches and trains believers to develop the discipline of obedience.

I created a discipleship curriculum at the Great Commission Bible Church, which my wife and I started in 2000. It is based on the acronym DISCIPLERS. It contains twelve lessons on the significant spiritual disciplines that can lead to spiritual maturity and Christlikeness.

Father God, may every church be a disciple-making church
that changes people's lives. In Jesus's name, amen!

_____

_____

_____

_____

The Prevailing Church
Dean De Castro

I will build my church.
—MATTHEW 16:18

The last letter *S* in the twelve discipleship disciplines of the acronym DISCIPLERS stands for "small group."

To become mature disciples of Jesus Christ, we need to belong to a local church and join a small group to grow spiritually with other believers.

Recently, I read an article entitled, "Satan's Beatitudes." It said that if the devil were to write his own Beatitudes, they would probably go something like this:

- Blessed are those who are too tired, too busy, too distracted to spend an hour once a week with their fellow Christians—they are my best workers.
- Blessed are those Christians who wait to be asked and expect to be thanked—I can use them.
- Blessed are the touchy people. With a bit of luck, these over-sensitive people may stop going to church—they are my missionaries.
- Blessed are the troublemakers—they shall be called my children.
- Blessed are the complainers—I'm all ears to them.
- Blessed are they who are bored with the minister's mannerisms and mistakes—for they get nothing out of his sermons.
- Blessed is the church member who expects to be invited to his church—for he is a part of the problem instead of the solution.
- Blessed are they who are easily offended—for they will soon get angry and quit.

- Blessed are they who do not give their offering to carry on God's work—for they are my helpers.
- Blessed is he who professes to love God but hates his brother and sister—for he shall be with me forever.
- Blessed are you when you hear this and think it is about other people and not yourself—I've got you.

The church is not a museum of perfect people. It is a hospital where God uses people, especially difficult people, to save us from ourselves.

In Matthew 16, our Lord predicts His bride will be under attack by Satan and his allies. Nevertheless, not even death, the "gates of Hades," has the power to impede the church's progress. The blood of martyrs, in fact, has sped church growth in size and spiritual power.

Lord Jesus, You are the Architect, Builder,
Owner, and Lord of Your church. Amen!

_____

_____

_____

_____

The Discipline of Support and Accountability

Jay Adams

Adapted from *Winning the War Within*

Bear one another's burdens.
—GALATIANS 6:2, ESV

We can't win our battles with sinful patterns alone. Galatians 6:2 teaches us that each Christian must come to assist others whenever he discovers them losing the fight. We need the support of other Christians as well as accountability to them.

Call for reinforcement. At many points in the Christian life, not every follower of Christ can engage successfully in the hand-to-hand combat that the war within requires. As such, there is nothing wrong with asking for help. So, don't hesitate to call for reinforcements when you find yourself in trouble.

Unfortunately, many Christians lost their spiritual battles because they were too proud to call for help. They were too proud to admit their failures for fear of embarrassment. Moreover, it is also pride that keeps people from receiving the support they desperately need.

As soon as you feel yourself sinking and know that your efforts to extricate yourself are useless, shout for help. Don't wait until you have lost the battle. Instead, call for others to stand beside you and help you so that you may win the battle for the sake of Jesus Christ.

For the sake of Jesus Christ. You are not merely fighting a battle of your own; this is *the Lord's* battle, and it is to be won for His glory.

How dare you assume that this battle is yours? Who do you think you are? How can you say, "It's my business whether I win or lose?" How can you tell others who want to help you to "mind their own business"?

Fighting the Lord's battle is the business of the church. That's why the Bible commands every believer to "encourage one another daily...

so that none of you may be hardened by sin's deceitfulness" (Heb. 3:13). "Let us not give up meeting together...but let us encourage one another" (Heb. 10:25).

God provided not only the Holy Spirit but also the church, through which the Spirit often offers such help. That is why Christ has provided support in His church and ordered His troops to help one another fight sin.

Father God, let us support one another and win
battles for Your Son's sake. In Jesus's name, amen!

_____

_____

_____

_____

Two Are Better than One

Charles Swindoll

Adapted from *Living on the Ragged Edge*

Two are better than one.
—ECCLESIASTES 4:9–12

Solomon is not talking about marriage here. His advice is for humans on this lonely earth wondering how to survive in our dog-eat-dog culture of ragged-edge reality. The preacher mentions three reasons why two are better than one.

Mutual encouragement when we are weak (v. 10). When we could easily stumble and fall on our faces, we need a companion to keep us from getting too bruised and bloody. When you feel troubled, God graciously steps on the scene and provides you with a friend.

In 1 Kings 19:4, the same strong man who stood boldly in front of Ahab and Jezebel was now praying that God would take his life. It was at this juncture that God gave Elijah a good friend—Elisha.

1 Kings 19:21 says Elisha followed Elijah and became his attendant. There's a renewed strength, as Elijah survives thanks to the presence of a companion.

Mutual support when we are vulnerable (v. 11). Solomon's point is that when we feel exposed, unguarded, and vulnerable, we need somebody to warm us up.

Any time or place you feel self-conscious and your major battle is "How am I going to make it through this right now?" be reminded that you are cold and need help keeping warm. A friend like Jonathan, who strengthened David again and again, would help.

Mutual protection when we are attacked (v. 12a). We all fight the same adversary—Satan. There is also an entire demonic force that is against us. When either Satan attacks us or people bear down on us with verbal spears and swords of slander, there's nothing like a companion to get us through.

Verse 12 concludes with, "A cord of three strands is not quickly torn apart." This is not simply a reference to Christ, who indeed is our best Companion; it's a reference to more than one companion, maybe two or three.

A cord of three strands is held with comforting words or arms around the shoulder or visible presence so that the waters of your soul are calm.

Father God, let us encourage, support, and protect each
other during times of adversity. In Jesus's name, amen!

You Won't Make It Alone

Drew Hunter
Adapted from desiringGod.org

But there is a friend who sticks closer than a brother.
—PROVERBS 18:24

One of the deepest regrets of the dying is not prioritizing friendship. Most of us, on our deathbeds, wish we connected more often and deeply with friends. So why is developing friendship worth all our effort? Here are five reasons you need good friends.

You are human. You need friendship because God created you in His image. God is not solitary but eternally exists as a triune fellowship of love. Our triune God made us reflect Him, which implies God wired us for lives of relational fullness with other people.

Friendship is the "highest happiness." Pastor and theologian Jonathan Edwards once wrote, "The well-being and happiness of society is friendship. This is the highest happiness of all moral agents." When Edwards claims that friendship is our highest happiness, I wonder why we do not seem to think or speak about friendship that way?

You won't make it alone. God brings us to faith, and He will cause us to persevere in this faith (Phil. 1:6). And one of His primary instruments is His people. True friendship is an affectionate bond between people who persist in the faith with truth and trust (see Heb. 3:13; 10:25).

Friendship halves your sorrows. One of the greatest gifts we can give one another in depression is our companionship. Bishop J. C. Ryle writes, "This world is full of sorrow because it is full of sin. It is a dark place. The brightest sunbeam in it is a friend. Friendship halves our sorrows and doubles our joys."

Many of us carry great pain and sorrow. Yet faithful companions cut those sorrows in half with their mere presence and rightly placed words.

Friendship points to the meaning of the universe. The cross is the most significant expression of love, and Jesus wants us to understand it as a sacrifice for friends (John 15:13). The single greatest moment of history, where we see God's glory shine most brightly, is a cosmic act of friendship.

With God's help, let's make it to our deathbeds without relational regret.

Father God, let us develop authentic friendships despite all
the mess and pain of relationships. In Jesus's name, amen!

_____

_____

_____

_____

Eternal Community

Larry Crabb
Adapted from *Connecting*

You [God] loved Me [Christ] before the creation of the world.
—JOHN 17:24

Consider the fictional conversation below among the persons of the triune
God sometime in eternity past.

"Let's create creatures who can share the unique joy of an intimate relationship with us. They are personal beings like us who can fathom the very depths of our glorious nature.

"These beings must be built with the freedom to love us and thereby experience a life of connection or to love themselves more and experience the misery of disconnection.

"They will, therefore, believe the lie that we're holding out something valuable that they could find through their efforts. But we can work their faithless choice to our advantage. It will allow us to reveal that our love is so profound that we will sacrifice the joy of our community to welcome them into the community."

"Son, at just the right time, I'll send you to become one of them and to accept the guilt for their sins. Then I'll break our connection and let you experience the death of separation from me all that sin deserves."

"Father, what you ask is painful beyond description to even contemplate. I cannot imagine what the experience will be like not seeing your face. Is there any other way?"

"No."

"Then I will go gladly."

"Spirit, you will come upon various people who will advance my purposes until my Son dies as a man and is resurrected. Then you will take up residence in everyone you have drawn to me, and you will incline their hearts toward loving me so that obedience will become a joy and not mere duty."

"It will be my incomparable thrill to advance your purposes and to create within all those who accept my gracious offer of forgiveness an appetite to know you. And I will nurture that appetite until it becomes stronger than all others. I will not rest until they live in my strength and overcome all desires to find life apart from you."

"It's time to get started. Let's see what we can do with this bit of clay. I have a vision of what it could become."

Father God, thank you for bringing us into Your eternal community. In Jesus's name, amen!

_____

_____

_____

_____

The Intercession of Believers

Erwin Lutzer

Adapted from *How to Say No to a Stubborn Habit*

For where two or three gather in my
name, there am I with them.
—MATTHEW 18:20

Scripture informs us that God's people's first responsibility is persistent prayer for one another, not merely individual prayer, but corporate prayer.

Prayer *as a group* is essential. It is good to form special friendships in the church. As we develop confidence in them, we can turn to them in the time of need.

First, we need to enlist God's people's prayer support, particularly when there are besetting sins that we can't overcome on our own. We need the added help of others who will *stand in for us* in the presence of God. We need the persistent prayers and encouragement of God's people to help us come to terms with our problems.

Second, there is supportive value in sharing our heartbreaks with a group of God's people. Jesus wanted the disciples to be at His side during His agony in Gethsemane. It wasn't only their prayers that He desired. He wished someone could be with Him during those agonizing moments, encouraging Him.

Thirdly, we need people to whom we can be responsible and accountable. We can agree to report to the group, or at least one individual, on our spiritual progress. If I know someone is going to ask me, "How's that problem coming?" I'm going to be more inclined to flee from temptation. When we develop responsibility toward others, it helps us to do what we ought.

We cannot live a victorious Christian life independent of God's children. We are all members of the Body of Christ, and each of us affects others' functions. Our successes and failures are always a team effort.

It's humbling to realize that we need the support of God's people, but we do. If we are wayward, spiritually mature Christians must restore us; if we are weak, others must share their strength with us. At no time ought we to think that we are making it alone with God— for we need His redeemed people too.

Father God, let our struggles and temptations humble us to enlist other believers' prayer support. In Jesus's name, amen!

_____

_____

_____

_____

Admonish One Another

Gene Getz

Adapted from *Building Up One Another*

...able also to admonish one another...
—ROMANS 15:14, NASB

The word "admonish" in Greek, *noutheteo,* doesn't refer to informal communication or standard teaching.

Instead, it implies a definite appeal, a correction. Paul used it to confront Christians who were idle and lazy (1 Thess. 5:14). As members of one Body, we should admonish others who stray from the straight and narrow path outlined in Scripture. We do this because we care enough to confront them (see Paul's example in Gal. 2:11–14).

Not everyone responds positively—even when we "speak the truth in love." There are times when we don't handle these confrontations well ourselves. We need to look at the biblical guidelines and some practical steps for engaging in this kind of communication.

Biblical guidelines. In Romans 15:14, Paul mentions two requirements for admonishing others with competence.

Full of goodness (v. 14a). The Roman Christians could admonish one another because they were making progress in their own Christian lives.

Though not perfect, they had removed the "plank" from their own eyes before they tried to remove the "speck of sawdust" from a brother's eye (Matt. 7:3–5). So, likewise, we must make sure we "clean up our own act" before we try to help others clean up theirs (See Gal. 6:1).

Complete in knowledge (v. 14b). An adequate knowledge of God's Word is the other requirement.

Admonition must be based on God's specific will and ways—not on what we think other Christians should or should not do. Thus, when we admonish other Christians, it should be based on sins mentioned in Scripture, not a list we have added to the Bible.

Practical steps. Each of us must evaluate our own lives before trying to admonish others. The following questions can serve as personal criteria:

- Can I say my own life is "full of goodness"?
- Do I know what the Bible teaches about godly and righteous living?
- When I encourage another Christian, do I reflect deep love and concern?
- Am I persistent in my admonishment without being obnoxious and overbearing?
- Do I admonish others to help them become complete and mature in Christ?

Father God, help us to offer admonition and
receive it if needed. In Jesus's name, amen!

The Discipline of Church

R. Kent Hughes

Adapted from *Disciplines of a Godly Man*

I will build my church.
—MATTHEW 16:18

Today, we have a phenomenon unthinkable in any other century: churchless Christians.

A vast herd of professed Christians exists as church hitchhikers, without accountability or membership. However, membership in an invisible church without participation in its local expression is never contemplated in the New Testament.

Church hitchhikers. The hitchhiker's thumb says, "You buy the car, pay for repairs and insurance, fill the car with gas, and I'll ride with you. But if you have an accident, you are on your own!"

So it is with the ideology of many of today's church attenders: "You serve on the boards and committees, you grapple with the issues and do the work of the church and pay bills—and I'll come along for the ride. But if things do not suit me, I'll criticize and complain and probably bail out."

Some hitchhikers attend one church for the preaching, send their children to a second church for its dynamic youth program, and go to the third church's small group. Church hitchhikers' vocabulary includes "I go to" or "I attend" but never "I belong to" or "I am a member."

Church disciplines. Whoever you are and however busy you may be, the church must be at the center of your life. It involves the following:

- The discipline of regular attendance. You need to commit yourself to attend the worship services of your church regularly.

- The discipline of membership. If you are not a church member, you need to covenant before God to find a good church, join it, and commit yourself to support and submit to her discipline.
- The discipline of giving. Your financial support of a local church should take precedence over your para-church commitments. It should be regular and systematic (10 percent is a good starting point).
- The discipline of participation. You must pour your time, talents, expertise, and creativity into your church to the glory of God.
- The discipline of love and prayer. Learn to love God's family by praying for the church leaders and working with other believers to fulfill the Great Commission.

Father God, let us avoid a cavalier disregard for
the local churches. In Jesus's name, amen!

_____

_____

_____

_____

The Importance of the Church

Tony Evans

Adapted from *God's Glorious Church*

You are the salt of the earth...the light of the world...
—MATTHEW 5:13–15

When talking about the church, it is crucial to understand this spiritual principle: Everything that is physical and visible—the world and life around us—is controlled by the things that are invisible and spiritual.

The only way to fix what is wrong in the visible and physical realm is to ensure that the invisible and spiritual realm is working right. Human institutions of power and influence can't fix society's most profound problems and address people's deepest needs.

The church is the most critical institution on earth. The church, and only the church, has been commissioned by the sovereign Lord to be His representative agency in history. God has given the church the sole authority to unlock the spiritual realm's treasures to bring them to bear on earth's realities.

Thus, as the church goes, so goes everything else. God designed the church to be the epicenter of culture, and the church's strength or weakness is a major determining factor in the success or failure of human civilization.

When the church is strong, it impacts the culture positively—even if the "powers that be" in a particular place don't realize that impact and seek to marginalize and persecute the church. But when the church is weak, its influence deteriorates, and so does the culture.

It is essential to understand the church's importance for cultural reasons since Jesus called His people to be salt and light, a city on a hill.

One example of the church's impact, both positively and negatively, is the institution of slavery in America. Many segments of

American culture condoned and sanctioned slavery even though it served as the catalyst for a civil war that cost thousands of lives and helped produce ongoing cultural upheaval.

And Christendom at large justified slavery, even leading some to find a basis for slavery in Scripture. But in the end, it was the strength of the church bringing its influence to bear that helped lead to the collapse of slavery.

Father God, may Your will be done, on earth
as it is in heaven. In Jesus's name, amen!

_____

_____

_____

_____

Is Church Optional or Essential?

Greg Ogden

Adapted from *Transforming Discipleship*

I will build My church.
—MATTHEW 16:18

Many people today like to say, "Jesus, yes; church, no."

For these Christians, joining and committing to a local church is optional. In their view, being integrally involved in the church is not a necessity for Christian living. It is unnecessary for discipleship.

My wife and I visited a well-known Southern California church the Sunday following Easter. The speaker preached to the twenty-one hundred people who had indicated they decided to receive Christ during the Easter services.

The preacher asked the congregation, "Is it necessary to go to church or be a part of the church to be a Christian?" His answer? "No. It is not necessary." I almost bolted from my seat and shouted, "Yes, it is necessary to a part of the church if you are a Christian!"

The Scriptures picture the church as an essential, chosen organization in whom Christ dwells. The Apostle Paul's favorite and most fundamental image for the church is that of the Body of Christ (1 Cor. 12:27).

When Paul uses this phrase, it is far more than a nice word picture or metaphor. He is not saying that the church is like the Body of Christ but that it *literally* is the Body of Christ. The church is the place where Christ dwells. The church of Jesus Christ is nothing less than His corporate replacement on earth.

The late Ray Stedman succinctly describes Christ's relationship to the church: "The life of Jesus is still manifest among people, but now no longer through an individual physical body limited to one place on earth, but through a complex, corporate body called the church."

The church is not an optional afterthought for those who name Christ as their Lord. The church is central to God's plan of salvation. God saves people into a new community, which is the vanguard of a new humanity. To be called to Christ is to throw in one's lot with His people.

To be a follower of Christ is to understand that there is no such thing as solo discipleship.

Father God, let the local church we belong to transform us into Christlike disciples. In Jesus's name, amen!

Three Pictures of the Church

Warren Wiersbe

Adapted from *The Bible Exposition Commentary*

...the church of the living God...
—1 TIMOTHY 3:15

The Apostle Paul wanted the church leaders and church members to know what a local church is. In 1 Timothy 3:15, Paul gives three pictures of the church.

The family of God (v. 15a). One of Paul's favorite words is "brethren" (see 1 Tim. 4:6). When a sinner believes in Jesus Christ as Savior, he immediately is born again into God's family (1 Pet. 1:22–25). Paul advised young Timothy to treat the local church members as he would treat his own family.

"Exhort him [an older man] as if he were your father. Treat younger men as brothers, older women as mothers, and younger women as sisters" (1 Tim. 5:1–2).

The assembly (v. 15b). The word "church" is a translation of the Greek word *ekklesia*, which means "assembly." It referred to political assemblies in the Greek cities (see Acts 19:29, 32). It is used about one hundred times in the New Testament to refer to local churches, congregations of believers.

There are many different kinds of assemblies, but the church is the assembly of the living God. Because it is God's assembly, He has the right to tell church leaders how to govern His church. Church officers must not become religious dictators who abuse the people to achieve their own selfish ends (1 Pet. 5:3–5).

The best counsel for managing a local church is found in the three Pastoral Epistles (1 and 2 Timothy, Titus).

The pillar and ground of the truth (v. 15c). The church as a pillar is an architectural image that may have reminded the Ephesian believers of the Greek goddess Diana's great temple, which had 127 pillars. The local church must put Jesus Christ on display in the lives of faithful members. We are like statutes put on a pedestal so the world can see them (Phi. 2:16).

The word "ground" suggests a bulwark. As a bulwark, the church protects the truth and makes sure it does not fall. Sometimes, church leaders must take a militant stand against sin and apostasy. It does not make them popular, but it does please the Lord.

Father God, let the church leaders manage Your
churches with love and truth. In Jesus's name, amen!

_____

_____

_____

_____

Church: God's Family

Philip Yancey
Adapted from *Church: Why Bother?*

...God's household, which is the church of the living God...
—1 TIMOTHY 3:15

It grieves me to see local churches that are run more like business institutions than a family, for the New Testament presents the church as more like a family than an institution (1 Tim. 3:15).

I think that God invented the human institution of the family as a training ground to prepare us for how we should relate within other institutions, including the local churches.

Human family. Institutions are based upon and held together by status and rank. In the business world, title, salary, and other "perks" signify status. In families, however, status works differently. A child "earns" the family's rights solely by birth.

An underachieving child is not kicked out of the family. Instead, a sickly child who "produces" less may receive more attention than their siblings. As John Wesley's mother puts it, "Which child of mine do I love best? I love the sick one until he's well, the one away from home until she's back."

Every family contains some successful individuals and some miserable failures. But these differences become insignificant in a family because we were born of the same ancestors, and the same genes coil inside our cells.

As novelist John Updike writes, "Families teach us how love exists in a realm beyond liking or disliking, coexisting with indifference, rivalry, and even antipathy."

God's family. Similarly, in God's family, "there is neither Jew nor Greek, male nor female, slave nor free" (Col. 3:15). All such artificial distinctions have melted under the sun of God's grace. As God's adopted children (Eph. 1:5), we gain the same rights, clearly undeserved, as those enjoyed by the firstborn, Jesus Christ Himself.

Family is the one human institution we have no choice over. We get in by simply being born. And as a result, we are involuntarily thrown together with a group of strange and unlike people.

However, God calls for another step: to bond voluntarily with a strange community because of a common bond in Jesus Christ. Such a community more resembles a family than any other institution.

Father God, may every church be the place where people
are welcomed and accepted. In Jesus's name, amen!

_____

_____

_____

_____

Church: A Living Organism

Greg Ogden

Adapted from *Discipleship Essentials*

Now you are the body of Christ.
—1 CORINTHIANS 12:27

The Body of Christ is the fundamental biblical image of the church. By this, we understand the church to be a living organism.

Christ's relationship to the church. The Body of Christ points to the reality that the church is not a human organization but a divine organism mysteriously fused to the living and reigning Christ. He continues to reveal Himself in His people.

Paul understood the church as an organism when the resurrected Christ appeared to Paul and charged him with persecuting Him (Acts 9:4–6). However, Saul was not persecuting Jesus but His followers.

This dramatic incident shows that Jesus lives in each of His disciples. Therefore, if you touch a Christian, you have touched Christ. Paul quickly realized the living Lord is the vital essence of the church, both now and in the past.

Church's relationship to Christ. The nature of the church's relationship to Christ is implicit in the idea that Jesus is "head over everything for the church" (Eph. 1:22). It means that the church is under Christ's direct authority.

It also means that He arranges life in His Body. Each member is directly connected to the head and therefore can receive signals from the head.

Just as the head sends forth the signals through the nervous system, which activates the body parts; likewise, Christ as the head of the church motivates and equips every member to fulfill the role God has assigned to them. That's how the church can function as a living organism.

Our relationship to each other. According to Paul's body image, all the parts are interdependent and necessary for the health of the whole. Thus, the underlying message of 1 Corinthians 12 is that everyone is valuable.

In His wisdom, God designed us not as well-rounded, multitalented, thoroughly complete, and independent people. Instead, He made it so that we need each other and that each of us brings something of value. We are not self-sufficient. In other words, "We don't have it all together, but together we have it all."

Father God, together, as parts of Christ's Body, may we
extend His life to the world. In Jesus's name, amen!

_____

_____

_____

_____

The Church as a New Culture

Peter Scazzero
Adapted from *Emotionally Healthy Spirituality*

Accept one another, then, just as Christ accepted
you, in order to bring praise to God.
—ROMANS 15:7

To love well, we will need the power of God and a commitment to learn, grow, and break with unhealthy, destructive patterns that go back generations in our families and cultures—and in some cases, our Christian cultures as well.

Remember, Jesus formed a community with a small group from Galilee, a backward province in Palestine. He chose twelve disciples with whom He lived day and night for three years. But unfortunately, they were neither spiritually nor emotionally mature.

Peter. As the leader of the group, he had a big problem with his mouth and was a bundle of contradictions.

Andrew. He was Peter's brother and was quiet and behind the scenes.

James and John. They were brothers who were given the name "sons of thunder" because they were aggressive, hotheaded, ambitious, and intolerant.

Philip. He was skeptical and pessimistic. He had limited vision. "We can't do that" summed up his faith when confronted by the problem of feeding the five thousand.

Nathaniel Bartholomew. He was prejudiced and opinionated.

Matthew. He was the most hated person in Capernaum, working in a profession that abused innocent people.

Thomas. He was melancholy, mildly depressive, and pessimistic.

James, son of Alphaeus, and Judas, son of James. They were nobodies. The Bible says nothing about them.

Simon the Zealot. He was a freedom fighter and terrorist in his day.

Judas. He was the treasurer, a thief, and a loner. He pretended to be loyal to Jesus before finally betraying Him.

However, all of them, except for Judas, did have one excellent quality: They were willing to grow and change. And that is all God asks of us.

> *Father God, help Your church demonstrate Your*
> *unconditional love and acceptance for the world*
> *to see and desire. In Jesus's name, amen!*

_____

_____

_____

_____

The Fruit of the Holy Spirit

Gene Getz

Adapted from *Building Up One Another*

But the fruit of the Spirit is love.
—GALATIANS 5:22

The following statements are positive "one another" exhortations. Notice how these exhortations reflect the fruit of the Spirit, which is love.

- members of one another (Rom. 12:5)
- being devoted to another (Rom. 12:10a)
- honoring one another (Rom. 12:10b)
- being of the same mind toward one another (Rom. 12:16; 15:5)
- loving one another (Rom. 13:8; 1 Thess. 3:12; 4:9; 2 Thess. 1:3; Heb. 10:24; 1 Pet. 1:22; 1 John 3:11, 23)
- edifying one another (Rom. 14:19)
- accepting one another (Rom. 15:7)
- instructing one another (Rom. 15:14)
- greeting one another (Rom. 16:16; 1 Cor. 16:20; 2 Cor. 13:12; 1 Thess. 5:26; 1 Pet. 5:14)
- waiting for one another (1 Cor. 11:33)
- caring for one another (1 Cor. 12:25)
- serving one another (Gal. 5:13)
- carrying one another's burdens (Gal. 6:2)
- bearing with one another (Eph. 4:2; Col. 3:13)
- being kind to one another (Eph. 4:32)
- submitting to one another (Eph. 5:21; 1 Pet. 5:5)
- esteeming one another (Phil. 2:3)
- encouraging one another (1 Thess. 4:18; 5:11, 14)
- confessing sins to one another (James 5:16a)

- praying for one another (James 5:16b)
- offering hospitality to one another (1 Pet. 4:9)
- fellowshipping with one another (1 John 1:7)

A church manifesting "the fruit of the Spirit" practices the "one another" injunctions that build up the Body of Christ and lead to unity. Practicing these "one another" exhortations in a small group context is the essence of love.

Father God, enlighten and empower us to understand
and apply these exhortations. In Jesus's name, amen!

_____

_____

_____

_____

Threats to the Body of Christ

Greg Ogden

Adapted from *Discipleship Essentials*

*The same Spirit...gives them [gifts] to
each one, just as He determines.*
—1 CORINTHIANS 12:11

The church as the Body of Christ is the prototype of unity in diversity.

When people in the Body take responsibility before the Head (Christ) to know and exercise their assigned function, the church becomes a living organism. However, when we forget this, the Body ceases to function according to its design.

In 1 Corinthians 12, Paul identifies two devaluing attitudes that undercut the proper functioning of the Body.

The attitude of inferiority. "If the foot should say, 'Because I am not a hand, [therefore] I do not belong to the body...' If the ear should say, 'Because I am not an eye, [therefore] I do not belong to the body'" (vv. 15–16).

When we compare our gifts to others, we declare ourselves deficient. This attitude of low self-esteem is detrimental to the health of the Body. We play the "if only" game: I would have significance and value *if only* I could be like so-and-so.

When we secretly envy the skills of others, we denigrate ourselves and the unique design God has placed in us. The Lord designed us just the way we are so that we are needed in the Body of Christ.

The attitude of superiority. "The eye cannot say to the hand, 'I don't need you!' And the head cannot say to the feet, 'I don't need you'" (v. 21).

Independence and self-reliance are enemies of community. Without vulnerability and awareness of need, there is no basis for community. Vulnerability is a gift to the community that says, "I need you. I welcome you into my life. I want you to be a part of me."

Yet we often devalue others in the Body because they don't think as we do or have the tastes we do. Instead, the right attitude should keep this complementarity in mind: "I need you. You have gifts and perspective that I don't have."

Instead of inferiority or superiority, we need an attitude of inter-reliance. Inter-reliance means you are incomplete without me, and I am incomplete without you. You need me, and I need you.

Father God, let us seek unity in
diversity. In Jesus's name, amen!

Why Join a Local Church

Dean De Castro

Every day they continued to meet together in the temple courts.
—ACTS 2:42–47

This passage tells us five reasons why every Christian should join a local church:

*To **understand Gods' Word.*** "They devoted themselves to the apostle's teaching" (Acts 2:42a). Look for a church where you can understand and apply biblical principles in everyday life. Join a church that wins converts and disciple them to grow in every area of life.

*To **love God's people.*** "And to fellowship" (Acts 2:42b). Somebody once said, "Relationship is the essence of everything, the essence of our existence." We all need relationships to receive acceptance, affirmation, and accountability continuously.

The best place to develop meaningful relationships is through the structure of a small group. Since close connection usually takes time to develop, I suggest attending a local church near where you live, allowing you to be an active participant in the community.

*To **witness God's power.*** "Everyone was filled with awe at the many wonders and signs performed by the apostles" (Acts 2:43). The early church also devoted themselves to prayer (v. 42b). As a result, miracles happened.

At the last church where I served, our congregation had witnessed how God heard our prayers by healing an older woman who had cancer and still lived to a hundred some years old. A praying church is a powerful church!

*To **share God's wealth.*** "They sold property and possessions to give to anyone who had a need" (Acts 2:45). Choose a church where the pastor is not shy in teaching about stewardship. For a Christian, giving is a significant expression of worship.

When we give our tithes and offerings to our local church, we're telling God that we are owners of nothing but stewards of everything. We must sacrificially support our church just as King David had provided everything to God's holy temple out of love (1 Chron. 29:3).

To honor God's day. "Every day they continued to meet together in the temple courts...praising God" (Acts 2:4a, 47a). Every day belongs to God. But Sunday is the Lord's day to celebrate Christ's resurrection from the dead. Therefore, we should approach it expectantly.

Father God, help us love Your church the way King David loved Your temple. In Jesus's name, amen!

Reasons to Join a Church

Mark Altrogge
Adapted from theblazingcenter.com

So in Christ we, though many, form one body,
and each member belongs all the others.
—ROMANS 12:5

Do you need to join a local church? Can't believers worship Jesus on their own? Yes, we can and should worship Jesus individually. But we should also worship, pursue, and love Him with others. It is vital to our spiritual growth.

Unfortunately, it seems like a growing trend that many Christians don't think they have to be a part of a church. But here are twelve crucial reasons why every Christian should join a local church:

- We need to be built together with other believers (Eph. 2:20–22).
- We need brothers and sisters to encourage, exhort, challenge, and build us up in our faith, and we need to enable and build others up (1 Thess. 5:11).
- We need to worship together with others (Col. 3:16).
- We need to be stirred up by others to love and good deeds (Heb. 10:24–25).
- Jesus is uniquely present when believers gather together (Matt. 18:20).
- The church grows as believers meet together and use their gifts (Eph. 4:16).
- We need to benefit from the gifts of others and serve others with our skills (1 Pet. 4:10–11).
- We need to pray for one another (James 5:16).

- We need pastors and teachers to teach and feed us (Eph. 4:11–12).
- We need to witness to unbelievers together with others (John 13:35).
- We need to love others, bear with the weak, help new believers (Rom. 15:1–2).
- We need to be a part of a church for the sake of our children (Eph. 6:4).

You need the church, and the church needs you! God never intended for us to live the Christian life alone! Remember, you are not just a body filling a spot in a pew. Look around. Others need you! You may not feel like you have anything to offer others, but God's Word says that you do.

So, if you're not involved in a local church, ask the Lord to guide and show you where He wants you to be.

Father God, let us see that joining a local church is essential to our spiritual health and maturity. In Jesus's name, amen!

Seven Good Reasons to Leave a Church

Brett McCracken

Adapted from crosswalk.com

So Paul left them.
—ACTS 19:9

Some people leave the church because the preaching is boring or the children's ministry isn't fun anymore. Those are real issues, though not usually enough to warrant leaving the community. But what are some *legitimate reasons* for leaving a church? Here are seven:

The church abandons orthodoxy. Look for another church if your church places cultural relevance or social gospel initiatives above sound doctrine and biblical authority. If your concerns go unheeded, leave (see Acts 19:8–10).

The church becomes more about politics than Jesus. If your church succumbs to the culture's "politics is everything" orientation, placing political activism above Jesus's worship and gospel proclamation, you should look for another church.

Transformation is absent. A church should be a living, growing organism where the Holy Spirit sanctifies believers, changes lives, and transforms communities.

If your church never sees people being saved or baptized, if church members never grow, and if nothing in the surrounding city is changing for the better because of the church, it might be time to find a new church.

You live too far away. Perhaps you've moved a bit further away from your church, and you find yourself going to fewer church events and meeting fewer people in your neighborhood who know about your church. That might be a good reason to find another church.

You have no opportunity to serve. Every church member should be serving in their church, whether that is by welcoming guests at the door, taking up the offering, teaching Sunday school classes, or helping out in some other way. If you are in a church with no opportunities to serve, look for another church where you can help.

You cannot submit to leaders. If you are unable to defer to the authority of your church's appointed leaders, and you've tried but can't seem to resolve your issues with the leadership, it might be time to look for a different church.

The church is homogenous and insular. If everyone in your church looks the same (life stages, socioeconomic status, culture, ethnicity, etc.) and your church feels more like a country club than an outward-minded community on mission, look for another church.

Father God, grant us wisdom to leave a church with good reasons and with Your Spirit's guidance. In Jesus's name, amen!

The Fellowship of the Church

Tony Evans

Adapted from *God's Glorious Church*

...so that you also may have fellowship with us...
—1 JOHN 1:3

When we really talk about fellowship, we are not talking about having punch and cookies in the church's fellowship hall. There's nothing wrong with that, but the topic is much more substantial.

The church is more than a school for spiritual instruction, a theater for a spiritual performance, or an organization carrying out spiritual programs.

The church is a living entity made up of people God has called to live in a relationship with Him and each other.

Three admonitions. There are three critical warnings to the church in Hebrews 10, which the writer delivers in the context of Jesus Christ as the high priest over the family of God.

Since we have Jesus Christ ministering as our great high priest, we need to do three things. "Let us draw near" together before Him in worship (v. 22), "let us hold fast" to our common faith (v. 23), and "let us consider how to stimulate one another to love and good deeds, not forsaking our own assembling together" (vv. 24–25).

We could summarize these commands by saying, "Let us not stay at home and draw back from one another in isolation, but let us draw near to God and to one another so we can hang in there together and be strong."

Two illustrations. The church's fellowship reminds me of a wicker chair. One or two strands of a wicker chair could not hold a person's weight by themselves, but when enough strands are woven together, the chair can easily bear it. The total of the wicker strands joined in "fellowship" makes the chair work.

I also like to compare the church's fellowship to logs in a fireplace. It's hard to burn a single log because it takes a lot to get it lighted and keep it burning, and it doesn't provide much warmth or last very long anyway.

But a stack of logs burns for a long time and draws people to the heat and the light. It is the picture of a church that is practicing biblical fellowship.

Father God, let us enjoy our fellowship with You
and with each other. In Jesus's name, amen!

_____

_____

_____

_____

The Covenant of Church Membership

Stephen Olford

Adapted from *Basics for Believers*

Let all things be done decently and in order.
—1 CORINTHIANS 14:40, NKJV

Except for the thief on the cross, all the believers in the early church were baptized. Baptism symbolizes Christians' oneness with Jesus and their unity with His people and His Word. To express their commitment to the local church that baptizes them, Christians must sign a covenant of membership.

This covenant below includes guidelines based on Scripture so that individuals seeking to align themselves with a local church might not come in confused but rather "decently and in order" (1 Cor. 14:40, NKJV). These terms remind us to be loyal, loving, and living members of the local church.

I acknowledge the Lord Jesus Christ as Lord of all my life and seek to confess Him as such before others by the testimony of both life and lip (see Rom. 10:9; 2 Cor. 5:15).

I trust in the power of the Holy Spirit, who lives in my heart to keep me, guide me, and lead me in the way of purity and holiness (see John 14:26; Rom. 8:2–4).

I accept the Bible as the inspired Word of God and my final authority in all matters of faith and practice (see 2 Timothy 3:16; 2 Pet. 1:20–21).

I recognize my responsibility by tithes and offerings to extend the kingdom of the Lord Jesus Christ both at home and abroad (see Mal. 3:8–10; 1 Cor. 16:2).

I recognize my responsibility to pray regularly for the work of this church, for its pastors, officers, and members, that the witness of all concerned may be to the glory of God and the salvation of souls (see Eph. 6:18–19; 1 Thess. 5:17, 25).

I recognize my responsibility to be regular in my attendance at the church's services and the Lord's table (see Acts 2:42; Heb. 10:25; 1 Cor. 11:26).

I have been baptized in obedience to my Lord's command, thus signifying my union with Christ in His death, burial, and resurrection (see Matt. 28:19–20; Rom. 6:4).

Church members should regularly review this covenant and reaffirm the pledge they made to the Lord.

Father God, let us fulfill the terms of this covenant
with Your strength. In Jesus's name, amen!

The Accountability of the Church

Tony Evans
Adapted from *God's Glorious Church*

...correct, rebuke...with great patience and careful instruction.
—2 TIMOTHY 4:2

Because life brings problems, one of the church's essential ministries is to call its members to account for how they live.

But whatever form accountability takes, the church cannot escape its responsibility to see that its members live lives worthy of Christ (Eph. 4:1). Accountability in the church can take two primary forms: directive and corrective.

Directive discipline. This has to do with the church pointing out how people should live, directing them in the course of godliness. The church does this by exercising its teaching ministry, encouraging and exhorting the saints to deal with sin and live holy and fruitful lives.

Directive discipline also has a much more positive implication. It's what happens when believers respond to the church's ministry and seek to get their lives to line up with Christ.

Corrective discipline. When a believer rejects the church's directive discipline and decides to continue in a sinful direction, the church is to apply corrective discipline. It may involve using biblical discipline with a sinning saint for correction and restoration.

The saint who will not listen to the church and its duly appointed leaders is a candidate for corrective discipline. If a person won't hold themselves accountable for their sin, it's up to the church to hold them responsible.

The necessity of judging. When we mention church discipline, someone will inevitably quote Jesus's statement, "Do not judge so that you will not be judged" (Matt. 7:1).

However, based on verses 2–5, Jesus did not say we are not to judge under any circumstances. His warning was against hypocritical judgment, someone with a "log" in their eye passing judgment on someone with a "speck" in theirs (v. 3).

In other words, Jesus's concern was over whether we are qualified to judge. He says, "First take the log out of your own eye, and then you will see clearly to take the speck out of your brother's eye" (v. 5).

Instead of prohibiting judgment, Jesus tells us to make sure we judge righteously. Therefore, judging situations and practicing discipline are necessary to distinguish between right and wrong.

Father God, empower Your churches to apply church discipline when it's needed. In Jesus's name, amen!

_____

_____

_____

_____

The Qualifications of Church Leaders

Tony Evans

Adapted from *God's Glorious Church*

He must not be a recent convert, or he may become conceited.
—1 TIMOTHY 3:6

Some Christians believe that the church needs to function like a business; hence, they look for corporate CEOs to chair the church board and accountants to do its books. There is nothing wrong with tapping business leaders to serve in the church *if they are spiritually qualified.*

Here are a few godly qualifications listed in 1 Timothy 3:1–13 and Titus 1:6–9 for leading God's people.

Aspiring to serve. A potential church leader should aspire to lead in the Body of Christ (1 Tim. 3:1). This doesn't mean he should campaign for the job, but he should be willing to serve if asked. The church should not be pressuring reluctant candidates into leadership positions just because there are vacancies to fill.

Even temperament. Church leaders cannot have a violent temper that causes them to be always ready for an argument or a fight and pound their fists on the table when things don't go their way (1 Tim 3:3; Titus 1:7). A habitually angry, disagreeable, and harsh-spirited rather than a gentle and peaceable person is not biblically qualified to lead in the church.

Manage family well. "If a man does not know how to manage his own household, how will he take care of the church of God?" (1 Tim. 3:5). Church leaders need to be faithful husbands, literally "a one-woman man" (1 Tim. 3:12; Titus 1:6).

The reference to the conduct of a leader's children doesn't mean there are never problems in the home. It may even be that an elder or a deacon is dealing with a rebellious child. The issue isn't the problem itself but how the leader handles it.

Faithful to God's truth. Since the church is "the pillow and support of the truth" (1 Tim 3:15), church leaders must have a track record of demonstrated spiritual maturity, commitment to the truth of Scripture, and an ability to handle God's Word.

They are godly people holding fast to the Word so that they can "exhort in sound doctrine and refute those who contradict" (Titus 1:9).

Father God, may every church choose godly leaders who are spiritually qualified to lead Your people. In Jesus's name, amen!

Prayer in the Church

Warren Wiersbe

Adapted from *The Bible Exposition Commentary*

...first of all...prayers...
—1 TIMOTHY 2:1

When a local church ceases to depend on prayer, God ceases to bless its ministry. "Much prayer, much power! No prayer, no power!"

The priority of prayer (v. 1a). "First of all" indicates that prayer is most important in the church's ministry. It is sad to see how prayer has lost its importance in many churches.

"If I announce a banquet," a pastor said, "people will come out of the woodwork to attend. But if I announce a prayer meeting, I'm lucky if the ushers show up!"

Not only have special meetings for prayer lost stature in most local churches, but prayer in the public services has also been greatly minimized. Many pastors spend more time with the announcements than they do in prayer! Pastors must also carefully prepare "the pastoral prayer" so it doesn't become routine, humdrum, and repetitious.

The attitude in prayer (v. 8). "I want men...in prayer." Paul stated that "men" should pray in the local assembly. Both men and women prayed in the early church (1 Cor. 11:4–5), but the emphasis here is on the men.

It is common to find women's prayer meetings but not men's prayer meetings. If the men do not pray, the local church will not have dedicated leaders to oversee its ministry.

Paul identifies three essentials for effective prayer. The first is "holy hands." It symbolizes a holy and blameless life (2 Sam. 22:21; Ps. 24:4). If we have sin in our lives, we cannot pray and expect God to answer (Ps. 66:18).

"Without anger" is the second essential and requires that we be on good terms with one another. A person who is a troublemaker rather than a peacemaker cannot pray and get answers from God.

"Without disputing" is the last factor in effective prayer. When we have anger in the heart, we often have open disagreements with others. Christians should learn to disagree without being disagreeable. We should "do all things without murmurings and disputings" (Phil. 2:14).

If we spend more time preparing to pray and getting our hearts right before God, our prayers will be more effective.

Father God, raise more men of prayer to lead
Your churches. In Jesus's name, amen!

_____

_____

_____

_____

The Lord's Prayer for Church Unity

M. Scott Boren

Adapted from *Making Cell Groups Work* by TOUCH Outreach
Ministries

...that they may be one as we are one...
—JOHN 17:22B

The night before Jesus was crucified, He prayed for the eleven disciples and the future church to be *one*, just as the Father and the
Son are *one.*

Theologians through the centuries have misinterpreted this prayer.
Some have applied this prayer to ecumenical cooperation between
churches and denominations. Others misused this prayer to promote
interfaith conferences, councils to discuss theological differences,
and cooperative ministry efforts.

While not inappropriate, such an application seems premature. How can churches that lack unity within become unified with
other churches?

Jesus used the radical unity between His relationship with the
Father as the model for church unity. The relationship between the
Son and the Father manifests itself by personal interaction, mutual
submission, and reciprocal love.

Love is not lordship; it is mutual life together, with no one claiming
power or authority over the other. The Son willingly submits to the
Father, and the Father blesses the Son. The Father loves the Son, and
the Son loves the Father. The church is only the church when it enters
into this love for one another.

The church is not the church because it preaches orthodox doctrine and meets for worship. Just because people meet in small groups
doesn't mean the church has come to life. Small groups function

God's way when believers experience a life of unity and learn to sacrifice for one another.

The church's ministries may include teaching, worship, and small groups, but these are not the cornerstone of the church's nature. Life in Christ and love for one another characterize the true church of God.

Some of the more practically minded might have some important questions: Where's the evangelism? Where's the church growth? Where's the group multiplication? What about assimilation and closing the back door?

According to John 17:23, Jesus prayed that we would be one "so that the world might believe that You have sent Me." True biblical unity leads to evangelism and results in church growth. When God is genuinely flowing through a small group, it will spontaneously grow.

Father God, may we experience genuine biblical community in our small groups. In Jesus's name, amen!

_____

_____

_____

_____

Jesus As A Small Group Leader

Neal Mcbride

Adapted from *Discipleship Journal*, issue 59 (1990)

He...chose twelve of them, whom He also designated apostles.
—LUKE 6:13

Small groups are not just a sociological fad. They are neither a clever gimmick to pump up church attendance nor a panacea for all the ills that confront the church. Small groups are, however, a ministry format with a solid biblical foundation.

Jesus's involvement in a small group is the most convincing argument for including them in the local church's life. The Gospels picture Jesus Christ as the most excellent small group leader in history. As either group leader or participant, you are walking in His footsteps.

Why was the small group such an essential part of Jesus's ministry? What can we learn from Jesus about its importance?

Jesus began His earthly ministry by establishing His "small group," the apostles (Matt. 4:18–22; Luke 6:13). The Son of God certainly didn't need the companionship or assistance of the apostles. Yet, from the beginning, He elected to establish and minister within a framework of interpersonal relationships.

Jesus spent the majority of His time with His small group. They were together constantly: They traveled together, shared meals, experienced mutual hardship, and lived together. As Jesus's crucifixion drew closer, He spent more and more time with His small group and less time with the multitudes sought after Him.

Jesus used the small group context to teach and model spiritual knowledge, attitudes, and behavior. It was not a formal or academic experience; the small group members participated with Christ in whatever He did. They saw and experienced the attitudes and actions He was admonishing others to adopt.

Through this intimate association, Jesus granted the apostles "the knowledge of the secrets of the kingdom of God" (Luke 8:10). The apostles' small group was their living-learning laboratory.

The small group was Jesus's method for leadership training. Jesus devoted Himself primarily to the task of developing a select group of men, the apostles. They would carry on the work of the gospel after He returned to the Father. It would be "through their message" (John 17:20) that the world would come to believe.

Father God, may every local church see small group ministry
as a necessity, not an option. In Jesus's name, amen!

_____

_____

_____

_____

Discipleship Groups

Greg Ogden
Adapted from *Discipleship Essentials*

Go and make disciples.
—MATTHEW 28:19

Discipling, in the minds of many, is associated with a one-on-one, teacher-student relationship.

In my many years of discipling Christians, however, I have come to see groups of three or four as the optimum setting for making disciples.

Here are five reasons why I believe that a triad or quad is better than one-on-one:

- One-on-one discipling puts pressure upon the discipler to be the answer person all the time. When a third person joins the group, the dynamic shifts to a process in which everyone can contribute to the discussion.
- Triad discipling shifts the model from hierarchical to relational. Every participant views discipleship as a come-alongside relationship where we are on a mutual journey toward maturity in Christ.
- The sense of the Holy Spirit's being present in our midst occurs much more often in the group versus the one-on-one.
- There is wisdom in numbers. Adding at least a third person multiplies the perspectives on Scripture and application to life issues.
- Finally, by adding a third or fourth person trained to disciple others, the multiplication process is geometrically increased.

If three is better than two, why isn't ten better than three? The answer is that the larger the group, the more you water down the essential elements that make for transformation.

- *Truth.* Learning occurs in direct proportion to the ability to interact with the truth. As group sizes grow, it becomes increasingly difficult to tailor the rate of learning to the individual.
- *Transparent relationships.* Self-disclosure is integral to the transformation of every group member. Openness becomes increasingly complex in direct proportion to the size of the group.
- *The larger the group, the easier it is to hide.* Accountability requires checking to see if group members have completed the assignments and maintained their commitment to obedience. Large numbers decrease access to a person's life.

Implementing reproducible disciple groups of three or four in all local churches is the best tool to nurture Christians' spiritual growth and successfully fulfill Christ's Great Commission.

Father God, may more local churches establish
small discipleship groups of three or four to
revitalize Your church. In Jesus's name, amen!

Small Group Covenant Example

Dean De Castro

Be devoted to one another in love.
—ROMANS 12:10

A small group covenant is a valuable tool to assist the group's spiritual development for both leaders and members.

Below is a sample of a small group covenant for you to consider.

We agree to abide by the following covenant to assist us in achieving our mission and guiding us in our mutual commitment to one another as brothers and sisters in Christ:

- *Grace.* I am willing to love you with the love of the Lord. I am eager to accept you unconditionally and affirm you, regardless of your past history and present situation and behavior (John 15:12; Rom. 15:7).
- *Transparency.* I am willing to be open and honest with you by sharing my joy, sorrow, frustration, and disappointment. I want you to understand me, and I also want to enter into your world and share the life that God has given to us (Rom. 12:10; Eph. 4:3).
- *Sacrifice.* I will renew my decision daily to consider your needs as necessary as my own. I will be sensitive to the leading of the Holy Spirit to care for you, help you, and pray for you (1 Cor. 10:24; 12:25).
- *Confrontation.* I permit you to confront me when you see my wrongdoings. I need your correction, and I will try not to be defensive (Col. 3:16; Phil. 2:1–2).

- **Responsibility.** Lord willing, I will attend all small group meetings and not be absent. I am eager to fulfill all my responsibilities in the small group (Acts 2:44).
- **Confidentiality.** I will never repeat outside the meeting anything of a personal nature said in the group (Prov. 11:13; 1 Tim. 5:13).
- **Evangelism.** I am willing to help and pray for the unsaved friends and relatives of my small group's members to become Christians and join our small group or church in the future (1 Cor. 9:23).

In full acceptance of this covenant, I, _____, recognize my commitment to God and the members of this group and will keep this document as a reminder of the voluntary covenant I have entered into on this date: _____.

Father God, let us honor the commitment we made to You
and the members of our small groups. In Jesus's name, amen!

_____

_____

_____

_____

Six Small Group Killers

Neal McBride
Adapted from *Discipleship Journal,* issue 59 (1990)

Watch and pray.
—MATTHEW 26:41

Here are six dangers that stalk small groups. But if you know what they are, you can overcome them with God's help.

Aimlessness. It's essential to determine the purpose of your group ahead of time. People will tolerate aimlessness for a while, but they'll soon drop out when they don't know why they're involved. So, identifying why the group exists and what you hope to accomplish is critical to a successful group experience.

Poor leadership. No single factor can kill a group more than its leaders. However, too much or too little leadership can be fatal. The domineering taskmaster is just as dangerous as the spineless leader.

Leaders should be in a growing relationship with Christ and be eager to assist others in that same process. No leader is perfect. Look for leaders who are faithful, available, and teachable.

The wrong mix. Groups that merge all types and ages often don't work. Most people will feel uncomfortable with others who do not share their interests and experiences.

On the other hand, homogenous groups can fall into the trap of exclusivism. Members can be so familiar with each other that the group lacks a healthy stimulation from within.

Group people who are approximately the same age. The same age group is more likely to have similar needs and interests. A ten-year spread tends to work well.

Shallowness. When members keep each other at an emotional arm's length, their interaction quickly deteriorates. Try to structure discussions and activities into your group sessions that encourage the expression of personal attitudes, opinions, and feelings.

Individualism. A day may come when you must confront a group member with an individualistic orientation that is damaging the group. Your goal should be to correct the problem without crushing the person. Approach this person in private and with a humble attitude. Be honest but sensitive in your choice of words.

Competition. Is your group just one of many programs, or are small groups integral to the life and existence of your church?

Once you have addressed these issues, clearly establish the expected level of commitment and participation with your group members.

Father God, bless every small group with Your
guidance and protection. In Jesus's name, amen!

_____

_____

_____

_____

Why Small Group Isn't Enough

Richard C. Meyer

Adapted from *Discipleship Journal,* issue 59 (1990)

*They continued to meet together in the
temple courts...in their homes.*
—ACTS 2:46

I have studied, prayed, cried, and laughed with the same group of people for several years.

My small group is an excellent source of encouragement and support, and I wouldn't trade it for any other. But it's also not enough. I also need the church, the larger Body of Christ. So, here's some reasons why we all need to belong to this extended family.

Family gatherings. Acts 2:42–47 shows that the early Christians not only met in small home groups; they also attended larger gatherings in the temple courts "every day."

When we join the church and attend these extended family gatherings, we strengthen the network of believers in a local community.

More gifts to receive. In becoming part of the church, we benefit from the gifts of the larger community of faith.

The choir lifts my spirit to God in a way that does not happen in my small group. In addition, the Tuesday evening services challenge me with messages that I don't usually receive from my small group meetings during the week.

The bigger picture. I rub shoulders with people from different backgrounds in my small group. But even though we're a diverse group, we're not diverse enough. Our view of reality is, at times, too parochial. I need broader group experience to open up the tunnel vision I have sometimes suffered from.

The need for the sacraments. My spiritual health is impoverished without the sacraments of the church. I need the spiritual nourishment of Holy Communion. Through these sacraments, I affirm my connection with the worldwide fellowship of believers in a way not possible in my small group.

When I watched people being baptized, I was reminded that God is alive and well in the world, even though He had been strangely silent in mine. The baptism encouraged me to go on.

I wouldn't go without my small group. But neither will I go without the larger Body of Christ. Each renews my faith and expands my horizon. I need them both.

> *Father God, let us faithfully join a small group and attend our local churches' larger gatherings. In Jesus name, amen!*

Discipleship Group Discussion Questions

Dean De Castro

But grow in the grace and knowledge of
our and Savior Lord Jesus Christ.
—2 PETER 3:18

Below is a sample of discipleship group discussion questions that relate to all the elements of DISCIPLERS in our daily lives.

It's best to use these questions as guidelines for group sharing after listening to the Sunday morning messages. These reflective questions will assist us to grow spiritually (2 Pet. 3:18).

1. What is God telling you to do in this morning's message?
2. What are you going to do about it?
3. Do you have any questions about the sermon?
4. *Devotion.* Did you spend time with the Lord in the last week, completing the Bible reading plan and praying to God?
5. *In love with people.* Have you hurt another person by your words, either behind their back or face to face?
6. *Suffering.* What personal problems did you encounter last week? How did you deal with them?
7. *Character.* What good habits do you feel God wants to form in your life? Have you taken specific steps to develop those habits?
8. *Investment for eternity.* Have you been faithful in your tithing and offering to God?
9. *Pursue holiness.* Have you given in to any temptation or any addictive behavior this week? How did you respond?
10. *Lordship of Christ (time).* What task have you been procrastinating on? When are you going to do it?

11. *Lordship of Christ (talent).* What opportunities did God give you to serve others since our last meeting? How did you respond?
12. *Lordship of Christ (temple).* Have you taken care of your body, making sure it gets a balanced diet, sufficient exercise, proper rest, and medical attention?
13. *Evangelism.* Have you shared with a nonbeliever this past week about your faith in Jesus Christ? With whom?
14. *Reproduction.* Are you discipling another Christian? Are they growing in the Lord? Please explain.
15. *Small group.* Have you been completely honest with us?

Questions # 1, 2, 3, 4, and 15 are mandatory for each member in the discussion. Members can choose to answer any of the other questions under the guidance of the Holy Spirit and as time allows.

> *Father God, help us diligently apply all the*
> *means of grace to grow in our ever-deepening*
> *intimacy with You. In Jesus's name, amen!*

_____

_____

_____

_____

Bibliography

Adams, Jay. *Winning the War Within.* Revised edition. Woodruff, SC: Timeless Text, 1994.

Adsit, Christopher. *Personal Disciple Making.* San Bernardino, CA: Here's Life Publishing, Intervarsity Press, 1988.

Alcorn, Randy. *Heaven.* Carol Stream, IL: Tyndale House, 2004.

———. *Money, Possessions, and Eternity.* Carol Stream, IL: Tyndale House, 2021.

———. *The Treasure Principle.* Portland, OR: Multnomah, 2005.

Anderson, Neil and Joanne Anderson. *Daily in Christ.* Eugene, OR: Harvest House, 1993.

Bethany World Prayer Center. *Finding the Rock.* Baker, LA: Bethany World Prayer Center, 2005.

Blue, Ron. *Master Your Money.* Nashville: Thomas Nelson, 1991.

Boa, Kenneth. *Conformed to His Image.* Grand Rapids, MI: Zondervan, 2002.

Boren, Scott. *Making Cell Groups Work.* Houston: Cell Group Resources, 2003.

Bridges, Jerry. *The Discipline of Grace.* Colorado Springs: NavPress, 1994.

———. *The Practice of Godliness.* Colorado Springs: NavPress, 1983.

Chapman, Gary. *The Five Love Languages.* Chicago: Northfield Publishing, 1992.

Chappel, Bryan. *Holiness by Grace*. Wheaton, IL: Crossway Books, 2001.

Coleman, Robert. *The Master Plan of Evangelism*. Second edition. Old Tappan, NJ: Revell, 2010.

Collins, Steven. *Christian Discipleship*. Revised edition. Tulsa: Virgil W. Hensley, 1989.

Cook, William H. *Success, Motivation, and the Scriptures*. Nashville: Broadman Press, 1974.

Crabb, Larry. *Connecting*. Nashville: Thomas Nelson, 2005.

Epp, Albert H. *Discipleship Therapy*. Henderson, NE: Stairway, Discipleship Inc., 1993.

Evans, Tony. *God's Glorious Church*. Chicago: Moody Press, 2003.

Eyre, Stephen. *Quiet Tines Dynamics*. Downers Grove, IL: Intervarsity Press, 1989.

Farley, Andrew. *The Naked Gospel*. Grand Rapids, MI: Zondervan, 2009.

Foster, Richard. *Money, Sex and Power*. Colorado Springs: NavPress, 1991.

Getz, Gene. *Building Up One Another*. Colorado Springs: Victor Books, 1980.

Gilham, Bill. *Lifetime Guarantee*. Eugene, OR: Harvest House Publisher, 1993.

Green, Michael. *Evangelism: Now and Then*. Downers Grove, IL: Intervarsity Press, 1982.

Groeschel, Craig. *Winning the War in Your Mind*. Grand Rapids, MI: Zondervan, 2021.

Heller, Alfred L. *Your Body, His Temple.* Nashville: Thomas Nelson, 1981.

Henrichsen, Walter. *Disciples Are Made Not Born.* Colorado Springs: David C. Cook, 1988.

Hughes, R. Kent. *Disciplines of a Godly Man.* Wheaton, IL: Crossway Books, 1991.

Hughes, Selwyn. *Christ Empowered Living.* Nashville: Broadman & Holman, 2001.

———. *Divine Love.* Surrey, UK: BPCC Poulton Books, 1985.

———. *How to Live the Christian Life.* Sussex, UK: Kingsway Publications, 1981.

Hummel, Charles. *The Tyranny of the Urgent.* Downers Grove, IL: Intervarsity Press, 1994.

Inrig, Gary. *The Parables.* Grand Rapids, MI: Discovery House Publisher, 1991.

Jeremiah, David. *Everything You Need.* Nashville: Thomas Nelson, 2019.

———. *Overcoming.* Nashville: Word Publishing Inc., 2018.

———. *When Your World Falls Apart.* Nashville: Thomas Nelson, 2004.

Kehl, D. G. *Control Yourself.* Grand Rapids, MI: Zondervan, 1982.

Kent Jr., Homer. *The Freedom of God's Sons: Studies in Galatians.* Winona Lake, IN: BMH Books, 1976.

———. *A Heart Opened Wide: Studies in 2 Corinthians.* Winona Lake, IN: BMH Books, 1982.

Kreider, Larry. *The Tithe: A Test in Trust.* Booklet edition. Litiz, PA: House to House Publications, 2022.

Littleton, Mark. *Delighted by Discipline.* Colorado Springs: Victor Books, 1990.

Lucado, Max. *How Happiness Happens.* Nashville: Thomas Nelson, 2019.

———. *A Love Worth Giving.* Nashville: Thomas Nelson, 2002.

Lutzer, Erwin. *How to Say No to a Stubborn Habit.* Wheaton, IL: Victor Books, 1979.

MacArthur, John. *Giving: God's Way.* Carol Stream, IL: Tyndale House, 1978.

———. *The Body Dynamic.* Wheaton, IL: Victor Books, 1986.

———. *The Gospel According to Jesus.* Grand Rapids, MI: Zondervan, 1994.

———. *The MacArthur New Testament Commentary on Romans 1–8.* Chicago: Moody Press, 1991.

———. *The Quest for Character.* Nashville: Thomas Nelson, 2006.

Mayhue, Richard. *The Healing Promise.* Eugene, OR: Harvest House, 1994.

McCallum, Dennis and Jessica Lowery. *Organic Disciplemaking.* Houston: Touch Publications, 2006.

McGinnis, Alan Loy. *The Balanced Life.* Minneapolis: Augsburg Fortress, 1997.

Meyer, Joyce. *Good Health, Good Life.* New York: Faith Words, 2016.

———. *Making Good Habits, Breaking Bad Habits.* New York: Faith Words, 2013.

———. *Overload.* New York: Faith Words, 2016.

———. *Seize The Day.* New York. Faith Words, 2016.

————. *The Love Revolution*. New York: Faith Words, 2009.

Miller, Paul. *Love Walked among Us*. Colorado Springs: NavPress, 2001.

Murray, David. *The Happy Christian*. Nashville: Thomas Nelson, 2015.

Nee, Watchman. *The Normal Christian Life*. Wheaton, IL: Tyndale House, 1977.

————. *The Spiritual Man*. 3 vols. Anaheim: Living Stream Ministry, 1992.

Newberry, Tommy. *Success is Not an Accident*. Carol Stream, IL: Tyndale House, 2007.

Ogden, Greg. *Discipleship Essentials*. Downers Grove, IL: Intervarsity Press, 2007.

————. *Transforming Discipleship*. Downers Grove, IL: Intervarsity Press, 2007.

Olford, Stephen. *Basics for Believers*. Colorado Springs: Victor Books, 2003.

————. *Windows of Wisdom*. Greenville, SC: Emerald International, 2001.

Osteen, Joel. *The Power of I Am*. New York: Faith Words, 2015.

————. *Your Best Life Now*. New York: Warner Faith, 2004.

Platt, David. *Follow Me.* Carol Streams, IL: Tyndale House, 2013.

Porter, Mark. *The Time of My Your Life*. Wheaton, IL: Victor Books, 1983.

Posterski, Don. *Why Am I Afraid to Tell You I'm a Christian*. Downers Grove, IL: Intervarsity Press, 1983.

Prince, Joseph. *Grace Revolution*. New York: Faith Words 2015.

Purves, Andrew. *The Crucifixion of Ministry*. Downers Grove, IL: Intervarsity Press, 2007.

Rasnake, Eddie. *How to Develop a Quiet Time*. Chattanooga, TN: AMG Publisher, 2004.

Reynolds, Steve. *BOD4GOD*, Grand Rapids, MI: Revell, 2009.

Sanders, J. Oswald. *Spiritual Leadership*. Chicago: Moody Press, 1994.2014.

Scazzero, Peter. *Emotionally Healthy Spirituality*. Nashville: Thomas Nelson, 2006.

Sherman, Doug and Bill Hendricks., *How to Balance Competing Time Demands*. Colorado Springs: NavPress, 1989.

————. *Your Work Matters to God*. Colorado Springs: NavPress, 1987.

Sjogren, Steve. *Conspiracy of Kindness*. Bloomington, MN: Bethany House, 2008.

Stanley, Charles. *Success God's Way*. Nashville: Thomas Nelson Publisher, 2000.

Stebbins, Tom. *Friendship Evangelism by the Book*. Camphill Drive, PA: Christian Publications, 1995.

Stone, Dan. *The Rest of the Gospel*. Eugene, OR: Harvest House Publisher, 2000.

Stoop, David. *Self-talk: Key to Spiritual Growth*. Old Tappan, NJ: Fleming H. Revell, 1982.

Stott, John. *Romans*. Downers Grove, IL: Intervarsity Press, 1994.

Swindoll, Charles. *Good Morning, Lord...Can We Talk*. Carol Stream, IL: Tyndale House, 2018.

———. *New Testament Insights on Romans.* Grand Rapids, MI: Zondervan, 2010.

———. *Growing Strong in the Season of Life.* Portland, OR: Multnomah Press, 1983.

———. *Improving Your Serve.* Waco: Word Books, 1981.

———. *Living on the Ragged Edge.* Waco: Word Books, 1985.

———. *New Testament Insights on John.* Grand Rapids, MI: Zondervan, 2010.

Tan-Chi, Peter and Deonna Tan-Chi. *MOTIVATE.* Manila: OMF Literature, 2017.

Warren, Rick. *Bible Study Methods.* Grand Rapids, MI: Zondervan, 2006.

———. *The Daniel Plan.* Grand Rapids, MI: Zondervan, 2020.

———. *The Power to Change Your Life.* Wheaton, IL: Victor Books, 1990.

———. *The Purpose Driven Life.* Grand Rapids, MI: Zondervan, 2002.

Whitney, Donald S. *Spiritual Disciplines for the Christian Life.* Colorado Springs: NavPress, 1991.

Wiersbe, Warren. *The Bible Exposition Commentary.* Vol. 2. Wheaton, IL: Victor Books, 1989.

Wilkinson, Bruce. *A Life God Rewards.* Portland, OR: Multnomah Publisher, 2002.

Yancey, Philip. *Church: Why Bother.* Grand Rapids, MI: Zondervan, 1998.

Websites

Beliefnet | https://www.beliefnet.com

The Blazing Center | https://www.theblazingcenter.com

Brandon A. Cox | https://www.brandonamacox.com

Christianity Today | https://www.chrisianitytoday.com

Chuck Lawless | https://www.chucklawless.com

Crosswalk.com | http://www.crosswalk.com

David Jeremiah/Turning Point | https://www.davidjeremiah.org

Desiring God | https://www.desiringgod.org

Dr. Carol Ministries | https://www.drcarolminsitries.com

Emotionally Healthy Discipleship | https://www.emotionally-healthy.org

Got Questions Ministries | https://www.gotquestions.org

Grace Notebook | https://gracenotebook.com

iBelieve.com | https://www.ibelieve.com

In Touch Ministries | https://www.intouch.org

J. D. Greear Ministries | https://www.jdgreear.com

Lifeway | https://www.lifeway.com

Our Journey of Hope | https://www.ourjourneyofhope.com

Outreach Magazine | https://www.outreachmagazine.com

Paul Lee Tan Prophetic Ministries | https://www.tanbible.com

Preaching Magazine | https://www.preaching.org

Replicate Ministries | https://www.replicate.org

Soul Shepherding | https://www.soulshepherding.org

Strategic Renewal | https://www.strategicrenewal.com

Magazine Articles

Hughes, Selwyn. "The Crucifixion of Jesus." *Every Day with Jesus*, March/April 1996.

McBride, Neal. "Jesus as a Small Group Leader." *Discipleship Journal*, issue 59, 1990.

———. "Six Small Group Killers." *Discipleship Journal*, issue 59, 1990.

Myers, Richard C. "Why Small Group Isn't Enough." *Discipleship Journal*, issue 59, 1990.

Nelson, Alan. "Brokenness." *Discipleship Journal*, issue 94, 1996.

———. "Christ's Continuing Afflictions." *Every Day with Jesus*, March/April 1996.

Toussaint, Stanley. "7 Things the Bible Will Do for You." *Veritas*, January 2012.

Walters, Ron. "Pain: A Touchstone." *Preaching*, May/June 2015.

Sermons

Chan, Edmund. "Redeem Your Time." Sermon delivered at Cebu Gospel Church, Cebu City, Philippines, March 21, 2021.

Soriano, Joby. "No Regrets with Money." Christ's Commission Fellowship, Philippines, April 18, 2021.

CPSIA information can be obtained
at www.ICGtesting.com
Printed in the USA
BVHW031519260922
647991BV00012B/138